THE MEDIA
AND POLITICS

THE MEDIA
AND POLITICS

Dean E. Alger
Moorhead State University, Minnesota

 Prentice Hall, Englewood Cliffs, New Jersey 07632

Library of Congress Cataloging-in-Publication Data

Alger, Dean.
    The media and politics / Dean E. Alger.
       p.   cm.
    Bibliography: p.
    Includes index.
    ISBN 0-13-572553-4
    1. Mass media--Political aspects. 2. Mass media--Political
aspects--United States. 3. United States--Politics and
government--1981-   I. Title.
P95.8.A44 1989
302.2'34--dc19   88-29230
                                                        CIP

Editorial/production supervision
and interior design: Virginia L. McCarthy
Cover design: Diane Saxe
Manufacturing buyer: Peter Havens

 © 1989 by Prentice-Hall, Inc.
A Division of Simon & Schuster
Englewood Cliffs, New Jersey 07632

Printed in the United States of America
10   9   8   7   6   5   4   3   2   1

ISBN 0-13-572553-4

Prentice-Hall International (UK) Limited, *London*
Prentice-Hall of Australia Pty. Limited, *Sydney*
Prentice-Hall Canada Inc., *Toronto*
Prentice-Hall Hispanoamericana, S.A., *Mexico*
Prentice-Hall of India Private Limited, *New Delhi*
Prentice-Hall of Japan, Inc., *Tokyo*
Simon & Schuster Asia Pte. Ltd., *Singapore*
Editora Prentice-Hall do Brasil, Ltda., *Rio de Janeiro*

This book is specially dedicated to my late wife

Sara Nelson

whose vibrant life tragically ended at a young age
not long after completion of this book. Many said
"integrity" was the first word that came to mind
when they thought of her. Caring for others and a
commitment to working for a more just world were
also central to her life. Her courage in dealing
with an insidious disease was striking. Her spirit
lives on in many other people and in this book.

CONTENTS

PREFACE

A book on the mass media and politics is, at least in part, an exercise in paradox. A significant part of the discussion in this print medium is about the vivid, "living color" motion-picture medium of television. The experience of television is quite different from that of a print medium such as a book. This book seeks to verbalize a logic of analysis of both print and broadcast media and to present results and conclusions from empirical studies on the impact of the TV medium. Still, the full reality of television, as employed for political ads, presidential appearances, campaign events, and so on, must be directly experienced to be thoroughly grasped. Correspondingly, individual readers or classroom users of this book are strongly encouraged to expose themselves to video tapes of various programs and forms of political television.

This book is intended to serve two basic functions. One function is to serve as a main textbook for upper-division Media and Politics courses or as a second book for Political Behavior or similar courses. As the main text it is intended to be what most other such books are not: comprehensive. It is also intended to be a thoroughly coherent, integrated, step-by-logical-step treatment of the subject.

This book is also intended to provide a good, serious treatment of the media and politics field of research. It is intended to provide a unique framework for a better understanding of the field and a sequence of discussions of areas of the field within that framework which (hopefully) clarify central questions and help frame and stimulate further research. A prime element of that effort to provide a fully adequate framework is the attempt to consistently place this subject in a political system context, including a grounding in the theory of democracy and the democratic process. This is emphatically a media and *politics* book.

There are a number of people I would like to thank for assistance of one sort or another. A simple perusal of this book makes evident my abundant intellectual debt to many scholars in political science, communications studies, and cognitive psychology, as well as to a number of reflective journalists. I would especially like to thank Professor Doris Graber for her many outstanding contributions to the field, for graciously reading and responding to some of my other work, and for the encouragement to continue work in the field which accompanied those responses. Thanks are also extended to Professor Larry Sabato for his generous comments on a paper of mine and the accompanying encouragement. And speaking of reflective journalists, I have benefited from and have enjoyed many stimulating discussions with WDAY-TV's News Director Al Aamodt. (I hope this acknowledgment will not ruin his standing in the journalistic community.)

The research reported in Chapters 3 and 4 was supported, in part, by a grant from the MSU research fund, for which the author is grateful. I have benefited from interaction with and the fellowship of many fine members of the faculty at Moorhead State University, Minnesota. I am especially appreciative of the intellectual stimulation of Professor David Flint and the excellent departmental environment he has done so much to maintain in his service as chair—and of his friendship, as well. The stimulation, shared efforts, and friendship of my political science colleagues Andrew Conteh and David Feldman (now at the Oak Ridge National Laboratory, Tennessee) are also appreciated. Thanks also go to my colleagues in the Math Department for their understanding and assistance and to Martin Grindeland and Melva Moline. Further, thanks are extended to Sid Morton, Bob Schieffer, and Darel Paulson, the crack audio-visual experts at MSU, for their assistance. And I want to thank Sheryl Jones, who word-processed the manuscript with good cheer, dedication, and a sharp eye, despite being under heavy work pressure and operating in office conditions most closely resembling a zoo.

The assistance of Prentice Hall editor Karen Horton was appreciated (as was that of her predecessor Elizabeth O'Brien, who saw a diamond in the rough and initiated the project). Steven Finkel, at the University of Virginia, Lawrence G. Flood, at Buffalo State College, and David Whiteman, at the University of South Carolina, reviewed the manuscript and made many helpful suggestions.

Truly special appreciation goes to Sara Nelson for her inspiration, her sunny good cheer when this project weighed heavily, her service as my "editor of first resort," and simply for putting up with me on a daily basis. This book is dedicated to her. Thanks also to Vern and Arlene Nelson for their support and for graciously welcoming me to their bit of Eden on Big Turtle Lake in northern Minnesota. Further, appreciation is expressed for the steadfast support, for so long, of my mother, Vera. This book is also dedicated to her. Finally, the many discussions I had with my brother, Ardon Alger, the photographer, on visual media and expression were enriching and stimulated me to pursue this work. (So did the arguments.) My chief regret in this project is that economics did not allow more visual material to be included.

Dean Alger

THE MEDIA
AND POLITICS

CHAPTER ONE
MODERN DEMOCRACY
AND
THE VITAL
CONNECTING LINK

INTRODUCTION AND HISTORICAL PERSPECTIVE

In 1970, Senator J. William Fulbright observed the following: "Television has done as much to expand the powers of the President as would a constitutional amendment formally abolishing the co-equality of the three branches of government."[1] Senator Fulbright was suggesting a particularly dramatic case of how major changes in technologies and techniques of communication tend to engender significant changes in the social, economic, and political systems in a society.

Change in communicational capacities in human society has certainly been dramatic over the past couple of centuries, and especially so over the course of the twentieth century. To illustrate:

> In 1776, it took 29 days for the news of the Declaration of Independence to reach Charleston from Philadelphia.[2]
>
> In 1981, four *minutes* after the first shot in the attempted assassination of President Reagan, ABC-TV had communicated the news to the nation, followed shortly by continuous live coverage of the event by all three TV networks (which included reshowings of videotape of the actual shooting—nearly instant replays of the event itself).[3]

For further illustration, in past ages the citizenry could be directly exposed to a political debate only by their physical presence at the debate site (thus severely limiting the numbers so exposed). But since 1960, 70 to 100 million Americans could and did (in 1960, 1976, 1980, and 1984) see and hear "debates" between presidential candidates in the United States through "live" national television broadcasts.

The tale of such changes in humankind's capacity for communication also involves corresponding changes in the social and political dimensions of societies. This is because communication is central to how communities and societies of people go about their operations. Indeed, any larger-scale human endeavor involving a sizable number of people requires substantial communication for success. When many people get together to work on a common project, especially if they are in different locations, and if they are to stay together and coordinate their efforts, they must share thoughts and information on the effort. The same applies to the whole of a particular community and to a general society—only more so. By the same logic, the larger and more complex a society is, the more critical a factor is such communication.

The origin of the English word *communication* is the Latin word *communis,* meaning "common."[4] Communication allows the establishment of a "commonness" among people, a sharing of specific thoughts and feelings as well as the more general orientations and perspectives, including loyalties, that enable a people not only to work together on particular projects, but also to maintain a social order and to operate a stable political system. Somewhat more formally, communication, in a societal context, can be defined as the process of social transaction which people use to construct meanings that constitute their images of the world, on which they act, and to exchange those images through the use of symbols (which can be linguistic or visual).[5]

Corresponding to the nature and central role of communication in society, when the means and capability for communication change significantly, the social and political systems in society change as well. As communications scholar George Gerbner has pointed out, for most of human history, "the messages and images that compose the fabric of popular culture were woven by the tribe and village out of the same homespun yarn of everyday experience. . . . The process was mostly interpersonal. It was slow-moving and fixed. . . ."[6]

The communication process was overwhelmingly of a personal nature; the means were direct interpersonal interaction and written messages. Even the edicts of kings and other governing authorities would appear to have actually reached what today we call the general public through interpersonal means. That is, the few formal notices that were posted and passed down tended to be filtered through and interpreted by local leaders and clergy, especially since most people had little or no literacy. (In fact, there was no "general public" in the sense that we know it today; most people's "world" was simply the village or local area together with its ascribed social structure and social relations.)

The introduction and gradual spread of the printing press in Europe, from the fifteenth century on, began to change those age-old communications capacities and patterns, and it upset traditional notions of who should have access to information and ideas. Such change was sped along by the advance of the industrial revolution, especially from the late eighteenth century into the twentieth century, and the resulting transformations in society. Increasing urbanization occurred, with a great migration of people from rural areas to cities to work in factories and supporting businesses. In the United States in the nineteenth century, immigration brought to major cities large numbers of people who had little or no connection to the traditional social network of an American community, although immigrants often located in ethnic enclaves. A mass society thus developed,[7] a society increasingly composed of large masses of people who no longer lived under the conditions of a traditional community with its long-established social ties. The middle class that evolved, and then greatly expanded, was increasingly literate following the establishment of a complete system of public education. Hand in hand with those developments was an increasing demand for political rights and participation, which received its first major push in the movement and era of Andrew Jackson in the later 1820s and 1830s.

All of those changes produced a populace more receptive to new sources of information and ideas and more desirous of learning about developments in the world beyond their immediate areas. Correspondingly, the first true medium of mass communication was established and took hold in America during the middle third of the nineteenth century: the mass circulation newspaper, originally called the "penny press."[8]

The twentieth century brought further developments in communications capability—notably radio and television—truly dramatic developments considering the scope of the audience reached by TV and the pervasiveness of that medium in modern life. Indeed, "pervasive" is the key word for the phenomenon of TV in American society. By the 1980s, 98% of households in the United States had at least one television set (more than had telephones or flushing toilets!). At the height of prime time (8:00–9:00 P.M.), 90 to 100 million people will be tuned in on an average night (at least in nonsummer months). As of the mid-1980s, the average household had a TV on over seven hours a day.[9] Here is a communication medium that incorporates striking new dimensions in its communicational capacity. It can communicate developments virtually instantly—even such unique developments as the assassination attempt noted earlier, and can do so to a nationwide audience. Above all, it does its communicating using not just dry ink on a page, but with "realistic" sound and motion pictures—views of people captured in actual activities, speaking in their own voices.

Many analysts believe that the development and universal adoption of radio and television has radically altered how human communication is performed in society—and, in turn, central elements of our social and political experiences and processes.[10] George Gerbner has reflected on those changes especially well:

> The shared communicative context of messages and images through which a culture reveals the varieties, limitations and potentials of the human condition is no longer woven out of a homespun yarn of private everyday experience. Even the meaning of everyday experience has changed. . . . The fabric of popular culture that relates elements of existence to each other and structures the common consciousness of what is, what is important, and what is right, is now largely a manufactured product. The new situation is a radical transformation in the ways members of our species [learn about being] human. . . .
>
> To sum up: The ways we reflect on things, act on things and interact with one another are rooted in our ability to compose images, produce messages, and use complex symbol systems. A change in that ability transforms the nature of human affairs. We are in the midst of such a transformation. It stems from the mass production of symbols and messages—a new industrial revolution in the field of culture. New media of communication provide new ways of selecting, composing and sharing perspectives. New institutions of communication create new publics across boundaries of time, space and status. . . . Along with other dramatic changes, we have altered the symbolic environment that gives meaning and direction to human activity.[11]

With such changes come profound implications for the political system. What role do the mass media of communication play in political systems, especially those that are—or are striving to be—democracies? To that fundamental matter of perspective we now turn. In succeeding chapters we discuss the realities of the media's role in the American and some other political systems. In the next section of this chapter we outline the place the mass media of today occupy in a representative democratic system, and then the concept of democracy is discussed to present a standard by which to evaluate the performance of media operations in the American and other political systems.

An extended discussion and analysis of the concept of democracy is not possible within the scope of the book. Our discussion here of the concept of democracy is intended to set out central elements of that concept, particularly those relevant to an evaluation of media's role in the political system. Several major figures in twentieth-century scholarship in political theory are quoted and their ideas put forth, but details of lengthy debates cannot be dealt with here. It is hoped that the following discussion will provide readers with sufficient background to alert them to the implications for democracy in the material presented in subsequent chapters. Those who wish a more comprehensive review of the concepts and associated issues and debates are encouraged to consult the literature cited.

THE DEMOCRATIC SYSTEM AND THE VITAL CONNECTING LINK: AN OVERVIEW

The centerpiece of a representative democratic system is the process of selection of representatives by the public through elections. Elections are intended to be the principal form of political participation on the part of the public. As Giovanni Sartori writes, in his landmark study of democratic theory: "Since in order to have democracy we must have, to some degree, a government of the people, let us immediately ask: When do we find a 'governing people,' the demos in the act or the role of governing? The answer is: . . . [T]he democratic process is . . . encapsulated in elections and electing."[12] But how do the voters make decisions on what candidates to elect? How do people in Peoria, Illinois, Moorhead, Minnesota, and Los Angeles, California, learn about candidates so they can make intelligent choices?

First, it should be remembered that most people have an array of (often intense) home, work, and other personal concerns on which they focus most of their attention. Thus most people do not have the time—nor do they usually have the inclination—to seek out detailed, authoritative information on candidates' positions and performance in office, or on the issues themselves. Most people do not seek out and read such sources as the *Congressional Quarterly* or the *National Journal* or even *Time* or *Newsweek*.

Traditional sources of information on candidates have been the political parties and their regional and local organizations. But in the American system in particular, the parties have declined notably during the past 25 years or so as forces in the organization and guidance of peoples' political behavior; the public relies on parties far less than it used to as sources of information and for cues on voting. As William Keefe has pointed out regarding parties and elections: "At virtually every point associated with the recruitment and election of public officials, the party organizations have suffered an erosion of power." As he further notes, direct primary elections are a prime example: "The party label has lost significance as candidates of all political colorations, with all variety of relationships to the organization, earn the right to wear [the party label] by capturing primary elections."[13] The substantial decline in the percentage of the public identifying with either major party, especially in the category of "strong identifiers," and the rising percentage of independent voters, testify to the low level of public reliance on the parties. It should also be noted that many people receive information and cues on political choices from interest groups with which they are affiliated or identify (although the policy areas covered tend to be within a rather narrow range compared with other sources; moreover, the public is very unevenly represented by organized interests, as certain scholars have systematically shown[14]).

What people have increasingly relied on for information and impressions is the mass media. Even when decisions are based partly on conversations with family and acquaintances, the media are most often the indirect source of information for most people. The Roper polls have documented a steady rise, through the 1960s and 1970s, in the percentage of the public that "usually get[s] most of [its] news about what's going on in the world today" from television compared with newspapers—from 58% for TV and 56% for newspapers in 1964 to 67% for TV and 49% for newspapers in 1978; only 5% indicated "other people" as their prime source.[15]

For the vast majority of the general public, with their attention focused primarily on personal concerns, there is a great physical and psychological distance from political affairs. That distance between political actors and the public (during elections and between them) is bridged by the communications of the mass media. The public receives its information on and impressions of candidates and other political actors principally from the media. As Walter Lippmann memorably put it, people respond to political matters on the basis of "the pictures in [their] heads" of what the world is like—pictures largely selected and arranged by the media.[16] The mass media are, then, the vital connecting link in the political system today. Indeed, as one observer commented in a speech to the nation's broadcasters: "The flow of ideas, the capacity to make informed choices, the ability to criticize, all of the assumptions on which political democracy rests, depend largely on communications. And you are the guardians of the most powerful and effective means of communication ever designed."[17] That observer was President John F. Kennedy. His thoughts lead us to a little deeper reflection on democracy.

THE MEANING OF DEMOCRACY AND THE MEDIA FACTOR

To understand fully the importance, nature, and implications of the media in our political system, we should probe a little more deeply into the meaning of democracy. It is appropriate to begin by spelling out essential elements of a representative democratic system. Then a little more complete discussion is added regarding how democracy has been conceived of by some prominent thinkers and scholars.

Two elements are essential in a true democracy. First, alternative choices must be available to the public. Central to the idea of an operative democracy is alternative choices competing for public acceptance, the principal form of which is, of course, alternative candidates for election. Given the fact that the average person cannot (or does not) devote substantial time to study of offices and issues, it is in the competition among alternatives that the public is made aware of the choices in directions for governance. Choice is at the core of democracy; the absence of choice means that democracy is lessened to one degree or another, depending on the nature of the lost choice.

The second basic element of democracy is that the public must have "in its hands" what it takes to make a political decision on those choices in a meaningful fashion—that is, to make such choices, as they relate them to their own values, beliefs, and concerns, as effectively as they are able to—and to act on them. If the public is intended to serve as the foundation of the democratic process and hence to indicate basic directions for government through their electoral choices[18] and other political participation, the people must have in their "possession" the means of adequately making such decisions, so that they can act on them in an appropriate fashion.

These two basic elements are important not only as a way of opening a discussion of the meaning of democracy; they will also be used specifically in later chapters as standards in assessing various aspects of the media's role in the political system.

What must the public "have" to enable it to make electoral as well as other political choices? Clearly, adequate general education and a perception of the freedom to select among options are necessary for most effective use of such a right. But of greatest importance for the present subject, the people need sufficient information on the *substance* of available choices. For democracy to work, the public needs to have substantial and accurate information in five areas in the case of electoral alternatives. First, they need information on the qualifications of the candidates for the particular office or leadership position: namely, the formal education and other training of the candidate, offices held and other relevant experience, and so on. Second, the voters need information on the positions taken by the candidate on issues of concern, as well as the candidate's general political orientations and philosophy. Third, information is needed on the personal leadership qualities of the candidate, as well as on other personal characteristics that might present problems in the person's conduct of the office. Fourth, information is needed on the nature of the office involved, including its responsibilities. Fifth, information is needed on the elements of and arguments concerning significant issues.

In general, information and full access to it is a cardinal principle of a democratic system, as various scholars have pointed out.[19] That is why a review of the concept of a democratic system is vital to an adequate framework for thinking about the media's role in political systems. Indeed, as Carl J. Friedrich observed in a landmark work: ". . . freedom of the press is considered a cornerstone of constitutional democracy."[20] After criticizing political science for neglecting the role of the media, Professor Friedrich pointed out that "The will of the people was treated as if unrelated to the information available. . . . Actually the emergence of constitutional government, and in particular the crystallization of the systems of popular representation as we know them, are inextricably interwoven with the growth of the modern press. Without it constitutional government is unimaginable."[21] And as Giovanni Sartori points out: "Electoral power per se is the mechanical guarantee of democracy; but the substantive guarantee is given by the conditions under which the citizen gets the information and is exposed to the pressure of opinion makers."[22]

Friedrich's use of the term "constitutional democracy" raises an issue that should be discussed briefly. What has just been presented is a concise review of central elements of what various scholars have called "classical democratic theory." But certain scholars have distinguished another general line of theory about democracy, which is usually called "constitutionalism."[23] Friedrich is, in fact, a principal modern expounder of this version of democratic theory. In constitutionalism the emphasis is on the division ("separation") of powers in government and restraints on government (thus avoiding dictatorial power and preserving popular freedom). As Friedrich has expressed it: "Division of power is the basis of constitutional democracy. It is what is meant by Constitutionalism. . . . [T]o render a government constitutional required the establishment and maintenance of effective restraints upon political, and more especially upon governmental, action. It is the function of a constitution, in this sense to organize such a restrained government."[24]

The constitutionalist conception of democracy is an important one, with its emphasis on restraint of government to prevent dictatorial governance and to preserve civil liberties. The latter element is of special relevance for a study of the media and politics, given the keystone position of the free press principle in civil liberties (a point that we will return to in Chapters 5, 6, 8, and 12). However (simplifying a bit), that line of thought concentrates on only half of the function of democracy as a system of governance.

There is more to the concept of a democratic basis of governance than restraint of excess and arbitrary governmental power and the preservation of individual freedoms. The second half of the function of a democratic system is the affirmative side of the popular basis of governance, namely, the role of the public in affirmatively indicating (at least basic) policy directions for government by political choice and action, especially in and through elections. Indeed, Friedrich himself felt it necessary to include the following in his discussion of "milestones in the process of democratizing constitutionalism": "Nowhere has the progressive spirit of democracy found more eloquent expression than in [Lincoln's] Gettysburg address: '. . . that government of the people, by the people, for the people shall not perish from the earth.' "[25]

Robert Dahl, in a classic work on democratic theory (which examined alternative conceptions of democracy), included this summary statement: "But at a minimum . . . democratic theory is concerned with processes by which ordinary citizens exert a relatively high degree of control over leaders. . . ."[26] Adding a more emphatic note, Benjamin Barber has eloquently argued that if democracy is to avoid subverting itself, it must involve far more than simply restraint of government and formal protection of individual rights (which conception of democracy he and others call standard "liberal democracy"). Rather, Barber states that democracy means and requires real, affirmative participation by the people. Participation is needed not only for the democratic function of ensuring that government action is in accordance with the public's wishes, but also for creating and maintaining a harmoniously working community which enables a democracy to sustain itself:

> [L]iberal democracy may not be a theory of community at all. It does not so much provide a justification of politics [i.e., a people debating and discussing, interacting and acting to decide directions for their common society] as it offers a politics that justifies individual rights.
>
> Liberal democracy is thus a "thin" theory of democracy, one whose democratic values are prudential and thus provisional, optional, and conditional—means to exclusively individualistic and private ends. From this precarious foundation, no firm theory of citizenship, participation, public goods, or civic virtue can be expected to arise.[27]

But how can ordinary citizens effectively exert that high degree of control, and how can they affirmatively act to ensure "government of the people and by the people"? The answer brings us back to the information that the public must have if they are to effectively make political choices. Another theorist in political science, G.E.G. Catlin, has tied all of this together: "'[F]reedom of the press' . . . is a civil liberty under law, logically justified for the specific purpose of . . . the development of an objectively informed or intellectually vigorous democracy. . . ."[28]

The mass media role of providing adequate information to enable people to realize the intent of a democratic process is even more crucial in today's world. This is especially so in the United States, where, as noted earlier, the political parties have significantly declined as information networks and cue-givers on political choice. Further, in the world of the late twentieth century, especially in America, we have a far more mobile, less "rooted" society. In an economy increasingly dominated by national (and international) corporations, and the multitude of job transfers and national job searches that go with it, a far higher percentage of the public does not have the experience of long-term, stable social networks which help share information on political matters and assist in its interpretation. As Vance Packard has written, we have increasingly become "a nation of strangers."[29] This encourages more dependence on the mass media for information and perspectives.

There is, additionally, a consequence of the nature of society in the twentieth century which it is of importance to note. Although it is difficult to document precisely, various analysts have suggested that societies in the large, more developed nations, with their full evolution of industrialization and urbanization, have increasingly become *mass* societies, key elements of which are the high mobility, even "rootlessness," just noted and an "atomized" individual condition. As William Kornhauser has expressed it: "People are divorced from their community and work, and they are free to unite in new ways. Furthermore, those who do not possess a variety of relations with their fellows are disposed to seek new and often remote sources of attachment and allegiance. Where proximate concerns are meaningful, people do not spend much time or energy seeking direct gratification from remote symbols."[30] With this loss of long-term ties to community and social networks, it is feared, comes a loss of capacity to interpret happenings in the world in a stable fashion. More ominously, scholars note that a consequence is little or no insulation between the ruling elites and the masses. This is a recipe for the effective use of propaganda, a high level of manipulation of the public, and for instability in general. This danger would appear to be heightened in the age of television. Friedrich provides some enlightening thoughts—both on the danger just noted and on the positive potential:

> Broadcasting: new medium of political influence. The possibility of broadcasting the spoken word and projecting visual materials to the four corners of the globe has profoundly altered the realities of modern politics. Whether political leadership is contested, as in the democracies, or imposed, as in the dictatorships, the opportunity of reaching millions in the direct, personal way which only the spoken word and the actual view of the speaker offer has turned the modern community into a market place. Their potentialities [of the new means of mass communication] have been further reinforced by the development of communication satellites. Inevitably, therefore, the issue of who shall control this channel of communication presents political problems of decisive importance, at least in a constitutional democracy.[31]

The reasons for the two central themes of this book—the democracy perspective and the media as the vital connecting link—should now be clear. Understanding the nature of that link and analyzing the implications for democracy of the role played by the media are crucial to an understanding of our present social and political system.

THE PLAN OF THE BOOK

If we are to understand the democratic process, we must analyze the foundation of the process, we the people. That is, we must consider who receives what communications, how people receive those communications, and what factors are involved in people's decision making. We need to discuss such subjects as the nature of public opinion, people's backgrounds and socialization, and psychological tendencies (such as selective perception) relevant to how people receive communications and how they make political decisions. The latter are, of course, important to study if we are to understand the impact of media communications on people's political actions. The study of people's decision-making also involves analyzing how people process information (called "information processing theory"). Those subjects are discussed in Chapter 2.

What of the act of communication itself? To understand how mass communication, through the various media, affects people and their political behavior, we must analyze how that communicating is done. There are two aspects involved. First, how do political actors go about communicating? Specifically, how do they use symbols and other techniques of persuasive communicating? We discuss these matters in Chapter 3. While reviewing those techniques, it is vital to keep in mind key parts of what is discussed in Chapter 2, namely, people's backgrounds and socialization, including attitudes developed toward various symbols, as that is what the various techniques of communications are drawing on and appealing to. In Chapter 3 we make that connection in some detail.

The second aspect of how communicating is done is that of the nature of the mass media themselves through which such communication is accomplished. The characteristics of each medium (TV, radio, newspapers, etc.) as a means of communication, especially political communication, must be identified and analyzed. What do the characteristics and corresponding capabilities of each medium mean for political communication, how are they used by political actors, and what are the implications? In Chapter 4 we explore those questions. A further question is: What is the nature of ownership and control of the media, and what are the consequences and implications of the existing patterns? Further, the nature of governmental regulation of the media, the laws involved, and the issue of people's access to the media need to be examined. These are the subjects of Chapter 5.

TV news and the newspapers and news magazines are the main media sources of information on public affairs. Correspondingly, a key subject to investigate is the making and presentation of the news. Why were those stories you saw on last night's network news chosen rather than other stories? What factors are involved in the choice by news organizations of what stories to cover, which to emphasize, and how to present them in a newspaper or on TV? We discuss those questions in Chapter 6. Included is a special section on issues in news decisions, included in which is coverage of terrorism. Chapter 7 does the same for news coverage of foreign affairs. In Chapter 8 we discuss the principal source of much of the news—government institutions and officers—and how media personnel interact with them.

Chapters 9 and 10 serve as the special focus section of the book. There we give special and extended attention to the crucial matter of the media's role in elections, with the principal focus on presidential elections. We introduce the subject in Chapter 9, put it in the perspective of a democratic system, and review methods of study. In Chapter 10 we discuss what scholars have found regarding the nature of media coverage of elections and the impacts of that coverage on voters.

The nature of the media and politics in another nation—which provides instructive comparisons with U.S. media and politics—is presented in Chapter 11. In the final chapter we return to the major questions raised throughout the book, and consider the balance of scholarly assessments and the implications for democracy of the various findings.

CHAPTER TWO
FOUNDATIONS
Public Opinion,
Political Socialization,
and Information Processing

INTRODUCTION

"We the people" is the classic beginning phrase of the Preamble to the U.S. Constitution. As that phrase suggests, the people are intended to be the foundation of a democratic system. If the operation of a democratic system and the role of the mass media in such a system are to be understood, attention must be focused on the public. The people are the receivers of political communications and are political choice makers in elections and other political activities. The nature of the public as receivers of political communications and the bases of people's political choice making are then fundamentally important to analyze in the effort to understand the subject of the mass media and politics—and the realities of an operating democratic system.

The appropriate place to start is with a discussion of who "the public" is. To analyze political communication through the media and its impact, we need to identify just who is actually receiving those communications— what "public" is being communicated to. Patterns of media use by the public are also discussed. The concept, nature, and origins of public opinion, together with people's political socialization, are then reviewed. This is followed by a discussion of the question of how people mentally "process" information and impressions. Finally, a note is added on the level and nature of the public's knowledge of political matters—and some of the very important implications involved.

THE PUBLIC/THE AUDIENCE: TARGETING COMMUNICATIONS/RECEIVING COMMUNICATIONS

"The Public" and the Targeting of Political Communications

As noted in Chapter 1, the development of the mass media of radio and television has enabled political figures to communicate directly to the general public, without parties or opinion leaders or the interpretations of newspapers as intermediaries. In the United States, those communications are sent out to an adult society of over 150 million people. The peak of such communications—presidential debates, prime presidential addresses, and principal presidential campaign ads—reach audiences of up to 100 million people. This is the most general dimension of the public reached by communications through the mass media. This capacity is, as noted earlier, unique in human history; correspondingly, it demands special attention. As one part of that attention, the nature of the general public as receivers of such communications is the subject of this chapter. This includes identifying the sources of shared orientations and perceptions, which form a common base enabling political communications to reach and affect a mass public.

The general public is not, of course, a monolithic whole. The general public is made up of various segments which differ in personal characteristics and interests. Indeed, the general public that receives communications from the major mass media is not only large, it is also heterogeneous.

Political communicators are interested in maximum effectiveness in influencing members of the public—they do not have unlimited resources to communicate fully with the entire public, especially in election campaigns. Consequently, political figures want to reach those members of the general public who will do them the most good (i.e., be most likely to vote for them in an election, be good prospects for being "converted" to the politician's candidacy or to support their bills in the legislature, etc.) As a result and in recognition of the various types of people making up the general public, political communicators often seek to *target* certain sections of the public. Targeting is an increasingly key element in political communication,[1] as it is in commercial advertising. To understand the use of the media, it is therefore important to analyze the various segments of the public at which such communication is aimed.

We can identify three basic categories of more specific publics. The first and simplest is that of geographic area. In a representative democracy, a typical way of organizing the election of representatives is by geographic constituency. The United States, with its federal system and traditions of localism, is perhaps the strongest example of this. (In Great Britain, for a partially contrasting example, there are distinct boundaries for the parliamentary districts, but candidates for a seat "from" the district need not actually live in the district; candidates run more fundamentally as representatives of their political parties.) So, corresponding to that geographic organization, specific parts of the nation are targeted. "The public" for some political communications is a state, for others a legislative district, for still others a general region of the country such as the South or Midwest. Thus, even in a presidential race, political ads, speeches, and so on, can be specifically designed for a particular state or region. An interesting and revealing example from the 1968 Nixon campaign was reported by Joe McGinnis:

> Chicago was the site of the first [of] ten programs that Nixon would do in states ranging from Massachusetts to Texas. The idea was to have him in the middle of a group of people, answering questions live. . . .
> One of the valuable things about this idea, from a political standpoint, was that each show would be seen only by the people who lived in that particular state or region. This meant it made no difference if Nixon's statements—for they were not really answers—were exactly the same, phrase for phrase, gesture for gesture, from state to state. Only the press would be bored and the press had been written off already. . . .
> And, to carry it one step sideways, it made no difference either if the answer varied—in nuance—from state to state. No one, unless he traveled a lot, would hear any statement but the one designed for him. So, a question about law and order might evoke one response in New England and a slightly different one in the South. Nothing big enough to make headlines, just a subtle twist of inflection, or the presence or absence of a frown or gesture as a certain phrase was spoken.[2]

The second category of more specific publics is a crucial one for analysis of the use of the media: demographics. Not only for political ads, but also for various other types of communications, women, blue-collar workers, minorities, farmers, and other demographic categories of "sub-publics" are increasingly being targeted. The substance of, and the symbols used in, political communications are increasingly being tailored to appeal to particular segments of the public. As political ad-man and analyst Mark Shields once said about political ads in specific, "a good ol' vanilla, one-size-fits-all [communication] will no longer do." One way this is done is by selection of TV or radio programs that are watched or listened to predominantly by a particular demographic category.

The third category of more specific publics is that of groups—both those which are formally organized and those which are simply sets of people with common interests wherever they are located. Thus members of labor unions are often targeted; or environmental groups can be targeted, along with people who have environmental concerns but do not belong to a formal group.

The Audience for the Mass Media: Patterns of Usage

Exploring the sub-publics at which political communications are aimed led us to note the existence of particular audiences for particular TV and radio programs. A brief note should be added at this point on the audience for the various media, specifically, the basic patterns of usage of the mass media by the principal demographic categories. With regard to television, the average time a TV set is on per day and the peak prime-time audience were noted in Chapter 1; here attention is focused on audience patterns for the various mass media.

Perhaps the most striking development has come in the category of socioeconomic status. The common notion has been that those of lower socioeconomic status watch a great deal of TV, whereas the upper socioeconomic class watches little. Through the 1960s this was true. But by the mid-1970s, as George Comstock and colleagues point out, "viewing was greater by those of higher socio-economic status than it had been a decade earlier by those of lower status."[3] Although people of lower socioeconomic status do, indeed, still watch more TV, the gap between the amount they watch and the amount those of higher status watch has narrowed considerably.[4] The advent and spread of cable TV has made this accounting more complex, however, since people of higher status are more likely to subscribe to the pay cable channels. Network TV continues to be the dominant force in the medium, however, especially with respect to political matters and the news; so far only the Cable News Network (CNN) has had any notable impact in that category in the realm of cable TV.

Comstock and colleagues offer this important perspective on that narrowed socioeconomic gap in TV watching: "This appears to represent a final step in the pervasive adoption of television by our society in which those at first most resistant—possibly because of greater affinity for 'print' and 'book' culture—began to approach the amount of viewing of those who turned to television more readily."[5] One other, related, note should be added here. It is likely that a substantial part of the reason for the significant increase in TV viewing by people of higher socioeconomic status—the overcoming of the resistance just noted—is the fact that the first "TV generation" was reaching maturity starting in the late 1960s. For those who grew up with television, the medium was an accepted part of life, a legitimate presence and source of communication. Indeed, as of the mid-1980s, over half of the public was born in the TV era (given the median age of 28–29).[6]

As of the mid-late 1970s, as documented in the study by Comstock and colleagues, children watched TV a little less than 30 hours a week (although during different prime hours than adults), while teenagers watched just over 20 hours a week. Women from 18 to 49 years of age watched about seven more hours of TV a week than did men in the same age category. This gap may have narrowed in the 1980s, given the significant increase in percentage of women in the work force. Men and women 50 and over (with an additional three hours a week for women) watched the most TV—over 30 hours a week. The level of schooling completed by the head of the household made a significant difference in how much TV children and teenagers watch: those with less than a college education had six more hours of TV watching by the young.[7]

Minorities (with blacks being the principal source of evidence) tend to watch somewhat more television than whites—about 15% more, according to one account.[8] This difference may be best accounted for by higher levels of unemployment and hence more available time. It also appears that minorities tend to rely on newspapers less than whites, 59% saying that they read a daily newspaper compared with 72% of whites saying they do.[9]

More highly educated people do rely more on newspapers and other print media, the most substantial "drop-off" of newspaper usage coming in those with less than a completed high school education.[10] The audience for the principal national news magazines is markedly "upscale," with subscribers who are predominantly middle class and "above" and more highly educated than average. The upscale public, and especially the more highly educated, also tend to rely on multiple media sources.

Finally, it should be noted that the reliance on TV for news, which the Roper polls and other sources have suggested, may require some qualifications. As Comstock and colleagues summarize the findings: "The term 'television news' to which the public responds in most studies encompasses both network national news and local news. A large proportion of the adult public—in one national sample more than half over a two week period—do not watch network national news. Reading of newspapers appears to be more frequent. The viewing of local news, ignored implicitly or explicitly in many studies, is greater [than national network news]."[11]

Further, Lawrence Lichty[12] has argued that newspapers are still the prime news source. This conclusion is based on a large market research survey of people's expressed exposure to the different media. Two things should be noted regarding those findings, however. First, what amount of hard news, as opposed to comics, sports, and so on, is actually read in newspapers by those claiming to "read" a paper is quite unclear. Second, "reading" a small-town, eight-page, local paper is far from the same thing as reading a major metropolitan daily—indeed, such papers *do* contain primarily local news. Consequently, the conclusions just suggested should be considered with caution.

THE NATURE AND ORIGINS OF PUBLIC OPINION

On Public Opinion

In seeking to understand the political world, a key question that must be asked is what causes people to behave the way they do in making decisions on and then voting in elections, as well as in deciding and acting in other realms of political activity. A major part of the answer is that people choose and act on the basis of their *opinions*. To build a very important foundation for much of what is discussed in succeeding chapters, a review of the nature and origins of public opinion is essential.

There is general consensus among scholars that people's opinions derive from their *beliefs, values,* and *attitudes* as well as from their more short-term perceptions. Beliefs are what people think the world is like (i.e., the physical and social realms of the world). The formal term for a roughly related concept, which applies more to the present tense, is *cognition:* the process and condition of knowing—that is, both being aware of something and of having decided that it is of such and such a nature.

To operate in this world you must have a set of beliefs about what it is like; that is what tells you what you can and cannot do, or what would happen or would likely happen if some action were taken. Most beliefs about the nature of the physical world are so obvious that you do not consciously think about them (gravity, the physical composition of a candle, etc.)—only philosophers and physicists do such a thing. People also have beliefs about the political world. They believe certain things about what the U.S. Constitution says and how it determines what the U.S. government is like, what various presidents are and were like, what the various political parties stand for, what the economy or military in the Soviet Union is like, and so on. Clearly, what you believe is "true" about the world will affect how you respond to relevant developments in the world.

It should also be pointed out that beliefs held by people may not correspond to objective reality (when it can be determined objectively), and they need not be in accord with objective reality to have a strong effect on opinions. What the U.S. Constitution says, what Presidents Washington and Lincoln were like and did, and what various aspects of the Soviet Union are like are areas of belief about which millions of Americans have factually erroneous beliefs. Those are classic areas of myth for Americans. Indeed, as one perceptive political observer pointed out: "Mythology distracts us everywhere—in government as in business, in politics as in economics, in foreign affairs as in domestic policy. . . ."[13] That observer was President John F. Kennedy, himself now the subject of a good deal of myth! The crucial point is: If we are to understand people's opinions and their ultimate behavior, and the related question of how they respond to political communications through the media, we must understand what people believe, factually correct or otherwise.

Values are just as crucial to be aware of in an analysis of public opinion and political behavior. It is especially important to be aware of them when analyzing political communication through the mass media.

Put simply, values are basic feelings about what *should* be and what is good or bad. More formally, they are the basic normative components of opinions. People have values regarding family life (i.e., protecting the family is a good thing, forces that "tear families apart" are bad things), values regarding "self-reliance," conservation of nature, the desirability of free enterprise, and so on. It should also be kept in mind that not all values are of equal importance to the person holding them. Some values are truly fundamental to a person's idea of what is "right" and what life should be like (as well as what the political system should be like). Other values are of secondary importance; many of them are, in fact, *instrumental* values, that is, values which indicate types of activities or manners of action which help attain more fundamental values. Additionally, we should remember that in any given person, various values are held with different intensity.

Two interest sectors in American and world society can serve as good exercises in value and belief analysis: the "right to life" interest sector and the Greenpeace organization and corresponding interest sector. The key questions: What are the fundamental values exhibited; what are the intensities compared with other values; what beliefs are involved; and what has the combination of beliefs and values led each interest sector to do, acting sociopolitically, which overrides other values of people otherwise quite similar to those in each interest sector? Another good example of value and belief analysis, which is highly relevant to analyzing political communications in the United States, is that involved with the word "freedom." For *you*, what value *combined* with what beliefs are involved?

The idea of freedom can be used to illustrate another important point about values: values are culturally determined. That is, people tend to learn their values from the society and culture in which they grow up and live. Freedom illustrates this very well. Especially in recent years, various Americans, most prominently President Reagan and members of his administration, have repeatedly pointed to the lack of freedom and of human rights violations in the Soviet Union. Most American citizens seem to have agreed—probably with a sense of superiority. Any suggestion from the Soviet side that there are violations of human rights or some limitations on "freedom" in the United States has been roundly dismissed. But according to *Soviet* values, with hundreds of thousands of homeless and malnourished people, and with millions of chronically unemployed in the face of the great wealth of the country, the United States is a nation with human rights abuses and limted freedom. A central aspect of "freedom" in such a socialist nation is freedom from fear of unemployment and homelessness.[14]

An attitude is a preference for or a predisposition toward something. An attitude is based on one or a cluster of beliefs and is directed by one or more values. An attitude is generally enduring; it normally lasts a substantial period of time. Most people reading this book have an attitude toward the Republican Party, for example. This attitude is based on beliefs regarding what it stands for and what its officeholders have done, and it is based, in some fashion, on how the party's general orientation and specific stands on issues, according to the reader's beliefs, are in accord with reader's values related to supporting business, helping the poor and needy, and so on.

Perceptions are what a person's senses take in; but all perceptions but the simplest are filtered by the person's beliefs and values. The senses, of course, receive stimuli directly from physical experience and from interpersonal interaction and communication through the mass media. In using the concept of perceptions, we are referring to a more temporary phenomenon—that of a person's perceptions of this president or that event at this particular time. A consistent pattern of perceptions over a period of time will lead to a belief.

Finally, as Bernard Hennessey has articulated it, an opinion is "a normative and/or pragmatic judgement about an object. Opinions are more specific than attitudes. Opinions are usually consistent with the attitude or attitudes to which they are related in the perception of the opinion holder."[15]

For the study of the media and politics, the key point of all this is: When, for example, people watch on TV a political ad or event in the news, or read of a presidential speech or action in the newspaper, those beliefs, values, and attitudes affect how they interpret and even perceive what has been communicated, and hence what their opinion and ultimate behavior will be. Walter Lippmann, in his early book on public opinion, expressed this in a way that has not been surpassed: "For the most part we do not first see, and then define, we define first and then see. In the great blooming, buzzing confusion of the outer world, we pick out what our culture has already defined for us, and we tend to perceive that which we have picked out in the form stereotyped for us by our culture."[16] That thought leads us to the next question: How do people acquire those values, beliefs, and attitudes?

On Political Socialization

Political socialization is the name for the process of learning values, beliefs, and attitudes in a society. The traditional agents of socialization are parents and family, school, peers, community, and church. Carefully thinking through how people acquired their values, beliefs, and attitudes, and consciously identifying their content, is very important in an effort to understand communication through the media and its impact on people's political behavior. It is also important to remember that many of the basic values and beliefs that people have were acquired in a long process of learning orientations over the formative years, and that the process involved, especially in the powerful case of parents and family socialization, is as often subconscious as it is explicit and conscious.

A person's response to a specific political communication such as a political ad, or to a pattern of communications from a particular political actor, will be powerfully affected by the orientations the person learned from the various socializing forces in his or her "world." Keeping in mind that such communications through the media can be verbal and/or visual, speeches and/or performances before the cameras, responses to a pattern of communications are the principal basis for evaluating an officeholder or candidate. As political parties have declined as organizations that guide people's political choices, it is increasingly individual *candidate evaluations* that are primary in people's electoral choices. Since very few people meet candidates directly, they respond to communications about and from those candidates through the mass media. Central to their responses are their socialized values, beliefs, and attitudes. To look at it from the opposite direction, such orientations are what the astute political actor is seeking to tap in people through communication.[17]

Clearly, then, the deeply ingrained basic values and beliefs people have as central parts of their mental makeup, and the attitudes that build on those values and beliefs, are key elements to analyze in attempting to understand the impact of political communications through the media. Perhaps a brief review of an illustrative example (which is discussed further in Chapter 3) will make the point clearer. Consider the principal theme of the Reagan presidential reelection campaign in 1984 and the TV ads that were its prime articulation and depiction. The theme was "Morning in America," and the ads depicted rosy sunsets over the great American landscape; workers hard at work and some happily *back* to work, including one, obviously of immigrant origin, who says "God bless America"; renovation of the Statue of Liberty; single-family-home construction being carried on vigorously, accompanied by talk of "the American Dream" of owning a home; and President Reagan in a mistily focused shot of the White House Oval Office. What values, beliefs, and attitudes of the majority of the public were being tapped, consciously and subconsciously, by those visual and verbal messages? Theodore White has summed up Reagan's appeal to main American orientations: "He saw the future in the lost summertime of the nation's past, when neighborhoods were safe, when families held together . . . when U.S. power bestrode the world. He wrapped both past and future in the American flag."[18]

Another basic product of people's socialization which was being tapped by the Reagan campaign appeals is an attitude, with underlying beliefs and values, toward the presidency. This attitude, with its primary genesis in the childhood years, is one of virtual reverence for the office of the presidency, a feeling that this office is something approaching the embodiment of the American system, the first symbol of the republic, with its associations of semimythical, heroic past presidents. Research in the late 1950s found children's perceptions of the president to be exceedingly, indeed, almost magically positive: "he gives us freedom," "he takes care of the United States," and so on.[19] Some post-Watergate research, on the other hand, found changes in young persons' images of presidents; they seemed to have more fallible images of presidents.[20] This led many scholars to the conclusion that young people—and adults even more so—are increasingly cynical about politics in general and presidents in particular. Yet caution is in order in interpreting these findings. The public would still appear to hold attitudes of an extremely positive, even glorifying nature, toward the institution of the presidency. As Kinder and Abelson have observed: "The American Presidency is a special office . . . [with presidents serving as] both monarch and minister. As a consequence, the Presidency becomes the focus of deep if ordinarily inarticulate feelings."[21] Correspondingly, the public would appear to retain a remarkable image of the presidency and to be receptive to striking leadership in the White House. The response to Ronald Reagan as president would seem to be very good evidence to that effect.

As introductory courses review the basics and other books treat the subject thoroughly,[22] the traditional agents and processes of socialization will not be elaborated upon. The newer agents, namely, the mass media, do need to be discussed here. The focus will be on television.

Television in American Society

What is needed first is a little perspective on the "place" TV holds in society today and on the reach of television in modern developed societies, especially America. Since midcentury, TV has evolved into a truly pervasive presence in American society. It is not easy to "pin down" precisely what a prominent place TV holds in American society. The widely noted fact that public opinion surveys in the 1970s repeatedly found CBS News anchorman Walter Cronkite to be the "most trusted man in America" provides an interesting hint. More generally, the Roper polls have documented a dramatic change in how the public responds to TV news compared with that in newspapers. In 1959, slightly more people said they would be "inclined to believe" a newspaper story over a corresponding TV news version of the same story if they were conflicting (by 32% to 29%). But by the mid-1970s, half of the public said they would believe the TV version. (People could also choose other mass media.)[23] One other indicator of TV's place in our society is appropriate to mention. As George Comstock and colleagues have pointed out:

Television viewing as a primary activity, excluding very disrupted viewing while doing something else, consumes more of the leisure time of Americans than any other activity. . . .

One of television's most marked effects appears to have been to reduce time sleeping. It also appears to have reduced time spent in social gatherings away from home, in radio listening, in reading books, in miscellaneous leisure, in conversation, in travel related to leisure, in movie-going, in religious activities, and in household tasks.[24]

Television does have extraordinary pervasiveness throughout American society. As noted earlier, 98% of households have a TV set, and virtually half have more than one. As of the 1980s, by the time teenagers graduate from high school, they have already spent more total hours watching TV than being in school. The direct *and indirect* reach of television is suggested by Michael Hughes:

[T]elevision in American society may be related to the diffusion of culture and to alterations in social structure, both of which affect the behavior of virtually all persons in the society regardless of how much television they watch. For example, persons who watch television may be carriers of cultural innovations, ways of conceptualizing the world, and variations in lifestyles which, through social interaction in the real world, are diffused to persons who had little, if any, contact with the original messages.[25]

Television has also been a highly unifying experience, in that essentially the entire nation has watched programs produced by, in the American case, the three networks, although cable TV development broadened that experience somewhat in the 1980s. That is, for the past three decades or a little more, the nation as a whole has shared the experience of a single tiny set of common entertainment, news, and other programs. (Such common mass media experience actually began with national radio networks a generation earlier, of course.) Communications scholar George Gerbner and colleagues have described the reach and basic role of TV in a modern developed society:

Television is a centralized system of storytelling. . . . People are now born into the symbolic environment of television and live with its repetitive lessons throughout life. Television cultivates from the outset the very predispositions that affect future cultural selections and uses. Transcending historic barriers of literacy and mobility, television has become the primary common source of everyday culture of an otherwise heterogeneous population.

Many of those now dependent upon television have never before been part of a shared national political culture. Television provides, perhaps for the first time since preindustrial religion, a strong cultural link, a shared daily ritual of highly compelling and informative content. . . .[26]

(One interesting and important political development of the past three decades may, in some significant part, be a consequence of the period of TV-induced more unified sociocultural experience. During essentially the same period as the rise and dominance of TV, there has been a reduction in political isolation and one-party political systems in the United States, most notably in the South—especially for presidential and congressional office. The author does not know of research on this specific question; it would be an interesting subject to investigate.)

Television as an Agent of Socialization

The next thing to note and reflect on is the basic ways in which TV can socialize people. The news shows, with scenes and reports of institutions and their officeholders and of classic symbols of the nation, certainly serve as socializing instruments.[27] They can also, on occasion, shake some socialized attitudes—although seldom basic values and beliefs—by coverage and portrayal of key institutional figures gone wrong. Richard Nixon and the Watergate events were the best example.

The news programs are not, however, the only shows that socialize, which depict, portray, and discuss, often implicitly, established values, beliefs, and attitudes. The entertainment programs also serve as socializing agents. We need to reflect for a moment on the ways they can socialize, and introduce some implications. Two important observations must be made first, which set the scene. First, socialization begins in early childhood. So does watching television—a considerable amount. Indeed, TV can, with only slight exaggeration, be called the nation's baby-sitter. Further, although this is difficult to document with any precision, a substantial amount of TV viewing by children and teenagers is unaccompanied by adults, which means that such communication is subject to little, if any, parental interpretation. This substantial TV viewing, engaged in throughout the formative years, would seem likely to have a significant impact on young persons' perspectives. Political scientist Austin Ranney has written of an incident that illustrates the power of entertainment programs on TV to affect how young persons see the world. Ranney tells of taking his 15-year-old son and a friend to visit the Smithsonian's Air and Space Museum. After the tour, which showed exhibits from the Wright brothers' plane to the *Apollo XI* moon capsule, Ranney

> asked the boys which sight they found the most exciting. Without hesitation they replied, "The Enterprise"—that is, a model of the fictitious space ship featured in the long-running television series "Star Trek." Somewhat taken aback, I remonstrated [must have been a professor if he "remonstrated"], "But you saw a lot of famous *real* airplanes and space ships, and that's only a model of a stage set for a TV show." My son explained, "Look, Dad, most of the things we've seen here we've already seen on TV. We've both been watching 'Star Trek' ever since we were little kids, and the Enterprise is just as real to us as all the other things in this museum, and more exciting."[28]

Second, it is important to think about the social patterns portrayed over the general course of TV programs. Specifically, what types of people (demographic categories) are seen to what extent in TV programs, what is the pattern of roles the different demographic types play, and what is the range of behavior, occupations, and basic economic and political orientations and philosophies portrayed and discussed? Especially over the formative years, if young people consistently see certain types of people in the vast majority of roles and certain types playing the dominant and the obviously skilled and admired roles, it seems likely this would serve to inculcate the idea that these are the legitimate, "properly" dominant social patterns. The same function would seem likely to obtain with regard to the range of social behavior, occupations, and basic economic and political orientations. One interesting question, with significant political implications, is: What of a young person from a family of a demographic type *not* portrayed in desirable roles (either not seen much at all or portrayed in *un*desirable roles); would the sense of political efficacy held by that young person be strongly depressed (or more so than other socializing forces have induced)? The child of a miner or a cleaning woman or a Hispanic are examples. It is also important to remember, since we are speaking of political socialization of the general public, including the *current adult* electorate, that the social patterns portrayed on TV in *past* periods—the 1950s and 1960s, in the case of TV—must be considered. Those were the formative years for a sizable percentage of the electorate of the 1980s and 1990s.

Those are questions for everyone to think about regarding television and its socializing impact. Some scholars have researched various of those questions and have arrived at some interesting and, in some cases, striking conclusions. The most substantial and perhaps the most significant such effort is the research conducted since 1967 by George Gerbner and his associates at the University of Pennsylvania's Annenberg School of Communications.[29]

The Gerbner team's principal research employed a two-pronged approach in their "Cultural Indicators" project. First, in what they have called "message system analysis," the team recorded a week of TV programming each year since 1967 and then analyzed the content of those programs to identify social patterns portrayed. They found distinct patterns which, in various ways, are not representative of the demographic and social realities of American society. They found the middle and upper middle classes heavily overrepresented (seven out of ten characters) compared with their percentage of the (actual) American populace. They found that only 10% of TV characters were from the blue-collar and "service" class, whereas 67% of the actual populace fall into that general category. People over 65 on TV comprised but one-fifth of their actual percentage in the American populace. There were at least three times the number of men's roles as women's and "[m]ost women attend to men or home . . . and are younger (but age faster) than the men they meet."[30]

Another research effort analyzed that pattern of the portrayal of women in greater depth. The direction of conclusions is the same, but this study, by Lichter, Lichter, and Rothman,[31] fills in further details. These scholars reviewed and identified the social background, personal traits, and activities of over 7000 characters from a sample of program episodes selected yearly from 1955 through 1985. Themes, morals, and social commentary were also recorded and analyzed from a total of 620 episodes. These researchers also found that male roles greatly outnumber female roles (although the gap has narrowed slightly since 1975). Two out of three men were involved in an occupation, whereas only two of five women were. From 1955 to 1985, 93% of all judges, 93% of all doctors, 86% of all corporate executives, 87% of all lawyers, and 87% of all college professors were played by males; and more generally, nine of ten educated professionals were men. Perhaps even more strikingly, of those characters whose education was made known, men accounted for 85% of college graduates and 89% of those with graduate school in TV-land.

Clearly, women, overall, have been depicted in a distinctly (traditional) secondary light, that is, as characters with lower status and less authority. Assessing themes, women's activities have most often been portrayed as concerned with the home or with men. Interestingly, however, women have been portrayed in a quite positive light in other respects: They commit only half as many crimes as men, are only half as likely as men to be portrayed as villains, and are only half as likely to experience defeat. This, of course, is also a traditional perspective. One positive aspect that is not of a traditional nature is contained in shows that raise issues of women's rights. The researchers found a noteworthy change in orientation in such shows. Although almost one-fourth of shows that raised such issues rejected the feminist position before 1965, thereafter none of the episodes analyzed "derided" notions of sexual equality.[32]

Some interesting particular examples of nontraditional role patterns appeared in the mid-1980s, which suggested some change in portrayals. The visibility—and image of competence—of senior citizens got boosts on TV with the appearance of shows with seniors in starring roles, such as "Murder, She Wrote," "The Equalizer" (at least for the over-50 set), and (with a sizable dash of senior-relevant humor) "Golden Girls." On the racial side, the hit of the mid-1980s was "The Cosby Show," featuring a black family. The show was criticized, however, for portraying an extremely atypical black family (husband and wife being successful doctor and lawyer) and hence missing central elements of the black experience in America.

George Gerbner and his research team also went beyond documenting the demographic patterns played out on TV. The second dimension of their approach to studying television and its effects has been what they call their "cultivation analysis." In this side of their studies they constructed multiple-choice questionnaires which included answers containing correct statements about actual demographic and social patterns in American society, together with answers that reflected how TV portrays the world (as discussed above). These questionnaires were submitted to representative samples of the public. Respondents who were "heavy viewers" of TV (those watching for over four hours a day) and those who were "light viewers" (those watching less than two hours a day) were distinguished. Gerbner and colleagues found that heavy viewers tended to choose the TV portrayal of the world rather than the answer corresponding to social reality, whereas light viewers tended to choose the latter.

Two specific examples most remarkably illustrate the impact on perspectives. First, as noted above, people over 65 have been drastically underrepresented on TV shows compared with the percentage of seniors in American society. Corresponding to that TV portrayal, heavy viewers perceived seniors as making up a *smaller* proportion of the population today than 20 years ago. This is especially striking since, in reality, the over-65 age category is the fastest-growing category (or one of the two fastest, depending on how one measures the "baby boom" generation). Second, one of the patterns of TV portrayals Gerbner and colleagues found was a high level of crime: "Crime in prime time is at least 10 times as rampant as in the real world. An average of five to six acts of overt physical violence per hour involves over half of all major characters."[33] Corresponding to this, heavy viewers of all demographic types and from all types of neighborhoods overestimate the likelihood of being victims of crime and the general level of crime. Gerbner calls this the "mean world syndrome," and researchers speculate that this can "be expected to contribute to receptivity to repressive measures and to apparently simple, tough, hard-line posturing and 'solutions'"—significant political implications if their conclusions are correct.

If accurate, these are findings of striking significance. Certainly, they compellingly demonstrate the importance of further research to document more completely TV's impact on the public's perceptions of social reality. The research process will go on for some time, as this is a very complex, challenging matter to analyze. This is demonstrated by the fact that other researchers have challenged various of the findings of Gerbner's team. Two scholars, Hirsch[34] and Hughes,[35] reexamined the data used by the Gerbner group and reanalyzed the relationships between amount of TV exposure and various of the categories of responses found by Gerbner's team. Their results called into question various of the conclusions of the Gerbner group. Stay tuned; more is to come on this important subject.

THE PSYCHOLOGY OF MEDIA USE

The studies just discussed analyzed the amount of exposure people have had to television and how various of their beliefs and perceptions were affected by that exposure. Particularly when combined with carefully con-

structed questions and careful analysis of good samples of people's responses, this is an important approach to studying the mass media and
their impact. Various scholars point out, however, that people's statements
that they "rely" most on one or another medium do not tell us precisely
what amount of actual exposure to that medium they had. Such scholars
also point out that a statement of a general amount of exposure to one
medium does not tell us precisely what message content was actually
received.

In studying the media to understand how they affect people's beliefs
and perceptions, it is important to probe more deeply into what has actually been communicated. But that raises two further categories of questions. First, if we are to understand what media communications people
actually get exposed to and what message content they actually receive, it
would make sense to ask how people come to pay attention to a particular
medium and various specific programs and stories; in short, why are people moved to watch, listen to, or read a particular program or story? Some
researchers have investigated this basic question, the general name for
which is "uses and gratifications" research. Second, and probing still more
deeply, we should ask how people specifically receive and mentally process
messages from the media. Various scholars have studied those questions;
two lines of study are important to review. First, they have considered
whether people employ selective perception and attention in watching,
listening, and reading. Second, researchers have drawn on "information
processing theory" to help sort out how people mentally receive and process communications. We now turn to these various aspects of the "psychology of media use."

Uses and Gratifications Research

Early studies of voting[36] and of the political effects of the media[37]
operated under a conception of the media as a powerful force that would
directly and simply "inject" messages into people (dubbed the "hypodermic
needle" effect); and correspondingly, the public was essentially conceived
of as just passively receiving those messages. Not too surprisingly, those
studies found "minimal effects" on people as a result of exposure to the
mass media. More recently, particularly by the 1960s and 1970s, it was
recognized that a more adequately complex conceptualization was needed
of how people interact with the media. Uses and gratifications theory conceived of people as playing a more active role in their interactions with the
media. Researchers pursued questions of why people choose to expose
themselves to particular media communications by considering what *uses*
they make of the media and what *gratifications* they receive from doing so.

Communications scholars Katz, Blumler, and Gurevitch[38] have summarized to what this "uses and gratifications" conception directs our attention in studying media impact: "(1) the social and psychological origins of (2) needs, which generate (3) expectations of (4) the mass media . . . which lead to (5) differential patterns of media exposure (or engagement in other activities), resulting in (6) need gratifications and (7) other consequences. . . ."[39] So, to understand what communications people expose themselves to and what they tend to pay more or less attention to, and hence, what message content they are likely to actually "take in," "uses and gratifications" theory suggests the following question for study. What needs do people have that can be met, to some degree at least, by attending to media communications? McLeod and Becker, like some other scholars, say that people's *motives* for exposure to the media should be distinguished from their basic needs; and motives are more measurable, specific reasons for such exposure. As those two scholars state, motives, which originate in people's basic needs, their social backgrounds, and their current circumstances, "can be defined as expressed desires for gratification in a given class of situations."[40] Motives are also easier than needs to measure.

One motive—the classic reason—for paying attention to the front section of the newspaper or the evening TV news would be to garner information to enable better choices in elections, "better," that is, with regard to one's political philosophy and assorted tangible and symbolic needs and wants. Another motive might stem from one's social and/or work situation: A certain current event may have been the center of discussion and one or more members of the group or job circle might turn to the news so as not to be left out of the conversation next time or to be perceived as "dumb" or simply "out of it"—which motive would involve the underlying fundamental need of social acceptance and "belongingness."[41] Somewhat different exposure to the various media is likely to result, and different information and impressions are likely to be remembered by people with those two different motives. Very different patterns of effects, and perhaps exposure, are likely for persons who watch or read the news principally for exciting and dramatic events, for those who tend to have the TV on anyway from watching a previous show, or for those who have the TV on out of habit or to have something to do. These people may merely "perk up" their ears and eyes when a well-known person or celebrity is brought up or appears on the screen; that may be most of what they "learn" from their exposure. Further, many of the people with these different motives might respond to a formal questionnaire about their extent of news watching, for example, by indicating the same or nearly the same totals for a given week or month, but they are likely to retain very different information and impressions. They will also have quite different expectations of what gratifications they will get from watching or reading a medium.

As a guide to thinking about how people expose themselves to the media and what they are likely to get out of that exposure, all the above makes good sense. Obtaining accurate measurement of such motives for use and of the resulting gratifications—and, from those, the ultimate effects—is a difficult matter, though. Some researchers have simply used age, gender, and other demographic variables to infer motives from them. For an obvious example, people over 60 are likely to have different types and intensities of motives from teenagers for paying attention to and remembering programs and stories on long-term health care. Other researchers have given samples of people previously developed lists of possible motivations to choose from, or open-ended questions (with appropriate probes) that allow people to report on their own motives.[42] This, of course, raises the problem of how fully conscious people are of their own motives regarding such a common enterprise as attending to the media, let alone their underlying basic needs.

With less than two decades of work by a relative handful of social scientists doing work that relates in any substantial way to the political realm, there is not enough evidence of relevance on this subject for anything close to definitive conclusions. Let the following illustrate some of the principal types of studies that have been done.

Two British researchers, Jay Blumler and Dennis McQuail,[43] as a result of repeated use of open-ended questions and probes, developed a list of eight motivations that people have for the use and nonuse of political communications. But further testing of them found that under various circumstances the motives could not be empirically verified as separate and distinct factors. The current consensus seems to be that there are three basic categories of motives: (1) seeking information; (2) seeking diversion, escape, and/or excitement; and (3) seeking communications that serve more specific personal needs (which covers a lot of ground).[44]

Some other scholars have looked at how people rate the helpfulness, and hence the resulting gratification, of the various media in assisting them in making political decisions. Jack McLeod and his team explored that question with a sample of people with specific regard to helping people judge candidates' stands on issues and their personal qualities in the 1976 presidential election. McLeod and colleagues produced findings of considerable interest for some central issues discussed further at several points in this book. They found that people felt helped as much or more by news in newspapers compared with news on TV in an effort to clarify issue stands. Mendelsohn and O'Keefe[45] found a clearer advantage: Newspapers were rated as distinctly more helpful than TV in satisfying informational motives in a campaign situation. But another study found that the newspaper medium was rated well behind TV news in helpfulness when illustrations of the candidates' personal qualities were the question.[46]

On Receiving and Mentally Processing Media Messages

Selective Exposure, Attention, and Perception Seeking to identify and explain the uses and gratifications people make and receive from exposure to the media has given analysts one good way to study how people come to expose themselves to the media and pay varying levels of attention to it. Another important dimension of that process of exposure and attention is, in a sense, a psychological close cousin of the "uses and gratifications" theory. It is the concept of selective exposure, perception, and attention.

In essence, with respect to people and their interaction with the media, there are the following elements: the individual human being, with his or her various sense organs enabling direct perception, and some medium through which a communication is sent. Most simply, there is a stimulus (the communication) and a response. But for real persons in their actual social situations, just how they receive the stimulus is certainly not a simple and automatic matter. Rather, some social scientists concluded that, for various reasons and to varying extents, people selectively expose themselves to the stimuli of media communications and selectively pay attention to, perceive, and remember those communicative stimuli.

Most fundamentally, our very sensory capacities, our basic perceptual system, naturally focuses our attention on certain parts of all the stimuli that are "reaching" us. As psychologist Henry Gleitman observes: "We focus on the figure [in our view], not on the [back]ground; we are more likely to notice shapes that are moving, rather than those that are stationary. Such examples indicate that perception is selective. . . . Our ability to take in and interpret the myriad stimulations around us is finite, and so our perceptual system is forced to choose among them."[47]

Psychologists have relatedly found what they have dubbed the "cocktail-party effect," referring to how, in the midst of all the noise of different conversations, people "tune out" others to focus on the person with whom they are talking (at least most of the time). This phenomenon has been demonstrated in experiments by placing headphones on someone, then running two different audio messages through the two headphones and asking the person to pay attention to one rather than the other. As a rule, the subject is not able to remember the "other" message at all; it is tuned out. But not absolutely. When a name or other item is highly familiar to the listener, the person tends to suddenly tune in.[48] The application of this finding to people watching TV or listening to radio, in their normal daily situation, should be obvious.

The central conclusion is that, due to inherent perceptual limitations, as well as to people's values, beliefs, attitudes, and readily available store of knowledge, people tend to have selective attention, and that attention "acts as a kind of filter." Thus as Gleitman reports: "This filter is . . . interposed between the initial sensory registration and later stages of perceptual analysis."[49] Further, and very interestingly: "In humans, the major means of physically selecting the stimulus input are the movements of the eyes,"[50] which formalizes what is intuitively recognized, that the eyes are the most powerful, determinative perceptual mechanism. The implications of these fundamental psychological observations, especially the latter, are profound for understanding the political use of the medium of television, as is discussed in greater detail in Chapter 4.

There is another dimension to the analysis of selective exposure and attention. Roughly speaking, there have been two basic stages in the findings produced in this dimension. Social psychologists and political scientists, guided by "cognitive consistency" theories, concluded that people, with their established values, beliefs, and attitudes, do not like to encounter information that contradicts those beliefs and attitudes; they find it disturbing to be confronted with such inconsistencies. Correspondingly, it was suggested that people tend to avoid such messages; they selectively expose themselves and selectively pay attention to those programs and stories that are consonant with their orientations. More recently, however (second stage), with a substantial amount of research evidence accumulated, the general scholarly conclusion is that selective exposure and even selective attention occur far less than was earlier thought to be the case.

There are a couple of main reasons for that revised conclusion. First, the very nature of TV and radio make selective exposure (especially) and attention much more difficult. Many people simply watch TV as such, rather than just tuning in for specific, isolated programs. Further, the nature of the medium of TV and of radio makes the message "keep coming at" the viewer/listener, who is normally in a passive mode of interaction (unlike the print media, where one must actively choose a story and read it). This is especially the case with the series of stories in, and political ads during, the TV news. Second, research has found information at odds with people's beliefs not to be as troubling for them as once thought. Some people even seem to be curious about different views or have a self-image as an open-minded person.[51]

Those findings apply to selective exposure and, to some extent, to selective attention. How great the attention, how much and what part of the communication are remembered, and also just how the communication is originally perceived are realms where there still appears to be selectivity in operation. As Patterson and McClure found in their study of the 1972 presidential election:

> Viewers' reactions to campaign story after campaign story reveal the strong pull of bias [i.e., selective perception] on what they see. . . . For those people whose politics were in tune with McGovern, his televised image was indeed a

positive one: "He looks so able. I think he's very able."—42 yr. old housewife; "He's a good honest man. You can see that."—25 yr. old secretary.

But to people whose politics were opposed to McGovern . . . : "I don't like him. I wasn't impressed."—52 yr. old housewife . . . ; "He's a weak sister. You can see that immediately."—27 yr. old worker.[52]

Information Processing Theory   Beginning in the 1970s, political scientists sought to probe still more deeply into how people receive communications from the media and how they mentally process such communications. The approach used in this work is called "information processing theory" or "schema theory." This theory was borrowed from psychology, which had been developing and employing the theory for some years.

Underlying the schema approach is the recognition that people have a limited capacity to "take in" and mentally sort through the mass of messages they are bombarded with through the various mass media. Here we refer not simply to the physical nature of the sense organs, but to psychologically limited amounts of attention, capacity and inclination to store information, and so on. A principal line of research in political science had prepared political scientists to accept that foundation of schema theory: Public opinion survey research done in the 1950s and 1960s[53] consistently found a public with limited amounts of information about the political system, despite relatively ready availability of so much information from the mass media.

Information processing theory contends that the way people with limited time, inclination, and capacity deal with the flood of information and impressions they are variously exposed to is by having developed structures of understanding from the accumulation of past experience. These structures of knowledge and impressions called "schemas" are relatively organized, having a more general conception which "ties" a cluster of particular bits of knowledge and impressions together—that is, which, in some way, draws a common connection between those bits.[54] These schemas, then, assist people in receiving messages and sorting them into meaningful categories.

This schema conception appears to provide the best description and explanation of the nature of people's knowledge use and the structure of their thought processes as they receive and consciously or semiconsciously try to sort out the meaning of communications to which they are exposed. Doris Graber, in a major study done on mental processing of political matters, found the schema concept to be very helpful in an explanation of "how people tame the information tide."[55] As Graber has pointed out, despite the modern wealth of information sources, the perceptions of average Americans "about the nature of politics, and the meanings they extract from media stories, often seem scant compared to media offerings. The content of their reported recall is often out of synch with the information base provided by the media."[56] Graber found that the use of existing schemas in people's heads was the best explanation for what they did with the communications to which they were exposed.

> [T]hey scan the information haphazardly to extract portions which are useful to them either to flesh out existing perceptions, or amend them, or confirm and, occasionally, disconfirm them. The failure to retain a wealth of details, or to always mirror the media stimulus faithfully, springs from media consumers' practice of limiting processing to information suitable for incorporation into their schemata. Questions [asked people] about media content thus tend to tap what remains of the original stimulus after processing, as well as what has been recalled from previously stored information as a consequence of the media stimulus.[57]

Much research still needs to be done for a fuller understanding of the nature (structure and content) of people's politically relevant schemas and precisely how they are used in processing communications.[58] But, as indicated, information processing theory has been very useful and holds even greater promise for furthering explanation of how people mentally process what they receive from media communications, which, in turn, is a central reason for why people vote and take other political actions the way they do. That question of the bases of people's voting and other political actions leads us to the final section of the chapter, and some research findings with strikingly important implications.

LEVELS OF POLITICAL KNOWLEDGE; COHERENCE OF POLITICAL OPINION

For several decades one of the central enterprises of political science has been the conduct of survey research, principally to determine the bases of people's political behavior. One category of finding produced by that work has been evidence on the general public's level of knowledge regarding issues, candidates and officeholders, and institutions in the United States. What has been found (with what one might call depressing regularity) is a very low level of such knowledge. Political scientist W. Russell Neuman has expressed the point very well:

> [T]he available data show overwhelmingly that even the basic facts of political history, the fundamental structure of political institutions, and current political figures and events escape the cognizance of the great majority of the electorate. Moreover, the media coverage of politics and interpersonal conversations peak at election time. Thus, since most of the studies were conducted at the height of an election campaign, these results may represent a relatively conservative estimate of public ignorance.
>   The basic fact of political relevance to the voter is the names of political candidates. Simple recognition of the candidates' names represents the minimum necessary awareness for a functional political life. It is difficult to imag-

ine an individual with a sophisticated sense of a candidate's policy positions, background, and political style who is unable to identify the candidate's name. . . . Over the past two decades, however, on the average 56 percent of the population have been unable to identify any congressional candidate in their district at the height of the congressional campaign. . . . On the average, only 22 percent are able to name both of the major party candidates in contested races in their district.[59]

Two other specific examples, among many major domestic and foreign policy issues that could be listed, are: In one major survey, only about a third of the public was able to give a basic identification of NATO;[60] and in 1979, at the height of Senate consideration and media coverage, only about one-fourth of the public could accurately identify which two nations were involved in the SALT treaty negotiations.[61]

For those concerned about an informed electorate serving as the base of a democracy, this is not an encouraging picture. Another category of findings from survey research adds to that picture; rather little coherence in the structure of people's opinions is in evidence. According to some major studies, most people do not seem to have a general conception of politics, a consistent package of ideas which are related to one another, or to consider cause and effect when responding to policies and issues. Someone who does think like that, political scientists have called an "ideological thinker." Rather, people tend to respond to political matters on the basis of particularized, gut reactions. The most prominent of the studies found that fewer than one in twelve Americans have such coherent political thinking. (The connections required to qualify were quite simple; people merely had to mention things like: "The Republicans believe in big industry. Besides, they've passed a lot of labor bills I don't approve of."[62]) Such a low level of coherence is also troubling for those concerned with democracy.

It should be noted that there has been some debate in political science about (1) whether there has been some increase in the public's attention to issues, as suggested by one study,[63] and (2) just what the low levels of knowledge and opinion coherence mean for people's real ability to act as adequate citizens[64]—and, in fact, whether the "ideological thinker" standard is unrealistically high for any society in the real world.[65] Still, the findings regarding the basically low level of knowledge and opinion structure have not been effectively challenged.

These circumstances of the nature of public opinion, along with the decline of the role of political parties, raise a question of central importance. If the general public has such low levels of knowledge and systems of thinking, and if they rely far less on the parties for cues on what to do, then *on what bases* do people make their political decisions? Further, given such circumstances of knowledge and opinion, are people more easily manipulated by the way that messages and images are communicated? People would appear to use schemas to help them sort through political messages, but how are those schemas formed, what are they based on, and how are they tapped by communications? These questions are of the first order of importance for a democratic society.

One way that such schemas are tapped is by the use of symbols in communication. We turn next to the use of symbols and persuasive communication in general.

CHAPTER THREE
THINKING ABOUT COMMUNICATION
Symbolics and Persuasion

INTRODUCTION AND POINTS OF PERSPECTIVE

Introduction by Way of Paradox

In the presidential election of 1984, incumbent Ronald Reagan won in a landslide—in fact, the fifth greatest in the century (in popular vote). This result would appear to be a clear example of "the people's choice, of a mandate for action in government." Yet there were some striking paradoxes involved in that election, paradoxes that raise important questions.

First, despite that landslide vote, major public opinion surveys in 1984 (and at other times) routinely showed majorities of the public holding opinions on policy issues that were contrary to positions or actions taken by President Reagan. In a number of cases, those were very large majorities. For example, a Gallup poll conducted September 28 to October 1, 1984 found strong to overwhelming majorities favoring the Equal Rights Amendment, "increasing spending for social programs such as education and Medicare," the nuclear freeze, and maintaining cost-of-living increases on Society Security benefits, and it found a strong majority in opposition to "relaxing pollution controls to reduce costs to industry." In each of those major issue areas, and in a number of others, Reagan's positions and actions were at odds with public opinion.

Second, it has been noted by scholars for many years that people have a general conception of what candidates for high office, especially the presidency, ought to be like; that is, what characteristics and capabilities they should have. Presidential scholar Stephen Wayne has articulated one key characteristic: It is "important to appear competent, to exhibit sufficient knowledge and skills for the job."[1] Indeed, political scientist Roberta Sigel, in her survey of what people see as ideal traits of presidents, found that "intelligence" ranked number two in importance (second only to "honesty").[2] Yet, as a number of stories in leading news media noted[3] and as could be observed in many of Mr. Reagan's press conferences (before the Iran-Contra revelations), he frequently gave incorrect statements of facts, made up stories and/or took them from movies and told them as real, and generally demonstrated a weak grasp of the substance of policies and issues. As presidential scholar Thomas Cronin pointed out: "By several usual standards of presidential leadership performance, Reagan might be judged a failure. He often lost track of his facts, or simply got them wrong. He once mistook his Secretary of Housing and Urban Development for just another visiting mayor. . . ."[4]

This would seem to be at odds with the public's idea of what a president should be like, in a very important respect. A further dimension of this paradox is that the public, as of 1984, perceived President Reagan as a strong *and competent* leader, according to various surveys.[5] Interestingly, Scott Keeter found that "on the issue of knowledgeability, Mondale did no better (in public opinion) than the President among those voters who said that this mattered."[6]

One other interesting and more recent paradox is worth mentioning. In December 1986, a Gallup poll found a majority of Americans favoring development of a "space-based 'Star Wars' system [President Reagan's proposed "Strategic Defense Initiative"] to protect the country from nuclear attack."[7] Yet there is good reason to conclude that only a tiny fraction of the public (almost certainly fewer than 10%) had anything resembling a good idea of what the system was to be like[8] or what the nation's physicists thought of the likelihood of the system working. (A majority of physicists thought it was unlikely to work.) Further, according to Gallup polls for the *same period,* nearly half the public thought "the government is spending too much for defense and military purposes" and just over a third thought the spending level "about right."[9] In light of the tens or hundreds of billions of dollars the system was projected to cost, those are interesting opinions!

How can we explain these paradoxes? Certainly, the perception of good economic times by much of the public was a factor in the 1984 election results; but that does not explain those other elements. The central subject of this chapter gives us an important part of the answer: the effective use of symbols in political communication to persuade the public. Could the verbal symbol of President Reagan and America "sitting tall in the saddle" again, along with the frequently seen visual symbol of Reagan pictured literally doing that on a horse at his ranch, have affected people's perceptions of him as a strong leader? Would the consistent rhetorical challenge of the Soviet Union, with speeches insisting on "negotiating from strength," bolstering our "military might," and being "number one again" have done the same? As Wilson Carey McWilliams observed: "In speech [and in TV appearance] Reagan is almost invariably firm and decisive, certain of his values and his direction, and inclined to strong language and striking expression."[10] Furthermore, regarding the first of those paradoxes (the disagreement between Reagan and the public on policy issues), Henry Plotkin has given us an important part of the explanation, which suggests a central role played by symbols: "Reagan's success, in no small measure, was his ability to redirect the memories of many Americans away from painful experiences toward more pleasant ones. [He] tapped into a powerful need of many Americans to forget the struggles of the past and present."[11]

How was that "redirection" accomplished? The effective use of symbols—and understanding how people would receive them—is the main answer. As Theodore White has said, Reagan presented to the public the symbols of "the lost summertime of the nation's past, when neighborhoods were safe, when families held together . . . when U.S. power bestrode the world" and "wrapped [it all] in the American flag."[12]

The use of symbolics and other forms of persuasive communication is thus an important subject to think about in understanding political communication. It is even more important in the age of television, with the ability of that medium to powerfully project symbolic portrayals and presentations to all realms of a society.

To discuss the use of symbols and other persuasive communication efforts adequately, we need first to set the scene by reemphasizing and adding to a couple of points made in the first two chapters. We then discuss what symbols are, the basic role they play, and how to analyze them. This is followed by a review of other facets involved in persuasive communication efforts and how they are received by readers, listeners, and watchers.

Points to Remember, Laying a Foundation

We should first remember what was pointed out in Chapter 1 about economically developed societies today, especially one such as the United States. Such societies are mass societies in which many people lack long-term ties to community and social networks which help their members interpret occurrences in the world in a stable fashion. As Kornhauser has observed, people who do not have strong, lasting involvement in local communities and social networks will tend to "seek new and often *remote* sources of attachment and allegiance [emphasis added]."[13] It seems that increasingly people have looked to such remote leaders and institutions and have invested in them their hopes and feelings. Presidents are, of course, the prime example. Does that remoteness make it more difficult for people to really know about those leaders and institutions with which they are identifying and in which they invest hopes and feelings? The crucial question is: How do people "know" about matters with which they (and any close friends and co-workers) have little or no direct experience? The answer is, with considerable difficulty; and the result is that symbols are decidedly more central to what people "learn" about such things. The way people learn about leaders, institutions, and issues (i.e., again, impressions and information) is by relying much more completely and directly on what the mass media communicate about them. Murray Edelman, in his classic work on symbolics and politics, has given us the best articulation of this point:

> For most [people] most of the time politics is a series of pictures in the mind, placed there by television news, newspapers, magazines, and discussions. The pictures create a moving panorama taking place in a world the mass public never quite touches, yet one its members come to fear or cheer. . . .
> There is, on the other hand, the immediate world in which people make and do things that have directly observable consequences. In these activities [people] can check their acts and assumptions against the consequences and correct errors.
> Politics is for most of us a passing grade of abstract symbols. . . . It is central to its potency as a symbol that it is remote, set apart [distant, in the psychological as well as geographical senses from the mass public].[14]

In fact, as Edelman points out, the actual impacts and consequences of leaders' political actions are often difficult for the average person to sort out, precisely due to that remoteness: "Conclusive demonstrations that their heros' policies may often be futile or misconceived are impossible simply because the link between dramatic political announcements and their impact is so long and tangled. . . . There is no necessity, and often no possibility, of continuously checking [people's] convictions against real conditions."[15] This makes the use and impact of symbols on the public even more of a significant element of the communication about politics—and hence, of politics itself.

The other basic point to remember from previous chapters is what was said in Chapter 2 concerning the nature of people's beliefs, values, and attitudes and how people generally acquire them through the agents and processes of political socialization. The symbols used in persuasive political communication are tapping those values and beliefs for a response. The strength of a person's political socialization regarding such values and beliefs, and the symbols with which such values and beliefs are associated, affects how intensely and in what way people will respond to symbols used in communication.

ON PERSUASION IN MASS COMMUNICATION

Definition and Basic Purposes of Persuasion

Political communication is persuasive communication. Human society governs itself by debate and discussion, negotiation and compromise between some or many officeholders, organizations, and groups, and interested individuals in the society regarding particular policies and basic "rules of the game" of policy making. That discussion involves efforts by different people to persuade others as to how things should be done. Persuasive communication is the essence of politics. Consequently, we should have a look at persuasive communication before we turn to symbolics in specific.

Successful persuasion is the communication of something to another person or group which affects the behavior of the other person or group. Persuasion is usually conceived of as *changing* the behavior of someone. But especially for political purposes, a second important variety of persuasion is the effort to *reinforce* existing orientations. As communications scholar Gerald Miller has pointed out: "Rather than aiming at changes in attitudes and behaviors, much persuasive communication seeks to reinforce currently held convictions and to make them more resistant to change. . . ."[16] A prime political example is the case of a Democratic Party nominee for president seeking to persuade people who have been Democratic Party identifiers to remain so and vote Democratic again.

Paralleling those two points, there are two basic ends toward which persuasive efforts strive: assurance and arousal. Being conscious of these techniques is helpful in analyzing political communication. Some persuasive communication is designed to assure people that a particular problem is being or has been solved or that things in general are all right. Other such persuasion assures people that an action is good or nonthreatening: for example, a president who gives a speech containing some data and some word symbols designed to assure the public that his economic policies are helping the economy, which, in turn, will generate enough tax revenues to balance the budget. Or the president or other leading official could give a name or a characterization to something that would serve a reassurance purpose. A good example was the naming of the MX missile system the "peacekeeper" by President Reagan. Many contended that the MX added unnecessarily to the arms race, but the name "peacekeeper" was intended to assure people that it was a benign development. So dubbing the MX missile also exemplifies one specific assurance technique: euphemism. Euphemism is the substitution of a pleasant or nonthreatening term or description for a designation of something which people tend to see as negative or threatening. Referring to a tax increase as "revenue enhancements" is another good example. Such an effort seeks to persuade people that a prominently stated policy of not accepting tax increases has not been altered, as well as to assure them that budgetary and economic matters are actually on the intended course.

It should also be clear that persuasive communication that offers assurance to people can come in forms other than the use of words. As we will be discussing more completely in the sections on symbolics, visual images and concrete activities, as carried over the mass media, can also be used to assure people, most powerfully so on television. A good example is the case of a proposed trip by President Reagan to a coal mine in 1982 (which was carried out and was dutifully broadcast on the network news shows). The president's assistants discerned from polling data that the president had lost some important political ground due to perceptions of lack of concern for minorities and the economically less fortunate. As *Newsweek* reported: "Advisors are now considering ways for Reagan to 'show compassion' for the problems of the poor and minorities. One possibility is a visit to a coal mine so Reagan could dramatize his commitment to continued benefits for miners afflicted with black-lung disease."[17] The trip was not exactly taken in private and incognito. The point was to get that visual symbol of concern on the evening network news programs.

Another example, a striking one, was that of the education initiative of the Reagan White House. Steven Weisman of the *New York Times* has described the effort well:

> Confronted by a growing public impression that the Administration was slighting education—an impression caused in part by Mr. Reagan's cuts of Federal student-loan programs and aid to schools—the White House chose to isolate the problem and focus on it. Mr. Reagan traveled around the country, calling for improvements in educational quality, meeting with students and teachers *in front of the television cameras* [emphasis added].[18]

There was no *policy* initiative here; no new education programs or budget increases were offered (indeed, the federal education budget had been cut). Were people assured that the Reagan administration was concerned about educational quality and acting on it, in the climate of opinion following the report of the President's Commission on Excellence in Education (called "A Nation At Risk")? Weisman continued: " 'The polls absolutely flip-flopped,' said Mr. Deaver [assistant to the president]. On the educational issue, 'He went from a negative rating to a positive rating overnight.' "[19]

Arousal, the second goal of persuasion, is the effort to persuade people that one or more things are *not* all right and that people must mobilize and action must be taken to solve some problem. This effort to arouse people can be intended either to persuade people to move directly to support some policy action, or can be used to engender more generalized support for a leader. One example of the latter which has been used repeatedly in the United States since about 1920 is alarms raised about the "communist threat." A particularly striking case of this was President Reagan's statement to the effect that the Soviet Union "is the source of all evil in the world." A different version was the assertion of President Lyndon Johnson and his administration of the "domino effect": If Vietnam fell to the communists, each of the other Southeast Asian nations would fall in turn (if not other nations, as well). The domino effect is also a good illustration of another specific technique of persuasive communication: the use of *metaphor*. The metaphor of dominoes falling is an easy one for a general public to grasp. It is much easier than an adequate review of the history and an analysis of another people's unique conception of their society. It also plays well on the short and dramatic story segments on the TV news. The general "communist threat" example of arousal also illustrates another technique in persuasion, *scapegoating*. It is often used to generate or reinforce general support for a leader or regime. Put simply, scapegoating is identifying some group, category of people, or nation outside one's own and assigning blame to them for many of one's problems. The ugliest example of this in modern times was, of course, the Nazi scapegoating of the Jews. (See page 51 for a note on the psychological foundations of people's response to this technique.)

Effects on People of Persuasive Efforts; Acceptance of Persuasive Communications

The reader should be "on the lookout" for the use of these techniques in political communication. But in general, are they effective in persuading people? The reader should remember what was discussed concerning how the average citizen has been socialized to see various aspects of the world (including, for example, U.S. citizens' beliefs about the Soviet Union and, conversely, Soviet citizens' beliefs about the United States). Second, the reader should remember what was noted above regarding the distance of most political affairs from average people's lives, and hence their lack of experience with such matters and consequent probable lack of understanding of them. The low level of knowledge and opinion coherence in most people should also be remembered.

These factors make for a fertile ground for planting persuasive seeds, if the communication is well calculated. A variety of other factors are involved, as well, some of which limit people's receptivity to persuasive communication. First, carrying on from Chapter 2, the more the public see an important value of theirs involved, the more likely they are to be persuaded.[20] Additionally, people have a variety of needs and desires (variously linked to their values) which incline them (1) to pay attention to persuasive communications, and (2) to consider the message. Communications scholars Cronkhite and Liska note an interesting and important implication of this and also raise the next factor: "Sometimes . . . listener [and viewer] needs are satisfied by sources who are competent and trustworthy, but frequently they are not; likability, novelty, and entertainment are often valued more highly."[21] This is a thought with interesting implications for political ads (see page 52 for evidence on this) and other forms of political communication.

Next, communications scholars have long noted the significance of how the receivers of persuasive communications perceive the credibility of the communicator. (In recent years, the old conception of communicator credibility has been broadened by scholars and has been deepened by drawing on psychological theories of cognition and information processing.[22]) Fundamentally, as Cronkhite and Liska point out: "Classic studies by Asch and Sherif[23] demonstrated early and persuasively that humans have a tendency to 'construct' social 'reality,' and much of social psychology and communication research since then has consisted of reaffirmation of that conclusion."[24] That is, through their own casual experience and mental inclinations (and again, strongly influenced by their socialization), people tend to develop their own impression of the physical and human world around them. This impression may or may not accurately correspond to "objective reality." The point here is that people will tend to "read into" or attribute to a communicator characteristics they did not directly observe, which in turn affects how receptive they are likely to be to the communicator's persuasive efforts.

Some important factors that affect how people perceive the credibility of a communicator, and hence what they tend to accept of the persuasive communication, are as follows.[25] "Reputed characteristics" are the name given one such factor. These are reports that others have given to us of what a communicator is like—important to the degree that we trust the other(s). A second factor involves nonverbal characteristics such as general physical appearance, nature and changes of facial expressions, and bodily movements, including breathing rate, respiration, eye movements, and so on. (Consider many people's responses to Richard Nixon in this light.) A fascinating bit of recent evidence regarding this factor was found by Doris Graber in her landmark study of information processing. She found:

> Judgements about peoples' honesty were especially common. In part, this was true because honesty was deemed to be a crucial element in determining whether to take messages conveyed by individuals seriously.
>
> And how did people decide who was an honest public figure? Our panelists' schema contained a number of criteria for assessing honesty. If physical appearance could be judged, people were described as having or lacking an "honest look." [Further,] avoidance of eye contact in televised encounters was universally interpreted as a sign of dishonesty, whereas a straight look into the eye [and camera] and firm, unhesitating responses were interpreted as evidence of honesty.[26]

(This was, in fact, the only articulated criterion for judgment of honesty that Graber was able to draw out of the people she studied.) As that evidence illustrates, television is the only medium that enables the receivers of communications to observe such characteristics. Hence it adds a dimension to people's judgments regarding mass political communications.

A close cousin to those factors is the human voice and how it sounds. For example, D.W. Addington found, from experimental research, that people rated speakers who had a "nasal" tone of voice as having a substantial set of undesirable personality attributes, whereas those having considerable variations in pitch were rated as having largely desirable personality attributes.[27] Such findings are interesting to contemplate in light of the case of the long career of a political communicator like Ronald Reagan. He spent his early career as a radio announcer (his livelihood depended in part on the quality of his voice) and most of his later career in front of the videocamera and microphone. Indeed, there is evidence to indicate the significant impact of this in the case of Mr. Reagan. One source of that evidence is a small-scale, in-depth panel study by the author. Asked in mid-1987 to describe their impressions of "President Reagan, as best you can recall, as of election day 1984," over 90% (of the not strictly representative sample) said that the characteristics of "likable and warm" and "sincere" applied to Reagan. About 90% even said "yes" to the "honest and straightforward" characteristic. ("Even," that is, after seven months of revelations on the Iran-Contra affair and in the midst of the televised congressional hearings on the affair. Separating present political feelings from past is, of course, very difficult for the average person to do.) A common reference was, as one put it: "He always appears with a smile on his face." Even an identifier with the Democratic Party who was "not impressed with Reagan's ideas" said Reagan "always appears [on TV as] real friendly." This person was also one who found Reagan to be "honest and straightforward" (at least as of 1984). From the overall pattern of responses, it appeared that the nonverbal characteristics of facial expression, general physical appearance, and demeanor, along with voice tones, contributed significantly to perceptions of Reagan's credibility.[28] The impressions of many also suggest that the sonority, pitch, and other qualities of Franklin Roosevelt's voice contributed considerably to people's acceptance of his credibility in the age of *radio*.

ON SYMBOLICS IN MASS COMMUNICATION

Definitions and Basic Conceptions of Symbolics

A symbol is something (word, object, visual image, activity) that stands for or suggests some meaning. Some symbols are simple and direct and are products of the basic need that people have to communicate using language or other means. The English letters making the word "chair" and a line drawing of a chair are what we call "referential symbols" for that class of objects on which we sit. They simply refer directly to all such particular, concrete objects. Of far greater importance for political communication are what Edward Sapir first called "condensational symbols."[29] This concept and the function performed by such symbols is very important. Some laying of groundwork is required before we describe more specifically what condensational symbols are and review some examples.

A few paragraphs above we noted that some classic studies showed that people tend to "construct" social "reality." The general society and the political system governing it are vast, complex, often confusing, and in most respects seem quite distant to the average person. People just don't have the time and/or the psychological energy to gather and sort out the knowledge needed to authoritatively understand such distant complexities. Despite that, political systems, if they are to function effectively, must have people cooperating, feeling like they are part of a single whole ("one nation . . ."), and accepting verdicts and actions of the system. For these reasons, people tend to build and rely on a kind of mental shorthand, a simpler set of ideas and impressions to enable them more easily to interpret and respond to developments in their society. Over the course of a nation's history, a number of such notions are developed on a society-wide basis to signify what the sociopolitical system is like and what principles are supposed to be central to it. Emotional feelings are linked to those "capsulized" ideas, through the process of political socialization. Principally, this encourages people to identify with and feel positively toward main elements of the system and the system as a whole. People are also socialized to feel negatively toward things not developed as part of the system, or considered antithetical to it.

These "shorthand ideas" centrally involve symbols—condensational symbols. As Joyce Hertzler has expressed it: "[Symbols] are the instrumentalities whereby [people] codify experience, or create a 'map' of the territory of experience."[30] Condensational symbols condense a set of notions of meaning about elements of society and condense emotions (formally called "affect") toward them. Myths and rituals, it should also be noted, are special forms of condensational symbols.

One additional point is important here. The process of socialization is a general one; especially for symbols of the national system, most everyone is taught the same basic meaning of the symbol. As Hertzler has said, the usefulness of these symbols "depends upon the fact that all [societal] members are conditioned to react more or less uniformly to them."[31] This common significance people are conditioned to attach to a symbol is why noted philosopher–social psychologist George Herbert Mead called all such symbols "significant symbols."[32] But somewhat paradoxically, such symbols still leave room for a fair amount of ambiguity in application to specific situations, issues, and policy matters. Indeed, as Hugh Duncan has observed, "perhaps it is the ambiguity of symbols which makes them so useful in human society,"[33] and also so useful in persuasive communication, and even in manipulation. Such generality is especially useful in political communication. An effective user of a symbol can indicate to a general public that he or she stands for a basic vaue the great majority holds, while also encouraging different individuals to read their own specifics into the symbol's application to the issue or issues with which it is linked by the communicator. Elder and Cobb have summed up the role played by symbols, and the potential consequences of their use, given the level of knowledge and coherence of opinion of most of the public: "Because they are simultaneously elements of the culture and objects of individual meaning, these symbols provide a linkage between the individual and the larger social and political order. They mediate the relationship between the individual and social reality, structuring people's perceptions and allowing them to find meaning in events beyond their own immediate experience. By the same token, symbols serve to constrain people's vision and make them vulnerable to manipulation."[34]

The special form of symbolics called myths is best defined as a story and/or a sort of stylized, "nutshell" explanation of historical persons, events, or circumstances which has developed over the course of part or all of a society's existence. Myths become part of the traditions of the society and serve to present part of the basic orientations and ways of viewing the society and its political system. Further, as Nimmo and Combs point out, a myth is

> A credible, dramatic, socially constructed re-presentation of perceived realities that people accept as permanent, fixed knowledge of reality while forgetting . . . its . . . imaginative, created and perhaps fictional qualities. . . . [That is,] myth is something thought to be real and believable; . . . it adds dramatic color and force to an otherwise inchoate reality; . . . it gives us a world that we can cope with and understand.[35]

Myths, as commonly held beliefs with emotional charges involved, are also one of the ways by which a society holds itself together, a way to make people feel part of a collective whole. A myth can have a specific object, such as the American myths about the character and accomplishments of George Washington or Abe Lincoln or the similar Soviet myth about V. I. Lenin. They can also be more generalized, such as the myth of the elevating and ennobling power of the presidency or (more broadly) myths regarding the original U.S. Constitution as a document that ensured democracy. (Murray Edelman has written on the uses of myth and symbol for political purposes.[36]) Rituals perform similar functions in a political system. The prime example in the United States is well explained by Dan Nimmo: "The inauguration of the president of the United States . . . is a ritual that melds a rich combination of significant symbols beyond the words of the administered oath: for example, the flag-draped setting on the Capitol steps, the presence of diplomatic dignitaries, the intonations of the chief justice administering the oath, the Holy Bible, even the mode and style of dress. All set the stage for a rite of passage, the bestowing of legitimacy upon the person elevated to presidential office. . . ."[37]

Examples and Explanations

The most obvious example of a condensational symbol is the flag of a nation. The object itself is simply a multicolored piece of cloth, but the meanings and emotions it condenses are striking. The Statue of Liberty in America is a similar symbol. It is interesting to note that in the 1980s, NBC Nightly News adopted a scene of the statue, with a rosy sunset as background, for the opening of their news show. The White House, and the Oval Office in particular, are condensational symbols that carry associations with great presidents and great events of the past.

Those are examples of objects that are visual symbols. In any given culture, various *words* also serve as key condensational symbols. Words such as "liberty" and "free enterprise," with their associated notions and emotions, have long been prime symbols in the American system. "Family" is another, as presidential aspirant Gary Hart discovered the hard way in the spring of 1987! Indeed, following the episode of the news media's zealous pursuit of Hart's personal life and his exit from the race, candidates for the 1988 nomination of both parties went to great lengths to have the tangible symbols of their spouses and other family members visibly with them at all times, especially for network cameras. A *National Journal* review of 375 political ads shown in 1986 in 14 key Senate and gubernatorial races and a scattering of others around the country found evidence of the political value of the family symbol, in word or visual form:

> For all their creative variety and differences in technical quality, the commercials, featured candidates of amazingly similar character, interests and values. . . .
> The Senate and gubernatorial contenders are uniformly depicted as hardworking family men and women who 'get the job done.' 'I-pulled-myself-up-by-my-bootstraps' stories are popular with all candidates except scions of wealthy families. . . . Even unmarried candidates are photographed frequently with children."[38]

A good exercise for the reader (especially the nonprofessional reader) would be to take a major political speech (e.g., a State of the Union message), a political ad, or a network news show and do the following: (1) carefully pick out all the visual and verbal symbols used, (2) analyze at least several for shared, socialized meanings and for all the primary and secondary values the symbols are designed to tap in people, and (3) analyze them for the beliefs involved, that is, which beliefs the communicator is seeking to tap. This should be done *with* the *persuasive purpose* of the speech, appearance, or activity in mind. As part of that effort, especially in the case of political ads, look for what commercial marketing specialists call "hitting the hot buttons" of emotional response.[39] For an excellent example of this, see the discussion at the end of this chapter.

Another example of symbols will lead us to an important point of perspective in our analysis of the use of symbols. It also leads us to note this era's most accomplished purveyor of symbols: Ronald Reagan. In the 1980s, a substantially increased number of political communications (as well as commercial ones) contained verbal and visual symbols of small-town America, often with allusions to an earlier age. These images included suggestions of how (or when) such people are more down-to-earth, honest, with basic values held clearly and forthrightly, etc., and included hints of a less problem filled, less confused past. These communications presented symbols that tapped strong beliefs, values, and emotions in many Americans. *Time* magazine summarized well Ronald Reagan's use of these symbol complexes:

> Reagan has been a master of public symbols. He worked an alchemy of nostalgia and hope, visions of the past and future collaborating. He gave the people reassuring images of a mythic American past—the Olympic torch, the tall ships, the Statue of Liberty, the heroes in the visitors' gallery on the State of the Union nights, Tom Sawyer come back to life as a yuppie—a sweet, virtuous America recrystallized by Reagan after the traumatic changes of the '60s and '70s.[40]

That brings us to an important point of perspective. Another factor that affects how people accept persuasive political communications in general and the use of symbols in specific is the nature or temper of the times. This is, of course, affected by significant events, trends, and patterns of developments of the relatively recent past. The most important dimension of this factor for the United States during the later 1970s and the 1980s was the series of dramatic developments that shook America from the late 1950s through the 1970s. These events included the civil rights activities and conflicts, the Vietnam war, Watergate and other political scandals, and international problems. Theodore Lowi has summarized the results in concise but striking fashion: "The decade of 1962–1972 was one of the most remarkable in the history of American Government. It began in almost unprecedented optimism and ended on the eve of despair."[41]

The use and acceptance of symbols in political communication in the 1980s has been powerfully affected by that recent historical context, which had a significant impact on the nation's collective psyche. The response to Lt. Col. Oliver North's nationally televised testimony before the Iran-Con-

tra committee of Congress in July 1987 is one of the more striking illustrations of this impact. On the one hand, after Americans had suffered
through Vietnam, the year-long Iran hostage affair, and so on, many vigorously cheered North's patriotism, "America is number one" attitude and
"can do" approach to his job, and in general found him an admirable
figure. On the other hand, with the Vietnam experience in mind, the
majority still was not accepting of the end he sought of American money
for the "freedom fighters" and involvement in Nicaragua. Nor were they,
with Watergate in mind, accepting of many of his methods and his "above-
the-law" attitude.

It should be added that Mr. Reagan was by no means the only major
political figure to tap the feelings noted above by the astute use of appropriate symbols. Jimmy Carter—from Plains, Georgia—did so. So did
Gerald Ford, with most conscious and elaborate design in his 1976 campaign ads, whose theme (and theme song) was "I'm feeling good about
America (again)." This was a clear precursor to the Reagan efforts in 1980
and 1984. It is also interesting to note, reflecting on the climate of feeling
and symbol usage, that one of the most successful and widely noted commercial ad campaigns in the 1980s was the Chrysler corporation's series
with the theme (and theme song) "The Pride Is Back: Born in America—
Again." It included classic scenes of America, especially of old-fashioned
American activities such as small-town picnics, Fourth of July celebrations,
and other such rites.

Further Points of Analysis in Understanding Symbol Usage in Politics

The historical point of perspective and the various examples just
discussed implicitly lead us to refine and specify something alluded to
earlier. It has been observed that symbols not only stand for some person,
event(s), or process, but also involve and evoke an emotional dimension.
The formal way of expressing these two basic, functional components of
symbols is, respectively, the *cognitive* and *affective* facets. The substantive
meaning that a person associates with a symbol, involving what the person
"knows" of what the symbol refers to (i.e., what the person believes to be
the reality of what is referred to) is the cognitive component. The emotive
feelings people have for various symbols comprise the affective component. To understand fully how persons are influenced by the use of a
symbol, one must (1) analyze the content of the symbol communicated, (2)
analyze the specific communicational context and the general time context
in which it is used, and (3) analyze the cognitive and affective associations
made by the person receiving the symbolic communication.

To help analyze the content of the symbols used, as well as their
reception, Elder and Cobb suggest that there is a set of types of symbols,

which form a basic hierarchy.[42] At the "top" and most general level of the hierarchy are symbols of the entire, long-established political community. Examples are the flag, "America," the "Constitution," and perhaps such terms and ideas as "liberty" and "free enterprise." These "higher-order" symbols, they point out, are "objects of widespread and intense affective sentiment," which sentiment "will normally be acquired earlier and held longer than those directed toward lower-order" symbols.[43]

The second basic type and level of political symbols Elder and Cobb call "regime norms, structures and roles." This refers to the institutions, norms, and roles of the established form of the political system. Examples are the "Presidency," the "Supreme Court," and "one man, one vote." The third level and type are called simply "situational symbols" and include less fundamental and more short-term symbolics. This level involves three categories: (1) current authorities, such as the "Reagan administration" or the "Rehnquist court"; (2) nongovernmental political actors, such as Ralph Nader or the NRA; and (3) policies and policy issues, such as the "Superfund" (for toxic waste cleanup), "right to life," or "welfare." (The reader is encouraged to consult the Elder and Cobb book for an excellent, more extended discussion than is possible here of the "dispositional structure" of people, which "defines the individual's world view" and "gives substantive meanings to his or her symbolic orientations." This structure includes the more fundamental "empirical premises" and "normative premises," plus the somewhat less psychologically fundamental "political prescriptions."[44])

One other dimension of the psychology of response to symbols is important to point out. Elder and Cobb have expressed the point well:

> Externalization is . . . another potential source of people's orientations toward political symbols. The affective and the cognitive linkages that serve this function are a product of psychic defense mechanisms that people use to assuage anxieties and to cope with personal problems they are reluctant to confront directly. The symbolic object serves as a convenient focus for affections or hostilities that may have little or nothing to do with the substantive content through which they are rationalized.[45]

The scapegoating technique of persuasion is a prime example of this externalization coming into play, in response to appropriate symbols.

One additional note should be added regarding how the circumstances of political decision for people affect their receptivity to the use of symbols and of persuasive communications in general, especially in the context of election campaigns. Communications scholar Charles Atkin, whose research was specifically focused on campaign ads, has given us some points that can be applied to the reception of communications and political decision more generally.[46] Atkin found that three "situational factors" are particularly important to consider. The first factor is the degree of "definition" respecting candidate differences (or differences respecting other major political choices). A high-definition situation for the individual and voter, for example, is one in which there are distinct differences in candidates' party affiliations, demographic and personal characteristics, and/or substantial differences in their ideologies. The second situational factor is that of involvement: how involved and engaged the voter is in the specific electoral or other political contest. The prominence of the office and race and the intensity of mass media coverage would, of course, be an influencing element here. A low level of involvement means a low level of attention to political communications and less reception of relevant information and impressions by the individual. The third factor is the decision state, referring to whether the voter is still undecided about the candidate or has reached a decision, although some "decisions" are, of course, tentative and "shaky."

As Atkin points out, the degree or stage of each factor that a person is in and the combination of the three factors will affect the reception of and response to persuasive political communication and the symbols involved. For example, if a person is relatively highly involved but has not yet made a decision, and if this occurs in a low-definition campaign situation, the influence of communications through the mass media will be stronger and the (effective) use of persuasion and symbolics is likely to have greater effect. People whose minds are not made up and who are actively paying attention, but who do not have candidate choices that are selected or rejected using long-established personal decision rules (such as "I'm a Republican but she's a Democrat" or "He's clearly very conservative but I'm a liberal"), will be more affected by symbolics and other aspects of persuasive communications. This includes the nature of news coverage of events. Primary elections in American politics often present a situation such as the one related just above as a hypothetical example—there are no party differences, by definition, as well as other minimal differences. Thomas Patterson has documented the impact of communications through the media in this situation in *The Mass Media Election*.[47]

One final note from Atkin's research should be added here. It concerns our general subject of people's receptivity to communications, specifically the question of attentiveness. Interestingly, Atkin found the following (specifically regarding political ads on TV): "Attentiveness is mainly a function of the entertainment quality of the messages and the partisan dispositions of the receivers. Those who feel that a candidate's ads are entertaining pay more attention, particularly uncommitted voters."[48] It appears that being entertaining is another factor enhancing persuasiveness. Is this, perhaps, a more important factor in the age of television? Neil Postman has recently published a book with some provocative thoughts on that question.[49] Indeed, in the study discussed above by this author of people's response to President Reagan, the entertainment factor loomed large in people's receptivity to President Reagan. Including in that entertainment category only citations of humor, verbal "come-backs," and as one subject put it, "the pizzazz other presidents didn't have, but [Reagan] does," that study found that a majority of the sample expressed the positive effect of this factor.

A Final Example and Explication

An exceptionally good example of persuasive communication using an array of symbolics in an effective way was displayed and employed in the 1984 presidential campaign. We will complete the chapter with a review of this example. The example and its discussion will also lead us into the next chapter. The foundation of what is actually a multipart example was the film made on the person and President Ronald Reagan (at a cost of over $400,000), which was shown at the Republican National Convention. Segments from the film provided most of the material for the "Morning in America" ads used so prominently by the Reagan campaign in the general election period.

First, it should be noted that the film used Ronald Reagan himself as the narrator or as on camera speaker—looking straight into the camera at close range. His professional background before microphone and video camera was profitably employed. The film used a sizable set of symbols in its effort to persuade the public to vote for President Reagan. There were scenes of Reagan on horseback galloping at a good rate of speed; scenes of the classic American symbols of the Statue of Liberty, with the renovation scaffolding around it, perhaps to suggest the renovation of liberty under the Reagan administration; and there were scenes of the White House and Oval Office with President Reagan hard at work at the big, ornate desk. There were also scenes of the natural splendor of America, the prime example being Niagara Falls. And there were scenes associating Reagan personally with military strength, a prime example being a scene of Reagan, clad in military outfit with flak jacket, greeting and vigorously shaking hands with a group of soldiers. We have already discussed what use of these symbols seeks to tap in the cognitive and affective sides of people's minds, but let us examine two sections of the film more closely.

The first section constitutes the Reagan response to the "fairness issue," that is, the response to the prominently made charge that the Reagan administration had been unconcerned with and had done little for minorities, women, and the economically less fortunate. The frames pictured represent the core of the response to this issue in the film. The film here shows faces of women, blacks, and senior citizens looking pleased, talking of positive developments, and in general showing a strong optimism. This is a visual and visceral display designed to demonstrate that Reagan's critics on this issue are wrong. The keynote of this section is a scene of a working man with a hard hat on in a construction work environ-

ment. He is talking with a foreign accent; thus he is an immigrant, visibly and verbally demonstrating the "land of opportunity" theme, and he is saying, in an assertive, upbeat fashion: "He put me to work. He's gonna keep me there. The man did a good job, and I hope he's gonna go for another four years. God bless America."

The second section of the film is also the most strikingly effective. It is of a ceremony, at Normandy, of the fortieth anniversary of D-Day. Part of the time Reagan is narrating in "voice-over" fashion, and part of the time Reagan is giving a speech to an audience of veterans and their families. There are many close-ups of the men and their families, which result in quietly powerful images of stalwart (now aging) veterans-as-middle-Americans, in a solemn ritual of patriotism and recognition of valorous action for country. This was an action that came in a war with clear, undisputed enemies fought in a time of unity, a war the United States led in winning and which led to U.S. preeminence in the world. The close-up shots also showed the drama of these Americans being increasingly moved emotionally, many to the point of tears, by President Reagan's speech on that occasion.

One of the two keynotes of President Reagan's remarks was as follows. Referring to the veterans at the ceremony and other veterans elsewhere, Reagan said: "They were what General Marshall called our secret weapon (dramatic pause): the best damn kids in the world. (dramatic pause) Where do we find them; where do we find such men? And the answer came almost as quickly as I asked the question. (dramatic pause) Where we'd always found them in this country: in the farms, in the shops, in the stores, in the offices. They just are the product of the freest society the world has ever known."

The second and truly climactic keynote of this section of the film showed Reagan reading a letter from the daughter of army private Peter Zanatta, veteran of the Normandy invasion. Private Zanatta had wanted to return to Normandy to commemorate his comrades and the effort, but died before he could do so. The daughter promised her father she would go in his stead, and it was her written promise that Reagan is seen dramatically reading, with his voice gradually breaking and his eyes welling up with tears. In reading from the letter he begins with the daughter quoting her father: "Someday, Liz, I'll go back." He then reads the daughter's promise to her father: "I'm going there, dad. And I'll see the beaches and the barricades and the monuments. I'll see the graves and I'll put flowers there, just like you wanted to do. I'll feel all the things you made me feel through your stories and through your eyes. I'll never forget, dad; nor will I let anyone else forget. And dad, I'll always be proud." Then President Reagan added his own words: "Through the words of his loving daughter who is with us here today, a D-Day veteran has shown us the meaning of this day far better than any president can."

Was this persuasive communication, with the symbols used, effective; did it have its intended impact? I know of no studies testing this specifically. One striking anecdote of evidence did present itself to this author, though. A colleague who was emphatically not a Reagan supporter told me of how struck, indeed, moved he was by the film; he thought it was immensely effective.

In any case, the reader is encouraged to analyze what is presented here for the elements and techniques discussed in this chapter, although use of an actual copy of the film would be far better.

Finally, in analyzing this election communication, what is it that makes it such a powerful persuasive communication? The answer follows a question: If this presentation by Mr. Reagan at the D-Day ceremony had simply been described in a newspaper ad, or even on radio, would it have had the same impact? The answer is: not even close. It was the audiovideo medium actually showing President Reagan and the veterans and their families, the lifelike visual image and sound, that produced the powerful impact. It is only the mass medium of television that has the capacity to so communicate. In Chapter 4 we discuss why that is the case.

CHAPTER FOUR
THE NATURE
OF THE BEAST
Basic Forms
and Conceptions
of the Mass Media

INTRODUCTION

In early 1968, with many people urging him to challenge President Johnson for the Democratic nomination, Senator Robert Kennedy told a group of reporters that "under no foreseeable circumstances" would he run for president. This statement was carried by the wire services and ran in newspapers. But when CBS News asked him to speak to them about it, he "adamantly refused to repeat" that flat statement on camera. Kennedy's press secretary Frank Mankiewicz later explained that while Senator Kennedy was undecided, "such a statement could be made for newspapers, but not directly on television, which would have given it too much impact. . . ."[1]

That little story impressionistically, but rather dramatically, illustrates the fact that there are significant differences in the nature of each of the mass media and very significantly different impacts, if the Kennedy–Mankiewicz assumption is correct. Another tale—nonpolitical in this case—humorously suggests the unique impact of TV, specifically given its capacity for "live" broadcasts. In 1983, some 50 stations in America, along with the BBC in Britain, carried a broadcast of actual heart surgery done on a Mr. Schuler (with a two-man panel of narrators). Manifesting what we might call tele-confidence before the surgery, Schuler said: "There is no way in hell they are going to lose me on live TV."[2]

More seriously (for the purposes of this book), what was it that gave such impact to the Senate "Watergate Committee" hearings and to the testimony of Lt. Col. Oliver North in the congressional Iran-Contra hearings of 1987? Would the impact have been the same if both events had simply been fully reported in the newspapers, with transcripts of all key segments, or even if carried "live" on *radio?* Or was it the live pictures and sound of television that provided the cutting edge of the impact? (One amusing indicator in the Col. North case was the following. Usually, when a political event is carried live or when a report of a breaking story interrupts TV programming there are numerous complaints. But "the editor of *Soap Opera Digest* reported there was no uproar from fans over the preemption of their favorite television shows. 'What,' she asked, 'could be more dramatic than Ollie North?' "[3]) We will come back to the illustrative "Ollie" North case later in this chapter for some details and comment.

To understand the role of the various mass media in politics, it is important to consider the essential nature of each medium, that is, the specific characteristics of each medium as a medium of mass communication. One of the best expressions of the need for an investigation like this was presented by communications scholar Neil Postman:

> [Walter Lippmann] wrote: "There can be no liberty for a community which lacks the information by which to detect lies."
>
> I want to advance here the cause of a slightly different proposition, namely, that there can be no liberty for a community which lacks the critical skills to tell the difference between lies and truth. . . .
>
> [W]e would be wise to consider what is the nature of the information we want to be critical about. Information may come in many different forms—through the spoken word, the written word, the printed word, the painted image, or the electronic image. . . . What critical equipment we think essential to have may, therefore, vary, depending on what form of [communication] is dominant in one's culture. . . . The printed word has moved to the periphery of our culture and the electronic image has taken its place at the center.[4]

In short, in this age a new electronic visual literacy is needed in addition to the traditional verbal literacy. The rest of this chapter details why that is the case.

We will proceed in this effort by basic analytic description of each mass medium and by drawing on some notable conceptualizations of the nature of the respective media. Empirical studies which provide systematic evidence for those conclusions, as well as for the impact of the various media on the public, are also reviewed. Following the central theme of the book, the implications of the nature of the media for the democratic system will also be considered. [For the musically inclined, let me recommend listening to John Fogerty's song, "I Saw It on TV" (from his album "Centerfield"), as an excellent pop music effort touching on some of what we discuss in this chapter.]

BASIC CHARACTERISTICS OF THE MASS MEDIA

The medium of communication of the printed word was the sole means of human communication, other than direct speech, for the vast majority of organized human history. Today, the printed word comes in several specific forms as mass media. Of principal political interest are, of course, newspapers and magazines.

On the Audience Reached

In thinking about each mass medium and in comparing them, we should take note of the scope and nature of the audience for each. Newspapers have basically reached local or state or regional audiences. Some, such as the *New York Times,* through their prestige and use by elites, have had much greater scope of influence than the base of their circulation would suggest.

Some newspapers have distinctly different types of audiences than others. Two examples are the more "upscale," more highly educated readership of the *New York Times* compared with that of the more "average Joe" and working-class Jane readership of the *New York Post.* Of special note are the *Christian Science Monitor* and the *Wall Street Journal,* which have had selective national audiences for a number of years. In 1982, *USA Today* was launched as the first truly national newspaper (its content is broadcast by satellite and printed at various regional plants around the nation). The major news magazines have national audiences, but as noted in Chapter 2, are read predominantly by upscale subscribers (amounting to 1 to 4 million each). TV news has both local (local stations) and national (network news) dimensions. Radio has been primarily local but does have a national dimension, with the network affiliations, and an increasing level of syndicated programs.

Two Characteristics of TV Compared with Print: Reviewability, Visual versus Verbal

Much more important for the purpose of this chapter is the essential nature of each mass medium itself. Various of the basic elements of each medium may seem obvious at first, but considering the basic elements of print with the broadcast media, the implications are highly significant.

The print medium comes printed on a page. One significant consequence of that simple fact is that the reader can go back, immediately or later, and reread a statement by an office-holder, candidate, interest group leader, or whomever and thereby reconsider what the person said. Did it make sense?; Were there facts to back up an assertion?; Was it really just nice-sounding symbolics? Under normal circumstances this cannot be done with communications over the broadcast media, which are transmitted over the airwaves. Technically, it could be done today, but only such strange creatures as a few political scientists and communications scholars actually tape the TV or radio news or other political programs. Now on occasion, a major political figure makes a statement, captured on video or audio tape, which directly contradicts either a previous statement of his or her own or the accepted facts on some significant matter, or he or she just makes an exceptionally foolish statement. Sometimes the statement is replayed by, say, a network news show. This does allow people to reconsider the statement (if they happen to be watching that broadcast). The view and hearing of it may give the contradiction even greater impact because of the nature of the medium. That is precisely why Robert Kennedy would not make his statement for the TV cameras; his statement running in the newspapers would minimize the reactions of Lyndon Johnson and his political allies, while avoiding any lifelike picture showing Kennedy actually saying something he might (and did) later contradict. It may be that a key reason that President Reagan lost a good deal of trust among the public after the Iran-Contra affair was because of the showing of such film (50% or more said, in spring and summer 1987, that he was not telling the truth about the affair). These instances of rebroadcast of statements are very rare, though; people must be watching or listening to the broadcast and doing so at the right time. The vast majority of political communications do not receive such attention. On TV or radio, such communications tend to "pass by" on the airwaves without a chance for reconsideration.

The second sort of characteristic to distinguish is closely related to the characteristic of the print compared with broadcast media which we just discussed. The distinction involved is a centrally important one. First, on the print side, the main politically relevant print media consist of ink words on a page and still photos (more photos and more in color in the news magazines). The written word is of central importance in these media, though, of course, the photos can add to the effect, sometimes notably.

Television, on the other hand, is fundamentally visual. The moving pictures and corresponding sound are absolutely central to the medium; they are, in fact, the essence of this mass medium of communication. Correspondingly, they are the primary material sought for TV news. (Incidentally, it is clear that the nature of the dominant medium of TV has influenced the splashy, colorful layout of *USA Today;* that is, the national newspaper of the late twentieth century felt the need to emulate television to make a go of it.)

The great impact of the medium of television is a result of the seeming realism of actually seeing and hearing persons and/or events. One analyst has expressed the point very well:

> [B]ecause television news and current affairs programmes convey action, movement, facial expression and demeanor, scenes and actors, as well as verbal messages, they seem *more* complete, more satisfactory than any account provided by newspaper. *"Viewability" is easily construed as reliability* . . . and . . . the *dramatic intensity* of film and video recording carries conviction and *guarantees authenticity in ways words cannot* [emphasis added].[5]

Cognitive psychologist Henry Gleitman's specific perceptual explanation of why this is the case, noted in Chapter 2, is worth quoting again: "We focus on the figure [in our view], not on the [back]ground; we are more likely to notice shapes that are moving, rather than those that are stationary. Such examples indicate that perception is selective. . . . Our ability to take in and interpret the myriad stimulations around us is finite, and so our perceptual system is forced to choose among them."[6] And most fundamentally: "In humans, the major means of physically selecting the stimulus input are the movements of the eyes."[7] These are social scientific confirmations of the old saying and notion: "Seeing is believing." Further, regarding the pictures and words, as well as the context in which they (seem to) take place in news casts, as Gaye Tuchman has observed:

> News film casts an aura of representation by its explicit refusal to give the appearance of manipulating time and space. Instead, its use of time and space announces that the tempo of events and spatial arrangements have *not* been tampered with to tell this story. By seeming *not* to arrange time and space, news film claims to present facts, not interpretations.[8]

We can take this point a little further. A print medium is, as Neil Postman has written, "line-by-line, sequential, continuous"[9] and "has a content: a semantic, paraphrasable, propositional content."[10] Postman further contends that virtually every scholar, from "Erasmus in the sixteenth century to Elizabeth Eisenstein in the twentieth," who has considered what reading does to people's habits of mind "has concluded that the process encourages rationality; that the sequential, propositional character of the written word fosters what Walter Ong calls the 'analytic management of knowledge.'"[11] That is not the essence of a moving-picture-based medium, however. Consider, for example, the mode of thinking exhibited by James Lake, press secretary for the Reagan reelection campaign of 1984, discussing how the president and events "play" on TV: "People like to see the trappings of the Presidency. If you add . . . the popularity factor, you get excited, enthusiastic crowds that *convey* on television. A blue-collar, ethnic crowd in Hammonton, N.J., puts out a message that *conveys* in Bakersfield,

California [emphasis added]."[12] "Conveys" what? There is no proposition to mull over here, just a vague, pleasant image projected through TV pictures. It should be added that the nature of the TV medium encourages what historian Daniel Boorstin called the "pseudo-event,"[13] that is, an event which is planned and executed primarily to be "reported"—especially *shown*—in the media.

Implications

Considering the essential nature of each medium of communication leads us to a general conception and an important corresponding political implication. Each mass medium is a distinct technology for communicating. But as Neil Postman rightly notes: "Every technology has an inherent bias. It has within its physical form a predisposition toward being used in certain ways and not others."[14] Political scientist E. E. Schattschneider, in conceptualizing political institutions and activities in general, has stated that "organization is the mobilization of bias."[15] That is, the very nature of organizing means that some people, issues, and so on, are naturally organized in or favored and others are not. The political implication is that with print media as the sole or dominant mass medium, certain types of people will find a natural advantage; certain types of activities and modes and techniques of communication will be favored, perhaps even certain types of issues as well. A different set of people, modes of communication, and types of activities, and even issues, will find a natural advantage with the medium of radio (especially in the era in which it is dominant). The same is the case for the medium of TV.

Earlier, Franklin Roosevelt's vocal tone and ability were mentioned. It is no accident that his reign came during the height of the radio era. Ronald Reagan evidently found a strong advantage in the medium of TV. For contrast, find a source with a *variety* of pictures of Abraham Lincoln (such as the work of Mathew Brady[16]) *and* find a description and at least some text of the Lincoln–Douglas debates.[17] Would or could Lincoln have been elected in the TV age? Would three-hour debates, with hour-long statements and half-hour to one-and-a-half-hour replies, "play" on TV today? In fact, would they be accepted and attended in any fashion? Such length (if not Lincoln–Douglas caliber) was apparently rather common in the nineteenth century. For a brief illustration of the appearance of such debates and how they might have played on TV, consider the following description of Lincoln at one of the debates: Lincoln approaches, "his furrowed face and long neck conspicuous above the crowd. He shambles on to the platform, displaying a rusty frock coat the sleeves of which stop several inches short of his wrists, and well-worn trousers that show a similar reluctance to approach a pair of enormous feet. His face . . . has an air of settled melancholy. [And the crowd could see] the frenzied gestures of

Douglas, and Lincoln's awkward habit of bending his knees and then rising to his full height with a jerk, in order to enforce a point. . . ."[18] One is certainly compelled to wonder whether Lincoln could have gotten elected in the TV age. Is this irrelevant for the 1980s and 1990s? Consider the response of the media and others to former Governor Bruce Babbitt after his appearance in the first generally televised debate among candidates for the 1988 Democratic presidential nomination (in the summer of 1987!). Much was made of his awkward facial and speaking style *as* it appeared on TV.

One final illustrative example of the visual nature of the TV medium and of the political implications stemming from it is in order. Public opinion analyst Kathleen Frankovic noted a fascinating aspect of the 1980 Carter–Reagan debate, which occurred one week before election day and was watched by over 100 million people:

> Throughout most of the fall, well over a third of the potential electorate feared the possibility of war under a Reagan administration. That proportion dropped somewhat after the Carter–Reagan debate, in the last week of the campaign. But, after the election, the proportion who worried about a war rose again to pre-debate levels. This suggests that Reagan's *presentation* during that debate . . . alleviated, if only temporarily, serious concerns about him held by the electorate [emphasis added].[19]

In other words, Mr. Reagan's delivery, using his well-cultivated, soft, friendly-sounding voice and "aw shucks" demeanor (as many characterized it), created an impression on TV that did not *look* or *sound* warlike. This impression, lasting for the period of the crucial last week of the campaign, countered the one that many in the public had developed over the rest of the campaign. This impact did not appear to result from the substance of the discussion: "While the 1980 presidential debates had some effect on qualitative assessments of Reagan, they appeared to have little effect in transmitting knowledge about his issue positions. If anything, they clouded the public's perceptions of his stands."[20] With a significant percentage of the electorate making up their minds in the final week, was this benign-appearing image a key to the result?

A Third Characteristic: The Attention Factor

We now turn to description of a third category of characteristics of the mass media. This category we can informally call the attention factor. Inherent in print media, compared with broadcast media, especially TV, seem to be different requirements of attention and involvement. First, with a newspaper or magazine, the choice of what story to read is up to the news consumer. Although main headlines and the front page(s) are designed to grab attention, readers can still easily skip to another story from the one their eyes first see. Relatedly, reading a given story requires an active, affirmative effort; those ink letters on a page do not leap out and grab the reader's attention.

Watching stories on the television news, on the other hand, requires no such affirmative effort. In fact, the reason that many people watch a given TV news program in general is simply that the TV was already tuned in to that station. Second, the TV viewer cannot choose which story to watch, since the stories are not all laid out for selection. Rather, the viewer just sits there exposed to each new story as it comes. This is why TV news viewers have been called the "inadvertent audience." Looked at from another angle, as mentioned in Chapter 2, selective perception and selective attention are more difficult. The television medium does have the visual and verbal characteristics to capture more actively the attention of the viewer. We should add, however, that many people do other things while watching the TV news (such as eating dinner), so their attention can be divided. Still, the nature of the medium of television makes it unique in its potential for impact. The following brief recounting of the case of Oliver North illustrates this strikingly.

Lt. Col. Oliver North appeared before the combined House and Senate Select Committees on the Iran-Contra affair. His testimony was awaited with much anticipation, as he was seen as a central player. The news media's treatment of him and his likely testimony prior to his appearance were not positive. There was characterization of him as a "loose cannon on deck," and his veracity and even mental health were questioned. But the visual and aural image the public saw and heard on live TV made a very different impression on many of the 55 million people who watched (a larger audience than normally watches the three network news shows combined). *U.S. News & World Report* effectively summarized what happened despite the contradictions in the substance of North's testimony: "North had . . . stolen the show, not so much with *what* he said, but with *how* he said it—and with how it played on television." And the result was that "virtually overnight" the image of the man who had been seen as the villain of the affair was transformed, "even though—by his own testimony—North had lied to Congress and shredded documents. . . . His performance astonished even the experts. 'In 35 years of watching politics I haven't seen a comparable change,' said [political] scientist . . . Everett Ladd."[21]

Indeed, following North's appearance (in both senses), a survey conducted by leading pollster Louis Harris for the *Democratic* Governors' Association found, at least in the short term, a lessening of public opposition to aid to the Contras (down to 51% opposed, 44% in favor, compared with 62% opposed, 33% in favor before the appearance). Even more strikingly, Harris found a "47% to 39% plurality that feels Republicans will do better than Democrats in handling the Nicaragua issue, and he found a 54% to 42% majority saying they would favor "sending U.S. troops to fight in Nicaragua if it is the only way to keep Nicaragua from going communist"—

a direct reversal of opinion on military involvement. The question wording may have inflated the results somewhat compared with earlier polls; but then, the invocation of symbols (such as were involved in that question wording) is a significant part of what many in the public were responding to in North's appearance. In sum, veteran pollster Harris called it "the Oliver North phenomenon," and said these findings are "both a surprising and highly unexpected result."[22] (It should be noted, however, that the favorable impressions of North's performance did not seem to help public perceptions of President Reagan.)

A Fourth Characteristic: TV—Mass Medium but Up Close and Personal

Another characteristic of the medium of TV should be noted, particularly in light of the example just reviewed. Television enables such a communicator (paradoxically) to enter the living rooms of a huge mass of people, yet in a seemingly close and personal fashion. As communications scholars Jamieson and Campbell have observed:

> The language of the television screen is the language of close-ups. . . . These typical close-up shots reflect the personal and social contact that is characteristic of television as a medium. . . .
> Distance is related to intimacy. Television simulates intimate relationships. . . . The reliance on close-ups creates new rules for our sense of interpersonal space. For example, when viewers encounter newspeople [or regularly seen political figures] face to face, they tend to treat them as intimate associates despite the fact that they are total strangers.[23]

This is the reason Walter Cronkite came to be called "Uncle Walter." For those who have the attributes "favored" by the nature of the medium, the effects can be great. The discussion in Chapter 3 of people's perceptions of a communicator's credibility should be applied here.

A final general point of perspective on the North case should be added here. Fifteen years before North's appearance, Irving Kristol suggested the following, which effectively combines the discussion thus far in this chapter with the discussion in Chapter 3. It also raises a crucial question and troubling implication, to which we will return in the final chapter. "What television can do . . . —and with extraordinary power—is to mobilize the audience's emotions around a vivid, simplified, essentially melodramatic vision of the political world, in which praise and blame are the magnetic poles. What television can do, in other words, is what demagogic rhetoric used to do less efficaciously."[24]

IMPACT: RESEARCH EVIDENCE ON THE EFFECTS OF THE NATURE OF THE MEDIA

Systematic research has provided some interesting evidence of the differential impact of the mass media. We will focus most of our attention on television.

Believing TV versus Newspapers; Information Costs

The first note on the evidence is a reminder and further explanation of something mentioned earlier. For many years, the Roper Organization asked this question of a national sample of people: "If you get conflicting or different reports of the same news story from radio, TV, magazines, and the newspapers, which one are you inclined to believe? In 1959, 32% answered newspapers, compared with 29% answering TV. But by the 1970s, half said they were inclined to believe the television story, while fewer than one-fourth said they believed the newspaper.[25] These results have often been reported as finding TV to be the most "trusted" source of news. But the question is not phrased that way, and so stating it misses the *perceptual* element tapped by the key word "believable." It is surely the perception of what is happening on the screen, due to the nature of the medium—the seeming reality of the moving pictures and sound—that is the reason for that change in believability (as well as the pervasiveness of the medium).

A relatively old finding in political science provides another point that should be noted before turning to some studies relating directly to the effect of the nature of the TV medium. Political scientists have pointed out for many years that for the average person, acquiring political information does not come easily; it requires time and effort, both of which are quite limited resources for most people. In short, political knowledge involves "information costs." This basic perspective on people's political behavior can be applied to the findings of some of the key studies to which we now turn.

Studies of Nonlearning from TV

There has been a striking pattern of conclusions about what people "learn" in the way of "political information" from television, a pattern that seems to contradict most of what has been discussed: People learn far less such information from TV than from newspapers. Perhaps the most notable study to present evidence that leads predominantly to that conclusion is Thomas Patterson's *The Mass Media Election*. Patterson noted in summary: "[W]hile the newspaper makes a substantial contribution [to the increase in people's information about issues and candidates' political records], television actually does not add significantly to what people learn." Patterson even concluded that newspapers had a greater impact than TV on people's image of candidates.[26] (In Chapter 10 we discuss Patterson's study in some detail.) In fact, saying that people learn far more from newspapers appears to understate the case, as John P. Robinson has effectively summarized:

> [W]e have reviewed the findings of 15 different studies relating mass media use to a variety of measures of news information across a 20-year period. These studies involve a wide range of informational content, study designs,

age groups, geographical locations, and information settings. In *not one* of these studies do we find viewers of TV newscasts in general emerging as much more informed than nonviewers after other factors are controlled; that is especially true for people who claim that television is their main information source. Further, hours of television viewed is correlated with lower information of all kinds except one: knowledge of entertainers on television. Obviously, these results call into serious question the meaning and validity of the main source question. They also raise the possibility that TV itself may be almost inimical to the successful learning of news information.[27]

Further, Robinson and Davis have concluded that exposure to stories in newspapers or news magazines, or by talking with others, in *addition* to TV, "may be required for the point of these news stories to make a lasting impression on the viewer's memory."[28]

On the Other Hand: The Visual Factor and "Learning" Impressions and Images

But there is a basic problem with that research if we are to understand what people receive and retain from watching newscasts, material they subsequently use in political behavior. That research has missed a dimension of communications through television which *does* appear to make a "lasting impression."

The problem is that in all the research just mentioned, the questions asked tap information that is in *verbal* form (knowing candidates' names and party affiliations, elements or definitions of issues, etc.). But this ignores the impressions and images people develop from the *visual* content of the news shows. Those conclusions also forget the consistent findings noted earlier regarding the low-level of political knowledge and opinion structure possessed by most people. Doris Graber, in her important research on information processing theory, has added depth to those findings on the nature of people's information and opinions:

> All of [the people she studied] preferred simple stories and stories which readily fit into situations for which they had appropriate conceptual schemas available for information processing.[29] For the most part, [these people] would not read and study carefully the more extensive versions of election and other news in newspapers and news magazines. Masses of specific facts and statistics were uniformly characterized as dull, confusing and unduly detailed.[30] Most . . . stored only a small portion of each news story. They were unable to recall even brief passages verbatim.[31]

Given that, we must ask again what we asked at the end of Chapter 2: What impressions are people likely to retain and "take with them" into the voting booth? A growing number of studies are providing increasing evidence that the visual content of news film and other political communications on TV plays a significant role in the images that people develop of candidates and other political figures, images that are important elements in their evaluations of those figures, and hence, in their votes and other responses.

W. Gill Woodall has provided a fine review of a number of relevant studies. First, even in research concerned with how much specific, verbally based information people learn from the news, several studies found the visual content of film enhanced learning. Woodall's summary: "Their research has shown that visual illustration of *person* and *place* elements of a news story enhances recall of those elements of the news but not other story elements. Visual formats and illustrations linked to cause-and-effect story elements, however, tend to enhance recall of all of the story elements overall."[32] After noting two studies that variously supported those findings, Woodall cited a third (by the same researcher) which did not. The questions in the third study were in specific, structured, multiple-choice form, however, in contrast to the free-recall method used in the earlier studies. As Woodall explained (drawing on the researcher's own words), the third study "required deeper and more *semantically* involved processing due to the greater length of the [news] item [emphasis added]."[33]

Other studies add some striking evidence. Again, Woodall summarizes the results of several: "The *vividness* and *concreteness* of visual information have been shown to predict retention of information experimentally and are also likely to predict news retention."[34] Woodall added a fascinating conclusion, based on the studies just summarized and on research by Davis and Robinson.[35] This conclusion concerned the link between visual material and news content: "Vivid or concrete visual information that is loosely linked to story content is likely to be remembered, but the story content will not be. In effect, a visual distraction outcome is obtained under these conditions in the sense that *what is remembered is not story content but visual context* [emphasis added]."[36]

Gina Garramone and other researchers have reached a similar conclusion from their work. Garramone offers this conclusion, drawing on the concepts provided by information processing theory: "Dramatic visuals might draw attention to the video channel while diverting attention from the audio channel. Because visual content tends to stimulate visual encoding [mental processing], messages in which the visual content is dominant may facilitate iconic [visual object] rather than verbal encoding."[37]

If the latter pair of conclusions (from a limited number of studies) is accurate, the implications for manipulation of the TV medium are profound. In Chapter 10 we explore this question in the case of the incumbent's 1984 campaign for reelection to the presidency, and in Chapters 6 and 8 we explore the question with regard to such efforts in the nonelection period of that incumbent's activity.

Doris Graber has given us some of the most significant evidence on the impact of the visual dimension of television. First, she found that it was common for people to judge the honesty of a communicator and that this was "a crucial element in determining whether to take messages . . . seriously." Where "physical appearance could be judged" political communicators were described as having an "honest look" or lacking it; and a straight look into the eye and camera (as well as a "firm, unhesitating response") was seen as evidence of honesty, whereas avoidance of eye and camera contact was "universally interpreted as a sign of dishonesty."[38] For those who feel comfortable in front of a TV camera, especially those who have a professional background in front of the cameras (i.e., those "favored" by the medium), this would appear to constitute a formidable political advantage.

Graber provides further important evidence in two recent research papers. The first of these pioneering research efforts, conducted during the 1984 election campaign, did content analyses of the nature of the *visual images* on the TV news as well as what was said. Two related findings are most important. She found "a vast gap" between the nature of the public's mentions of the traits or characteristics of President Reagan and TV correspondents' verbal appraisals of him. The public's perceptions were vastly more positive on "competence," "leadership," "integrity," and "empathy" than were those of the TV news correspondents. "In all cases, television [news people's verbal messages] is far less positive than the polls. However, when pictorial news is considered, the story changes drastically." The visuals told a dramatically more positive story. In fact: "For leadership and empathy, television traits [visually portrayed] are actually more positive than mentions [by the public], running ahead by 17 points and 18 points, respectively."[39] This remarkable evidence suggests that the *visual images* contained in news film during the campaign had a fundamental impact on people's perceptions of and beliefs about President Reagan's traits, and were thereby central to their evaluations of him as a candidate.

In a 1987 paper, Graber presented further empirical evidence on the impact of the visual dimension of the television medium. This was an analysis of a large series of television news stories, "with special attention to the visual aspects." It involved assessing the nature of the visual content of the stories, their manner of presentation, and what a panel of 48 people said they "learned" from viewing and listening to a sample of the news stories. Graber found the following (among other things). First and most important: "Our viewers were most impressed by the fact that pictures make stories more realistic." A third of panelists' judgments stressed this.[40] She concluded: "The realism presented by television pictures enhances the credibility of news reports. People trust what they see more than what they hear. From watching television pictures, they gain a sense of actually witnessing an event. This, too, is bound to have an impact on opinion formation."[41]

Graber also "noted the important inferences that viewers are able to draw from the face and body language revealed by the plentiful close-ups of people shown on television"—the most prevalent finding of her visual content analysis. She also found that visual "cues are used to appraise the credibility of news personnel and the spokespersons they present to the public on television,"[42] which reaffirms the findings of various communications scholars reported earlier.

The results of another study should be noted here. McLeod et al. found that people rated newspaper news "well behind television when illustration of personal qualities was the criterion."[43]

A study of the case of Ronald Reagan, by the author of this book, added some suggestive evidence. This study (among other things) asked open-ended questions about perceptions of Mr. Reagan's image, as well as a series of specific trait questions concerning Reagan's characteristics as a person and political leader. The open-ended questions, which were asked first, required the people to supply the content of the answer themselves, which is much more demanding of the memory than is response to multiple-choice or yes-or-no questions. For the responses reported here,[44] the panelists were asked (in summer 1987) to state how they perceived Reagan as of late 1984.

A general positive image of Reagan was evident, and it seemed clear that the "live" visual material on television was a central contributor to that image, if not *the* central contributor. Half of the panelists specifically mentioned Reagan as friendly and/or personable and/or mentioned the impact of his smiling appearance. This was in addition to the 20 of 21 who answered "yes" to the specific trait question regarding whether they felt that Reagan was "likable and warm." Variously related to that basic trait category were mentions by a third or more (each) of his sense of humor and "come-backs," and how he and Nancy always appeared happily engaged with one another and family-like. Almost a third specifically mentioned seeing him as a "regular guy" or the like. Further, and more explicitly related to the impact of the TV medium, were specific mentions by a third of how adept Reagan was at answering questions and dealing with reporters in press conferences. As one panelist said: "The press conferences always went well. He was confident when he spoke; he would answer questions without hesitation." This impression is striking in light of the fact that the leading newspapers, news magazines, and even the network news programs at times commented on and gave examples of how President Reagan repeatedly got facts wrong, made up stories, and so on. How did people develop such an impression, given the substantive record?

Also mentioned by a third—and strongly expressed by those mentioning it—were images of Reagan personally caring about other individuals, with mentions of such examples as *seeing* Reagan showing deep concern for and consoling families of soldiers killed in Beirut or elsewhere or families of the *Challenger* crew. The images were of a tangible, personalized nature, not of an aggregate, policy-related sort of concern. On the specific trait questions, all but one saw him as "likable and warm," all but two saw him as "honest and straightforward," all but two and a marginal third saw him as "sincere," and all but three saw him as "a fair person."

Clearly, many, expressed in one way or another, had developed an image of Reagan that was very personal. The central content of that image was of a friendly, personable man who was strongly caring of (specific) others, who was a "regular guy," not "uppity," and who had a good sense of humor and an entertaining bent for "come-backs." It seems likely that Reagan's appearances on TV network news portraying and doing such things is the explanation of why he came across as a "fair person." This appears to have allowed him to minimize any damage from what seemed a major substantive vulnerability in 1984: what many commentators called the "fairness issue" (given Reagan's cuts in programs for the poor, seeming lack of commitment to pursuit of civil rights, and so on).

Let me add some panelists' specific comments, which allow us to see more directly the perceptions and thinking of the panelists. One person, who said she was "initially never a Reagan supporter," said: "In the campaign, Mondale was scowling a lot, he was more intense. Reagan was more relaxed, his manner made me like him more." And another said: "I remember with other presidents feeling more tense." One who "leaned Democratic" said, strikingly: "It's easier to trust him: that picture of him with his suit on, joking, always smiling; it seems like he's looking you in the eye." A Democrat who said, "I'm not impressed with his ideas; he leans too much toward big business," also said: "He seems to talk more down to earth, which puts him on a more human level. . . . He seems like more of a regular guy." The patterns of response and such specific comments give good indicative evidence of the impact of the TV image.

IN CONCLUSION

Earlier in the chapter we noted that each mass medium consists of a technology enabling communication to reach a general public. Television is the newest mass medium, a medium with unique characteristics and impact, as we have discussed, theorized about, and presented empirical evidence on in this chapter. TV is the newest basic medium, but technology did not stop developing with the advent of basic broadcast television. Many millions of people do not receive TV over the traditional airwaves; they receive the three original networks, plus several or many other newer "networks" or station programming through electronic cable. Further, a fascinating new capacity for direct public interaction with leaders (or conceivably involvement in policymaking) through presentations on TV has been shown to be technically feasible. The most notable technology involved is "interactive cable." This technology allows people with the right hook-ups to watch a program presentation on some issue, and send back their responses (such as, "yes, I support that"). So far, the responses cannot be very elaborate. The possibilities are fascinating, though, as are the potential hazards, such as manipulation and the eliciting of pseudo-opinions. The few experiments with such technologies, the potential involved, and various implications are discussed in Chapter 12.[45]

Those technological advances, according to some observers, have changed the situation of channel scarcity and have opened up access to the TV medium in a dramatic fashion. This raises the question of the law on the mass media and regulation of the media, as well as the issue of who has access to the media. The discussion through this chapter of the unique impact of the medium of television, considered in light of our continuing theme of democracy, also raises the question of who owns and controls these media. We turn to those matters in the next chapter.

CHAPTER FIVE
WHOSE MEDIA; MEDIA FOR WHOM?
Ownership of the Media, Regulation, Law, and the Access Issue

INTRODUCTION

In Chapter 1 we noted that communication is central to how communities and societies maintain a social order and operate an effectively working political system. We have also discussed how the development of new technologies of mass communication affects the way communication is accomplished in a society and affects the society more generally. The central nature of communication in a society and the impact of new technologies of communication are especially important in a modern democratic political system (or more accurately stated, a system striving to be democratic). It is worth requoting President John F. Kennedy on the mass medium of television in this regard (in a speech to TV broadcasters): "The flow of ideas, the capacity to make informed choices, the ability to criticize, all of the assumptions on which political democracy rests, depend largely on communications. And you are the guardians of the most powerful and effective means of communication ever designed."[1]

Also noted earlier was the fact that information and full access to it are cardinal principles of a democratic system, as President Kennedy suggested in the words just quoted. In the United States especially, a "free press" has been seen as the most vital means of giving the public access to the information needed to make their decisions, and it has been considered a crucial means of keeping watch on the government and keeping it responsive and responsible. In the American political system, the latter principle is enshrined in the most widely known and quoted Amendment to the Constitution, the First Amendment, which also establishes the related right of "free speech."

In a mass society, though, political communications of importance are mass communications transmitted to the public by mass media organizations. The First Amendment and the principle of a "free press" in the American system were established in the 1780s. But in the two centuries since then, the technologies and techniques of communication have developed dramatically. Have these changes altered the realities and application of the free press idea? Again requoting from Chapter 1, Carl J. Friedrich, in his renowned work on constitutionalism and democracy, said: " . . . freedom of the press is considered a cornerstone of democracy."[2] But he also observed: "The possibility of broadcasting the spoken word and projecting visual materials to the four corners of the globe has profoundly altered the realities of modern politics. . . . Inevitably, therefore, the issue of who shall control this channel of communication presents political problems of decisive importance, at least in a constitutional democracy."[3]

In this chapter we explore the questions and issues of ownership, control, and regulation of the media, as well as access to the mass media. The patterns of ownership and direction of the mass media in the United States are discussed first, and the implications for a democratic system are noted. The regulation of the broadcast media by the government is then discussed, along with the key patterns of decisions by the Federal Communications Commission and the courts which have determined the nature and extent of nominal and actual government regulation of the broadcast media. The interpretation of the First Amendment resulting from those decisions is also reviewed, along with the related issue of who has and should have access to the mass media. The focus in this chapter is on the media and governmental system in the United States, but brief mention is made of contrasting patterns of ownership, control, and regulation in other nations, a subject discussed more thoroughly in Chapter 11.

OWNERSHIP AND DIRECTION OF THE MASS MEDIA

The Commercial Media

The economic system in the United States is a capitalist one. Correspondingly, the mass media are mostly privately owned, "for-profit" organizations. In fact, even the "public" television and radio systems have private elements.

For the economically developed, more democratic nations, the pattern of overwhelming private ownership and control of the mass media in the United States is unusual. In the Scandinavian nations, broadcasting is a government-owned and government-operated system, and even the newspapers receive government subsidies. In most other developed nations, the government either largely controls the broadcast media or there is a public organization set up (separate from the current political administration) to perform most of the broadcasting.

The private corporations, ABC, CBS, and NBC—the "networks"— own some of the radio and TV stations and supply the great majority of the programs for the rest of the radio and TV stations, most of which have contracted with the networks as "affiliates." There are about 1700 individual daily newspapers, somewhat less than 900 commercial VHF TV stations, and somewhat less than 5000 AM and 4000 FM radio stations in the United States. There are also a few "superstations," transmitted via satellites and received by individual satellite dish or cable system. The "individual" broadcast stations, newspapers, and magazines, however, are not all individually owned, in fact, far from it. We need to explore the patterns of who owns, or at least partially controls, those media, together with the implications of such patterns.

The Commercial Media and the Economic Context   In the U.S. capitalist system, the great majority of the mass media are, indeed, private, profit-making organizations. Correspondingly, the ownership and direction of the media must be placed in the context of the general capitalist system.

In the United States the ownership and control of business is highly concentrated. As political scientists Dye and Zeigler point out: "More than 200,000 industrial corporations exist in the United States, but the [top] one hundred . . . control 52% of all assets in the nation. The five largest industrial corporations control 10% of the nation's assets themselves. Concentration in utilities, transportation, and communications is even greater."[4]

And the concentration story has two additional dimensions. The people who direct and are legally responsible for corporations are the presidents and the boards of directors. American business is even more concentrated than the figures just noted, due to interlocking directorates, where members of the board of directors of one corporation sit on the boards of various other corporations. Those directors are legally responsible for the economic well-being of the respective corporations. A U.S. Senate study, released in 1978, found that each of the 13 largest corporations reach an average of 70% of the 130 largest corporations "through a total of 240 direct and 5547 indirect interlocks."[5] Second, control of significant percentages of corporate stock by large financial institutions, such as the biggest banks, is another contributor to effective concentration. Finally, we should note that over the 1980s the trend has been toward even greater concentration. Indeed, the ten largest corporate mergers in American history all were accomplished in the 1980s.[6]

Concentration Patterns in American Media

Does ownership and direction of the mass media follow this pattern? The answer is yes; and like the general economic trend, the level of concentration has increased in recent years in the mass communications area. As Ben Bagdikian has pointed out, in the late 1940s, over 80% of the nation's daily newspapers were under independent ownership. Today, over 70% are "owned by outside corporations and fifteen of those corporations had most of the business." And more generally: "despite 25,000 media outlets in the United States, twenty-nine corporations control most of the business in daily newspapers, magazines, television, books, and motion pictures."[7]

The largest newspaper-based corporation is Gannett. Gannett, as of mid-1986, owned 93 daily newspapers, including the only wide-circulation *national* newspaper, *USA Today*, as well as 40 nondaily papers, eight TV stations, 15 radio stations, and owned 20% of Cowles Media Co., itself a sizable multiunit media corporation. (Gannett also owns the major polling firm of Louis Harris Associates.) Gannett's daily papers alone reached over 6 million in paid subscriptions, and hence at least twice that many people, which was a dramatic increase from the 3,563,000 the newspaper chain reached as recently as 1981.[8] As of the early 1980s, two other newspaper chains reached well over 3 million subscribers through many individual papers: the Newhouse chain and the Knight–Ridder chain.

That level of multiple ownership and control of newspapers is of particular concern given a development of major importance over the past couple of decades. In the TV era, newspaper competition in the *same "market"* (area) has declined dramatically. Thus, in 1923, "502 cities had two or more competing newspapers. By 1979, only 36 cities, or 2.3% of all cities, had newspaper competition."[9] And the number of such "newspaper monopolies" has increased since 1979.

Legal Restrictions   The Federal Communications Commission (FCC) has traditionally placed some limits on the total number of broadcast stations under single ownership. Further, since 1970, a company was prohibited from acquiring more than one AM and FM radio station or more than one TV station in the *same area,* and since the 1970s, no single company could make an acquisition that would result in owning two or more organizations in *different* media (called "cross-media ownership"). Combinations of such a nature existing *before* 1970, however, were *not* affected by that rule. Until 1984, companies were limited to seven TV stations, seven AM radio stations, and seven FM radio stations. In 1984, the FCC raised those limits to 12 of each.

Concentration, Conglomerates and Potential Consequences

Further, Ben Bagdikian notes that *interlocking directorates* are, indeed, legion in corporations involving the media: "The controllers of most of America's news and views are partners in industries such as agribusiness, airlines, coal and oil, timber, banking . . ."[10] and many other industrial areas. Another side of the same phenomenon should be made explicit: A good number of these media corporations are the core or are part of *conglomerates,* that is, corporations which have business operations in a number of different business areas. The most notable example is NBC, which has long been part of RCA. This giant corporation, in addition to owning one of the three TV networks, has included a huge consumer electronics division, RCA records, and other divisions, plus numerous subsidiaries, such as the Hertz Corporation, a gas company, three realty companies, other communications companies, and a sizable defense contracting section. In 1985, in the fifth-largest corporate merger in American history, RCA merged with General Electric Corporation. GE, the eleventh-largest industrial corporation before the merger,[11] has vast consumer electronics and appliances sections, large military contracting operations, is one of the few builders of nuclear power plants, and so on. Also in 1985, ABC was acquired by Capital Cities Communications Corporation, a large media corporation itself. That merger gave the "new" corporate giant 12 TV stations, 11 AM and 13 FM radio stations, and 55 cable TV systems.[12] In 1987, control of CBS was effectively taken by Laurence Tisch, head of Loews Corporation, a large conglomerate which includes Loews hotel and theater chain, Lorillard Tobacco, CNA insurance, Bulova watches, and many other investments. Tisch became chief executive officer of CBS.[13]

As Bagdikian observes, the crucial issue in all this is: "These media report the news of industries in which they either are owners or share directors and policies."[14] But does the concentration and interlocking nature of ownership really make a difference? News people generally see themselves as professionals and most would probably not agree with a suggestion that they are influenced by corporate concerns. But is there evidence the corporate and conglomerate connection has an impact on what is reported?

First, it should be remembered that we must consider both how a story is reported *and* individual stories and patterns of subjects which are *not* reported but that are of significance. The concern is with actual past patterns, as well as with the potential for abuse in the future (the "means and motive," to borrow from another realm). Bagdikian concludes that the corporate connection does make a difference, and he cites a number of examples. Let two of his examples and a third from another source illustrate the actual and potential problem.

Illustrative Examples   In 1969, a story on "imminent labor negotiations between hospital workers, who received pay near the poverty level, and the management of Johns Hopkins Hospital in Baltimore" was carried in the first edition of the Baltimore *Sun* (one of the nation's more respected papers) but was missing from each edition thereafter. Was it a mere accident that a certain Mr. Cooper was on the board of directors of the newspaper and was also on the board of the Johns Hopkins Hospital? Mr. Cooper was also on the board of the Mercantile Safe Deposit Trust Co., a prominent bank that held 61.3% of the shares in the newspaper company. The *Columbia Journalism Review* observed: ". . . it seemed evident that if Cooper or an associate in the ownership echelon had not ordered the story killed, a top editor, afraid that it might displease the owners, had done so. And one reason for growing concern over conglomerate ownership of news media was underlined."[15] Political scientists have long pointed out the fact that people's behavior can be affected by direct actions to influence them, or by "anticipated reactions," that is, where someone alters actions due to anticipation of the reaction of others—in this case, the owners and ultimate employers.

The second illustrative case involves the nation's most respected and influential paper, the *New York Times*. The *Times* board of directors interlocks with Morgan Guaranty Trust (financial giant), Bristol Myers, Charter Oil, IBM, and a number of other large corporations, including Ford Motor Company. In 1974, Henry Ford II told the publisher of the *Times* that

> federal safety and pollution standards would increase car prices. According to [publisher] Sulzberger, "I said it certainly would affect the advertising coming into our newspapers. I said I would set up a forum." Sulzberger sent a letter to major newspaper publishers announcing a meeting with Ford officials, adding, "I strongly urge you to bring with you your editorial page editor and your business and financial editor, for the story that Messrs. Ford and Iacocca wish to tell goes far beyond the scope of an 'automotive' story."[16]

The result was that all the major wire services carried the Ford case against the federal safety and pollution controls. "Most papers whose reporters attended the meeting put the story on page 1, including the *New York Times,* which ran it at the top of page 1 with a two column picture of Ford."[17]

The point here is not that the *Times* would never run an article that does not reflect positively on Ford Motors. Rather, it is a question of what gets emphasized, what gets very prominent, front-page news attention, as opposed to far less prominent attention. (Keep in mind that many people look *only* at the front page, or two, and then skip to the sports, entertainment, or other such section.) This little tale also implicitly suggests something relevant to the last subject of this chapter, the issue of access. As we shall be seeing shortly, the First Amendment rights of free press and free speech have been central principles referred to in communications regulation cases; but this tale raises the question of who really has access to the media.

The final case example, like the preceding case, is not simple and clear cut (at least regarding the second stage of the case), but the potential and implications are substantial. We have noted the 1985 merger of NBC's parent corporation RCA with General Electric; and GE's nuclear power plant division was noted. Nuclear power is a very difficult issue, with great potential consequences. Could that merger affect how NBC News covers the nuclear power issue? Again, NBC News people consider themselves professionals and would no doubt deny any interference (or even any anticipated reactions). But it is interesting to note that in 1979, General Electric canceled sponsorship of a Barbara Walters special with Jane Fonda (on ABC), who was to discuss her film "The China Syndrome." That film was critical of nuclear power. Did such an action "send a message" to networks inclined to do shows critical of nuclear power? The GE announcement, indeed, said: "[W]e decided not to sponsor the program . . . because it contains material that could cause undue public concern about nuclear power."[18] In March 1987, another interesting event occurred. Roughly two years after the merger, NBC aired a prime-time documentary (using the network's familiar evening news music) called "Nuclear Power: In France It Works." As the title suggests, this program was a rather glowing report on how well nuclear power works in France.[19] It is difficult to say whether NBC was influenced, directly or by anticipated reaction, to decide to air a show on nuclear power instead of one on some other notable topic, and to make it very positive. In fact, NBC did take some note of problems in the American case; and it should also be noted that the original planning for the show apparently began before the merger. In any case, the potential for impact of the corporate and conglomerate connection is well illustrated.

Interestingly, Bagdikian reports a survey by the American Society of Newspaper Editors which found that 33% of all editors "working for newspaper chains said they would not feel free to run a news story that was damaging to their parent firm."[20] To elaborate a little on the issue, the question is not only how a news organization reports a subject, but the level of emphasis given to it, whether a subject is reported at all, and also how vigorously a subject is investigated in the first place. Are reporters assigned to it, especially investigative reporters?

Cable TV: Concentration and Consequences   One final note on the concentration issue is in order. Cable TV systems have been perhaps the most

striking mass media development of the 1980s. In fact, we should prominently note that the networks' share of the total prime-time TV audience
declined from 99% in 1980 to 74% in mid-1985; cable TV stations had
"stolen" those viewers.[21] Various observers suggested that cable TV, with
its capacity to deliver a dozen or several dozen channels to the home, would
end the old problem of scarcity of TV channels and thus provide the
opportunity for great diversity of broadcasts. And they suggested this
would allow treatment of TV like print media. However, it has turned out
that cable ownership has begun to follow the American pattern of concentration. We noted above that Capital Cities–ABC owns 55 cable systems.
And then there is TCI (Telecommunications, Inc.): "One out of five cable
viewers in the United States . . . watches systems in which TCI has an interest."[22] It is important to remember that in the vast majority of areas,
there is only one cable system—it is a cable monopoly—and those on cable
receive *all* their TV stations off the cable. An interesting example of what
this can mean is as follows. Local government has a formal regulatory role
based on its control of the right-of-way cable systems need to run their
wires. Normally, the local government regulatory hand is far from firm,
though, until recently, approval for rate hikes had to be formally gained
from such government. In one case, TCI "asked for a rate increase in Vail
and was turned down. So one weekend it shut down all its programming
and, instead, *for 48 straight hours,* ran the name and telephone number of
the town manager in charge of the cable contract!"[23] TCI and its head,
John Malone, also have "substantial control of Turner Broadcasting" (after
Ted Turner got into debt trouble). The second largest cable company is
owned by Time, Inc. (which also owns the entertainment channel HBO).
Kenneth Berents, a media analyst for Butcher & Singer, has concluded that
TCI "can't exactly control the [cable] industry, but they can dictate what
will happen."[24]

A Note on "Public" Television and Radio

As noted earlier, the U.S. government has no direct involvement in
mass media broadcasting, nor is there a separate public organization that
plans and runs most of the broadcasting, as with Great Britain's BBC
(British Broadcasting Company). In the United States, we have what can be
called a "semi-public" television and radio system.

The 1967 Public Broadcasting Act established the Corporation for
Public Broadcasting (CPB) (a nonprofit organization), which receives funds
authorized by Congress and distributes the money to most of the public
radio and TV stations. A separate Public Broadcasting Service (PBS) is
responsible for producing specific TV programs, as is National Public Radio (NPR).

Between 1968 and 1972, the Ford Foundation provided more funds
than the government for public television. Federal government funding

increased from a few million dollars per year in the late 1960s to $162 million in fiscal 1982. Federal funds amounted to just under 30% as of that time.[25] However, due to budget cuts, in fiscal 1983 especially (initiated by the Reagan administration), federal support has declined to slightly more than 15% of funding for public TV.[26] The same thing has happened in public radio. It should be added that local and state governments provided one-fourth of public TV funding as of the mid-1980s.

The result of those budget cuts has been a much more intense scramble for funds and more reliance on corporate sponsorship. Even before those budget cuts dependence on corporate funding was substantial: "Between 1973 and 1980, business support increased sixfold. In fiscal 1980, 115 corporate underwriters gave just under 30 million dollars for public television. Four oil corporations contributed half of that total in 1980."[27] (This was an example of what is called "institutional advertising," whereby the organization seeks to improve its overall image, rather than sell a specific product; after huge profits during the energy crises of the 1970s, the oil corporations had major image problems.) From 1979 to 1985, corporate underwriting of stations' programs jumped from 10% to over 16% of the total.[28]

It should be kept in mind that corporate sponsorship is usually of specific programs, on both TV and radio. Further, a recent development has deepened business involvement: Under new FCC rules, corporate sponsors of national programs can now identify specific product brand names, rather than just the general corporate name; corporations can even "pay local public TV stations to air limited types of 15- or 30-second commercial ads."[29] As the president of New York's WNET has said, "The adequate financing of public television has become a continuous conundrum." The basic problem is, as the *National Journal* has observed, that a "station that increasingly relies on corporate contributions or advertising to survive runs the risk of becoming virtually indistinguishable from its commercial brethren."[30]

The question is, then: What is the purpose of *public* television? It is interesting to note that the United States spends little, in public fashion, on public broadcasting compared with other developed nations. In fiscal 1983, the federal government spent 69 cents per capita, whereas during "basically the same period . . . Great Britain spent $18 per person, Japan $10.09 and Canada $22."[31]

The ten members of the directing board of the Corporation for Public Broadcasting, it should be added, are appointed by the president. These can be very *political* appointees. For example, Sonia Landau, who was renominated in 1986 to serve as chairwoman of the board, once headed Women for Reagan–Bush, and one of Nancy Reagan's former press secretaries has also been nominated to the board. Other administrations have acted more or less similarly.[32]

Finally, a note should be added on the public TV audience. The good news (at least for my values) is that audience has grown considerably. The proportion of households viewing public television at some time during the day rose from 37.6% of all households that watched television in the 1977–1978 season to 56.6% in 1984–1985; and the proportion that viewed public TV in prime time (or at least some part of it) rose from 18.6% to 34% according to the audience ratings company A.C. Nielson.[33]

REGULATION, THE LAW AND ACCESS

Regulation and the FCC

In the United States, the free press principle has meant that the print media have been left essentially free of government regulation. But from early in the radio era, the broadcast media have been seen as different. After chaotic circumstances at the beginning of the radio era (where stations interfered with one another's signals, among other problems), the conclusion was reached that broadcast channels were scarce; only a limited number of channels existed on the usable spectrum for radio and then television. As a consequence, choices had to be made as to who would be allowed to own a station and use a given channel to broadcast. Additionally, these new media of communication were seen as different. As one prominent official commented on the broadcast medium, it "has passed from the field of an adventure to that of a public utility. Nor among the utilities is there one whose activities may yet come more closely to the life of each and every one of our citizens, nor which holds out greater possibilities of future influence, nor which is of more potential public concern. Here is an agency that has reached deep into the family life."[34] That official was none other than the public embodiment of unfettered private enterprise, Herbert Hoover, speaking as secretary of commerce, and speaking about the medium of *radio!*

Drawing on the existing model of federal regulatory agencies, Congress first set up the Federal Radio Commission, and then, in 1934, the Federal Communications Commission (FCC) to regulate the broadcast media (as well as interstate telegraph and telephone). The FCC had seven members until 1984, when it was reduced to five members, four of whom are appointed for seven-year staggered terms by the president. The chairperson is named by each president. The membership is to be "bipartisan" (three from one major political party and two from the other), although presidents have found it easy to appoint people of like mind who were formally in the other party. Because many commissioners have resigned before the end of their term, most presidents have had a majority of their appointees on the Commission by the end of their first term in office. This has given presidents considerable influence over the FCC. But Congress passes on the FCC's budget each year, and it enacts the laws on which FCC actions are based. Especially through the Commerce Committees in each house and the telecommunications subcommittees, Congress has considerable influence over what the FCC does, as well. One study suggests that this influence is often very great.[35]

Because of the scarcity of channels and (less explicitly) the nature of the medium, the FCC was charged to regulate the broadcast media in "the public interest, convenience, or necessity." That is a very vague, general instruction. Neither in the Federal Communications Act of 1934 nor since has Congress specified exactly what that crucial phrase means; it left the matter up to the FCC to establish rules and guidelines for its implementation.

Licenses for stations to broadcast were the key mechanism established for implementation. A number of other rules have been established, most of which are requirements which are, theoretically at least, taken into account in making license decisions. (Rules limiting ownership of total number of stations and of different media in the same area were noted above.)

We turn next to the more important of those rules and the pattern of FCC implementation of them. Special attention is focused on the licensing instrument. Significant court decisions interpreting those rules, FCC case decisions, the basic law, and the First Amendment's relation to them are also discussed. The history of FCC rules and decisions and the courts' responses is a complex one, with a multitude of such decisions and many twists and turns in the regulatory road. There is space here to cover only the more significant decisions. There are a few very good sources for those wishing more detailed discussion, though, Fred Friendly's *The Good Guys, the Bad Guys and the First Amendment* being the most marvelously readable.[36]

Deciding Whose Media; Media for Whom?: FCC Licensing and Related Rules and Court Decisions

The fact of channel scarcity* and the idea that the public interest must be protected in the use of these broadcast media led to the requirement that a station and its owner must obtain a broadcast license to operate from FCC. Until the 1980s, TV licenses were for three years; they are now given for five years (in standard cases). Note that it is the *stations* that are licensed; the networks themselves are not licensed by the FCC, although certain other rules and court decisions have involved them more directly. In principle, if a station does not perform in the public interest, the owner organization can lose its license; in principle, any new channel assignments

---

*The broadcast channel scarcity question is discussed more fully in the final section of the chapter.

are made on the promise of good performance, as spelled out in a programming plan submitted with the license application. That is the principle established in and by the Federal Communications Act. The reality is something else. In exploring why that has been the case, we will be led to the other more important rules and actions in broadcast regulation.

On Licensing   The reality of FCC's implementation of the regulatory instrument of licensing was summed up well by the U.S. Court of Appeals (D.C. circuit) in 1982. With a mix of irony and incredulity in the Court's "voice," the Court commented:

> Finally, we must note that we are still troubled by the fact that the record remains that an incumbent *television* licensee has *never* been denied renewal in a comparative challenge. American television viewers will be reassured, although a trifle baffled, to learn that even the worst television stations—those which are, presumably, the ones picked out as vulnerable to a challenge—are so good that they never need replacing. We suspect that somewhere, sometime, somehow, some television licensee *should* fail in a comparative renewal challenge, but the FCC has never discovered such a licensee yet.[37]

A "comparative challenge" is one where another organization challenges the existing license holder, in effect claiming that it would serve the public interest better than the existing licensee, and usually contending that the licensee is not performing well in the public interest. This court statement applies to the FCC itself. In one instance, a court directed the revocation of a license, as we are about to see.

The case of station WLBT-TV in Jackson, Mississippi, an NBC affiliate, illustrates just how reluctant the FCC can be to end license privileges. Thurgood Marshall, chief attorney for the NAACP (and later on the Supreme Court), who argued the famous 1954 *Brown* v. *Board of Education* case before the Supreme Court, appeared on the NBC "World At Home" show on September 7, 1955. As he was explaining the Court's ruling that the old "separate but equal" concept and practice was unconstitutional, an interruption slide flashed on the TV station's signal which read: "Sorry, Cable Trouble From New York." It was reported that WLBT's general manager boasted of having cut off Marshall. During the racial crisis in Little Rock, Arkansas, in 1957 (over integration of the schools), a program on that matter on WLBT included only white segregationists and (like-minded) Mississippi officials. And when Medgar Evers, NAACP field secretary for the state, asked for response time, he was refused. Further, in 1962 when James Meredith, with help from various groups, sought to integrate the University of Mississippi, and while the racial crisis that came with it occurred, WLBT's general manager "went on the air to rally white supremacists," encouraging them to "go out to Oxford and stand shoulder to shoulder with Governor Barnett and keep that nigra out of Ole Miss." In another NBC broadcast relating to civil rights (a documentary), another "Sorry, Cable Trouble" slide interrupted the program on station WLBT.[38] And so it went.

In 1964, when WLBT sought renewal of its license, it was challenged on the specific practices just noted and the general pattern underlying them. The challenge was spearheaded by a New York–based minister, with support from the United Church of Christ, civil rights groups, and some local citizens. The FCC at least recognized some hint of the problems— WLBT was given a one-year renewal instead of three. Despite the fact that blacks constituted almost half of the population "served" by the station's signal and despite that record, FCC let the ownership retain its license. (FCC did say that a full three-year license was to be conditioned on increased fairness in future broadcasts, and two commissioners did strongly dissent.) On appeal, the U.S. Court of Appeals reversed that FCC decision and sent the case back to FCC for reconsideration. FCC took two years to do so, and then granted a full three-year renewal to the station ownership! Some effort had been made during the latter period to moderate the racist pattern of WLBT, but the result is still striking; indeed, a U.S. Court of Appeals decision (again) reversed the FCC and *demanded* that the license be rescinded.[39]

What is the meaning of the "public interest" and of granting an organization the privilege of using one of the standard (VHF) TV channels, if such a (non-)decision on even such a licensing renewal case is made? That concerned question raises another: What have been the bases of FCC decision making?

Criteria for Licensing Decisions Congress has never spelled out the criteria the FCC should use in making the crucial license decision; it left that up to the Commission. The FCC has never precisely spelled out criteria for granting new or renewal licenses either. From a 1965 "Policy Statement" and various statements of particular case decisions, we can discern some prime criteria. The chief criteria (at least in theory) are as follows:[40]

1. Diversity in control of the mass media, meaning that the concentration of media ownership will be taken into consideration, especially any multimedia combinations in the same area. This is a matter for which there is a specific rule for acquisitions after 1970 (as we noted above).
2. Full-time participation in operation of a station by the owners, called "management–ownership integration," in preference to absentee ownership. The idea is to have the ownership of a station as closely connected to the actual, daily management of it as possible, so as to maximize direct responsibility for what is broadcast and to maximize sensitivity to the local area's (evolving) needs.
3. The actual performance of the program services proposed in the initial or previous application. That is, to receive a license, an owner has proposed a programming plan; the question is, has it been followed?

4.   Past record in broadcasting—what has been the pattern of actual performance?

5.   "Character," which in practice has meant: Has the ownership told the truth about criteria 1 to 4, and has it been involved in any misbehavior in other significant areas of activity?

These criteria were reinforced and elaborated on, at various times, by other rules. In the mid-1970s, the FCC ruled that 5% of total programming had to be devoted to local affairs, 5% to news and public affairs, and 10% to nonentertainment programs. More fundamentally, TV and radio stations had been required to keep rather detailed logs of all programs broadcast, which would document the amount of time the station spent on news, public affairs, and so on. In 1981, however, the FCC ended the log-keeping requirement for radio, and in 1984 did the same for television. In so doing, the specific requirement to air at least a minimum of public affairs programming was ended. This has not, of course, ended stations' presentation of news programs; and in theory, the license renewal process can serve to assure that basic news responsibilities are met. But the move would appear to symbolize a lessened commitment to nonentertainment programming, and it certainly does nothing to encourage public affairs programming beyond the regular news programs.

Realities of Licensing and the "Expectation of Renewal"   In principle, licensing was and is the chief instrument for ensuring broadcasting in the public interest. In reality it has not been so used. The criteria just reviewed have been used, with varying specificity and intensity, and varying consistency, to gently encourage responsible behavior. In practice, through many statements of case decisions, as well as some court rulings and occasional pronouncements from some person or section of Congress, the dominant orientation has been the "expectation of renewal," however. That is, under more-or-less normal circumstances, the existing owner and license holder can expect essentially automatic renewal. As one FCC commissioner commented on the decision process involved: "To the perceptive observer . . . [it is] apparent by now that there is less to such [renewal] 'contests' than meets the eye, that in fact, it is not a real contest between two applicants but a pretend game played between the Commission and the public. The outcome of the game is predetermined. . . ."[41]

One reason for this orientation is recognition of the existing investment in the station, its equipment, and so on, and the idea of maintaining stability in station ownership so as to encourage more investment in equipment, personnel, and so on. Further, a serious challenge can require a large sum in legal fees in the process of renewal hearings ($100,000 and more), a burden not to be imposed lightly. A more prominent reason is the idea of protection of a "free press." The free press principle involves the idea that government should not be routinely interfering with what the broadcasting news media are producing, and correspondingly, that the news media should not feel inhibited about investigating news matters. This prominently includes those matters involving the government.[42]

Yet some serious questions are raised by this expectation of renewal if the broadcast media are involved in the economic structure as described above, if the nature of the broadcast media is as discussed in Chapter 4, and if they are vested with a public trust. Before we pursue the difficult, fundamental questions in broadcast ownership, regulation, and free "press," three specific rules and principles that have spelled out key areas of the responsibilities of broadcasters need to be noted.

The Media for Whom?: FCC Rules and Court Decisions on the Issues of Responsibility and Access

Three other rule areas relate to the general idea of responsibility of broadcasters to the public. These rule areas have been quite controversial. Each of these rules is also a factor in the general, hotly debated issue of "access," of who has had and who has a right to access to the mass media to send their message over it.

Equal Time Provision   The Equal Time Provision applies to (and only to) candidates in and during an election period. The principle involved is that of inhibiting a station from shutting one or more candidates out while giving the other (or others) ample opportunity to send their message, and hence, giving unfair advantage to the one candidate. The Equal Time Provision, enacted into law by Congress, says that if time on a station is given or sold to one candidate, the same opportunity must be given to the other candidate(s). This provision does *not* apply, however, to "bona fide news coverage and interviews of candidates."[43]

A problem with the Equal Time Provision has been a tendency, in practice, to apply it only to the *major* party candidates. The most notable example is that of the presidential debates. In 1976 and 1980, the FCC ruled that if some private organization (namely, the League of Women Voters, which organized each of the debates) arranged a debate between candidates of "their choosing," it was a news event, so the Equal Time Provision did not apply. Frankly stated, this was a ruse, by those friendly to the two dominant parties, to exclude candidates from any other party from such events. It was a way to get around the equal time principle. In 1983, FCC dropped the pretense and simply allowed news organizations themselves to arrange debates among candidates of their choosing. In the TV age, this is a further blow to minor parties, already struggling against large obstacles. This position seems to contradict the principle, oft-stated by the FCC, Congress members, and the courts, that there must be a "free market of ideas" in the broadcast media. It would also seem to be at odds with the key democratic principle of *choice* reviewed in Chapter 1: "Central to the idea of an operative democracy is alternative choices competing for public acceptance. . . ." Does limitation of public exposure, on the broadcast media, to two parties' candidates constitute a true free market of ideas and maximized choice for the public? (Separating legitimate candidates and parties from crank or frivolous ones is, of course, a necessary and less-than-easy task. But democracy is not the tidiest and most easily managed form of political system.)

Fairness Doctrine   The Fairness Doctrine is the second, and easily the most controversial, rule of broadcasting responsibility and public access. Again, with the limited number of channels available, the pervasiveness, reach, and nature of the broadcast media, and given the allocation of a channel of "airspace" by public authority, many have said that fair treatment of issues and individuals must be assured. The Fairness Doctrine is the result of those concerns.

There is a long, elaborate history of FCC, congressional, and court statements involving this doctrine.[44] A series of key cases forced the issue onto the agenda, the content of some of those cases being truly startling. The principal original stimulus for the doctrine came from the case of the owner of three major radio stations, who, in the 1940s, ordered his news staff to "slant, distort and falsify" news against such "enemies" of his as President Roosevelt. Among other things, he ordered stories about Roosevelt to be placed with those about "communists and criminals so they might seem related." When the issue of fairness was raised, the owner said: "This is my station and I'll do what I want with it."[45]

In response, the FCC issued a report in 1949 directing license holders to "operate in the public interest." The two points of articulation of this principle came to be of central importance: "(1) to devote a reasonable amount of time to the coverage of controversial issues of public importance; and (2) to do so fairly by affording a reasonable opportunity for contrasting viewpoints to be voiced on these issues."[46] A decade later in 1959, while in the course of writing the Equal Time Provision into law, Congress enacted the following amendment to the Communications Act (specifically, Section 315): "Nothing in the foregoing . . . shall be construed as relieving broadcasters in connection with the presentation of newscasts, news interviews, . . . and on-the-spot coverage of news events from the obligation imposed upon them under this act to operate in the public interest and to afford reasonable opportunity for the discussion of conflicting views on issues of public importance."[47] As Fred Friendly has pointed out: "In the ensuing years a long series of FCC findings and court rulings have reiterated the fairness concept. . . . "[48] The Fairness Doctrine does not specify exactly how contrasting viewpoints should be expressed, or by whom; this was left to broadcasters, although appeals to FCC and the courts were certainly open.

In the mid-1980s, however, with an FCC dominated by strongly business and laissez faire—oriented commissioners appointed by President Reagan, the commission showed an inclination to abolish the Fairness Doctrine. In 1986, the U.S. Court of Appeals issued an opinion saying "that Congress in its 1959 amendments to the Communications Act did not obligate the FCC to uphold the doctrine" and hence the "FCC has the discretion to overturn the doctrine."[49] This is a rather strange decision in light of the 1959 amendment to the Communications Act. (Indeed, as Friendly observed in 1976 in regard to that amendment: "Henceforth the lawyers' argument that Congress had never passed Fairness Doctrine legislation would be hard to justify."[50]) In any case, in 1987, at least partly in response to the 1986 court decision, Congress passed a formal, specific (re-)affirmation of the Fairness Doctrine (by nearly two-to-one margins in both houses). President Reagan then vetoed the bill. Two weeks thereafter, the FCC voted to abolish the doctrine. That decision was challenged in court and some key members of Congress vowed to reinstate the doctrine by law. (There matters stood as of this writing.)

Right of Rebuttal   The third rule concerning the responsibility of broadcasters and the issue of access is a close cousin of the Fairness Doctrine: the right of rebuttal to personal attacks. The case of the Red Lion Broadcasting Company, station WGCB, was the key case leading to this rule. An extremely conservative "radio minister," the Reverend Billy Hargis, attacked a book by and the person of a writer by the name of Cook. Cook (with help from elements of the Democratic Party) sent a request for free reply time to the 200 stations that carried the Hargis program. To make a long story short,[51] the owner of WGCB adamantly refused to grant free reply time (though an advertising rate card was sent with the "offer" to sell time to Cook). The Supreme Court eventually ruled that stations which run programs attacking individuals or groups were obligated to supply free air time for rebuttal.

This was a striking ruling. Exactly when the rebuttal would be aired and how much time would be devoted to it was left to broadcaster discretion. Still, broadcasters and some critics maintained that this rule, especially in conjunction with the Fairness Doctrine and the need for FCC's licensing approval, would inhibit, would have a "chilling effect" on broadcasters' investigation of controversial issues. They also said that many stations would simply not do programs on controversial issues at all for fear of having to provide too much reply time or spend too much money defending themselves from doing so. Doris Graber suggests that this decision "led to sharp curtailment of air time for controversial broadcasts,"[52] although she does not provide evidence for that conclusion (an unusual occurrence for her). In sum, the concern was that the rebuttal rule leads to the reverse of the first of the two basic elements of the Fairness Doctrine: devoting a reasonable amount of time to coverage of controversial issues. Broadcasters and others also maintained that this rule, as well as the more general Fairness Doctrine, violated their First Amendment rights of free press and free speech.

The Supreme Court, in the Red Lion case, did speak directly to the latter issue. The court held: "There is no question here of the Commission's refusal to permit the broadcaster to carry a particular program or to publish [his/her] own views. . . . Such questions would raise more serious First Amendment issues. But we do hold that Congress and the Commission do not violate the First Amendment when they require a radio or television station to give reply time to answer personal attacks and political editorials."[53]

This opinion of the court and the three rule areas we have just discussed point to the need to think through the fundamental questions of ownership and control of the mass media and public access to them, and to put those questions in perspective.

Before we do so, one other note should be added regarding an encouraging development, related most closely to the Equal Time Provision, but ultimately to the Fairness Doctrine, as well. After various sorts of skirmishing and pressures in the 1960s and 1970s, the networks have established the tradition of granting time to the "other" party to reply to major presidential addresses. This is an encouraging development for which the networks are to be applauded. It is a step toward the important democratic principle the British have called "the loyal opposition." This is the notion that prominent exposure should be given to critiques, by the "out" party, of the party in control of the central positions of government.

Whose Media; Media for Whom?: Further Details and Some Perspective on Ownership, Control, and Access

Four Basic Issues   There are four basic issues raised by the preceding discussion, four issues that are fundamental to the role of the media in our society. These issues affect one another. The first issue is: How unfettered and unregulated should ownership of the mass media be, especially that of the broadcast media, and what means should be used for control of a station and ultimately of a medium? A specific question is whether the *expectation* of license renewal is appropriate. Second, what is the meaning of the First Amendment rights of free speech and press, and how are they affected by existing and potential patterns of governmental regulation *and* of ownership concentration? The third issue is comprised of two matters related to the nature of each medium and its technology. They are: In the 1980s, is there a scarcity of broadcast channels, and if so, does that and the characteristics of the medium of TV compared with print justify or require different regulatory treatment for the former? Fourth, there is the question of the democratic perspective: What do the requirements of democracy in the current age suggest about the role the media *ought* to play and what responsibilities they ought to have? We continue the discussion, particularly of the fourth issue, in Chapter 12.

It is appropriate to deal first with the issues of scarcity and nature of the media, and then with the ownership and control issue, as they are at the foundation of current debate and official actions. Also, responses to the other issues depend in important ways on the conclusions regarding those issues.

The Scarcity Idea and Criticism of It   Through much of the nineteenth century, the press was mostly partisan. Some newspapers were unabashedly Democratic in orientation, in how they covered the news as well as in editorial statements, and were bought by Democrats.[54] Other papers were Whig or Republican in orientation and were bought by their party identifiers. In each sizable city there was vigorous competition between two or more newspapers. But with the development of the telegraph and the Associated Press wire service, which had to appeal to all sorts of newspapers to thrive, and with private ownership increasingly encouraging appeal to a larger mass audience, the partisan press gradually disappeared.[55] Then the twentieth-century developments of radio and television led to the conclusion that these were unique media in which channels were naturally scarce. There were only a limited number of radio, then (VHF) TV channels, on the technologically usable spectrum. Scarcity has been a prime justification for governmental regulation of the broadcast media, while leaving the print media untouched by such regulation (since in theory, there was no "natural" limit to starting up a newspaper anywhere).

Long-time scholar of politics and communications, Ithiel de Sola Pool,[56] has argued that scarcity is no longer a reality in the broadcast media. He has eloquently expressed his concern about the character of government regulation and the potential for that regulation to spread to means of communication other than the traditional broadcast media. The development of technology is the reason for both conclusions. Pool asserts that the technology of cable TV, with its capacity for dozens of channels and with its increasing availability, constitutes a prime contradiction of the scarcity notion. He also cites other technological developments which represent the potential for other means of electronic mass communication. He points out such developments as direct broadcasting from satellites to the home and multipoint distribution servies (a pay-television service where programs can be sent via microwave frequencies and directed to individual homes).[57] Further, Pool points to the fact that there are several or many radio stations in most areas, and to the fact that newspaper competition in a single city is now rare, while many such cities are served by more than one TV station. To him this contradicts the traditional scarcity argument.

In light of those contentions, Pool suggests we should look to alternative approaches to the system of mass media control and allocation in the United States. Two "options" that he suggests are the "common carrier" approach and/or using the market mechanism. In the common carrier approach (as used in the telephone and telegraph industries), the owner of a station or network does not develop and decide what is carried on the medium; rather, others do and the owner of the medium "is obligated to serve all on equal terms without discrimination."[58] But in the likely circumstance of demand for air time exceeding supply, especially in the case of standard VHF TV, how is it decided who in specific is served? The answer: "either selective licensing, or some rationing scheme, or a price mechanism must be used."[59] The former two methods, of course, bring us back to the same issue of deciding criteria for who gets on the air—and deciding who decides: public authority or private business. Pool favors a price mechanism, which is simply a specific variation on the market mechanism for general use of the broadcast media. (Pool does recommend that the government sell the initial license for the lucrative enterprise of broadcasting, which has been given free, and thereby capture some revenue for the public treasury.) The market or price mechanism allocates the channel or air time to the highest bidder.[60]

A Critique of Pool's Critique: Scarcity Is Still a Problem, and the Problem with the Market Mechanism   Pool's concern for freedom of expression and a democratic society are genuine and long held. But are his interpretations of current realities and of potentials for the reasonably foreseeable future accurate? There are good grounds for questioning those interpretations.

First, the potential of cable for a large number of channels has not materialized. The assumption that there would be 200-channel systems has turned out to be a faulty assumption.

Now in the mid to late 1980s, cable systems began to offer quite a few channels beyond the traditional broadcast stations. But the fact is that nearly all those channels have been simply entertainment or video merchandising. For public affairs purposes, with the exceptions of CNN, C-SPAN and the occasional exception of TBS, cable TV has been a noncontributor.

Second, the demand for space on the total broadcast spectrum is up substantially. The increased demand comes from such uses as police radios, mobile "cellular" phone systems for cars, and the like. Further, new technologies such as high-definition TV "may require the use of two adjacent TV channels instead of one."[61]

It should also be noted that there had been an FCC rule, called the "must-carry" rule, which required cable systems to carry the signals of all local TV stations normally received over the air, as well as to carry a "community access" channel. This included UHF stations, which in a number of areas meant the single public television station or several such stations in the region. But a 1985 decision of the U.S. Court of Appeals held that cable operators have the right to choose which broadcast signals to carry. More specifically, "Cable systems must carry only those stations [above] certain audience ratings, although most would still have to carry at least one public station located in their service area."[62] Basically, cable systems can now fill their channels with whatever attracts the largest audience (although in theory the local government, which grants the right-of-way for cable wires, can set some requirements).

The basis for the court decision just mentioned was that cable systems have potential competition from other cable companies which are free to build another cable system in the area, and they have competition from the new technologies noted by Pool and others. In the vast majority of areas, however, a second cable system is not economically feasible; they simply aren't being built, nor are they likely to be. The fact is that in the great majority of areas, the cable system is a monopoly; and as we noted earlier, the cable industry is becoming increasingly concentrated throughout the nation. All those facts and developments led to substantial moves in Congress in the late 1980s to reregulate the cable TV industry.[63]

There are further grounds to question the idea that the development of technology and the free press principle mean that regulation of broadcasting is no longer needed, especially in the case of television. First, the fact is, the standard, traditional VHF TV stations and networks are and will continue to be dominant in TV broadcasting, especially regarding news and public affairs. With the welcome if less than major exceptions of CNN and public TV, they are the place people look for their public affairs information and impressions, in the realm of broadcasting.

Scarcity and the Nature of Broadcast versus Print Media   Second, speaking of impressions, if the discussion in Chapter 4 is correct, the medium of TV in particular, compared with print, has a different and unique impact. The nature of that medium, in conjunction with the continued dominance in public affairs of the traditional VHF stations and networks, suggests the need for continued oversight and public control. Again, the TV medium is pervasive in our society, and unlike newspapers, it does not require an affirmative act to be exposed to a message. Rather (as with radio), if the set is on, everyone tends to be exposed. Further, TV has been found to be the most believable medium. As a Supreme Court opinion written by Justice Stevens held: The broadcast media are a "uniquely pervasive presence" which confront citizens "in the privacy of the home"—a phenomenon that "outweighs the First Amendment rights of an intruder." (The specific case at issue concerned profanity in a radio broadcast.[64])

The idea of scarcity and, implicitly, the idea of the nature of the medium were the bases for a notable Supreme Court decision which ruled against a right of access to the print medium for rebuttal (or other point of fairness). The case was that of the *Miami Herald v. Tornillo*. Tornillo was running for the state legislature when the *Herald* published two editorials attacking him. He was represented by noted law professor Jerome Barron, who had previously written arguments for such access to the print media. The court, however, saw those media differently and struck down the request for reply space. The fact that the typical newspaper runs critical letters to the editor and various and opposing opinion columns, unlike most of TV, seem to have affected the ruling, as well.[65]

Scarcity and Critique of the Market Mechanism   Third (and in response to another contention of Pool's), as former FCC Chairman Newton Minow has explained: "The test of scarcity cannot be measured by the number of newspapers. The proper test is the number of citizens who want a broadcast license and are unable to obtain one. At that point, a decision must be made as to who is to be allowed, and who denied, the exclusive license to use the channels. . . ." Minow notes that several major newspapers in large cities have gone out of business in the 1980s without replacement; but, "by contrast, when the FCC made RKO's channels available for competitive application, it quickly got 172 applications. . . . And when the . . . commission decided to permit new low-power television, it was inundated by almost 14,000 applications."[66]

Now with regard to the recommendation of use of the market mechanism to allocate stations, or even segments of time on a "common carrier" station, there are some serious questions to be addressed. The more obvious question is: Would such a system, as much or more than currently, mean that "access" to the broadcast media was available only to wealthy individuals and businesses? In such an open market, for such a resource, who could afford to join the competition?

In 1986, the three main TV networks had "combined operating earnings of about $400 million on revenues of $8 billion, . . . while the 600 affiliates [stations] will earn about $3.5 billion on $10 billion in revenues." Further, and reinforcing the point made above regarding the continued dominance of the three traditional TV networks and their affiliates: "The sale prices of affiliated stations also testify to the value they gain simply by carrying network programming."[67] A regular VHF TV station in anything resembling a populous area is highly profitable, as a rule, and an extremely expensive "property" to buy. Even radio stations, in the typical case, are highly expensive: Los Angeles station KUTE-FM sold for $15 million in 1985, and "even stations in smaller markets, like Fresno and Lompoc (California), have sold for more than $1 million,"[68] which was, in fact, just *under* the *average* price paid for a radio station in 1985.[69] Even in the highly unlikely event that there is a switch to common carrier status for at least some stations, who will have the money to outbid others for a "slice" of air time? Additionally, it seems likely that under a more total market mechanism entertainment programming would be even more heavily emphasized, since the feeling will be that such is the way to gain the largest audience and hence the best return on one's specific investment. Further, in a common carrier approach, the existence of a continuing media institution where responsibility for treatment of public affairs can consistently and easily be located would be wiped away. There are then, grounds for questioning Pool's "options." There are also grounds for questioning the automatic renewal tendency, given the discussion above.

Ownership, Regulation, the Public Trust, and a Democratic System: Perspective and Comment   Edward Jay Epstein has provided an excellent summary of some FCC statements and court decisions which, in this analyst's opinion, best enunciate "the public interest" in broadcasting *in a democratic society:*

> First, it is assumed as "axiomatic" that the "basic" purpose of broadcasting is, in the words of the Commission, "the development of an informal public opinion through the public dissemination of news and ideas concerning the vital public issues of the day." The "foundation stone of the American system of broadcasting" is then the "right of the public to be informed, rather than any right on the part of the government, any broadcast licensees or any individual members of the public to broadcast his own particular views on any matter." The broadcasting of news and information on matters of public importance is thus presumed to be an indispensable element in fulfilling the "public interest."
>
> It is assumed further that it is absolutely "essential to the welfare of the public" for these ideas and information to come from "diverse and antagonistic sources."[70]

The U.S. Court of Appeals (D.C.), in a revised version of a previous opinion, held that the existing broadcast licensees should have a substantial advantage toward renewal *if* they had performed "meritorious service."[71] This seems sensible if a broadcaster's actual performance is held to some significant criteria for public service; "meritorious service" should mean something. This presumably does not mean dictating specific content. But it also does not mean avoiding important, and contentious, issues. Nor is there reason for the Fairness Doctrine to inhibit such discussion. Indeed, point number *one* of the original statement of that doctrine mandated that a "reasonable amount of time" be spent on coverage of "controversial issues of public importance." Broadcasters should certainly be spared from frivolous fairness or license challenges and the expense that goes with them, although separating the frivolous case from one that represents an important principle is not always easy. In the absence of a reasonable amount of coverage of important and controversial issues, in a fair fashion, why should a particular owner be allowed to retain a license to operate the exceedingly valuable, effectively scarce, and powerful communications resource of a broadcast channel, especially a TV channel?

Something of an encouraging development has been the formation of some groups with the specific purpose of keeping a watch on, challenging, and ensuring access to the broadcast media. Challenging the broadcast media is certainly a healthy thing (subjected to the qualifications just noted). Examples are, on the conservative side, the amply funded Accuracy in Media (AIM) and, roughly speaking, on the liberal side, The Media Access Project (principally a law office). Some other groups, especially on the more liberal side, did not survive the 1970s.[72] [A new group was formed in 1986 as a liberal counter to AIM: Fairness and Accuracy in Reporting (FAIR), although with but a fraction of AIM's funding, it would appear.]

It should also be noted with regard to citizens' rights and efforts in challenging broadcasters, that the case of WLBT-TV in Mississippi gave citizens without a direct financial stake in a license case legal standing to challenge licensee performance.[73] A related step of an encouraging sort was taken by the FCC in 1976 with the creation of a Consumer Assistance Office to provide informational services to the public, which included a regular public summary of pending rule makings and inquiries. Further, in the late 1970s "under Chairman Richard Wiley the FCC held a series of mass public meetings at scattered sites across the nation, which, if nothing else, gave the regulators a feeling for what was on the minds of some members of the public."[74] The bad news is that Reagan administration budget cutbacks in 1981 ended publication of the public summary and other elements of citizen services.

These issues of ownership, regulation, and access are certainly not clear cut. Decisions on which approach to take and how to spell out the details are not only difficult, but each direction of decision is fraught with potential dangers for involved individuals and the public good of society as a whole. Hopefully, this chapter has lead to further reflection on these issues.

My concern remains, in any case, that we continue to place the key questions in the context of the political system as a whole and the constant struggle to maintain and enhance the democratic nature of the system. This includes a maximally informed and engaged citizenry, which must provide the base of such a system. Let me repeat what Catlin has observed, first quoted in Chapter 1: " 'freedom of the press' . . . is a civil liberty under law, logically justified for the specific purpose of . . . the development of an objectively informed or intellectually vigorous democracy. . . . "[75]

Perhaps the question we need to ask, in light of the needs of democracy, is not, "has an existing license owner done a grossly inadequate job," but rather, especially in the case of television, "how can this powerful medium be *best* used to support and enhance an informed and engaged citizenry?" Such a question leads us to the next chapter, on the making and presentation of the news.

CHAPTER SIX
WHAT'S NEWS?
The Formulation and Presentation of the News

INTRODUCTION AND PERSPECTIVE

November 22, 1963. President John F. Kennedy was assassinated. What exactly happened? How did it happen? What did it mean? Tens of millions of people asked those questions, and they turned to the news to find out.

Also in late November, 22 years later, President Reagan met with Soviet leader Mikhail Gorbachev. This "summit meeting" was the first time President Reagan had met with the leader of the Soviet Union (after virtually five years in the White House). During that time there had been massive further increases in nuclear and other armaments on both sides of this "superpower" relation, and a considerable increase in tensions. What did this summit mean? Could the arms race be slowed down or even stopped, and could the monumental sums of money spent on this arms race be lessened? Millions of people wanted to know, and they turned to their newspaper, TV news, or news magazine to find out more.

Whether it is to understand dramatic events such as those just related, or simply to "keep up with what's happening," people turn to the news media. For most, this is their "window on the world" (rather literally, in the case of television). Beyond this edifying function, the news media can also serve a unifying function when a sizable percentage of the public turns to the news media to find out about a particular development. The feelings develop that this is a common matter—"we're all in this together." This is especially the case when tens of millions turn to one of the three network news programs (or four, counting CNN); the shared national experience seems palpable in the case of the more dramatic developments such as the Kennedy assassination or the *Challenger* space-shuttle disaster.

There is, however, another side to this basic tale of the news. There are frequent headlines and other prominently placed stories of the latest murder or other violent crime, airline or train crash, fire or other malady, as well as the tribulations and escapades of celebrities—and basically, the more sensational in nature, the better. A great deal of the limited news space and time is devoted to such stories. This is especially notable in the front pages or front sections, which are most frequently and closely read or watched of hard news sections. There is also the trivial (fairly frequently under the banner of "human interest" story). The running of a trivial story is not trivial, however. With limited space and time, a trivial story will often push a more socially significant story off the front pages or the front section of a newscast—if not all of it.

Let one example illustrate the basic problem, an example of how overwhelming coverage of (possible) scandal took up large amounts of news space and drove much more important matters out of the news. Journalist David Broder relates this case: "Consider 'Billygate,' the on-going story of the connection between the President's brother, Billy Carter, and the Libyan government. . . . Between July 14, [1980], when Billy Carter registered with the Justice Department as an agent of the Libyan government, and October 3, when Senate investigators issued [a] report, the *Washington Post* published 117 stories on the subject—46 of them on page 1."[1] The *Washington Star* published even more stories on Billy Carter. Why such coverage? Broder observed: "George Lardner, Jr., one of the lead reporters in what eventually became a squad of *Post* writers on the case recalled, . . . 'I thought for a long time there was something to it. But it was also a matter of meeting the competition. . . .' [*Post* managing editor Howard] Simons recalled his concern that 'The *Star* was beating us on it and it looked like a good scandal.'"[2]

With all the space and all the time spent by reporters and editors on that story, what developments of true importance to society were given short shrift or ignored entirely? Robinson and Sheehan have provided a startling part of the answer to that question: "To appreciate how hot Billy was as news copy, compare his 140 news stories [on CBS News and the UPI wire] with the total of 19 stories given over principally to SALT II. Billy Carter attracted seven times as many news stories in 1980 as SALT II. . . ."[3]

That discussion raises a more fundamental question. This question is not a factual one, it is a normative one; it is intended to put the matter of news coverage in perspective. The question is: What is the *purpose* of the news—or are there multiple purposes, and if so, which is the most fundamental and important?

In Chapter 5 we noted that "freedom of the press" is protected in the First Amendment to the Constitution. Why are the news media the *only* private, economic enterprise given special mention and protection in the Constitution? At the end of Chapter 5 it was suggested that the primary reason for giving "the press" such a privileged position was the development of an informed and "intellectually vigorous" public, which is the guarantee of a healthy, operating democracy. Allowing and enabling the mass media to present such information to the public is clearly the central intent of the First Amendment. Correspondingly, the prime purpose of the news is surely an adequate amount and quality of information about developments of fact and opinion affecting the public.

But is that the sole purpose of the news? That question must be asked in both factual and normative fashion. On the normative side, it is hard to argue that no news items should be entertaining, or even that none should be primarily entertainment and diversion. (Perhaps such items draw people to reading or watching the serious news who would not otherwise.) Rather, the question is one of what events, developments, and patterns the public should know about and how much attention needs to be paid to those matters to help the public understand them and what they relate to. Thus the critical question is: Which such events have been inadequately reported or not reported at all?

Regarding the factual question, in most actual news operations, are other purposes evident? Obviously, the facts show other purposes, such as entertainment, being pursued. This then raises the question of why we get the news we hear broadcast and see in print.

This chapter explores that question, together with the impact of the news on the public. The main part of the chapter presents a framework for understanding decisions on what becomes news. In a preface to that framework we discuss news people's own prime conception of the essence of the news-making process and explore the implications involved of objectivity in the news—in this author's judgment, a crucial continuing issue in the making and presentation of the news. The framework itself then consists of a discussion and analysis of the various factors that affect decisions on what news is produced. An added note considers the question of bias in the news. In the next section we consider the impact of the news on the public, including public opinion about the news and the agenda-setting effect of print and TV news. In the final section we discuss the important and difficult issue of news coverage of terrorism.

A PREFACE TO UNDERSTANDING NEWS DECISIONS

What is happening in the world; in short, what is the news? The news that the public relies on for the information and impressions on which to base political choices is the product of decisions by news media personnel. A newspaper or news magazine, and especially radio and TV news, have limited amounts of space or air time. Consequently, decisions must be made about what to include and what to leave out of "the news." News media personnel are frequently called "gatekeepers" for this reason. Of all the events and developments in the world, some must be chosen to present as "the news" and others left out. In fact, as David Broder has pointed out: "All of us know as journalists that what we are mainly engaged in deciding is *not* what to put *in* but what to leave out [emphasis added]."[4] This raises a very important question: On what criteria are those decisions based, and what other factors affect news decisions?

Reflections in a Mirror?: On the Gatekeepers' Conception of News Decisions, and the Objectivity Question

Before laying out a framework for answering the question just posed, the conception of the news formulation process held by news media personnel themselves should be discussed. The centerpiece of their conception has long been that of the *mirror metaphor*. As Frank Stanton, then president of CBS, stated in the late 1960s: "What the media do is to hold a mirror up to society and try to report it as faithfully as possible."[5] The many journalists who offer this conception of news formulation and presentation are suggesting that what gets printed or aired as the news is not the product of biased human judgment (as many critics have said). Rather, such journalists are contending that they simply reflect what has been going on in the world; reporters and editors simply do "straight reporting" of what has actually transpired. [The journalists' contention is reminiscent of the line from the old "Dragnet" TV show (and 1987 movie): "Just the facts, ma'am."] This is the reason that journalists maintain they are "objective." This contention is reinforced by the journalists' conception of themselves as trained professionals. They do, in fact, increasingly have college and graduate degrees in journalism or mass communications. So who would know what the news is?: trained professional news people.

Such a metaphor or model of news decision making raises some difficult questions, however. Given the vast number and complexity of events and developments in the world and the limited space and time in the news media, evidently the news decision process is not simply one of holding a mirror up to society and presenting "the facts." In the following subsections we discuss the various factors affecting news decision making. But there is another implication underlying the mirror metaphor and the suggestion of a "just-the-facts" mode of operation which should be discussed here. It constitutes an issue of increasing importance in the "media age"—and the age of media manipulation.

To suggest that just the facts are presented is to suggest that "the facts speak for themselves," that the choice of certain "facts" to include in the news, as well as the meaning of those facts, is somehow self-evident. They are nothing of the sort. At the core of this news media issue is a notion of objectivity which has significant consequences for news reporting. Two specific dimensions of the issue are involved.

The first dimension involves both the choice of a news item and establishing the meaning of it. Objectivity is a nice thought and a nice goal; but in practice, the values held by journalists and related judgments about what the world is like (in conjunction with the factors reviewed in the next subsections) are primary determiners of decisions on which news items to run and what each means. Involved in such decisions is what can be called "reality judgments." As scholar Herbert Gans pointed out in his study on "deciding what's news":

> Values enter the news most pervasively in the form of reality judgements, the assumptions about external reality associated with the concepts which journalists use to grasp it. . . . When journalists must decide what is new, they must also make assumptions about what is old and therefore no longer newsworthy; when they report what is wrong or abnormal, they must also decide what is normal. If they favor the old or the new, and if they believe that what is normal should be normal, reality judgements then become preference statements.
>
> In any case, journalists cannot exercise news judgement without a composite of nation, society, and national and social institutions in their collective heads, and this picture is an aggregate of reality judgements.[6]

Shortly, we will take note of some of the values journalists hold that affect their reality judgments[7] and hence their choice of news items.

The second dimension of the issue of the mirror conception of news decisions and of objectivity concerns the question of the meaning of stories that appear in the news. The essential problem lies in the idea that "straight reporting" is what is needed for objectivity. An additional part of the problem lies in the standard definition of news as something new, striking, and different. Straight reporting is the notion that objectivity is practiced simply by reporting the overt "facts" of an event or development and/or the words of those involved—and that explanation and interpretation of circumstances, context, or general related patterns are either not needed or are illegitimate or simply not worth the time or space.

The act of selecting this particular story and these particular "facts" as opposed to many and various others, however, is itself an act of interpretation of what is worth communicating as news, of what is reality, and of what "it" means. If the news is to help people better understand the world, is it not important to establish the meaning of the particular event or statement through description and analysis of the general pattern in which it exists (or contradicts) and/or the context of the matter? A recent (excellent) biography of the great American broadcaster Edward R. Murrow has expressed the point well. The influence a BBC news official had on Murrow (during his years as a correspondent in London) was noted, "not, perhaps, for the handling of a story . . . [b]ut for the wisdom and historical comparisons, and the larger context of presenting the news."[8] A concise phrase sums up this concern with "straight reporting" and with establishing the more complete meaning of particular events and developments: As a rule, one cannot be objective without perspective.

Examples will make the point more concrete. Journalist Tom Wicker has provided one good example, and its critique. Wicker noted the typical journalistic tendency to report the (apparently) new and different. Then, with a categorical example, he effectively raised the question of perspective:

> A two-term senator safely being elected to a third term, for example, is hardly news at all, as American journalists define news; but if some unknown suddenly appears to be upsetting the same senator, the political press will flock in and cover the story exhaustively. Yet, depending on the constituency involved, the feat of that senator in making himself politically invulnerable might be of greater value in understanding politics and American society than the relatively commonplace story of one more young upstart knocking off an old head. What most appears as news to the press is often stale stuff in the long history of human events.[9]

The second example "speaks" directly to the "straight reporting" and objectivity issue. It comes from the Nixon reelection campaign of 1972, as recounted by Timothy Crouse. In the company of reporters Bob Semple and Peter Lisagor, Crouse noted the text of a speech by Nixon which "referred to certain proposals that would put the United States in the position of having the second strongest Navy, Air Force and Army. . . . 'It would be a move toward war.'"[10] Although not explicitly naming him, Nixon's Democratic opponent was obviously being referred to. Crouse continued:

> "All right," said Semple, "let's say we use a lead saying President Nixon declared today that Senator George McGovern's defense policies represented—you know this is simple, wire service stuff—a move toward war. . . ." [And Semple wondered about McGovern's indigant response.] "I mean, that's tough business." "Well," said Lisagor, "that's how it's gonna be handled. . . ."
> "And to be recorded flatly, it helps him more," said Semple. . . . [Lisagor

explained the basic reason:] "It's because Nixon is one of the best students of journalistic formats of any politician. . . . He understands the one-dimensional format of the wire service, where you can't qualify anything and where you've got to go with a hard punchy lead, and that's what this speech is designed to do. . . ."

"The rules of objectivity are such . . . that a man can make political capital out of them by being clever in the way he presents a particular issue. . . ."

"It becomes a problem for the press to put these charges in proper perspective. But a lot of reporters feel that they've discharged their obligation if they just report what the man said."[11]

The third example illustrates both the problem of straight reporting and the need for context and perspective in reporting on events and developments. In early May 1986, the major Western nations and Japan held the twelfth annual "economic summit," which was attended by the presidents and prime ministers of those nations. The coverage by the *Minneapolis Star and Tribune* of the meeting was typical of the news media. The principal headline on the front page was: "U.S. hails Tokyo triumph." The opening two paragraphs said:

> President Reagan hailed the 12th annual summit of industrial democracies as a "triumph in Tokyo," saying the meeting produced a "strong measure of allied unity" on economic, agricultural and antiterrorism issues. "All that we sought at the summit was achieved," he said today.[12]

The average reader, listener, or watcher of the news on this development had to come away with an impression (1) that an important event had occurred, and (2) that the Reagan administration had had striking success in economic policy matters. Such impressions were, however, seriously in error. Straight reporting and lack of perspective resulted in stories that did news consumers a disservice.

Newsweek, a week and a half later, ran an analytical story by their Chief Economics Correspondent which put the matter in perspective:

> This "triumph at Tokyo . . ." an exultant President Reagan called it when he met with reporters. . . . But this was, after all, an economic summit—and when it came to economics, the only American triumph . . . was one of blue smoke and mirrors. Reagan and his treasury secretary . . . failed to obtain any agreement at all on the two key issues that were before the summiteers: economic growth and the launching of trade talks. They salvaged nothing more than a technical victory on a third issue, reform of the international monetary system.[13]

Perspective is, indeed, needed. Regarding the news story just noted, the fact is that these "economic summits" have rarely produced anything remotely justifying the attention they have been given. What they do is give a chance to political leaders to look like they are doing important things in the international arena, which plays well with the folks back home—if reported in the fashion just noted. Indeed, as leading foreign affairs columnist William Pfaff pointed out following the 1987 edition of "the economic summit show":

> Of all the exercises in vanity to which the political world is given, the economic summits of the seven great industrial nations have become the most preposterous and the least warranted.
> The thousands of journalists writing or broadcasting accounts of these contrived events in Venice must acknowledge that they are accomplices in an immense and shameless fraud. The game is fixed, the communique has been drafted in advance.[14]

In sum, then, the quest for objectivity involves much more than concern for any partisan political bias of reporters and editors (which concern has preoccupied many critics and media personnel themselves). Ironically, the principal device the news media have used to ensure objectivity, namely, straight reporting of overt events and expressed words of leaders, has subverted truly objective reporting of developments and has allowed principal political leaders, especially incumbent presidents, to manipulate "the news" more successfully. A sense of perspective that fills out the meaning of an event or development is frequently lost in preoccupation with overt activities and excitement about personalities. In the next general section we discuss various factors that affect these tendencies in the news. (It is not suggested here that avoiding these tendencies is easy, or that more analysis and interpretation does not have hazards of its own. Rather, the need is to understand an existing problem that has not received adequate analysis.[15])

A FRAMEWORK FOR UNDERSTANDING NEWS DECISIONS

Personal and Professional Factors

An obvious place to begin analysis of news decisions is with the people who make news decisions. Three specific factors to be considered are the personal background and values, the political values, and the professional orientation of news personnel.

Sociologist Herbert Gans has provided the best study of the background and values of the reporters and editors of the major news media. Gans studied CBS and NBC News, *Time,* and *Newsweek,* but the findings apply to the major newspapers as well. Gans found the personal experience and life circumstances of those news media personnel to be middle class and upper middle class, corresponding to their incomes, education, and so on. There are still very few minorities. Women still comprise a much lower percentage of news people than they do in the general population. There appears to have been increases in both categories during the 1970s and 1980s, though.

News people have values that correspond to their midde–upper-middle-class status. This socioeconomic status affects their "reality judgments," and hence their decisions about what is news. "The reality judgments they use to determine newsworthy abnormalities generally reflect their own expectations of what constitutes normal [middle–upper middle class] parent, neighbor, friend, club member, churchgoer, and other everyday behavior."[16]

Gans also found a set of basic social and political values held by major media journalists, which he called "enduring values." These values affect what is seen as news and how an item should be presented. "Ethnocentrism" is most evident in both the limited amount of news included from other nations and in the tendency to "judge other countries by the extent to which they live up to or imitate [dominant] American practices and values."[17] A second enduring value is "altruistic democracy," that is, a tendency to indicate (implicitly or explicitly) "how American democracy should perform by . . . attention to deviations from an unstated ideal, evident in stories about corruption, conflict, protest, and bureaucratic malfunctioning."[18] As Gans also points out, this value and notion tends to focus overwhelmingly on the formal political institutions and processes, and pays little attention to the distribution and control of economic resources that profoundly affect the realization of that ideal of democracy.

Not unrelated to the latter (and perhaps, to the corporate ownership of the news media) is a very positive orientation toward private business and the general benefits it is said to bring to American society; this is the "responsible capitalism" value. Stories critical of failure or inefficiency in business (especially big business) tend to be far less reported. (The Wall Street and other business scandals and problems of 1986 and 1987 did lead to some increase in stories about problems in business, as well as some columns and even a few news analyses of "what's wrong with the business sector," but this was only in the short term.) The classic American value of individualism is also a part of the mental makeup of news people, Gans found. A tendency to focus on notable individuals, to celebrate "self-made" people and the like, is the result. This is reinforced, in TV news especially, by the inclination to personalize stories, to use specific people in news stories to illustrate a general phenomenon, since this is seen as more engaging than a story with abstract statistics.

Two final "enduring values" should be noted. First is an orientation toward the moderate in political and social matters, and suspicion of "excess or extremes." Correspondingly: "Individualism which violates the law, the dominant mores, and enduring values is suspect"; and "groups which exhibit what is seen as extreme behavior are criticized in the news through pejorative adjectives or a satirical tone. . . ."[19] This, for example, is why third or minor political parties get exceedingly little news attention, as a rule, and what time or space they do receive is frequently satirical. News people also tend to have political values very like the Progressives of the early twentieth century, with a focus on rooting out corruption (in government), an antipathy for political machines and often a low regard for party organizations in general, a distrust of bureaucracy (in government), and a desire to be "above politics."

The self-conception of news media people as professionals was noted earlier. This is also a significant part of their makeup. This, in conjunction with the Progressive-style political values, is why a number of journalists will say they have not voted in an election for some time. The feeling is that this enhances the credibility of their claims to objectivity.

It should be added that some studies have been done of the more specific partisan orientations of journalists, news executives, and owners (as self-identified in surveys). In summary, those studies have found the following regarding news people from the major media (network news, news magazines, and major newspapers). Among working reporters and other staffers, far more appear to identify with or lean toward the Democratic Party than toward the Republican Party, although independents are, indeed, very prominent. Among editors and other news executives, Democrats or Democratic leaners still appear to outnumber Republican identifiers, but the gap is far less, and independents appear to outnumber Democratic identifiers and leaners. Among owners, there appear to be decidedly more Republicans and conservatives. One interesting illustration of the latter is the fact that each time Richard Nixon ran for president, despite his claims of an unsympathetic press, the editorial endorsements of his candidacy far outran those of his Democratic opponent. Many of those endorsements came from nonmajor newspapers. It should be added that news reporters and staffers with those papers and with local broadcast stations appear to include nearly as many Republicans and Republican leaners as Democrats.[20]

The differences in party identification should not be taken too seriously, though. The enduring value of a moderate political orientation and of a Progressive-style antipartisan mindset and the self-conception as a professional are more dominant in major news media personnel. Additionally, editors and owners hire the reporters and staffers, so the latter are unlikely to get too far afield from the former. Further, on a more ongoing basis, news people work in a general organization. The organizational environment tends, as Gans has described,[21] to filter out those holding "nonmoderate" views; it isn't usually direct censorship, it is just a case of the nonmoderate sooner or later feeling uncomfortable or thwarted.

The fact that news people are part of large organizations brings us to the second general category of factors in news decision.

Organizational and Technological Factors

In all but the smaller broadcast stations and newspapers, news people are part of a large *organization,* and the news itself is the product of forces and processes in and of the organization, as several scholars have discussed.[22] The following subsections discuss·the various factors involved.

Economic Considerations   As was discussed earlier, the news media in America are or are part of private, capitalist enterprises. Making a profit is central to these organizations. Obtaining and retaining a large readership or audience is of central importance; the advertising revenues that support the corporate enterprise depend on it. The connection with news decisions is not simple and direct (at least in the case of the major media). The professional self-conception of news people certainly acts as a constraint on that connection. But it is obvious that economic considerations are very important.

The concern for the impact of profit maximizing on news decisions has been greatest in the case of television news (network as well as local news). In the spring of 1987, for example, "critics, including highly respected former news executives," testified before a subcommittee of the House of Representatives that "the proud heritage of [now-legendary broadcast newsman] Edward R. Murrow is being squandered by TV networks and affiliates, which have turned their public trust into a 'midway of junk entertainment' in pursuit of profit. . . ."[23]

Further, a major investigative report by the *Los Angeles Times* on the network news shows (run in late 1986) noted "the growing bottom line orientation of the last two or three years."[24] That concern is not new, however. In a speech that rocked the broadcast industry at the time, Edward R. Murrow himself referred to "the money-making machine" of television and said:

> One of the basic troubles with radio and television news is that both instruments have grown up as an incompatible combination of show business, advertising and news. . . . The top management of the networks, with a few notable exceptions, has been trained in advertising, research, or show business. But by the nature of the corporate structure, they also make the final and crucial decisions having to do with news and public affairs. Frequently they have neither the time nor the competence to do this. . . .[25]

He added this a little later: "This could be the most exciting and fruitful method of communication yet devised, but it is in the hands of timid and avaricious men and the public seems incredibly apathetic."[26] These conclusions were offered in 1958.

Why are these concerns expressed by many, including various prominent people who have been involved in television? The answer is the corporate, profit-making situation in which TV news, and other news organizations, exist, and more specifically, the audience ratings which determine revenues and hence profits. The basic corporate structure was discussed in Chapter 5. The ratings provide an estimate of the audience for the TV news shows using samples of the public, which samples are chosen in a fashion similar to samples in major public opinion polls. (As of late 1986, one rating point represented 874,000 homes, which was 1% of the 87.4 million households in the United States with TV sets.) See the box for an explanation of the ratings.

The A.C. Nielson Company principally does the ratings for the networks. The Nielson Company has used devices ("audimeters") which automatically record whether each set in the sample households is on and if so, to what channel it is tuned. There are about 1100 households in the sample. The Nielson ratings have also included data from about 2200 families who keep diaries of all the TV viewing for each week (although not all families send back complete diaries every week). These diaries have been the source of demographic data on TV watching. Arbitron (American Research Bureau) has had a competing ratings service, used primarily in local TV markets, which has used the diary method.[27] In September 1987 something called "people meters" were installed in sample homes (2000 in the Nielson case) to generate more precise data; in theory, they will also be less faulty than diaries. Participating households are interviewed to establish complete demographic information on each household member. Each person, as he or she begins to watch TV, must punch an assigned number into a remote control device, which then sends the viewing data to the central computer, and the computer, in turn, correlates all the demographic data with the viewing patterns "instantly." Whether some people will tire of always punching in their number (or forget sometimes) and whether the loss of such people will skew the sample somewhat (as now happens with the diaries) is a subject of considerable debate.[28]

The key question is: Are the networks sufficiently concerned about profits to impell the news programs to run stories and to present them in such a fashion as to maximize the audience? In short, are the networks' eyes focused as much on audience ratings as on gathering and presenting important news? There are several reasons to believe so. First, as noted earlier, all three of the traditional networks are now under the basic control of more general corporations which have *not* had major, distinguished news organizations as a central part of their identity for a long period of time.

Each of the three networks, in the later 1980s, has also experienced tighter financial conditions, along with increased competition from CNN and the cable entertainment channels for a share of the audience. (The network news shows reached 76% of *all* homes with the TV set on in 1979, but reached only 62% of such homes as of late 1986.[29]) With annual budgets of $225 to 275 million, the network news divisions have attracted increasing corporate attention. More specifically, covering a story for TV news is expensive, much more so than for print media, since videocameras and camera operators are needed in addition to reporters. This is especially the case on remote locations. In the past, the networks would appear to have been more accepting of news shows not showing much of a profit (i.e., advertising revenues generated during the shows not exceeding news costs by much, if any); the news programs were seen to some significant extent as a combination of public duty and as good for the network image. But somewhat ironically, the success of the quasi-news program "60 Minutes," with annual profits estimated at $50 to 70 million, and the (more modest) profitability of "20/20" and "Nightline," apparently convinced network executives that the news shows should be substantial profit makers. Indeed, as the vice-president of ABC News observed: "It's a bad thing [for a news division to lose money]. It's unhealthy . . . to be a supplicant in a corporate setup." Correspondingly, the ratings race between the news shows has received a great deal of attention.[30]

More direct reasons for concluding that the profit factor has affected the TV news operations have been cited by Fred Friendly, former president of CBS News and Edward R. Murrow collaborator (now journalism professor). He, like others, points to the dramatic decline in numbers of network documentaries. Through the 1970s, each network did a dozen or more documentaries, but by the mid-late 1980s, they were doing as few as two a year. He and others also point out the "pursuit of the sensational on the evening news," including far more coverage of crime and disaster stories, which had previously been left to local news coverage. More or less related is a greater emphasis on fast pacing and drama in the news, a change that a *Los Angeles Times* investigative team confirmed after watching "scores of network news programs, old and new."[31]

One scholar suggests the year 1977 as the principal point at which these changes took place. This was when ABC named its director of the sports division, Roone Arledge, the new head of the news division, with the ensuing changes throwing the "news business into a period of intense competition for ratings."[32] That scholar, Daniel Hallin, also found a dramatic shortening of the "sound bites" of all officials and ordinary citizens which were included in the news in 1985, as compared with 1965–1972.[33] (A "sound bite" is a tape segment with someone speaking.) This is empirical evidence of the increased pacing. It may also be that worry about mass audience appeal is why only one of the three networks had regular commentary in the later 1980s.

Local TV news, in medium-sized or large markets, is at least as fierce-

ly competitive, and it has gotten more expensive, with mobile camera operations, use of satellite time, and so on. Local TV news is also very profitable
as a rule. Correspondingly, in the major urban areas, local news time has
expanded to a total of two hours (and more in at least one area).

In most areas, newspaper competition no longer exists. Economic
pressures do still exist in and for such papers, though. The quest for more
resources leads to a quest for larger ad revenues and hence larger mass
readership. Ultimately, the question stemming from all this is how it affects
the way the news operations fulfill their most fundamental purpose in what
Bill Moyers has called "news as the conversation of democracy." Moyers,
with experience in public affairs programming for TV and in a high government position, has expressed the concern eloquently, reflecting on his
experience at CBS News:

> Instead of the role of gathering, weighing, sorting and explaining the flux of
> events and issues, we began to be influenced by the desire first to please the
> audience. . . .
> Pretty soon, tax policy had to compete with stories about three-legged
> sheep, and the three-legged sheep won. . . . And now we're trapped. Once
> you decide to titillate instead of illuminate, you're on a slippery slope, you
> create a climate of expectation that requires a higher and higher level of
> intensity all the time until you become a video version of the drug culture and
> your viewers become junkies.[34]

"Nightline"'s Ted Koppel, reflecting on the economic factor in general and, in specific, the network news budget cutting of the later 1980s,
observed:

> There is all this competition from CNN and syndicated news programs. The
> network executives see their competitors turning out a pretty good news
> product for a lot less money. . . . Our managers conclude: 'We can do it that
> way and survive.' They don't seem to realize that their network news will only
> flourish by being visibly stronger, deeper and of better quality.[35]

Criteria for Deciding What Is "The News"   It was noted earlier that limited time and space in the news media require choices to be made of what to
include as news and what to leave out. Various analysts have found that
certain criteria are used by editors and news directors, often implicitly, to
decide what is "the news."

First, two points that apply especially to TV news. As described in
Chapter 4, television is preeminently a medium of visual motion pictures.
Correspondingly, prime criteria for deciding TV news stories are the availability of good visual material on film, which involves action. Action stories[36] are far more likely to be chosen than "talking heads" or graphs and
charts, even those produced by the new computer graphics capacities. Ad-

ditionally, TV news people take the word "story" in the phrase "news story" quite seriously. (The print media do so, as well, though perhaps not as overwhelmingly.) Epstein relates a memorandum from Reuven Frank, then executive producer of "NBC Evening News," which classically expresses this basic criterion: "Every news story should, without any sacrifice of probity or responsibility, display the attributes of fiction, of drama. It should have structure and conflict, problem and denouement, rising action and falling action, a beginning, a middle and an end."[37]

Several other criteria apply to print as well as broadcast media. First, as was suggested by the example given earlier of the continued reelection or upset of a Senate veteran, a key criterion of what is news is something that is novel and very current. News, that is, is what is "new" and "different" from ordinary affairs. An immediate consequence is a tendency to see developments in the world as rather discrete events; as Gans puts it, "journalists see external reality as a set of disparate and independent events, each of which is new and can therefore be reported as news."[38] (The consequences of this orientation for coverage of and impact on the presidential nomination process are detailed in Chapters 9 and 10.) *Newsweek,* in an excellent example of the perspective that news analysis, including media self-analysis, can add, pointed out the all-too-frequent results of this criteria complex, especially in conjunction with the deadline factor discussed below. Noting that "the press has a short attention span," *Newsweek* observed:

> [N]ews . . . is often treated with . . . gullibility and lack of follow-through . . . [as was exemplified by the] nuclear-plant disaster at Chernobyl. In the Soviet Union, first-hand reporting was impossible. The resulting anger of Western reporters—combined with competitive pressures to come up with something—led to vastly inflated casualty-figure assumptions, which some news organizations then did too little to correct. . . . In the same vein, the early impression, conveyed largely by supporters of the American nuclear-power industry, was that the Chernobyl plant lacked safety features found in all U.S. plants. That turned out to be false, but by the time a truer picture was established—at least three weeks after the explosion—the networks barely mentioned it at all. . . .
>
> "It's as if there is an inflatable map of the world," says David Halberstam. "One month the Falklands is the biggest thing in the world, then it's a flyspeck again." [And] . . . the media's saturation coverage skips on to the next event, often passing over whatever new details that may fundamentally change the "old" stories.[39]

A second criteria complex is conflict, violence, disaster, and scandal: in sum, humans in circumstances or interactions that are dramatic and which involve trouble. The tendency to use sports metaphors involving conflict (and even violence) is also noted, such as references to the existence or nonexistence of a "knock-out punch" in a candidates' debate. One notable example from elections is worth mentioning here. It was coverage of a debate in New Hampshire between candidates for the 1984 Democratic presidential nomination. The only thing network news viewers saw that evening was a brief finger-pointing argument between Mondale and Glenn—just the argument, not what it was about or any other content from the debate. Viewers saw similar coverage of the first Republican candidates' debate for the 1988 nomination (in October 1987) involving George Bush and two others.

As Doris Graber points out, two other criteria concern relevance to viewers, listeners, and readers. For the nonnational newspapers and for local TV news, events that occur in the area receive a preference in news choice. For local TV news and most newspapers, there is a sense that they are, indeed, *local* news media, so such a criterion seems eminently sensible. It is also felt that the people who are "consuming" the news can relate better to such stories. Further, it is apparent that putting local people's events and other developments in the news is good public relations for the news medium; people like to see their or their friends' and associates' stories in the news. The second criterion of relevance to the audience Graber calls "high impact," meaning stories that have a substantial, distinct impact on viewers, such as health hazards.[40]

Partly related to the latter criterion and partly to the inclination to emphasize drama is a criterion of focus on individuals. TV news is especially given to this criterion since the impact of a general social development, such as unemployment, is easier to present and allows better visuals if the focus is one or more individuals. The picture of a distressed unemployed worker is easier to grasp and more engaging to the viewer, it is felt, than a set of abstract figures; the written description of a specific person's or family's case is also felt to be more engaging in print.

Finally, well-known people and celebrities are much more likely to make it on the news than others. Graber suggests that a sense of familiarity with such people is a central element of this criterion.[41] All sorts of activities of entertainment and sports stars are seen as news. This orientation toward "star"-as-news-subject also extends to government officials. (Has anyone heard of "Ted" Kennedy?) This criterion is even used in drawing on experts to offer their specially trained assessments of developments: The same small set of experts on foreign policy, Congress, the presidency, and so on, are sought out time and again. (Some wits have referred to this as the "round up the usual suspects" approach.) Another reason for this pattern is the fact that some of those experts understand the media's desire for brief, crisp comments with catchy lines, and they are good at providing such comments and lines.

According to one study, the criteria of conflict, locality (how close to the local area), and newness or "timeliness" are the most important. The study presented 64 news items, created by the researchers, to television and newspaper editors, who were then asked which items they would select as the news and why.[42] Interestingly, as Graber notes: "Conspicuously absent from their choice criteria was the story's overall significance."[43]

Two Case Illustrations of Use of News Criteria   In the spring and summer months of 1986, there was massive media coverage of what many news organizations called "the drug crisis." The chief focus was on cocaine abuse, especially on the "crack" form of its use. Time and again this was one of or was the feature story on the evening news programs and in the news magazines. (*Newsweek* even used a regular logo: "The Drug Crisis," with red border lines.) The same was the case, although to a somewhat lesser extent, in the newspapers. An NBC Nightly News report, for example, said: Cocaine, "America's drug of choice . . . [is] flooding America."[44]

Had there been a dramatic increase in drug abuse in general and cocaine in specific? New York University's News Study Group concluded: "TV news in particular hammered home stories of an increased drug threat ["A nationwide epidemic of cocaine and crack use was one of the biggest stories of 1986"] when, in fact, 'there was no evidence that the level of drug abuse had changed.' "[45] Why the magnitude and intensity of coverage, then? The criteria of news choice of conflict, drama, scandal, and human hazard are a prime part of the answer. A version of the celebrity criterion was also involved: The deaths of two star athletes, apparently related to cocaine use, helped touch off the increased coverage.

The consequences of such coverage are not just distraction and loss of space for more important matters. As Jim Fain of Cox News Service pointed out: "What we have is a sunburst of media and political hype that creates melodrama for exploitive purposes."[46] Politicians spent a good deal of time proclaiming their concern and their intent to act on this grave matter, especially in the two months before the November 1986 elections.

The second case illustration is that of the sagas of presidential candidates Gary Hart and Joe Biden. There is not enough space to go into details, but the basic issues involved should be raised. In May 1987, former Senator Gary Hart felt compelled to drop out of the contest for the Democratic presidential nomination for 1988 as a result of news media coverage of rumors and allegations about extramarital affairs. Senator Hart had been the leader in public opinion polls at the time. The principal precipitator of this news coverage was a stakeout of Hart's townhouse in Washington by reporters of the *Miami Herald* and the printing of a story, by that paper, saying that Hart had spent the night with a woman other than his wife. Whether the *Herald* had, with certainty, established the facts of the activities of the evening has been seriously questioned.[47] This itself raises serious questions; one would think a news organ would be absolutely certain of its facts in such a case, given the potential impact on a person and on the public's opportunity to hear and choose qualified candidates for the presidency. (It should be added that there had been rumors of Hart's extracurricular activities for some time, and supposedly, the *Washington Post* was ready to run another story indicating an affair, though it was not run after Hart dropped out.)

Another issue in this case is whether the personal life of a political figure is a proper subject for news media treatment. It was generally not considered so by the media until the 1970s. The post-Watergate era has brought a change in that orientation. No judgment is offered here; the reader is simply encouraged to think about it. (One is inclined, however, to ask whether Roosevelt, Eisenhower, and Kennedy were inadequate presidents because of rumored activities of that sort—and to ask whether we would have had the benefit of their services had they run for election in the media climate of the later 1980s.)

That raises the most important issue: Were the media concerned about "character" and "judgment," as they claimed, or did this story really get the attention it got due to such news criteria as scandal, drama, and general sensationalism? And did the news media lose perspective on what is important? The latter conclusions were reached by *New York Times* columnist Anthony Lewis, who said that there was a "sense of disproportion" in coverage of the story compared with what else was happening at the time. He suggested, "for all the talk about judgement, the real interest in the story was sex"; "too many editors and reporters salivated in their zeal to learn all and tell all."[48] The nature of the pictures of the woman in the matter (a model) run by much of the media at least partly supports the Lewis conclusion. (They were classic "cheesecake" pictures.)

The case of Joe Biden, U.S. Senator from Delaware, is an even more striking example of current news notions of "character" affecting a presidential candidacy. The initial major burst of media coverage (September 1987), including network news shows, was of lines Biden borrowed from other prominent politicians' speeches without always specifically citing the source. A tape supplied by a rival campaign to news media showing a Biden speech next to one from which he borrowed was the chief stimulus to major media attention. Was this a "character problem" of significant magnitude? A later "revelation" about an allegation of an incident of "plagiarism" in law school and a misstatement of his law school graduation rank (captured on video) led to feature media attention. He then dropped out of the presidential effort, without a single vote cast by a citizen.

One other case should be noted briefly: the saga of President Reagan's second 1987 nominee for the Supreme Court in November 1987, Judge Douglas Ginsberg. It was "discovered" and then Judge Ginsberg "admitted" smoking marijuana a few times in the 1960s and 1970s. This "revelation" resulted in massive media coverage, and shortly thereafter, Judge Ginsberg asked that his nomination be withdrawn. (Ginsberg had another source or two of trouble in his nomination; the media deluge about his extracurricular smoking was definitely not the only reason he withdrew.

But it was a prime contributor.) Did this activity justify the great media attention that it got, or did the media once again get carried away with private and/or minor matters of no real relevance to the conduct of public office—in short, did they again lose perspective? In initial surveys, the public seemed to think so by wide margins. Many of the media were sufficiently struck by rising criticism of such coverage that they did some reflective pieces on the issue. (In the Ginsberg case, various media, *after* the damage was done, acknowledged, as one major newspaper put it, that "a decade ago, experimenting with marijuana was the moral equivalent of double parking.")

Further, it is difficult to escape the conclusion that the media's concern for "character" and "judgment" seems to be somewhat selective. For example, if the media were so concerned about character and judgment, why did the formally alleged or proven improprieties of so many Reagan Administration officials receive relatively little attention prior to the 1984 election (compared with the massive attention that Hart's private personal activities and Biden's borrowings and single misstatement received)? As *Time* magazine summed up (as of May 1987): "More than 100 members of the Reagan Administration have had ethical or legal charges leveled against them. That number is without precedent." Although these activities might not have been "as flagrant as the Teapot Dome scandal or as pernicious as Watergate, they seem more general, more pervasive and somehow more ingrained than those of any previous Administration."[49] (Thus *Time* did give some attention to the matter, although belatedly.) This disparity in attention would not appear to result from political bias; rather, it is probably a combination of what items are more easily identified and portrayed (especially on TV), what has greater sensationalism, and other prime news criteria.

The Hart and Biden cases also illustrate what is called "pack journalism"; that is, when one prominent news organ runs a story, most of the rest follow in like fashion. The news media's "feeding frenzy" on private affairs questions became so great that the flimsiest of rumors led to reports on those rumors and direct questioning of candidates about whether they had "committed adultery." Vice President George Bush was the subject of such media behavior in June 1987[50] [thus demonstrating the nonpartisan (or bipartisan) nature of media inclinations].

Organizational Structure, News Space, and Story Competition   Earlier it was noted that TV news, news magazines, and newspapers are, or are part of, large organizations. The news operations themselves are sizable organizations. From this fact stem some consequences for deciding on and presenting the news.

A principal characteristic of any large organization is its hierarchical structure. What this means specifically for news decisions is that, as a rule, "higher-ups" decide what stories to cover and which will be reported in the news; the reporters do not make such decisions. In the networks, the following are the decision makers. A president of the news division usually enforces established news policy of a basic nature and refines that policy or makes new general rules as the need arises. An executive producer usually identifies stories to cover and decides which items, with what amount of film, to include in the news (an associate executive producer may be involved, as well). Occasionally, an anchorperson has been sufficiently valued to be named managing editor; CBS's Walter Cronkhite and Dan Rather have held that title and Rather has had substantial decision-making power not only in story selection but "in everything from who gets on the air to who gets hired and fired."[51] Others are involved in processing news stories, but they do not have primary influence in news decision making.

In local TV news, the decision makers are usually a news director, an assignment editor, and in varying degrees, one or both anchorpersons (in some cases, an anchorperson has the title "news director"). An executive director of the station may be involved, at least in setting out basic news policy. In major newspapers, an executive editor, a managing editor, and various section and area editors are the decision makers. The news magazines have a similar but more complex set of editorial personnel. (For a fascinating inside view of the newspaper editorial process, see Woodward and Bernstein's *All the President's Men*.[52])

Before turning to a consequence of the structure of news reporting and decision making, another distinct factor in news decision needs to be discussed, a factor stemming from the nature of each medium. This factor is the "news hole." The news hole is the amount of space or time a news medium has for news material once the commercial ads are in place. Thus the "30-minute" network news programs actually have only 22 minutes of news time after the commercials are figured in.

What should be readily evident is how much less room the network news shows have for news presentation than a newspaper (especially a major one) or a news magazine. As a number of analysts have pointed out, in total words normally expressed, the network news programs amount to less than the front page of a typical newspaper. (Given that, it is evident that the theme line used by ABC News in the 1980s—"uniquely qualified to *bring you the world*"—is not a remote possibility; a 22-minute newscast cannot bring you the world, even if "the news" is defined simply as what happened in the last 24 hours.) Because of this severe time limitation, the network news programs have been called mere "headline services" (although we will suggest some qualifications of that statement below).

The combination of the hierarchical factor in news decisions with the limited time or space of the news hole, together with use of the usual criteria for deciding what's news, leads to a consequence for the making and presentation of the news that should be detailed. The prime goal of reporters' professional lives is to get their stories in print or on the air. But with limited time and space, they must compete with each other for getting "their" story in. Reporters "sell" their story to those prime gatekeepers. Naturally, given the factors already discussed, at the center of that sales pitch are the key news criteria.[53] In consequence, the more striking of the news criteria—familiar personalities, drama, conflict, and so on—are further reinforced as news decision rules, and context and meaning are more easily lost. Gans notes an example. In the late 1960s, a press conference was held in Washington on hunger in the United States, with almost a dozen people, representing various organizations, making statements. One of them was Senator Robert Kennedy. The network reporter Gans followed highlighted "the piece with Bobby" and the producer of the news show "bought only Kennedy's participation in the conference"; even though "Kennedy's role in the actual press conference had been minor, . . . it became the centerpiece of the film."[54]

SOME QUALIFICATIONS REGARDING NEWS-MAKING TENDENCIES Some recent developments in TV news, and one development in print news, also need to be discussed. Over the past decade or a little more, the network news shows have evolved to something more than simply a headline service. Because they had become such prominent, even dominant, news media, yet had very limited time, the network news programs increased the use of *themes,* in the later 1970s and 1980s, to help tie things together and to help stories make more sense. One scholar argues strongly that much less in the way of simple acceptance of official pronouncements and events (less straight reporting) has been the result. Thus he finds the much shorter "sound bites" of officials now used in network news to be evidence that TV news is much more "mediated"; there is much less straight acceptance of what has been said and done and more editorial interpretation.[55] To the extent that this is an accurate analysis, it is an encouraging development in one major respect: It limits the capacity of officials to manipulate the news the public receives as political reality. In Chapters 8 and 10 we present evidence that raises questions about how complete (or successful) the change is in that regard, however.

Other developments in network news related to news time and space should be mentioned here. First, the news segments have increased somewhat in length compared with past decades, which gives a little more time for adequate treatment of stories. Second, there are more multipart reports, some involving serious investigative reporting; using the networks' high-priced talent and the video pictures, sound, and graphics that give TV news its unique impact, these reports can present a development or issue in remarkable fashion. (In 1986, for example, ABC News aired a five-part series on terrorism, a five-part series on immigration, a ten-part series on life in the Soviet Union, and others.) Third, NBC News has incorporated a four- or five-minute "special segment" story as a regular part of the newscast (although some of the subjects are "soft" news). And of course, beyond the traditional dinner-time half-hour news show, the most significant development in network public affairs programming in more than a decade is ABC's "Nightline." With respected interviewer Ted Koppel, with devotion of the entire half hour to one subject, and with the different news format of bringing principals or experts involved in the subject together on the show for debate, this program is both an effective addition to network news presentation, in late evening, and a great popular success. (Strikingly, ABC allows the program to "run over" the time allotted in the schedule if something significant or dramatic is happening in the discussion.)

It should also be remembered that the three traditional networks are not the only national broadcast news programs. Cable News Network's (CNN's) "Prime News" offers an hour of national news for those on cable or with satellite dish, a notable added dimension of TV news in the 1980s. The "MacNeil–Lehrer News Hour" on public TV begins with a news summary and then brings in key players in the world of public affairs for greatly respected debate and discussion on one, two, or three issues for the balance of the hour. After losing some viewership just after its expansion from a half-hour to an hour, the program regained viewers and now reaches almost 2 million people a night and 7 million at least once a week;[56] this is a very influential audience, as well. Finally, on another medium, National Public Radio offers the widely respected "All Things Considered," which provides for more extensive time than TV network news and generally runs news segments three or four times the length of those on network news. In the broadcast media, total news programming, in varied forms, is now strikingly abundant, for those who are aware of the options and willing to tune in. The broadcast news shows that are most relied on, the network news programs, remain severely restricted 22-minute shows, however. Prospects for a full hour of network news, called for by many, remain dim, due to the resistance of local affiliate stations. (The affiliates generally see the expansion to an hour as the networks trying to take still more of the principal time the affiliates have to generate revenue.)

Print news, as noted, has much more space, and the total amount of space is not strictly fixed. Correspondingly, the major newspapers and news magazines are able to devote large amounts of space to some matters. It is in these media that the greatest glory of journalism, namely, in-depth investigative reporting, can truly flourish. Multipart stories in considerable depth are a striking feature of America's major—and occasionally some not-so-major—newspapers. Many such stories are a remarkably substantial and highly accessible source of information on subjects of importance to the public. (For those who will make a little effort, major newspapers are surely the best value a "consumer" can purchase today.)

One other development, comparatively new in the extent of use, has been noted in the print media. As the *National Journal* has pointed out: "Largely in response to the 'headline service' that television provides [and its prominence], the print medium is turning more to background reports and analytical pieces that explain the meaning, importance and probable consequences of events and high-level government decisions."[57] Given the concerns expressed earlier regarding the consequences of "straight reporting" and the lack of context and perspective, this is an encouraging development (although the economic summit example suggests much room for improvement).

Deadlines, Limited Resources, and Beats Another significant factor in news decisions is the simple but consistent and overwhelming fact of deadlines. For TV and radio news and for newspapers, the daily specter of the deadline for stories to be in is a central constraint on reporting the news. This factor limits the amount of time available to gather information on a current development (especially a "breaking story") and to reflect on its content and meaning.

The deadline factor has a more specific consequence of considerable importance for coverage of political matters. Stated plainly, the daily deadline crunch allows the astute political figure (who understands the structure of media operations) to manipulate the news. Journalist Tom Wicker, of the *New York Times,* has provided an excellent illustration:

> I was called in to the office on the night of August 4, 1964, to cover President Johnson's speech announcing that he had ordered retaliatory air strikes against North Vietnam, following an attack on American ships by North Vietnamese torpedo boats in the Gulf of Tonkin. Later it developed that the facts of the Tonkin Gulf "attack" were unclear at best. . . . But that evening . . . it never occurred to me that the facts were in question or that Johnson was deliberately manipulating events. . . .
>
> Johnson spoke in prime time, on short notice, long after our regular deadlines. Working from a White House text and a television set, I had to crank out my story virtually as Johnson spoke. . . . A reporter able to deliver a smoothly written story under such conditions and in time to make most of the press run may be highly valued in the trade; but the truth is that if I or any other reporter had had doubts about the validity of Johnson's speech or actions, we would have had no chance to check them out that night—which meant that television and the morning headlines gave *his* version of events the initiative in the public consciousness. No other version would ever quite catch up.[58]

The example of Nixon's speech in the 1972 campaign noted early in the chapter also illustrates the deadline problem.

The news magazines have somewhat different deadline circumstances, since they are published only once a week. There is still a limiting deadline, but it happens once a week rather than daily. The fact of publishing weekly has the specific consequence of giving more time to sort out the news. Also, since the news magazines cannot compete with the daily news media on breaking stories, they have tended to focus more on noting themes in and suggesting interpretations of developments.

News organizations also have limited resources; they have only so many reporters and photographers, correspondents, and camera operators. These limitations are especially profound in the case of television, due to the expense of camera crews. A prime consequence of the limited resources factor, again especially for television news, is that the news media plan as much coverage as possible in advance. Correspondingly, predictability in news stories is highly valued. As a result, the news media tend to cover regularly the same institutions and activities. More specifically, they assign some of their reporters and camera people to institutional "beats" or to issue areas (such as "health/medical") and establish routines of which officials and places most reporters should check in with periodically. Media scholar Leon Sigal found that stories covered in regular beats of one sort of another totaled twice the number of other stories in the *New York Times* and the *Washington Post*.[59] In light of this and the typical news criteria described above, Sigal coined the interesting phrase "the standardized exceptional" to describe the news.[60] Sigal also documented the other side of the news media's use of beats and routines (as well as coverage of already well-known figures): political officials' use of media for publicity. Sigal found that two-thirds of the sample of 3000 stories he studied in the *Times* and the *Post* were stories the political figures had planned with a view to receiving media attention.[61]

There is another dimension of the story of the assignment of reporters, though. Epstein pointed out that the network news organizations, at least through 1970, assigned very few reporters to distinct beats. Reporters tended to be assigned on an ad hoc basis, and having reporters who are generalists "who can be expected to cover any subject" was seen as a good thing. This notion remains central in the news media in general. The main rationale for it is as follows. First, news executives think that "a generalist who, like most of the audience, is an outsider to a subject, will make it more interesting and comprehensible for most viewers," listeners, and readers. Second, and in light of limited resources, the feeling is that generalists allow a much more efficient use of reporting personnel: "Since it is possible to dispatch any available generalist to the nearest or most convenient happening, the news staff can be fully utilized. . . ."[62]

There are, however, some unfortunate consequences stemming from the reliance on generalists in reporting. This is an age of information explosion, of specialization, and of the increasing importance of technical detail. Generalists do not have the mastery in any of those respects to cover truly adequately developments in many subject areas. Further, without more training and background in a given field, there is a far greater chance that a reporter can be misled or even manipulated by someone involved in a story development who is a specialist. This does not apply only to a strictly technical area such as physics or medicine. It also applies to politics, whether it is covering the presidency, executive agencies, presidential nomination campaigns, or whatever. Without higher training in the particular area, not only is there greater chance of being specifically misled, there is also much less likelihood of adequately and accurately placing some action or event in historical context and in political system perspective, and thereby better establishing its meaning. Looked at from another direction, officials find it easier to manipulate reporting which is not deeply informed of *past* official efforts and of the nature of political institutions. Strikingly, even in coverage of the presidency, the generalist orientation was still clung to into the 1980s, as Grossman and Kumar observed:

> Unlike White House officials, who are aware of their need to understand the media, reporters tended to discount the importance of specialized education about the President in their preparation for a White House assignment. They indicated that before taking up their positions they did not receive briefings about White House operations from other reporters or from their editors. Edward Walsh of the *Washington Post,* who was assigned to the White House in late 1975, reported that his editors suggested that he read a number of books about the President by academics and reporters. He did not read them then, nor did he intend to in the future. "The White House is a general assignment beat," he said, repeating a sentiment shared by many reporters. "It's just like covering City Hall."[63]

Fortunately, there appears to be some increase in understanding of the shortcomings of this orientation, although the increase is mostly in the realms of law, science, economics, and medicine. As NBC's Tom Brokaw has recently written: "Most of us in this business were raised as general-assignment reporters. Now we require more specialists, reporters who can describe not just the dollars-and-cents side of the economy, but the impact of an ever-older American workforce . . . , the technology explosion, etc."[64]

Limited Resources, Technological Constraints, and Capacities   Limited resources also have another impact, an impact of particular relevance for TV news and the technology it involves. Again, central to TV news is video pictures. But to have film, cameras must be on the scene, or "the news" must be limited to where the cameras are. The newer "minicams" (smaller, more portable cameras) have made TV filming more portable. Satellite technology, including mobile vans that can send signals directly to satellites, have dramatically increased the capacity to send a TV report from virtually anywhere. But it is expensive. As Graber has summarized, "News organizations . . . generally station teams [of reporters and camera people] in only half a dozen cities. Locations are chosen for the availability of good resources in terms of equipment, support staff, and news personnel."[65] The end result is that the nation is very unevenly covered. In fact, one study found (in the 1970s) that 90% of film coverage originates in the few locations with camera crews regularly stationed.[66] In the 1980s, that percentage was lower, but the basic resource constraint remained.

Still, the new technologies have changed TV news, both network and local. The capacity to transmit news film instantly from anywhere adds a remarkable dimension to what TV news can present. But also, as NBC's Tom Brokaw has written, "There are some dangers" involved. "Speed is important in journalism: Get the news while it's hot. Furthermore, a live television picture of a major event is often irresistible. However tempting speed and excitement may be, they do not alone serve our long-term needs. If there is an undue emphasis on the speed of coverage, context will be overrun and there will be a diminution of accountability and memory."[67] Examples of such implications are discussed in the final section of this chapter in regard to the coverage of terrorism.

It should be added that local TV news has been given new access to Washington and other centers by this new technology. Network film feeds and new news services which tailor Washington coverage to local interests (such as what the local member of Congress is doing) have added a notable dimension to local TV news.[68]

ADDITIONAL NOTE ON NEWS DECISIONS: ON BIAS IN THE NEWS Considering the end product of news decision making, various critics (especially of network news) have accused the news of bias. Particularly regarding partisan bias, however, the evidence shows that the major media do not favor Democrats or Republicans. Further, as Doris Graber has summed up: "A number of content analyses of [coverage of campaign and other political] events definitely refute the charges of political bias, if bias is defined as deliberately lopsided coverage or intentional slanting of news. These analyses show instead that most newspeople try to cover a balanced array of issues in a neutral manner and do include contrasting viewpoints."[69]

Three qualifying notes should be added to that conclusion, though. First, most of the studies alluded to have concerned election campaigns and a few other situations with relatively clear-cut basic bias questions involved (i.e., is one party or one candidate or the other receiving better treatment). More study needs to be done to determine bias in more standard news story circumstances (more systematic study, that is, not ideologically grounded attacks). Second, in such standard news situations, there can be little doubt that the basic political orientations (although not party identification) of media management and editorship affect news decisions in the process of news story selection, at least at times. An excellent pair of examples from this author's home region illustrate the point.

In late 1982, the American economy was in the worst tailspin in decades, with the official unemployment rate in October at 10% and with factory utilization declining. Correspondingly, the trend in the economy was the single biggest issue in the 1982 "off-year" election. Interestingly, two newspapers in the same general region ran stories on the economic trend which were diametrically opposite in conclusions, although they were given essentially identical front-page treatment: the second-tier headline in the Fargo–Moorhead *Forum* was, "Key economic forecast shows recovery signs," whereas the *Minneapolis Star and Tribune's* similarly placed story for the *same day* (October 29) was headlined, "Fed forecasts sluggish economy." Which was "the news" on that important matter? It can hardly be an accident that *The Forum,* which regularly endorses conservative, Republican candidates and takes other conservative editorial positions, would run a headline and story that would make Republican economic policy look better. Nor is it probably accidental that the *Star and Tribune,* which (not quite as) regularly endorses more liberal, Democratic candidates and (many but by no means all such) issues, would run a headline and story that in effect supported liberal, Democratic contentions. This two-sided example is *not* necessarily representative of most papers (or perhaps even of most of the coverage of one or both of those two papers), but it does illustrate how political orientation can, at least at times, affect news decisions. Obviously, some papers, magazines,[70] and TV news programs are more subject to this effect than others.

THE IMPACT OF THE NEWS ON THE PUBLIC

Given the description and analysis of the factors involved in the news decision process, and given the discussion in Chapter 4 of the nature of each mass medium, what is the impact of the news on the public? Before taking up two important lines of research findings on that impact, it is well to discuss the public's feelings about the news media and their role in the system, which itself is, in important part, an effect of news operations.

The Public's Feelings about the News Media and the Implications

Following the events called "Watergate," in which investigative reporting by the news media played such a central role, the news media enjoyed high confidence and a very positive image in the public's mind. In the mid-1970s, over a quarter of the public expressed "a great deal of confidence" in the "press," and many more felt substantially positive about the news media, according to one survey. By 1983, however, the news media were seen in a different light by much of the public. The percentage of the public expressing a great deal of confidence in the press had plummetted to 13.7.[71]

A notable event in 1983 brought something of an outpouring of antipress sentiment. The event was the exclusion of the news media from coverage of the invasion of Grenada, an exclusion directed by President Reagan and the military. As *Time* magazine noted, "in 500 letters and phone calls to NBC, viewers supported the press ban in Grenada 5 to 1 . . . [and] *Time's* 225 letters on the issue ran almost 8 to 1 against the press." Further, while the "support for excluding the media was far from universal, . . . much of it was expressed in gleeful, even vengeful terms."[72] Why was a good portion of the public cheering the curtailment of First Amendment rights designed to protect the public? The impact of the nature of news criteria and news operations in general are a major part of the answer.

Time, in an excellent feature story examining the news media and their strained relations with the public, articulated the main reasons for the public's response. On a general societal level, there is "a perception that journalists regard themselves as utterly detached from, and perhaps even hostile to, the government of their country." And further, there is "the perception that as [journalists'] power has increased, so has their presumption of self-importance. Says William Woo, editorial page editor of the *St. Louis Post-Dispatch:* 'Arrogance, insensitivity, sensationalism, the sounding of First Amendment alarms at every provocation—these have all lost the press sympathy.' "[73]

Indeed, a Gallup poll commissioned for *Newsweek* in late 1984 found that 44% of the public thought nationally influential newspapers "arrogant" and about as many felt the same about network TV news.[74] Additionally, as the editor of the Oakland *Tribune* observed, the news media "are too hungry for blood—it sometimes seems to readers that we will not do the story unless we can do someone in."[75] At least the initial response of the public to news treatment of Gary Hart was of this nature: 22% called the treatment "fair," 64% "unfair."[76]

These phenomena and feelings are also apparently behind a surge of libel trial defeats for the news media: From 1976 through 1983, "nearly 85% of 106 major libel verdicts by juries have been defeats for journalist defendants, and almost two dozen involved damage awards of more than $1 million."[77] Two dramatic, widely publicized libel trials, *General Westmoreland* v. *CBS* and Israeli *Ariel Sharon* v. *Time,* were technically won by those two media, but they were expensive in both dollars and image of judiciousness and accuracy. What is ultimately more troubling is the potential chilling effect on vigorous news media investigations.

On the more personal side, as *Time* observed: "Some of the most controversial actions of journalists come when their desire for a good story causes them to collide with an individual's right to privacy. When 239 U.S. servicemen were killed in Beirut, the homes of the victims were surrounded by reporters and camera crews seeking to record the families' grief. . . ."[78] Indeed, in the *Newsweek* Gallup poll just noted, 62% felt that nationally influential newspapers and (58%) network TV news "invade people's privacy."[79]

The privacy problem can be equally stark, although of very different specific impact, when some heinous crime has been committed and the news media run stories on people accused of the crime *before any trial.* This would appear to be an especially compelling problem when the TV cameras are bringing "real life" motion pictures of these people into everyone else's homes. Even if found innocent, are these people effectively branded with suspicion thereafter? (This is an area that cries out for more research.) A striking example of this problem was 24 parents accused (formally by an apparently overzealous district attorney) of child molestation in Jordan, Minnesota in 1983. Their names and faces were splashed all over the print and broadcast media. Later one person pleaded guilty on a plea bargain, one couple was acquitted in a trial and charges against all the rest were dropped. Meantime many lives were turned upside down. Any rights to privacy were seemingly destroyed by this trial-by-media.[80]

In summary, news media operations, use of the typical criteria for news choice, and probably news competition and economic pursuits have resulted in news production that has left many in the public with resentment against the media. When this resentment results in popular support for government censorship of the news media's watchdog function over government—precisely the central purpose of the free press provision of the First Amendment—the political implications are serious.

Let me add one other note on news media operations and the analysis of them—an editorial comment, actually. For several years, Hodding Carter hosted and directed an excellent TV show on PBS called "Inside Story," which analyzed the news media and various issues involved in their operation. Sadly, the show was canceled in mid-1984 for lack of sponsorship. More, not fewer, such analyses are needed *in the mass media.* Also lost in the mid-1980s was the National News Council, intended to be an "independent and voluntary" forum to consider charges of inaccuracy and unfairness in the news media. It was never a very vigorous press critic, but it was there, and so was greater potential.

The News Media and the Agenda-Setting Effect—And Beyond

A key question follows from the description and analysis of the news decision process: Does the news that is produced actually affect the public's thinking on political matters, and if so, how? If the public's thinking is significantly influenced by what is printed and aired as news, there are important implications for a democratic society. One significant line of research has investigated this question and found some interesting (if still less-than-definitive) answers. This line of research is called the "agenda-setting effect."

The agenda-setting hypothesis (in light of early studies concluding minimal effects of the news media on public thinking) suggests that the news media may not directly affect *how* the public thinks about political matters, but it does affect *what* subjects people think *about*—in short, it sets the agenda for what political matters people think about. A number of studies have found positive evidence for an agenda-setting effect. Most of the studies have consisted of data showing a correlation between the amount and importance of attention one or more news media have given to certain issues and how significant the public considers the given issues to be. The cumulative effect of media coverage of an issue over time, not surprisingly, seems to have the greatest effect.[81]

Some have criticized these studies because most of them have not specifically demonstrated a *causal* connection between media agendas and the public's or individuals' agendas, and also because of less-than-strong statistical correlations in some of the studies.[82] But some more sophisticated studies have been done, using more complex models of how the news affects people's agendas of how important certain issues are, and they have considered varying conditions affecting that process. (The striking evidence on agenda setting in a presidential election found by Thomas Patterson is discussed in Chapter 10.) Some of those studies have also directly analyzed the counternotion that the news media is really just responding to the public's *existing* agenda (what the public already wants) and hence is not actually *changing* the public's agenda. Those studies have found good evidence to refute that conclusion and to support the news agenda-setting function.[83]

On the whole, the evidence indicates the news media have a significant effect on what people think about and what they see as important. Interestingly, included in that evidence was the finding that "the relationship between the content emphasis on the front page [of newspapers] and the saliences [the importance people saw in issues] was greater than the relationship between the content of the inside pages and the saliences."[84]

An important new book detailing research by two scholars of political communications has provided striking evidence on the agenda-setting effects of TV news. Shanto Iyengar and Donald Kinder, using a more experimental approach, carefully edited TV news programs to emphasize certain issues and then tested people on perceived importance of the issues (compared with control groups). Their summary of their findings:

Taken all together, our evidence decisively sustains the agenda-setting hypothesis [for television news]. The verdict is clear and unequivocal: It issues from sequential experiments that last a week, from assemblage experiments that last an hour, and from time-series data [correlating trends in network news coverage and national public opinion] that span seven years; it holds across different measures of importances; and it is confirmed for a variety of problems [including defense, pollution, arms control, civil rights, energy, social security, drugs, and education]. By attending to some problems and ignoring others, television news shapes the American public's political priorities.[85]

Additionally, like the study reported in the previous paragraph on newspapers, Iyengar and Kinder found the lead story in TV news to be more influential in agenda setting than later stories.

Iyengar and Kinder also concluded from their experiments that there is a dimension of effects beyond agenda setting. They call this the "priming" effect. The foundation of this effect is the fact that people do not have elaborate knowledge about political matters and do not take into account all of what they do know when deciding on political questions—they must consider what more readily comes to mind. Consequently, "through priming (drawing attention to some aspects of political life at the expense of others) television news might help to set the terms by which political judgments are reached . . . ," including evaluations of political figures. The results of their experiments demonstrated just such an effect: "When primed by television news stories that focus on national defense, people judge the president largely by how well he has provided, as they see it, for the nation's defense; when primed by stories about inflation, people evaluate the president by how he has managed, in their view, to keep prices down, and so on. According to a variety of tests, priming is both powerful and pervasive. . . ."[86]

One final fascinating finding of this research must be related. Iyengar and Kinder "expected that viewers' judgements of overall presidential performance would be primed more effectively than would assessments of presidential character," because of more diverse and personal factors involved in the latter. They expected the same for judgments of competence but not for integrity, since success or failure, as shown in the news, in an issue area would reflect more incompetence. They found the former expectations confirmed by their experiments, and the latter expectations confirmed for President Carter but *not* for President Reagan—in fact, the expectation was "sharply and consistently violated." Their explanation: "The public may be most susceptible to priming on those aspects of the president's character that are most open to debate"—for Carter it was a question of competence, for Reagan it was trust and caring, that is, "did he care for the welfare of all Americans?"[87] The present author would suggest that a better explanation is presented in Chapters 3 and 4 in this book (especially pages 49–56 and 68–71 and in the author's 1987 paper referenced therein).

ISSUE: THE NEWS AND TERRORISM

Terrorism and television; looked at one way, it seems almost inevitable that they would have become involved with one another in a big way. But that involvement raises important and very troubling questions, and it has become a major and contentious issue in the making and presentation of the news.

Terrorist acts are, in their essence, public acts. First, note that in most terrorist acts (as opposed to simple extortion or personal retribution) the specific victim or victims involved are not identical with the basic enemy; the real enemy is a nation, a regime, or the like. As two principal European experts point out: "If the meaning of a violent act no longer depends on the specific identity of the victim but can be constructed by the terrorists, almost anybody can serve as a target . . ."; and any such relatively random human targets can "serve as strong message generators as long as the terrorists' adversaries [namely, a *government* or regime] can be *held responsible for the lives of the victims* [emphasis added]."[88] The real intent of terrorism is well articulated by Brian Jenkins, terrorism expert at the Rand Corporation:

> Terrorism is aimed at the people watching. By carrying out inherently dramatic, deliberately shocking acts of violence, terrorists hope to attract attention to their causes and project themselves as forces to be reckoned with. To reach their audience terrorists depend on the news media.[89]

Terrorism is an intendedly public act of a sensational nature involving violence or its potential, dramatic conflict, and especially in the later twentieth century, a people's sense of (threatened) nationhood and national power. The news media, as we have discussed, have strong economic reasons for increasing their audience, and they make decisions on what is news based primarily on news criteria, which include drama, conflict, violence, and sensational events. Correspondingly, the temptation to give free reign to coverage of terrorism is well nigh irresistible. The consequences are profound, however.

First, we should present a historical note and a note on the evolution of the nature of the media. The increasing development of the mass audience newspaper was reviewed earlier. The increased audience provided increased specific exposure to the public of public figures, and an increased audience for terrorists. Then came television and related technological capacities. Corresponding to the discussion in Chapter 4 on the nature of the medium, coverage on TV would appear to have especially striking impact, with its capacity to air live coverage and for communication in actual sight and sound.

Two crucial questions are raised by the matter of terrorism and the news, especially by the television–terrorism connection. First, does media coverage of terrorist acts tend to exacerbate the situation itself? Is this especially the case for live television? Second, and ultimately more important, does such coverage tend to encourage further acts of terrorism, and hence, are even more profound questions raised of where the public good lies? What are the consequences for governments in dealing with terrorism? Again, the question of the principal purpose of the news should be considered to put things in perspective.

The answer to those two questions seems to be "yes." Regarding the first, a special report in the *Christian Science Monitor* summarized points on which "basic consensus" had developed, one of which was: "Television is no longer simply reporting *about* the story: It has become *part* of the story." Even the president of NBC News, Lawrence K. Grossman, acknowledged that TV is "the stage on which terrorist incidents are played." British Prime Minister Margaret Thatcher phrased it well in noting that the news media "provide the oxygen of publicity on which terrorism thrives."[90] And *Newsweek,* in an analysis article, noted what happened in the case of the TWA hijacking and hostage situation in mid-1985 (flight 847): "The question was whether the press was prolonging the ordeal by in effect handing the terrorists a megaphone. For much of the week, the Shiite hijackers—as savvy in the [electronic] 'global village' as in their own—got exactly what they wanted out of the news media: a conduit for their cause and their demands."[91] Studies have found similar effects in the Iran hostage case (along with other interesting elements and impacts of news coverage).[92]

Regarding the second question on encouragement of further terrorism, Rand expert Brian Jenkins reports: "Initial research tentatively suggests that heavy media coverage of [such acts] increases the likelihood that similar incidents will occur in the period immediately following. A recent Rand analysis of embassy seizures during the last decade shows them occurring in clusters, clearly suggesting a contagion effect."[93] Robert Oakley, director of the U.S. State Department's Office of Counter-Terrorism and Emergency Planning, says: "There's a long history of what you might call copycatism [and] competitiveness, [especially] among Middle East terrorist groups."[94]

Foreign Affairs columnist William Pfaff, reflecting on the various terrorist actions in the mid-1980s covered by the media, observed the media response and a significant consequence: "When television crews frantically compete to put hijackers and their victims on the air, dramatizing the victims' plight and the terrorists' conditions for their release, and correspondents and commentators assume a kind of negotiating role, the pressure on a government to make concessions builds until it is all but irresistible."[95]

The news media give two basic reasons for airing and printing stories

on terrorism: (1) the people involved are "newsmakers," these are news events, and it is the news media's job to report the news; and (2) the public "has a right to know" about such developments (ultimately referring to the First Amendment). There are some problems with this logic, however. The biggest problem is with live coverage, although the following reasoning applies to all immediate- or short-term reporting. To say "this is news" begs the question of what the event means, of whether and why it is important, and hence of whether and how it should be communicated to the general public. Correspondingly, claiming the "public's right to know" begs the question—"know" what? What does it mean, and why is it that the general public needs to see live hostage-bandying sessions and the rantings of people who have violated the most basic rules of social existence? The fact is, in the immediacy of the event and its excitement, there is no possibility of checking out statements and conditions to separate fact from fiction, and there is no opportunity to sort out specific background, basic related history, and present conditions which are or are not involved in what drove the people involved to engage in such acts. As Brian Jenkins reports: "Content analysis of coverage of terrorist incidents [even] in *The New York Times* and the *Times* of London shows that the news media provide little context in which the public can judge the events."[96] Hence the "people's right to know" is not served, only the people's right to be psychologically terrorized and frightened.

Does this mean that the government should censor coverage of terrorism in the mass media—and if so, who defines what can and cannot be so censored? As this author referred earlier in this chapter to the serious abridgement of First Amendment rights in the censoring of news coverage of the Grenada invasion, it is difficult to argue for it here. (The history of media involvement in U.S. military operations is, however, generally one of caution regarding American interests, whereas the history of media involvement with terrorism has little to do with caution in reporting.)

The American system is unused to such controls and the First Amendment is a central pillar of democracy in the United States. How, then, can the problem be dealt with? The general point is: somehow exercise more restraint in coverage. More tangibly, *Newsweek* News Media Editor Jonathon Alter, reflecting on the "Great Television Circus" of the '85 TWA hijack and hostage affair, suggested some principles for TV to follow. Perhaps with some sort of "media summit" on coverage of terrorism, such ground rules could be agreed to fairly formally, thus circumventing any move for government censorship (*perhaps* they might. . .). Three of the suggestions were:

> 1. Raw footage of hostages and terrorists should be pooled. The idea of pool reporting was developed to make covering wars and presidents less of a zoo. It makes even more sense in a terrorism crisis. Ending hostage "exclusives" would end the spectacle of the networks competing with each other for the favor of thugs. 2. Don't broadcast live or unedited coverage. . . . Live coverage of terrorists, captives, or even mediators is like giving them control over America's front page [and home television]. . . . 3. Downplay staged events. One lesson the networks learned from the Iranian hostage crisis was to ignore street protests put on solely for American cameras. As a result, Shiite demonstrations at Beirut . . . Airport received little coverage this time. But when the backdrop for the staged event changes, the lesson can sometimes be lost. . . .[97]

Coverage of terrorism affects the people of the nation, control of the news media, and various other domestic matters. However, many of the most striking cases take place in and involve foreign nations and peoples. This brings us to another basic element in understanding news coverage and its consequences: the coverage of foriegn affairs by the American news media. To that subject we turn in the next chapter.

CHAPTER SEVEN
NEWS FROM ELSEWHERE
Foreign Affairs and the News

INTRODUCTION AND PERSPECTIVE

Canadian theorist Marshall McLuhan first called it a "global village." The world has, in effect, shrunk. Both in terms of the capacity of humans to communicate from great distance and in terms of the capacity to transport people and materials physically, the world is effectively a much "smaller" place. Another, more dramatic illustration of the "closeness" of the different parts of the world is the fact that an intercontinental ballistic missile (ICBM) can travel from one "superpower" on one continent to another in less time than it takes to have dinner—about the time it takes to watch the evening news. Further, the world is increasingly *interdependent*. This is especially the case in economics, with world trade continuing to increase, with greatly increased foreign investment in the United States (and vice versa), and similar developments. It is also the case in cultural affairs, in science, and in other areas.

What all this means is that the need to understand what is happening in the rest of the world is extremely important, and increasingly so. That need includes understanding other nations' political, economic, and social systems, their histories, their leadership, and simply what the people of other countries are like. This understanding is perhaps most urgently needed in the case of the Soviet Union. Preferably, this understanding should be as accurate and complete as possible.

What *that* means for the subject of this book should be evident. The mass media are the "window on the world" for the American public; the media are the way people find out about events, conditions, movements, leaders, and systems in other nations. Because of the distance factor (and because of America's buffer of oceans and its traditional, rather isolationist orientation), the American public is even more dependent on the mass media for information on and impressions of foreign peoples and nations than for information on American political matters—much more. Correspondingly, it is important to investigate how news from foreign lands is covered.

FOREIGN NEWS COVERAGE

Amount of Foreign News in American Media

If the importance of knowledge and understanding of foreign affairs is greater than ever (and will increase in importance), and if the American public is even more dependent on the mass media for news about other nations and international matters than on American affairs, then it is important to know what foreign news the public receives. The first thing to consider is how much attention is paid to foreign and international news by American news media.

In one sense, the answer to the question of the amount of coverage of foreign and international news depends on how one defines foreign news stories (simply those that include mention of something about a foreign land or organization, or is a more stringent definition appropriate?). And it depends on what time period is examined. For example, an aggregate measure of foreign affairs news during the late 1960s and early 1970s or during the late 1970s and early 1980s would be a little misleading because of the vast attention to Vietnam in the first case and the Iran-hostage affair in the second. Coverage of these two matters was so great that it would skew the total upward, thus misrepresenting general patterns of international coverage. As in opinion polling, timing of studies is important to keep in mind.

Two other things should be noted before we review amounts of foreign news in the media. Much of the international news that appears in a given network news show, newspaper, or other news medium does not originate with that news organization. For media in the United States, much of that news comes from Associated Press, United Press International, or Reuters. For news film and videotape for television, Visnews and

UPITN are the two dominant distributors in the world. Visnews "distributes stories on film and videotape to 200 broadcasters in almost every nation where television exists."[1] The second thing to note here is that the technological developments of satellite communications and more portable cameras have increased the capacity to cover international news even more dramatically than domestic news. The costs of transmitting foreign video material over satellite has also dropped sharply over the past decade.

Regarding how much international news is covered in American media, let us look first at television. (The three major networks are concentrated on; CNN is still so new that studies including it are rare.) International affairs coverage on TV is a good example of the problematic questions on definition and timing mentioned above. Communications scholars Gerbner and Marvanyi[2] found that such coverage amounted to only 16% of the stories in the national newscasts in noncrisis periods (the data coming from the year 1970). From these (and other) data their conclusion was that the networks give poor coverage to international affairs—a conclusion reached by a number of other analysts. James Larson has studied the networks' coverage of foreign and international news in rather elaborate detail (using a sample of over 1000 news shows) and finds a very different aggregate total for international coverage. On the average, for 1972–1981, approximately 7 of 17 stories in each network news show, or 40%, "dealt with international affairs"[3]—quite a different total. His definition was very broad, however (i.e., any story that mentioned another nation in some way, and it included crisis periods and stories originating in the United States, such as the visit of a foreign leader). Further, when we examine the details that Larson presents, we find the complaints of inadequate coverage sustained. The details are discussed a little later.

Regarding newspapers, Doris Graber reports that foreign news comprises, on average and in noncrisis periods, only 11% of all stories.[4] A study by the Newspaper Advertising Bureau found that only 6% of total news items involved foreign news in 1982.[5] Further, the budgets of even the more prestigious newspapers reflect the modest commitment to coverage of international affairs: in 1986, 9.2% of the *Washington Post*, 8.2% of the *Los Angeles Times*, and 6.8% of the *Chicago Tribune* were devoted to coverage of foreign news. The *New York Times,* generally considered the American news medium with the best foreign affairs coverage, devoted 12.7% of its budget to such coverage.[6]

One other analysis of the amount of foreign news coverage should be mentioned here—a striking one. Clearly, the Soviet Union is a truly vital subject for foreign news coverage, perhaps *the* most vital subject on which Americans need to gain knowledge and understanding. An analysis of network news coverage of the Soviet Union was presented on an edition of the PBS program "Inside Story," hosted and led by Hodding Carter (former newspaper editor and State Department spokesman in the Carter administration). Harrison Salisbury, former *New York Times* reporter in the Soviet Union and distinguished journalist, reviewed network news coverage of the USSR for 1982, as a consultant to "Inside Story." His conclusion:

> The record is dismal, dismal in any kind of terms you want to judge it. In volume, the total amount of coverage is trivial. . . . Not only that, it is unimaginative. There seems to be little or no sense of responsibility for covering what I consider to be the most important, sensitive international story of the [time]. . . . [A typical] story was a 30-second squib about razor blades not being available in Moscow. Well, that's not exactly first-rate economic news.[7]

The *Washington Post*'s correspondent for the Soviet Union, Robert Kaiser, echoed that conclusion, and said it even more dramatically: "The treatment of the Soviet Union by U.S. media is a national disgrace."[8]

American Coverage of Foreign Affairs News Compared with Media in Other Nations   Do the American news media pay less attention to foreign affairs than the media in other nations? Further perspective is gained by making that comparison. The answer to the question is, "yes, they do." Gerbner and Marvanyi (again, from 1970 data) found that foreign affairs news comprised 17% of space in Soviet newspapers, *Pravda* containing 38% foreign news, 24% of space in West European newspapers, and 38% in East European newspapers.[9] (Compare that with the totals they found for American newspapers, using the same definitions, which are reported above.) In their review of network coverage of the Soviet Union, "Inside Story's" Hodding Carter and Harrison Salisbury found American network coverage "dismal compared with foreign electronic media." In 1982, for example, the three major American networks averaged a total of one hour of coverage for the entire year. "By contrast, one West German network (ZDF) carried a total of 2 hours and 51 minutes of news on the Soviet Union—virtually three times as much."[10]

The 1970s and 1980s: Decline and Signs of Resurgence   Since a World War II high of 2500, the number of foreign correspondents for American media declined considerably. And, as the *Los Angeles Times* observed in a special report: "In both actual and symbolic terms, the late[r] 1970s can be seen as the nadir of foreign correspondence."[11] By 1969 there were 929 full-time foreign correspondents (including many in Vietnam, and hence fewer elsewhere than that total would suggest), and by 1975 the total had dropped to 676, according to surveys by two communications scholars.[12] As the *Los Angeles Times* observed, the 1970s, especially, beginning in the later stages of the Vietnam war, were a time when the public and news people turned inward, when "the big stories seemed to be right here in the United States, starting with the anti-war movement itself, and including the campus protest movement, . . . feminism, environmentalism, . . . Watergate. . . ."[13]

In the mid to late 1980s there are, however, signs of resurgence in the amount of news media attention to foreign news. In the case of newspapers, for several examples, the *Washington Post* increased the number of foreign correspondents on staff from 13 in 1978 to 19 in 1986, the *Los Angeles Times, Christian Science Monitor,* the *Wall Street Journal,* and other major newspapers, as well as the Associated Press, increased their foreign reporting staff in similar fashion over that period.[14]

The *New York Times* has maintained its position as the premier news medium for covering foreign news, with 34 foreign correspondents on staff (including seven women as of the late 1980s).[15] It also has stories on foreign affairs on the front page every day and uses all the news space in the next 10 or 12 pages of its first section for foreign news each day. The *New York Times* is the number one example of the "prestige press" which is relied on by the foreign policy establishment in the United States—from Congress to the State Department. For higher officers, it is virtually required reading.

There are some examples of increased attention to foreign affairs by network TV news departments, as well. Most notable is ABC's "Nightline" program, which, on a good number of occasions, has aired shows on foreign affairs. These programs have included key foreign affairs participants or key advisors and spokespersons. For striking example, Philippine President Marcos was interviewed live during the final days of upheaval before his ouster by Aquino forces, along with major opponents of his regime; similarly, in the midst of major developments, key Soviet spokespersons and other officials have been interviewed, along with contrasting views received from U.S. officials. The TV "news magazine" programs "60 Minutes" and "20/20" have also aired some foreign affairs segments; some of these "60 Minutes" shows have had a notable impact. The regular "NBC Nightly News" program broadcast for 10 days in the fall of 1987 from China, with Tom Brokaw, Connie Chung, and other correspondents doing a striking series of reports from that country, and NBC did roughly the same from the Soviet Union in the fall of 1984. Finally, a major "special report" by CBS News should be noted. In the summer of 1987, a two-hour special investigation into Soviet society was aired in prime time (entitled "Seven Days in May"). Although attention to aspects of Soviet society was selective and the character of some of the segments was perhaps somewhat stereotypical or sensationalist, the magnitude of the effort constituted a significant addition to the traditional level of coverage. The sincerity of the effort to provide deeper coverage of Soviet society than had been typical was also evident. Mentioning the character of the CBS segments in "Seven Days in May" leads us to the next section of this chapter.

Coups, Earthquakes, Wars, and the American Angle:
Types of Foreign News Stories in the American Media

Beyond the amount of coverage, to get an understanding of the news on foreign affairs communicated to the American public, we need to consider the nature of the stories that usually appear in American media. Not surprisingly, the pattern of these stories parallels to a significant extent the news criteria detailed in Chapter 6. There are some unique elements, though, due to the different nature of covering news from other lands and political systems.

Crisis stories are a major type of story emphasis in foreign news in American media; in fact, it is fair to say, the greatest single story emphasis. James Larson found that 27% of all network TV news stories involving foreign affairs and over a third of all *video* ("film") reports from foreign lands carried crisis themes.[16] (Again, remember that his definition of "foreign news" was very broad; the study was of a sample of more than 1000 news shows for the period 1972–1981.) Veteran foreign correspondent and editor Mort Rosenblum, in his review of American news coverage of world affairs, suggested that the "rule of thumb" used by many reporters and editors is: "All anyone cares about is coups and earthquakes"—and wars.[17] That may overstate the case, but it is evident that crisis stories fulfill key criteria for news selection (drama, conflict, danger, etc.) and are the prime type of foreign news appearing in American media. This orientation was perhaps most revealingly articulated by Malcolm Browne, veteran foreign correspondent for AP and the *New York Times,* when he said: "Almost by definition, a foreign correspondent is a war correspondent."[18]

Competition within the organization for news space and time would appear to heighten the tendency to select crisis stories. Rosenblum noted the situation (which again, parallels the general progress of news selection discussed in Chapter 6): "Because of . . . competition for space, correspondents tend to squeeze the last drop out of stories they cover. . . . Few exaggerate purposely . . . [b]ut reporters often are tempted to reach for dramatic conclusions . . . to make their stories more attractive to editors." And further, the various editors (gatekeepers) involved in the selection process most often see things the same way—the majority may "sometimes throw in dull but important stories because they feel they must, but they generally follow what they think is the average taste of their market."[19]

One interesting example, which is a variation on this category of foreign news stories, is coverage of dissidents in the Soviet Union. This is the most notable example of a general tendency to cover internal conflict in major communist bloc nations, especially in the USSR, and protests and demonstrations in general if they are sufficiently large and threatening. Other than the succession of General Secretaries, dissidents were clearly the top story in the American news media through the late 1970s and much of the 1980s—so much so that West German reporter Fritz Pleitgen was moved to comment: "People could get the impression from [such] coverage that 80% of the Russian people are dissidents."[20]

The second category of story selection in foreign affairs that should be noted here is not really a single type of story, but rather is a way of looking at stories—the American angle. Stories on other nations (and international organizations) tend to be sought out and reported in light of the relation to American interests involved. Regarding network TV news, James Larson found: "The United States is referred to in about 60% of all international news stories broadcast. . . . Most often, mention of the U.S. indicates some direct involvement or interest in the affairs reported."[21] This finding (if not the exact magnitude) applies to newspapers and news magazines as well.[22]

The "geography of the news" comprises the third general category of foreign news selection—that is, the pattern of what nations and regions tend to receive what respective amounts of coverage. Coverage of the world is very uneven. The "world of U.S. newspapers," as Gerbner and Marvanyi[23] put it, is dominated by Western Europe and, to variously lesser extents, the Middle East, especially Israel, and the Soviet Union. In various periods other nations appear more or much more prominently as a result of selection categories one and two above (crisis and the American connection). James Larson found only 12 nations mentioned in but 4% or more of all international stories in American media in the 1972–1981 period.[24]

A fourth category is comprised of elections, especially if they are in the nations receiving principal attention, as just noted, and especially if there is a change in the head of government. Other types of more peaceful change in heads of government and/or state can be included as a subset here. A fifth category is coverage of royalty, primarily West European and most especially British.[25] Indeed, Bill Moyers has humorously complained: "There were periods when I thought the British royal family had signed on [with CBS News] as correspondents, so frequent were their appearances."[26]

REASONS FOR THE NATURE OF AMERICAN FOREIGN NEWS COVERAGE

Attitudes—Or Perceptions of Attitudes

One principal reason for the rather paltry coverage of international affairs in U.S. media, a reason that has been identified by news people, is a lack of interest by the American public in news on such matters. As Doris Graber has summarized: "Presumed lack of interest leads to less coverage."[27] Such has been the perception of most news people.

There is evidence that casts doubt on that perception, however. Mort Rosenblum cites evidence from the 1970s (which then raises questions about whether the decline in foreign correspondents and foreign news in the 1970s represented misperceptions by news executives of the public's desires, let alone its ultimate needs):

> The Louis Harris [polling] organization reported after a special nation wide survey in 1978 . . . : "Those who work in the [news] media . . . feel that only 5 per cent of the public are greatly interested in international news. A much higher 41 per cent of the public expresses deep interest in world affairs being covered in the news media."
>
>   Daniel Yankelovich surveyed readers for the *Washington Post,* asking a test group to check categories they found "interesting and important." The highest number, 66 per cent, listed foreign news.[28]

And in the later 1980s, the *Los Angeles Times* reports: "Recent studies . . . show readers more interested in foreign news—60% are 'very interested,' according to one survey, and 84% say they 'usually read . . . international or world news,' according to another survey (by the Newspaper Advertising Bureau)."[29]

The foreign editor of the *Wall Street Journal* articulated the current opinion of the prestige press: "Readers are much more interested in foreign news today than they were 10 years ago. The oil embargo in the late 1970s brought home the fact that the rest of the world is out there and can have an influence on us."[30]

Distribution of Foreign Correspondents

The distribution of foreign correspondents around the world is another reason for the amount and nature of foreign news coverage (in addition to the decline in the total number of American reporters in foreign affairs). There is substantial concentration of reporters for American news media in Western Europe, and moderate concentration in the Soviet Union, and in the 1970s and 1980s in the Middle East, especially in Israel. Japan has received an increasing delegation of correspondents through the 1980s. Elsewhere it varies greatly with dramatic developments (especially wars), and many nations or even regions of the world have very few or no full-time foreign correspondents. (In various areas, a few local "stringers" suffice.)

Journalist Mort Rosenblum has noted that pattern of distribution, along with what the news media do to compensate, as well as some consequences. In many developing and socialist nations, he pointed out, "news organizations have no representatives at all. They monitor official news agencies [but these are] seldom more than government propaganda services." The prime technique used to compensate for not having a journalist based in a nation can be called "parachute journalism." That is, when a story breaks, a reporter (and camera crew for television) must be rushed to the area and "parachuted in" to "do" the story. They are rushed either from a foreign bureau office some distance away—from which the reporter must cover several or many nations—or from the home office in the United States. Evidently, this means the stories that do get covered in such areas are even more likely to be of the crisis–drama–conflict type. This is clearly not the way to communicate an adequate understanding of those nations and regions; this solution to coverage "is a poor substitute for more resident correspondents spread throughout the world," as Rosenblum notes.[31]

As a rule, only journalists who have spent a fair amount of time in the nation and region will have enough knowledge and understanding of the society to give an adequate explanation of what events in the news really involve and to put them in perspective. Rosenblum points out another consequence of this approach: "Parachute journalism reinforces a pack mentality which has always plagued foreign reporting. Correspondents who hurry off to a new place tend to stick together, interviewing friends who arrived earlier and competing to find the most dramatic angle of the story."[32] There is one positive side, though: A reporter who does not have to stay living and working in a given nation, and hence be subject to officials' restrictions and harrassments, might feel more free to report material that would offend the authorities. This is, in most cases, a rather minor compensation, though.

A pattern and a consequence must be noted of the thin-to-nonexistent distribution of foreign correspondents in developing ("third world") countries, in conjunction with the story types usually selected. In his study on network TV coverage, James Larson found that such coverage of developing countries includes considerably more crisis stories than coverage of developed and socialist nations. Specifically, 36% of the stories mentioning only developing nations were on crises, compared with 26% for developed nations and 21% for socialist countries. Further: "The data concerning national origin of foreign *video* reports [are even more striking]. Nearly half (47.5 percent) of all stories reported directly from developing nations by network television correspondents deal with crisis, compared with only 32.1% of such reports from developed nations. . . . [emphasis added]"[33]

As mentioned above, these patterns of reporting are not an adequate way to communicate developments and circumstances in the developing nations or to assist the public in understanding such areas. The picture (in both senses) that the American public receives of the Third World would appear to be quite distorted. Otis Chandler, who, as publisher, was the principal force behind developing the *Los Angeles Times* into one of the nation's great newspapers, has thoughtfully put this matter in perspective:

> [T]he problem of obtaining pertinent information about Third World nations has assumed dimensions of such national importance that it should have

the attention of everyone. This is because the energy crisis plus recognition that accommodation must be reached with the Third World have impelled the United States to formulate new policies toward the non-aligned areas of the world.

Thus, the question arises: How can the government formulate and the public pass judgment on a sensible policy toward a country about which we know little or nothing . . . [or about which we have crisis images as the principal impression]?[34]

The Language Problem

A third reason for the amount and especially for the inadequate nature of foreign reporting in American media is lack of language ability. The fact is, especially outside Western Europe and the Spanish-language parts of Latin America, it is common[35] for correspondents not to have a mastery of the language of the nation (or area) they are assigned to cover. The *Los Angeles Times* reports the observation of *New York Times* reporter R. W. Apple on the source of this problem. He concluded "that too many foreign correspondents lack language fluency because too many American newspaper editors have 'a rather naive belief . . . that a good police reporter can cover anything.'" Indeed, in the informal survey conducted by the *Los Angeles Times*, "Most editors interviewed for this story did . . . voice that opinion."[36]

The consequences of such a notion are significant, however, as some leading journalists have recognized. First, without a good language capacity, especially in any location other than urban Western Europe, correspondents must rely on two very restricted categories of sources for stories. The first is official sources in the country, and usually the official translations. The chief of *Newsweek*'s Bonn bureau, Andrew Nagorski, has illustrated the problem with the case of the Soviet Union. He says that "most of the daily output with Moscow datelines is nothing more than a repackaging of Soviet propaganda." He observes that during the period he reported from Moscow, "an American wire service correspondent estimated that 90% of his bureau's copy amounted to rewriting dispatches and articles from Tass and the Soviet press. Few other [American news media] could claim substantially lower percentage."[37] The second category of sources on which reporters without language ability must rely on was expressed astutely by Mort Rosenblum. Those sources "are mainly fellow Americans or a small elite who have learned English for a particular reason."[38] The result of reliance on such sources is likely to be a skewed view of the nation involved.

The problem of inadequate language skills is certainly most critical in a nation such as the Soviet Union or China, where the language is very different from most Americans' experience and where a more authoritarian, more "closed" society makes accurate, knowledgeable reporting difficult under the best of circumstances. *Washington Post* Moscow correspondent Robert Kaiser has most eloquently articulated the consequence, in the case of the Soviet Union in specific. He noted that few American reporters speak Russian fluently, and he concluded: "To send a reporter to the Soviet Union who doesn't speak the language is to say [in effect] 'I'm sending a reporter who's going to be deaf and more or less blind.' "[39] For "America's overseas eyes and ears," this is a serious deficiency; the information and impressions American citizens have of nations so covered must be correspondingly deficient. ABC's Anne Garrells, whose reporting from the Soviet Union on various aspects of Soviet society won well-deserved praise, observed: "I was able to do those stories precisely because I spoke Russian and had a lot of Russian friends. Those friends showed me the real Russian world. . . . If you don't speak the language, you can't see that."[40]

The Background Problem: Education in the Culture and Political System

The fourth reason for inadequate foreign news coverage is really the second side of the basic problem of sufficient training for the job. R.W. Apple's observation, noted earlier, that many editors think language ability isn't needed "because a good police reporter can cover anything" applies to the education of a reporter in the culture, economy, and political system of the nation or nations to be covered. The fact is that a reporter who does not have special education and training in the social and political system of a foreign nation, especially one such as the Soviet Union or China or one in Africa or Asia, will have a difficult time finding his or her way around to search out and report on a story, let alone to accurately discern the meaning of some development.

A few news organizations take quite seriously the need for educational preparation. The *New York Times* and *Washington Post* give reporters newly assigned to the Soviet Union nine months to a year to prepare. The *Post* "usually sends reporters to Stanford or to the University of Michigan for courses in Russian and 'area studies'" and the *Times* "encourages its reporters to plan independent study programs at whatever institutions or with whatever private tutors they think best."[41] Apparently, most news organizations arrange for little or no such training, however. As foreign news reporter David Lamb puts it, the attitude of most news media seems to be: "Send them in with a parachute and [they] can do some stories [the] second day there and as [they] go on, they'll get better."[42]

Language and Background Inadequacies: A Further Consequence One further consequence should be noted of inadequate language skills and inadequate education in the social and political systems of nations assigned for reporting. Without such skills and training, correspondents are much more vulnerable to manipulation by political leadership and other officials. Political leaders and other officials in nations around the world are increasingly conscious of the presence and impact of the American news media and increasingly knowledgeable about how those media operate. They, like the terrorists discussed at the end of Chapter 6, are increasingly seeking to make good use of, indeed to manipulate, the news of their persons, regimes, and societies. Without language and background, "independent reporting" can be a euphemism for the reality of foreign correspondence.

Cost

The fifth reason for the amount and character of foreign news communicated over the American media is simple and logical: It is costly to cover foreign affairs. According to the *Los Angeles Times,* as of 1986, it cost a newspaper $150,000 to $200,000 per year "to maintain one-reporter bureaus abroad." The *Times* also observed the business situation and a logic discussed in Chapter 6 regarding news in general, as they apply to foreign news coverage: Many "newspapers, increasingly owned by large media conglomerates with bottom-line priorities, became more cost-conscious than ever; it's much cheaper to fill a newspaper with wire service copy than it is to staff a bureau overseas. . . ."[43] What is missed, however, is reporting with depth, reporting that more adequately explains another society and its political system; the wire services generally offer only stories on particular, usually more-or-less dramatic, events, results of major elections, and the like.

Socialization

Like other Americans, news reporters grow up in the midst of and are continuingly subject to the political socialization that is characteristic of American society. Foreign correspondents tend to have more formal education than the average American and as working journalists in news organizations, may have somewhat more skepticism about the government line (as was discussed in Chapter 6). But fundamentally, foreign correspondents carry with them the basic American socialization regarding what America stands for, its place in the world, what "communism" and communist nations are like, and so on. This inevitably affects how reporters see things—what matters they decide are "news" and how they present those matters. This is especially the case with the "communist" nations; American reporters have an especially difficult time removing the American-style lenses, filtered by socialization, when reporting on the Soviet Union and its ideological fellow nations. (Soviet reporters, of course, have an equally difficult time in the opposite direction.) Examples abound. A simple perusal of *Newsweek, Time,* or *U.S. News & World Report* stories on the Soviet

Union over the years, for the most accessible examples, shows use of unsubstantiated and extreme labels[44] and a tendency to reject out of hand or cast sarcasm on Soviet contentions and (in this subject area) to accept U.S. government contentions without much question. Fairly frequent editorializing in the midst of news stories is also evident.[45] (Observe the networks for similar or worse patterns.) An illustrative example follows.

Illustration: The Case of KAL 007   The case of Korean Airlines (KAL) flight 007 provides a revealing illustration of the basic filters that reporters see through as a consequence of socialization, and the resulting patterns of reporting just discussed. The KAL flight was shot down by a Soviet fighter plane over Soviet territory in early September 1983. That much is fact. Why the KAL plane, on a flight from Anchorage to Seoul, strayed so far off the normal path, what the Soviet Union perceived was happening and why they reacted the way they did, and how and why the Reagan administration acted are the subject of some debate and some interesting later investigations. How the news media reacted is not in much doubt, however.

The American news media's response to the story was one of immediate assumption of cold-blooded barbarity on the part of the Soviets, with corresponding labeling and editorializing accompanying the stories, and with complete or virtually complete acceptance of the explanations of the U.S. administration. The networks ran late-night specials the evening of the event, with coverage of the character just mentioned, complete with heated rhetoric of condemnation. *Newsweek*'s report in the issue following the event was representative of coverage at the time. The cover story carried the large title "Murder In the Air" and had a picture of a KAL plane with the cross-hairs and concentric circles of a gun scope superimposed. The title of the feature story inside was: "A Ruthless Ambush in the Sky." And so went the story.

Was this development a simple barbaric act, as depicted in the media? More important for the present purpose, did the media ask enough questions and review the context to allow sensible judgments? The answer appears to be "no." Rather, socialized preconceptions led to a conditioned response—a response made more stereotyped and extreme by deadline pressures (unresisted) and competitive pressures, along with use of classic news criteria as well as by pack journalism. To support this judgment, a note on relevant context and a note on some subsequent investigative reporting are required.

News people made little or no effort to place this event in context. Perhaps the most striking element of the context involved went completely unmentioned by the media. To explain, a little background is required. Ten months earlier, Yuri Andropov had succeeded Brezhnev as leader of the Soviet Union. After the long Brezhnev era, and as with any change in leadership of a superpower, there was much interest in who this man was.

As former head of the KGB, there was an early tendency to portray Andropov as a wily, "gaunt ogre." But the dominant media treatment quickly turned to depictions of his fascination with Western culture and his much better grasp of Western ways (than Brezhnev).[46] In one way, Andropov proceeded to demonstrate the accuracy of the latter. That is, as of September 1983, he had spent most of the ten months of his leadership carefully trying to build a positive, responsible image of the Soviet Union, which efforts were carried out in part through the international mass media. So, the question of context: Why would a man—one portrayed as wily and intelligent and aware of Western ways, who had spent the previous ten months trying to build a responsible, reasonable image for the Soviet Union, proceed to order or accept a "cold-blooded murder of an innocent passenger plane"? It does not add up. A little reflection on the context would have led to far greater caution and the raising of far more serious questions rather than the knee-jerk response that occurred.

Regarding details of circumstances of the event, news people did raise questions about why an airplane (Boeing 747) with such state-of-the-art guidance systems could have strayed so far. But only limited attention was given to the fact that the territory KAL 007 strayed into was on the charts as a restricted and sensitive military zone. Exceedingly little or no attention was given, especially in the initial TV and print reports, to other things happening at the time. Renowned investigative journalist Seymour Hersh detailed those other circumstances and the media manipulation of the U.S. administration in a book on this case:

> U.S. Air Force intelligence concluded within a day of the attack that the Soviets had *not known* it was a civilian airliner when they shot it down. They thought it was a U.S. spy plane, an RC135, that in fact had flown near the *same area* of the Soviet Union the *same evening* [emphasis added]. . . .
>
> Reagan [shortly after the event] made a television speech about what he called the "Korean airline massacre." He said it had been a deliberate "act of barbarism," arising from the brutal nature of Soviet society.[47]

But Hersh discloses "that the president, before making the speech, had signed a directive ordering that the Korean airline tragedy be used to darken the Soviet image."[48]

The media, with socialized preconceptions, along with the factors in news decision mentioned above, swallowed that line whole and failed to ask adequate questions. The result, frankly, was a distorted picture of what happened, which left an impression in people's minds that made future progress in relations between the two superpowers more difficult. And the media had been manipulated for political purpose by the administration. (It should be noted, however, that roughly a month later, some news media did carry stories noting the U.S. intelligence findings; others never made even a belated effort to correct the earlier stories.)

RECENT DEVELOPMENTS OF NOTE

Gorbachev, the Soviet Union, and the TV Age

Andropov sought to convey a positive image of the Soviet Union, in part through the international mass media. But compared with Mikhail Gorbachev, Andropov was a rank amateur in the public relations game on the international stage. In the Gorbachev era in Soviet society, the mass media have become a prime means of international diplomacy and influence (as well as a major, dramatically enhanced means of affecting the Soviet system itself).

General Secretary Gorbachev, along with a number of his colleagues, evidently have an understanding of Western mass media and an ability and flair for using them which are a quantum leap above previous Soviet leaders. Quite simply, in the battle for international public opinion, it is a new era from the Soviet side. Regarding Gorbachev himself, as *Newsweek* observed (in late 1985):

> The voice was warm, the handshake firm. Mikhail Gorbachev went to Paris last week and turned on the charm. Polished, pleasant and direct, he quickly dispelled the stereotype of the crude and imperious Soviet boss. He also revealed himself as a master of public diplomacy. . . .
> Even before leaving the Kremlin, he sat down for an interview with three French television reporters—and handled their toughest questions with aplomb. In France, Gorbachev held a major press conference with President Francois Mitterand—and quickly stole the show.[49]

And as *Time* observed, in the international arena, "Gorbachev has outcommunicated the Great Communicator [Reagan]. Some recent European opinion polls have found that the man in the Kremlin is more popular than the one in the White House."[50]

The understanding and making good use of the media by the Soviet Union goes well beyond Gorbachev's performances, though. To use a basketball metaphor (with a dash of pun), the Soviets now put on a full court press for the media. For example, for the November 1985 summit between Reagan and Gorbachev, in September, "already . . . Soviet advance teams [like those for the United States] have scouted Geneva for the best camera angles."[51] And more generally: "Once shy of Western reporters, Soviet officials at various levels have become more open and accessible. The Foreign Ministry spokesman, Vladimir Lomeiko, has instituted regular on-the-record press briefings that now attract more newsmen than the off-the-record backgrounders at the U.S. embassy."[52] Another example, as *Newsweek* expressed it: "Vitaly Churkin, 35, blow-dried first secretary at the Soviet Embassy in Washington, will be rewarded for five years of vigorously defending Moscow's disarmament strategies—and for his mastery of U.S. TV after the Chernobyl nuclear accident."[53] (He was given a position in the Central Committee's international department.)

To use another sports metaphor, covering the Soviet Union in the late 1980s became a whole new ballgame. In some ways, it is more challenging than ever to respond to Soviet developments fully and accurately while minimizing news manipulation. The move toward *glasnost*—more openness, acceptance of critique, and so on—certainly made for a more fruitful situation for Western reporters to gather information. Officials became more responsive and the Soviet media contained more searching and authentically informative articles.[54]

It should finally be added that the nature of Gorbachev's leadership and the changed conditions he is so centrally responsible for have stimulated some much more substantial media efforts at coverage of the Soviet Union. The two-hour CBS special on the Soviet Union, "Seven Days in May" (1987), for example, has already been mentioned. The news magazines have been particularly notable since 1985 in carrying major stories on the Soviet Union. Perhaps the most striking of those was *Time*'s long 1985 interview with Gorbachev (run as transcripts, only "slightly condensed"), with accompanying feature story.[55]

"Media Diplomacy"

Another development of note is a direct result of the advent of the medium of television and the remarkable place the network news programs came to occupy in the United States. It has come to be called "media diplomacy." Media diplomacy occurs when actions of news people—usually an anchorperson—result in actual developments in diplomatic relations between nations. That is, in such cases, the news operation has not just reported the news, it has effectively generated news developments in the international arena. The most famous instance took place in November 1977 when CBS anchorman Walter Cronkite, in an interview with Egyptian President Sadat via satellite, elicited a promise by Sadat to go to Israel if it would further the prospects for peace in the Middle East. Such a visit would be an unprecedented step in that troubled region. Cronkite then obtained a promise from Israeli Prime Minister Begin, in another interview, that he would personally welcome President Sadat at Jerusalem's airport. It was with that media effort that a dramatic meeting of Egyptian and Israeli leaders took place in later November. The capacity to "go live" via satellite and telecast an interview or event to the American public, or to hundreds of millions of people around the world, along with the prominence and power of the American network news operations in the public arena, has provided a remarkable ability to affect developments in international affairs. Several interviews and other stories by "60 Minutes" correspondents have had striking impact (e.g., Mike Wallace's interviews with Yassir Arafat of the PLO and the Shah of Iran). Interviews by Ted Koppel on "Nightline" have had similar impact.

Whether such a circumstance of media interrogation, before a mass public, of officials responsible for foreign policy is always (or even usually) a healthy thing for a nation's diplomacy or for the world's international relations is a subject for debate. Media news criteria, competitive concerns, and the like, as well as a simple lack of foreign affairs expertise on the part of news people, may result in questions and pressure on foreign policy officials to do something ill-considered. Further, in many cases, diplomatic relations require patient discussion over a period of time, enabling negotiation and compromise, to help nations involved take steps to meet one another while preserving established dignity and saving face. In the glare of TV lights and cameras, especially on live satellite hook-ups, such discussion and negotiation may be a casualty of TV technology and criteria for selection of dramatic news.

The "New International Information Order"

This chapter has been about coverage of foreign affairs news by the American media. But especially in the world of the late twentieth century, mass communications are far less neatly separable into media coverage for and by organizations from each particular nation. In accordance with the patterns discussed in the introduction to this chapter, mass media communications had become highly international in nature by the second half of the century, and were increasingly so over the ensuing decades. Correspondingly, we should expand the discussion a bit at this point.

That increasing internationalization has not simply meant an increased international flow of communications. Many observers throughout the world were concerned that very inequitable circumstances of mass communications had developed, with the more industrialized, richer Western nations dominating international communications (as they had dominated economics). The result of this concern was calls, especially from leaders of Third World countries, for a "new international information order."

More specifically, several charges were leveled regarding Western dominance of the communication of news and public information. First, it was said that "world news is defined by the West and distorts or excludes authentic but non-Western values of the Third World . . . [and third world] cultures and cultural evolution are seen in the rest of the world only through Western filters." Second, much of what happens in Third World nations is ignored, and what "does get into the world news system emphasizes fragile aspects of the Third World." Thus, while coups and other violent political events get coverage, progress in peaceful development of a

Third World nation gets no attention, said the critics. Finally: "Distorted, negative treatment of the Third World in the Western media is transferred to the Third World itself because of the latter's dependence on the Western news agencies."[56]

There are, indeed, some good reasons for taking these charges seriously. The types of news stories American media tend to report from developing nations, as discussed earlier, supports one of those charges (though more research is needed to add more complete data). Mustapha Masmoudi, former Tunisian minister of information and leading spokesman on the issue, has articulated the other main evidence. First, he pointed out that "almost 80% of the world news flow emanates from the major [Western] transnational agencies." That is, the great majority of the news flow comes from AP and UPI, Reuters (British), and to a lesser extent, Agence-France Presse (French, as you may have guessed). For TV, Visnews, UPI-TN, and to a lesser extent, CBS provide video footage for the world (American and British dominance being evident). Second, Masmoudi pointed out that those news agencies "devote only 20 to 30 percent of news coverage to the developing countries, despite the fact that the latter account for almost three-quarters of mankind."[57]

This is a significant issue in international communications. Unfortunately, it is beyond the scope of this book to discuss it in much further detail. The general conclusion on the issue is: "It is clear that the flow [and influence] of news and information is overwhelmingly . . . from a handful of industrialized nations in the West to the developing nations." But in accurately studying this issue we must be more careful than many in the past in defining terms and concepts; and it should be noted that much of the data on the issue are out of date. In short, some caution is in order in reaching those conclusions. Further, in response to the raising of some of these concerns, some new regional news services have been developed in and for Third World areas. And greater potential is there for using the gradually less expensive newer technologies to enable third world societies more international and intraregional communications capacity and influence.[58]

One final note will serve as an appropriate endspiece for the chapter and, as it were, as the moral of the story. In 1978, UNESCO (United Nations Educational, Scientific, and Cultural Organization) set out a declaration on the media (after much debate). This "Declaration of Fundamental Principles" is, in fact, a stirring articulation of an international news coverage version of the question raised in Chapter 6 regarding the basic purpose of the news. (Among other things), it said:

> [T]he mass media, by disseminating information on the aims, aspirations, cultures and needs of all people, contribute to eliminate [sic] ignorance and misunderstanding between peoples. [And such information can] make nationals of a country sensitive to the needs and desires of others [enabling] the

respect of the rights and dignity of all nations, all people. . . . [Further, by giving] attention to the great evils which afflict humanity, such as poverty, malnutrition and diseases, . . . the formulation by states of policies best able to promote the reduction of international tension and the peaceful and equitable settlement of international disputes [can be encouraged and assisted].[59]

CHAPTER EIGHT
CAPITAL COVERAGE
AND COMMUNICATIONS
The Media–Government Relation

INTRODUCTION

The image of the president addressing the nation is one most Americans can readily call to mind (". . . and now, the President of the United States," says the announcer). The picture of some dramatic congressional hearings, such as the Senate "Watergate" hearings or those of the joint House–Senate Committee hearings on the Iran-Contra affair, also readily come to mind for most people. But in general, what is the nature of the news coverage of our institutions and officers of government? Additionally, how do government leaders and other officials seek to communicate to the general public through the mass media?

The continuing theme of this book has been the role the mass media play in the democratic system. In a representative system, the public must make choices on legislators and a chief political and executive officer. The public, by its choices of the complete set of legislators and other elected officials, ultimately makes choices of which political party will control the basic directions of government, as well. If the public is to be effective in those choices, people must have information on what the incumbent officers and parties have done in office. This applies to people's political participation in other ways and times than elections, as well. The mass media are the prime sources of information on those governmental actions and the processes involved. Looked at another way, if the public is fundamentally dependent on the mass media for their understanding of what has transpired in government, the nature of what the news media communicate about governmental institutions and officers will presumably affect how the public carries out their democratic task.

In this chapter we discuss those matters. The focus is on American national institutions of government. Many of the patterns reported also apply to media–government relations at the state (and even local) levels. The chapter begins with a note on the general nature of the media–government relation as perceived by the public, by the news media, and by government officials from their different positions and perspectives. Following that, the Presidency and Congress are reviewed with respect to both the nature of news coverage of each and with respect to efforts by officials to use the mass media to communicate to the public (and each other). More brief treatment of the media–government relation for the Supreme Court and the executive agencies is then added. At the end of the section on the Presidency, the special category of media–government relations of officials' efforts at secrecy, censorship, and more general control of press coverage is discussed. In a final section we discuss some findings on the impact of news media coverage on public policy.

NATURE OF THE MEDIA–GOVERNMENT RELATION: ORIENTATIONS AND ROLES

In the United States, there is a peculiar, almost schizoid quality to feelings about both media coverage of government and government and politics themselves. Regarding government and politics, on the one hand, more than in any other developed "democratic" nation, Americans are inclined to feel the chief political officer—the president—is much more than simply that; rather, the president is seen as the national symbol, someone "we all must rally around," someone whose message must always be heard and whose leadership is primary in the nation and must not be fettered. On the other hand, there is a long tradition in America of an abiding suspicion of politics—virtually a sense that political matters are inherently less-than-honorable, even dirty activities. The word "politician" itself has a negative ring to it as used in American political culture. Further (at least in form), there is a long tradition of suspicion of governmental power, especially as reposed in a chief executive (the principal reason for the nonparliamentary, separation-of-powers form of government established in the Constitution).

On the media side, on the one hand, the First Amendment freedoms of press and speech are held to be foundation stones of the American system. The function performed by the news media of government watchdog has been applauded by the public as well as the intellectual elite in such cases as the Watergate affair and a variety of cases of corruption, misuse of power, and so on. On the other hand, the public seems to resent criticism by the media of presidents in specific and government in general as noted in Chapter 6. Further, the public (or sizable and vocal parts of it) have cheered when high officials have lashed out at the media and when such officials have sought to keep the media from covering activities (the case of the Grenada invasion, which is discussed below, being the most notable example in the 1980s).

Such is the general environment in which the media–government relation takes place in the United States. This environment was especially agitated by presidential action in and media coverage of Vietnam and Watergate, as well as the 1979–1980 Iran hostage and 1986–1987 Iran-Contra affairs. In sum, in the American political system, there are inclinations to support and encourage the news media to watch over and investigate government activity, but also inclinations to complain about news media harassment and excessive intrusiveness regarding officials and their actions. There are inclinations to support unfettered presidential action and nearly unquestioned loyalty to "the president" and to discourage critique of government in general, and yet concerns are expressed about excessive governmental power and the need to watch over it. This schizophrenia is also evident in news coverage of these governmental institutions, and in patterns of use of the media by officials.

The basic respective roles of news media and government would appear to be more clearly delineated. Prominent analysts have suggested that there is a basic "adversary relationship" between the news media and government officials. For political figures effectively to move other people in government, and other involved groups and organizations, to get something done, they often need to build carefully coalitions of officials. This normally requires bargaining, trading, cajoling, and so on, and doing so in the right order, with good timing. Much of that must be done in private so that delicate arrangements and agreements are not upset or proposals aired publicly before they and their coalitions are ready. But also, as scholars at least since Neustadt[1] have pointed out, the president's "public prestige" (general public approval) can have a significant effect on how other government officials respond to presidential initiatives, as can a wave of public support for a specific action. Presidents use the mass media to sustain general approval and to rally support on specific issues. Such reliance on the media has become an increasingly prominent part of presidents' efforts to provide leadership and move the government to act on problems.

The news media, on the other hand, wish to report the news, preferably more exciting news according to standard news criteria, and to beat the competition to a scoop. They also do see themselves as watchdogs of government, especially after Watergate. Correspondingly, the news media wish to poke into what is going on behind closed doors, report conflicts and wheeling and dealing, and so on. (Remember the "enduring values" and Progressive political orientation described by Herbert Gans and reviewed in Chapter 6.) In sum, as Graber interestingly phrases it: "Government wants its portrait taken in its Sunday best, from the most flattering angle. The media, however, want to take candid shots, showing government in awkward poses and off its guard."[2]

The relation is more complex than that, however. The fact is that the media and government need each other to fulfill their functions. Officials need to use the media to communicate with each other, and the public and the media need government officials as sources for many or most of their major stories. Further, the consequence is that they not only recognize the mutual need and put up with one another, but there is quite substantial cooperation, in various basic ways, both in news coverage and in officials' more direct use of the media for communicating. At the local level of government—or of media coverage of national government—that cooperation can be remarkable; it can, in fact, have more of a collaborative quality. In the following pages the specifics of this combination of conflict and cooperation are presented.

COVERAGE OF INSTITUTIONS; OFFICIALS' USE OF THE MEDIA

The Presidency, the Media, and the Political System

Perspective Presidents have long had an especially striking relation with the mass media. In the twentieth century, as the mass media came to hold an increasingly prominent place in society, increasingly greater emphasis and pressure was placed on that relation. Beyond the variations of cooperation and conflict in particular periods, more fundamental developments have taken place in the American system which have affected the relation between the president and the media. These developments are important to understand if we are to fully grasp the nature of that relation—as well as the relation between Congress and the media.

We have previously noted the decline in the role played by political parties in the political system and the corresponding rise in candidate evaluations in people's electoral and other political choices. As has been pointed out, people correspondingly rely more heavily on the mass media for information and impressions on candidates, officers, and issues. Further, various major developments in the twentieth century, such as the two World Wars, the Great Depression, and technological creations such as nuclear missiles, have moved the nation to look to the president in an increasingly primary way for direction of and for government.[3]

The consequences of the combination of those factors for the media–government relation, and for governance of society itself, are profound. Drawing on a remarkably prescient earlier report on parties and the American system by a committee of leading political scientists, Theodore Lowi has recently pointed out the consequences of those developments (in a striking, deeply concerned book on the presidency):

> A system that vests such [great] responsibility in the president can work well enough as long as the program has been democratically formulated within the president's party. However, when there is no party support for a broad program [or when it is not coherent], the president has no choice but to work up a program of his own and then go out and build the necessary popular support for it. Here, according to the committee, are the implications of that way of operating: "In effect this concept of the presidency disposes of the party system by making the President reach directly for the support of a majority of the voters. It favors a president who exploits skillfully the arts of demagoguery . . . and who does not mind turning into the embodiment of personal government."[4]

This is just what has happened, says Lowi: The "plebscitary presidency" is the result. As political scientist Samuel Kernell observes: "Impatient with Washington politics, [presidents] are inclined more than ever to 'go public'"[5] on each given issue, rather than seeking to build enduring party coalitions, for stable governance. The central means used for going public are speeches and appearances carried and covered in the mass media. Kernell has documented a dramatic increase in such public appeals by more recent presidents.[6] As Lowi puts it, we have an increasingly personalized presidency at the increasingly prominent and increasingly emphasized center of the American political universe. Correspondingly, the mass media have increasingly become the primary instrument of the conduct of this personalized political enterprise, both in news coverage and in use of the media for more direct communication to the public and other political people. This then places a premium on the media–government relation and on the need to understand it.

Five Functions of the Media–Government Relation for Presidents and Other Institutions   There are five basic functions performed by the media–government relation in the case of presidents. These functions are also performed with respect to Congress and the other governmental institutions, although at different levels and in different fashion.

The first basic function is to tell the public about how the Presidency itself is being conducted by the incumbent, *and* about the Presidency *as part* of the institutional structure and processes of the government as a whole. The second function is that of the mass media providing a means through which the president (and other officials) can communicate directly with the public. As was discussed in Chapter 4, the media of radio and then, more dramatically, of television added striking dimensions to the capacity to communicate directly with the public. The third function is the channel the media provide to the president to communicate with other officials, and vice versa.

The fourth function is partially related to the third: communication through the media of political feedback from other political actors and from the general public. For presidents, the mass media have long been crucial sources from which to learn the political response to what they have done. The media are even more so today. George Reedy, former presidential press secretary, has expressed the point best: "The significant impact of the press upon the president lies not in its critical reflections but in its capacity to tell him what he is doing as seen through other eyes." In fact, as Reedy points out, despite the complaints of a series of presidents about "their press," "the reality is that a president has no press problems [that is, they have no problems getting just about all the media attention they want], but [a president] does have political problems, all of which are reflected in their most acute form by the press."[7]

The fifth basic function of the media in relation to the government is to transmit to the president and other officials information about events and developments. The *New York Times* and the *Washington Post* normally get much relevant information to the president faster than official channels, even on foreign affairs. Another side of this function is the need of presidents to review principal news sources to know what the public is receiving as "the news" about public affairs. David Halberstam's recounting of President Kennedy's attitude best illustrates the point:

> The door to Kennedy's office was always open, a surprisingly large number of people could drop in and chat with the President of the United States. But when the Huntley–Brinkley [NBC News] or the Cronkite [CBS News] show was on, everything stopped. . . . He felt that what went on these shows was terribly important. Perhaps it was not reality . . . , *but it was what the country perceived as reality.* . . . He felt he could not respond to the country if he did not know what voices it was hearing.[8]

Coverage of the Presidency and Comparison with Congress

The Presidency: Focus of News Coverage of Government   The president has increasingly become the central focus of national news coverage of government. Now one study suggested a basic equality in coverage between the Presidency and Congress, with newspapers giving somewhat more coverage to Congress and network TV news paying more attention to the president (by a slightly greater margin).[9] This study is cited approvingly by

Graber, who adds data from her own study of three Chicago newspapers to support the same conclusion.[10] Further, Graber states that the advantage the president has in sheer amount of TV coverage is reduced in its "usefulness as a booster for the president" since "much television coverage was highly negative."[11] Those two studies were each conducted during a single year, however. And as was discussed and documented in Chapter 4 (see especially pp. 69–71), while the verbal content of network TV coverage may, at times, be rather negative, the *visual* content tends to be exceedingly positive, which has a big impact (more on White House control over those pictures a little later).

Beyond those points of critique, another more complete study has documented the emphasis on the Presidency in the news. Richard Davis did a content analysis of a large selection of news stories from CBS News, a major newspaper (the *Los Angeles Times*), and a medium-sized paper (the *Syracuse Post-Standard*) over the period 1969–1983. He omitted election years to isolate "normal" news coverage. Davis found that "the presidency dominated the news coverage of national governmental institutions. Over one-half of the stories [on institutions] in this study concentrated on the presidency as the primary institution of the story. Only slightly more than one-third of the stories sampled reported on Congress primarily."[12] Further, "two-thirds of the stories about Congress . . . included the presidency as a secondary institution," whereas only a third of stories primarily on the presidency mentioned Congress. In sum, "Congress, then, was viewed [by the media] not as a separate branch, but one that was important due to its relationship to the presidency."[13] A gradual trend through the century toward prime emphasis on presidents has, in fact, been observed for many years.[14] Davis found that "the frequency of presidency stories rose steadily during the period under study (1969–1983),"[15] a pattern Grossman and Kumar also found through the 1950s, 1960s, and 1970s in their major study of national media coverage of the presidency in the *New York Times*, *Time*, and CBS News. (They found a partial exception in CBS News, largely due to study timing and the availability of film records.)[16] Indeed, Grossman and Kumar found that "the President represents the single most important story that the network follows on a continuing basis," and "the White House stories in each issue or broadcast represented a major portion of the news space or time" in each medium (an average of almost nine White House articles, two on the front page, in each issue of the *New York Times,* for example).[17]

The Nature of Presidential Coverage and Phases of the Relation Grossman and Kumar also found that coverage of the presidency by the two national print media (*Time* and the *New York Times*) tended to be quite positive in tone; specifically, two favorable stories were presented to one unfavorable story. CBS News was found, at least at first glance, to present far fewer favorable stories and more negative ones. But since the late Vietnam and the Watergate eras comprised about half of the total period CBS was studied, those figures are distorted.[18] Further, strikingly, and affirming the discussion in the later parts of Chapter 4, Grossman and Kumar found the *pictures* in all three media to be very favorable (although somewhat less so in the case of CBS—again, the totals were affected by the late Vietnam and Watergate periods). In fact, "pictures often are favorable even when they accompany an unfavorable story."[19] A fascinating illustration of this is reported by David Broder:

> Lesley Stahl, CBS News's White House correspondent . . . learned to her chagrin how pictures can override even the most biting commentary.
> During the 1984 campaign [October 4, to be specific], she put together a four-and-a-half minute piece that showed how far the White House had gone in staging events for Reagan. "It was a very tough piece," Stahl said later. . . . "I was very nervous about going back to the White House the next day. But the show was no more than off the air, when a White House official called me and congratulated me on it and he'd loved it. I said, 'How could you love it?' And he said, 'Haven't you figured it out yet? The public doesn't pay any attention to what you say. They just look at the pictures.'" Stahl said she looked at the piece again, with the sound off, and realized that what she had shown was a magnificent montage of Reagan in a series of wonderful, upbeat scenes, with flags, balloons, children, and adoring supporters—virtually an unpaid campaign commercial.[20]

Speaking of pictures a note should be added here on a major change in the history of the president's relation with the news media. The change concerns the visual medium of television. As Grossman and Kumar observed: "The most conspicuous changes in the relationship between the White House and news organizations since the 1950s can be traced to the growing perception by White House officials that television is the most important medium for the President to dominate."[21] President Ford's press secretary Ron Nessen expressed it more colorfully. He said, "television is reality," and "if it hasn't happened on television, it hasn't happened."[22]

The nature of presidential coverage is not uniform through a given president's term (something most people already sense). But there are patterns to the changes in presidential coverage, Grossman and Kumar found. They concluded there are three basic phases through which presidential coverage and the White House–news media relationship tends to go. In the first phase, cooperation is great between the White House and the news media and the coverage is normally very favorable. The news media is eager for news and, in accordance with the traditional "honeymoon period" for a president, they are usually very accommodating in carrying the president's message. The White House is equally eager to assist the news organizations in gathering stories, both to build the goodwill of the news people and to get the White House's concerns and a good general image more completely to the public and other officials. But sooner or later, phase one cooperation breaks down and a kind of competition between the White House and the news media breaks out, with repeated efforts by the White House to manipulate coverage and "keep the lid on" some stories, and with accessibility to officials lessening. Meanwhile, reporters suspect White House motives and are less accommodating (in intent, at least) in carrying the White House message in unedited fashion. The third phase Grossman and Kumar call "detachment." White House officials " . . . are more concerned about preventing reporters from seeing their flaws than in getting them to prepare stories that will be favorable to their policies." White House officials are much less accessible to reporters and reporters more often look elsewhere for sources.[23]

The Nature of the White House Beat and the "Washington Reporters" Covering It   The Presidency is the reporting "beat" of first emphasis for American news organizations. What is that beat like? The first two things that should be noted apply not only to the White House beat, they apply to Washington reporting in general.

Washington reporters and their editors generally see "the news" on government institutions and their officers as "hard news," meaning, as a rule, new developments, especially tangible events (usually those occurring in the previous 24 hours). Stephen Hess found that 80% of Washington stories are about events.[24] This is in accordance with basic news criteria: some action involving prominent, well-known people. This is especially the case for presidents, who, as head of state, are involved in so many official events. Reporters have an interesting name for the constant news need to follow and cover the president; they call it "the body watch," that is, physically monitoring the president and reporting his activities (including the threat of assassination). Obviously, given this preoccupation with ostensible activities, there is little reporter time and news space for reports on the nature of institutions, processes, background, current facts and analyses of issues, or review of alternative policy proposals. Additionally, there are consequences that stem from the concentration on events—consequences for officials' manipulation of the news. This problem is discussed below, after other aspects and conditions of presidential coverage are reviewed, and after a second point is made about Washington reporters in general.

Now what methods do reporters use to cover the Presidency (and other institutions)? While Washington reporters, like all news people in major media, have increasingly higher levels of education, the techniques for gathering news "stories" have not changed much from earlier eras. Especially for the Presidency, and for Congress and other "political" areas, the physical coverage of events and the interview of relevant officials and interested parties are the techniques used. Documents (reports, etc.) are not usually used. Stephen Hess found that for three-fourths of their stories, reporters used no documents; and even when they did use some, other newspaper articles were the most frequent source. Documentary research by reporters for primary materials to verify assertions of interviewees and to raise further questions is rare—in fact, few news operations as a whole have facilities for serious documents research. The exception is the Supreme Court beat, which requires attention to court opinions, legal briefs, and so on, and which involves reporting circumstances that minimize interview opportunities. The noninstitutional, subject "beats" of economics and science are also exceptions to the nonuse of documents.[25]

What about the reporters themselves? The White House is the number one beat in coverage and in corresponding visibility for the journalist. It is thus a prime journalistic assignment, which in theory at least, attracts many of the best senior reporters or the better younger talents with bright futures. Again, White House reporters have increased higher education compared with past eras, although that education is mostly in mass communications/journalism. The pattern that was noted in Chapters 6 and 7 regarding lack of specialized training in the subject reporters are covering, in this case, the Presidency, is also found here. More White House reporters are "generalists with a broad background as political correspondents," Grossman and Kumar found; indeed, "reporters did not regard the presidency itself as an area about which it was necessary to acquire specialized knowledge and information."[26]

As discussed in Chapters 6 and 7, the consequences of the lack of such training are great for the ability to place presidents' actions and statements, and White House organization and policies, in historical context and for the capacity to resist manipulation. And Grossman and Kumar found, "as a result, White House correspondents skim the substance of many issues to focus on politics or personalities."[27] These problems are most painfully evident in many press conferences (discussed further below). The informational and educational value of news coverage for the public certainly suffers as a result of these problems.

There are also difficulties in coverage having nothing directly to do with reporters' training and news inclinations, but rather with the circumstances in which they must work at the White House (and with the "presidential road show"). Working in these special circumstances, physically inside a wing of the White House, largely under White House rules, makes for a very difficult reporting situation. Grossman and Kumar have described the situation well:

> The atmosphere there provides a life support system rich in the ingredients that enhance a journalist's status but thin in elements that encourage high-enterprise reporting. . . . [I]n order to cover the Chief Executive's activities, correspondents allow officials to herd them to [the daily news] briefings, ceremonies, and conferences where they are fed a diet of statements, [press] releases, and rehearsed answers. . . .

Reporters congregate in the briefing room and the adjoining press areas at the center of the public White House, where they hope to get a sense of what is going on inside the private areas. What they get are echoes of their own thoughts rather than cross-currents of information flowing among White House officials. "The press room is hermetically sealed," remarked *National Journal* correspondent Dom Bonafede. . . . [Reporter] Andrew Glass [said] . . . , "You have no idea of what they're really doing. . . . The only time you see them on the job is in a situation stage-managed by them."[28]

Over the past three decades another factor has contributed to the worsening of that situation: the threat of assassination and the White House reponse. Since the assassination of President Kennedy, each administration has restricted the physical contact of the president with the public—and, variously, with reporters. The Reagan White House affected a quantum increase in those restrictions. George Reedy, former press secretary for President Johnson, has reflected perceptively on the consequences of this restriction of contact. Reedy noted the increasing tendency to wrap tight security barriers around the president "whenever he ventures outside the grounds" and the increasing tendency to substitute the use of television for real human contact and interaction. This is especially troubling in the case of presidents who are so easily isolated in the White House, surrounded by ambitious aides who tend to tell the president what he wants to hear. The distinct danger of this combination of a security-buffered and isolated television-reliant president is: "It is a means by which a man can conduct a monologue *in* public and convince himself that he is conducting a dialogue *with* the public." This is a dangerous psychology.[29]

The circumstances in which reporters work in covering the White House have another unfortunate impact: They encourage pack journalism. Grossman and Kumar found this consequence, and they found quite a few White House reporters who recognized it and lamented it. Indeed, the frustration appears to be considerable, as Hess found:

> Just about every White House correspondent made a critical comment about the beat: "We're in small quarters with access to only a small number of official people, getting the same information. So we write similar stories and move on the same issues." "The focus is too much on surface events." "Too much pack or herd journalism."[30]

James Naughton of the *New York Times* expressed another consequence of profound importance: "There is no place where a correspondent can be more easily led than at the White House."[31] Veteran reporter Peter Lisagor expresses this consequence in a very revealing way. The restrictions and routines in which White House reporters are forced to operate constitute a principal reason that there is so little investigative reporting by White House correspondents; indeed, "the White House is the last place the Watergate story would have broken."[32]

President's Use of the Media: Means and Methods

The Presidency is in a class by itself as a position from which to communicate; no other position comes close. Even early in the twentieth century, Theodore Roosevelt called the White House a "bully pulpit" for communicating presidential concerns. George Reedy, in light of his experience as presidential press secretary, expressed it this way:

> As a stage [from which to send a message—or just get attention], the White House has no equal in the electronic age. It is equipped with props that cannot be matched by Hollywood, Broadway, and Madison Avenue combined. . . . And above all, it has the faculty of commanding the instant and total attention of television networks that dominate the largest audience in all history.[33]

What are the ways in which presidents use the media to communicate to the public and other officials, and how, in general, is the White House communication operation organized? We look at those questions next.

Organization of the White House Press and Publicity Operations   Even through the time of that early master of the media, Franklin Roosevelt, the White House press and publicity operation amounted to four or five staff people (fewer, before FDR). By the 1980s, the White House press and publicity operation had grown dramatically. In the Reagan White House, at least 50 staff members were assigned to such duties, and they operated out of an elaborate office structure.

Two general offices form the main parts of that office structure. The better known of the two is the Office of the Press Secretary. Using the Reagan administration for illustration, besides the Press Secretary himself, there were several assistants to the Press Secretary and a series of Deputy Press Secretaries and other assistants. There was also a News Summary and Audio Service, which provided summaries of news coverage of relevance to the White House, along with related services. The second office was the Office of Communications, headed by the Director of Communications. Beyond that officer's assistants, there were several suboffices. They included Speechwriting and Research, Media Relations and Planning, Public Affairs, Communications Planning, and Public Liaison. In addition, in the Reagan administration (through 1985) the Deputy Chief of Staff was Michael Deaver, whose principal duty, in practice, was the arrangement of media treatment of the president and the promotion of the president's image. A number of assistants in his office were involved in various specific elements of media strategy and operations.[34] Media strategy sessions were frequent and planning more elaborate in than ever before in the Reagan administration, before Deaver left and after.[35]

The Presidential News Conference   Since Franklin Roosevelt's administration, the presidential press conference has generally been seen as a principal way for the public and the press to hear and see the president discuss developments and issues of importance. The press conference has also been seen by many as one very public way to keep the president accountable—to keep him answerable for actions taken and proposed. In Britain, the prime minister must submit herself to a Question Hour before Parliament once a week. There is no counterpart to Question Hour in the United States (due in part to tradition and to interpretation of the separation of powers idea); the presidential press conference is the rough substitute. It is not an adequate substitute, in most cases.

The presidential press conference has its origins as far back as Theodore Roosevelt, although it was with Franklin Roosevelt that the press conference became something of an institution—and the expectation of regular conferences was established. The first live, televised presidential news conference was held by President Kennedy. With the use of television, press conferences (like many other political activities) changed dramatically. The press conference was transformed from a relatively simple interaction between president and press, where the former responded to developments and to reporters' questions, to a dramatic performance before a mass audience.

In form and in appearance, the presidential press conference is a forum where the president exposes himself to the questioning of many professional journalists. Indeed, at times the questions have probed presidential actions and elicited answers of a significant nature. But that is not the reality of the typical press conference. There are from several dozen up to 200 or so reporters at press conferences. Most want to ask their own question—and to be *seen* doing so on national TV (in front of their editors). "Their own question" means just that: There is virtually no coordination or collaboration on questioning and most have their question written out in advance. What this means, especially with dozens of reporters clamoring for recognition by the president each time he appears to finish an answer, is that there is no concerted follow-up, no consistent pressing of a question to pin down an answer. Even a moderately accomplished president finds it easy to give a nice-sounding generalization or a witty one-liner and skip on to something else. Presidents are also able to anticipate most questions in advance, with help from various assistants, and to prepare carefully crafted answers in advance (including those one-liners). Increasingly in recent years, presidents have also begun the conference with a "statement" of some length on matters they wish to express to press and (especially) public—thus partly turning what is intended to be a two-way question-and-answer session into a one-way free presidential speech to the nation. George Reedy has memorably summarized the experience (with irony dripping from his pen): "When televised, [the press conference] has become as spontaneous as a Javanese temple dance but without the grace which makes the latter such a deeply moving experience"; and "any president who has done his homework will emerge unscathed. . . . It is a breeze."[36]

Despite that situation, which is so favorable to the president, two presidents in the TV era have avoided press conferences assiduously: Nixon and Reagan. Nixon held only 37 in his resignation-shortened presidency, an average of only one every two months. As Nixon always distrusted the media and as he was not a very media-genic person, this was not too surprising—if lamentable for the American system. Reagan had held only 42 press conferences (counting one in Venice) as of late 1987—an even lower frequency level than Nixon.[37] This is puzzling for one who was so media-genic, who had been a professional before the camera and microphone, and who had been called "the great communicator." But in press conferences, as was noted earlier, Reagan had repeated problems in responding to questions. Despite increasing criticism from the news media and other politics watchers, fewer and fewer press conference appearances were made.

Two other implications of and responses to the Reagan approach to the press conference function should be pointed out. First, the attitude of the Reagan White House regarding the avoidance of press conferences was revealing, and troubling, given the implications for the democratic process in the media age. *Newsweek* summed up well: "Reagan's handlers admit . . . they have cut back on news conferences in favor of prime-time speeches because the president does better reading a prepared text than he does thinking on his feet. They also suggest that with national esteem for the press at an all time low, they can safely ignore complaints from the media."[38] Second, and strikingly, this author discovered evidence that the TV image overcame the substantive difficulties Reagan had in press conferences, in a number of people's minds (how many is unclear). In experimental research, some people *spontaneously* mentioned how *well* Reagan came across in news conferences. As one who "leaned Democratic" said, strikingly: "The press conferences always went well. He was confident when he spoke, he would answer questions without hesitation."[39] Reagan *looked* good and confident before the camera, which is what a good many people appear to have remembered, rather than the substance of his answers.

One other means of news dissemination by the White House should be mentioned here: "backgrounders." An interview "on background" is one in which a White House staffer, or the president himself, discusses developments and issues with one or more reporters *but with* the *ground rule* that the material will not be directly attributed to the person. (That "high administration source" you so frequently here about is the result.) Reporters get more material this way than they probably would otherwise. But especially since a high percentage of White House–press interaction is on this basis, there are troubling consequences. The potential for manipulation is higher, with no direct accountability, and it encourages self-serving, not necessarily accurate leaks.

Direct Communication through TV: Presidential Addresses   As was noted earlier, presidents have increasingly sought to use the TV airwaves, usually in prime time, as their direct channel to the public. The networks nearly always accede to requests for a presidential address. A striking example of that network accommodation occurred just 20 days before the 1982 "off-year" general election when President Reagan received time from two of the three networks (ABC was the exception) for a speech "on the economic situation." As the state of the economy was the number one issue in late 1982 and "Reaganomics" was at the center of the debate, network granting of evening time for a "presidential" speech was a striking example of the obeisance to presidential prerogatives. (That anyone could have misunderstood the political purpose of the speech strains credulity. Indeed, prior to the presidential request, the Republican National Committee had sought to buy a similar block of time but was turned down.) On rare occasions a president is refused air time, but it is rare. Partly moderating this striking political advantage, as noted in Chapter 5, is the response time normally given to the opposition party to reply to presidential speeches (although sometimes that response time is late in the evening or even on another day).

Leaks   Assistant Secretary of State for Inter-American Affairs in the Reagan administration, Langhorne Motley, testified before a congressional committee that Central American policy had been disrupted by "premature unauthorized partial disclosures."[40] These are better known as "leaks." Leaks have been a method of communicating to the public and other officials for quite some time, although the method may have intensified in use over the past three decades. Presidential complaints about leaks, usually directed at Congress or the bureaucracy, seem to have intensified during that time. In reality, the White House is at least as frequent a source of leaks as other institutions. Leaking is used for sending up trial balloons on policy proposals, for discrediting another person and their position (often related to internal White House struggles for preeminence), and for other purposes. The danger for reporters, especially given the high number of unattributable backgrounder interviews, is that they can be used for officials' personal agendas rather than reflecting authentic White House policy.

"Photo Opps" and the Presidential Picture Parade   In Chapter 4, theory and empirical evidence were presented which demonstrated the impor-

tance of the visual dimension of the news for public impressions of presidents—and ultimately for people's evaluations of them. Literally, the picture of the president that appears on the TV screen and in the news magazines and newspapers is a picture with impact. White House operations personnel, at least since President Kennedy, have been very aware of this. Especially since Nixon, each presidency has exerted major efforts to make that picture as cumulatively positive as possible. In the Reagan presidency this concern was raised to remarkable heights; it was, in fact, central to White House operations.

There are several aspects of this purveyance of the presidential picture. Increasingly, over the past few decades, "photo opportunities" (or "photo opps" as they are known in the business) have been prime elements of the presidential picture parade. Presidential pictures have been principal material for news organizations, especially for TV and for the news magazines (with their color photo layouts), but also for newspapers. Some significant questions are raised by the White House direction of photo opportunities and dissemination of photos and by the news media's preoccupation with presidential pictures.

The constant, large appetite of the news media for pictures of presidential activities gives the White House an excellent, ongoing opportunity to have positive pictures appear in the media. The direct method is to have a White House photographer take pictures and then distribute them to the news media. This is especially effective if the president is not very accessible, as in the Reagan case. An excellent example of what results in many cases can be seen in *Time,* September 9, 1985. The first and largest story in the national news section was of President Reagan's return to Washington from vacationing at his California ranch and the political and policy battles he faced. The story was headlined "Back in the Saddle Again" and was topped by a one-third page photo of Reagan sitting (tall in the saddle) on horseback. This all looks like a *Time* news-and-photo story. But it isn't (as the fine print shows); the feature photo, which obviously was used as the story theme, was a *White House* photo. For the casual observer, the White House got just the *picture* it wanted of Reagan in the leading national news magazine.[41]

Photo opportunities are appearances, normally by the president, at some place, usually with one or more people, where the White House allows the news media into the room or at the site to take pictures (a meeting with another head of state, business leaders, the Olympic hockey team, a tour of a new factory, etc.). The rules are set by the White House. In all recent administrations, this has meant substantial White House control over the nature of the pictures taken and hence of what the public *sees*. In the Reagan White House (as in the Nixon White House, but even more completely) that control was extreme.

One aspect of that control was most interesting: at these supposed "news events," the White House did not allow any questions of the president. (Reporters were particularly insistent in their questioning since Reagan rarely held press conferences and since the press were kept distant from the president elsewhere and hence could not effectively question him.) After the first couple of years, the Reagan White House absolutely banned questions of the president at these photo opportunities, or, they threatened, the reporters would be barred and only the cameras allowed in. Astonishingly, although the reporters protested, their superiors at the networks accepted these conditions. This raises a question: photo *"opportunity"* for whom?! As ABC's Sam Donaldson has said, representing TV correspondents: "They [the White House] don't need us as long as they capture our cameras."[42]

Full Court Press: Control of Media Access and Information in the Reagan White House

The control of pictures emanating from the Reagan White House was, in fact, only part of an extraordinary, comprehensive process of controlling news media access to and information from the Reagan presidency. Very troubling questions were raised by these news management efforts. Before turning to the Reagan control efforts, it should be noted that the Reagan administration drew on basic patterns and tactics of restriction of news media access and control of information established by the Nixon White House.[43]

There were three basic elements of the Reagan White House efforts in news and information control. First, they restricted news media access to the president to an extraordinary extent, even more so than in the Nixon presidency. As *Newsweek* said, "despite big smiles for the cameras, Ronald Reagan is the least accessible president in modern U.S. history. Helen Thomas, long-time White House correspondent for United Press International, says that even Richard Nixon during the depths of Watergate was sometimes easier to approach."[44] Although prime-time TV addresses and presidential appearances and speeches were many, the working press were allowed very little access to the President where they could ask questions. Indeed, reporters were physically kept at a distance from the president— and when the president was leaving the White House to helicopter somewhere, the engines were deliberately revved up to drown out reporters' shouted attempts at questioning. (Ironically, that need to shout, if reporters were to do their jobs and ask questions, appeared to many viewers of TV news as simply the acts of a bunch of rude and unruly reporters who did not respect the presidency.) In fact, President Reagan was so inaccessible to reporters that by later 1982 Helen Thomas had taken to calling him "the invisible man."

But "invisible man" Reagan was certainly *not* invisible to the *viewing*

public. The second element of the news control efforts, which built on the first to maximize its effectiveness, was a comprehensive and constantly applied media strategy. The construction and review of the media strategy was seen by the Reagan White House as central to their presidency and was a "major part of the workday of senior aides." These efforts, as David Broder has pointed out, were "designed to define and dominate primarily [the] night's network news programs and secondarily the next morning's newspaper headlines." Carefully staging presidential appearances, which were carefully crafted to reinforce the White House message, was a central part of these efforts. Broder notes a prime tactic involved—and the aide chiefly responsible for it: "[Michael] Deaver understood that providing certain pictures of the President—and no others—could largely determine that night's television story." That is, the White House mapped out a theme of the day, decided on a speech or event which would get across the message or image they wanted, and then would allow news cameras into no other activity involving the president.[45] Given the networks' focus on the Presidency and their insatiable appetite for film, the White House frequently got the story they wanted on the news, especially the visuals and the basic theme. (The White House understood the deadline and other news production constraints and made good use of them.)

    The culmination (or ultimate application) of those two basic elements of the Reagan news management strategy came in the invasion of the island nation of Grenada in the fall of 1983. Unlike major U.S. military manuevers of the past, the news media were not allowed to go along on the invasion and they were banned from going to the island in any manner for two full days. In fact, the military went to great lengths, including threats, airplane harassment of boats, and effective military confinement, to keep the news media out. For about a week thereafter reporters and camera crews were allowed only in small "pool" groups, and these groups went only where and observed only what the military directed. The result was that the public, during the prime news period, received *only* the administration's and the military's account of what transpired and only the pictures that the administration and the military wished seen.[46] No "TV war" as in Vietnam would be seen. These actions raised the gravest questions about the function of a free press, able to report to the public, on an independent basis, what was going on. How are officials to be held accountable if the only "news" people get is the government line and government-censored pictures?

   . . . And Secrecy and Information Restrictions, as Well (The Third Element)   The Reagan administration made efforts to take the control of news a step further; they sought to affect greater control of government information. As the *National Journal* summarized: "Constitutional lawyers, scholars, prominent journalists and public interest advocates widely agree that the Reagan administration, generally under the cloak of national security, has taken an unprecedentedly narrow view of First Amendment rights involving free speech and . . . press." This was done through a number of actions, the three most important of which (beyond what was reported above) were as follows.

   The administration took steps to broaden the *exemptions* from the Freedom of Information Act (FOIA), which was enacted to give citizens, including the media, access to government information, in accordance with basic democratic principles of official accountability for actions. The administration also took steps, principally through an executive order of the president (not subject to congressional approval), to expand the "discretion of federal agencies to classify information for an indefinite period. The order further allows the withholding of information that merely relates to national security or foreign affairs and provides authority to reclassify information already in the public domain." This was an effort to further restrict public access to information on the government's conduct of a variety of affairs. Finally, CIA Director William Casey publicly threatened to bring criminal charges against any news organization that supposedly violated certain national security laws, as determined by Casey. These were striking actions in restriction of the media's right to report and the public's right to know.[47] (It should be noted further that a program of "disinformation," of deliberate spreading of untrue stories through the media about Libya, was also engaged in by the Reagan administration, actions that raised troubling questions about what and who could be believed.[48])

David Broder has expressed an interesting thought on all this: "It is no accident, in my view, that we have had recurrent secrecy-caused scandals in the administrations of Presidents who refused to meet regularly with the press. Frequent news conferences [and other forms of real interaction with the press] are an antidote to secrecy and an effective deterrent against official misbehavior."[49]

Coverage of Congress

The Nature of Congress   Congress is a very different institution than the Presidency. This, in itself, is presumably not a news flash for the reader; but there are important implications for the media–government relation stemming from the different nature of that institution.

The Presidency is a single-headed institution. Congress, of course, is composed of 100 senators and 435 representatives. Even at the leadership level, the institution of Congress is multiheaded, with a speaker, a majority leader, minority leaders and whips from each party, as well as the various committee chairs in the House; and there are the majority leader and whip and minority leader and whip, plus the committee chairs in the Senate. The legislative process is fundamentally a multistage process, with normal legislation having to go through at least one subcommittee and committee, the Rules Committee, and debate on the floor in the House and the same stages in the Senate, except for the Rules Committee. Major bills usually require a conference committee, as well, to resolve differences in bills "coming out" of each house, followed by another floor vote in both houses. Further, the full House and Senate operate differently in floor debates. Additionally, most of the prime work of Congress occurs in the committees and involves complex bargaining, compromise, and other such person-to-person politically involved interaction which is not inherently visual in nature and which needs to be done out of the glare of cameras.

These characteristics do not lend themselves to easy coverage on 60 seconds of videotape. It is important to keep in mind when the nature of news coverage of Congress is reviewed below that the institution of Congress is the prime institution designed for the resolution of basic conflicts in society; that is a *main* function of the national legislature in a representative political system. Correspondingly, especially in difficult times, that there would be disagreement and conflict in Congress is not something which indicates that Congress is flawed or includes a bunch of mere bickerers; it is part of what the institution is there for. Finally, we should remember that Congress, especially the House, is a national institution *based* on more *local constituencies;* House members are elected from local (or statewide, at-large) districts, and Senators are elected from particular states.

Coverage of Congress

Amount of Coverage   In an earlier section we noted that the presidency has increasingly received more coverage than Congress. It would appear that coverage of Congress has declined, in general. Davis, in his study of non-election-year coverage of government institutions from 1969 through 1983, found that stories about Congress decreased, both compared with the presidency and in absolute terms. Specifically, in CBS News, the *Los Angeles Times* (elite newspaper), and the *Syracuse Post-Standard* (more a local paper) in 1969 and 1971, barely under half of stories about government institutions concerned Congress, and half concerned the Presidency. By 1981 and 1983, only one-fourth of such stories concerned Congress, while over 60% concerned the Presidency.[50] Greg Schneiders found the same sort of drop in his study of congressional coverage.[51] Further, stories about the Presidency were not only more frequent than those on Congress, but they were featured more prominently (more front-page coverage, etc.).[52]

Nature of Coverage: Institution and Individuals   The most striking aspect of the way that Congress is covered concerns the treatment of the institution. Although more research is needed to fully document this empirically, coverage of Congress as an institution seems to have a negative tone to it (in contrast to the overall tone of presidential coverage). Michael Robinson reports an instance that illustrates the tone of—and the attitude behind—a fair amount of reporting on the institution in the media. When, in 1976, the Supreme Court handed down its major ruling on the federal law regulating campaign finance (in *Buckley* v. *Valeo*), it gave Congress 30 days to refashion the Federal Elections Commission. David Brinkley of NBC News made the revealing comment: "It is widely believed in Washington that it would take Congress thirty days to make instant coffee."[53] Such a media attitude and corresponding pattern of reporting has led Congressman David Obey (D–Wisc.) to say: "[Network reporting] is a smirking way of covering this institution . . . just one more raindrop eating away at the rock of public understanding of a very complicated institution."[54] The consequences of such coverage are, then, significant for Congress in performing its role, the congressman contends.

Robinson and Appel have provided some empirical evidence of those reporting patterns. They reviewed all stories on Congress carried on ABC, CBS, and NBC network news over a five-week period in early 1976, coding each story as positive, neutral, or negative. Most stories were neutral by their criteria (86%), but 14% were negative and *none* were positive.[55]

A remarkable contrast to that coverage of the institution is found when we consider the coverage of *individual* members by the *local* news media. The local media tend to cover the local Congresspersons in a very positive fashion and to be readily accepting of press releases, appearances at events, video pieces from the floor of Congress sent by a Congressperson's offices, and so on.[56] This contrast between coverage of the institution of Congress and local media coverage of individual members is one of the key factors explaining a major paradox in American politics: For the last three decades the public expressed generally low and decreasing confidence in the institution of Congress, while at the same time the public was reelecting House members at an average rate of 90% and Senate members at a rate of 75% or more.

Corresponding to the media age in general and reelection needs in specific, Congresspersons have become increasingly attentive to the news media connection. To illustrate, as Cook reports, "the percentage of House [members] offices listing no press aide . . . has fallen . . . from 84% in 1970 to only 28% in 1984."[57]

Now that finding leads us to an issue that has received considerable discussion. A number of writers and some political scientists have suggested that the TV age has led to a new breed of Congressperson gaining prominence through the media—the "show horse"; and that they no longer need to "play by inside [House or Senate] rules to receive inside rewards or avoid inside setbacks." It has also been suggested that electronic media coverage has "given younger members and maverick members more political visibility—and consequently greater power."[58]

Media scholar Stephen Hess has found, however, that the great majority of senators receive little or no coverage in the national media, that a few senators receive the vast majority of coverage *because* of their leadership positions—or because they are seeking the presidency. He also found that mavericks and "show horse" senators who sought national media attention either received little or receive attention *because* they were in one of those leadership categories. These patterns, Hess found, had held rather constant for three decades.[59] These patterns are the reason "most members' press operations concentrate largely on the local media. . . . The local media . . . were generally [seen] as the principal, most dependable and most important customers for a member's press officers."[60]

Why this pattern of coverage of leaders rather than flashy news seekers? Hess explains that the media, *especially* TV, have limited reporting resources and news holes, so they can only follow some people and parts of the process, and the way to decide which to follow has been power—chamber and committee leadership, or presidential aspirations (if at all credible). As Hess observes: "The (major) print media exclude the powerless; the electronic media exclude the powerless and the inarticulate."[61] By roughly the same logic, the Senate (with fewer members and greater constitutional duties) usually receives more media attention than the House. (An exception occurred during 1980–1984 when the Democrats, as "opposition party," controlled only the House and Speaker O'Neill was looked to as that party's prime spokesman in opposition to President Reagan.)

Still, one should not take too far Hess's conclusion about the nearly sole focus of the media on the leadership; nor should one take his suggestion about the futility of others seeking media attention and conclude that the media, especially television, are not a decidedly greater factor in the congressional process than they used to be. There is simply too much testimony by principals involved that TV has had a major impact on how individual members act. Richard Bolling, central figure in the House through the 1970s and early 1980s, has said that TV is the "key change" in the media–government relation in two decades, and that "the independence of current congressmen is attributable in large part to their ability to maintain an image through television which is separate from their role in the actual lawmaking process." Joseph Califano, key aide to President Johnson and cabinet member for President Carter, said, "when you go up on the Hill now . . . and you hear [them] talk, they'll talk about did they make page one of the *Post* . . . , *and* talk about whether they got thirty seconds on the evening news. . . . All you have to do is look at the *Congressional Record* in the House on any significant debate and you can find fifty good quotes because they're all fighting to be one of those guys who gets into the Rather coverage."[62]

In summary, then, the party and committee leadership logically receive the lion's share of attention, but otherwise Congress, as an institution, tends to receive a rather negative press. This is ironic, since the Congress beat is far more appreciated by reporters than the presidential beat (which usually receives such positive coverage); it is "the best beat in town," as Kumar and Grossman[63] have summarized those feelings. This is because there are many sources for reporters to turn to, the principals in Congress tend to be more open and accessible than the president and senior White House staff, and there are always at least a few colorful characters in Congress to spice up a story.

Nature of Coverage: Process and Policy   As was reviewed above, the congressional process is an elaborate one, involving a complex process of political interaction and policy formulation and enactment. Unfortunately, that entire legislative process does not get covered, as a rule. Rather, floor debates, preferably dramatic ones with conflicting Congresspersons in full cry, and some committee hearings get most coverage. Investigative hearings, especially those with dramatic testimony, and some committee hearings on bills of obvious major public concern, receive principal attention at the committee stage.[64] Some committees receive more coverage than others (led in the Senate by the Foreign Relations, Judiciary, and Budget Committees). The earlier stages of the process receive little or no coverage, especially on TV news.[65] This is a serious problem in coverage because it is in those stages where the prime work on policy formulation is done. To wait until floor debates to cover a legislative issue is to report what is principally a ratification exercise. In a participatory democracy, citizens need information *before* decisions are "done deeds" if they are to have a chance to express their concerns.

As that observation suggests, the substance of policy considered in the congressional process receives rather little treatment in the news media, as well. Notions of who won or lost the battle and what it means for current political strategies and political futures are the prime focus of coverage. An example of striking importance was enunciated by Rep. David Obey (D-Wis.) at a conference on the media and Congress. He said Democratic complaints in 1981 about the economic assumptions and arithmetic underlying President Reagan's spending and tax-cut program received inadequate attention. "The focus was on who was winning and losing politically, not on the details."[66] What also tends to receive news attention (unsurprisingly, given news criteria) is scandal and congressional "junkets" (trips abroad). (The addition of the Cable Satellite Public Affairs Network (C-SPAN) has certainly been a welcome improvement in total coverage of Congress—on cable TV, but its viewership is evidently very limited, as yet.)

On the other side of the relation, a note should be added here on how congresspersons can respond to network news in the TV age. Veteran network reporter Dan Schorr has revealingly illustrated how TV can affect the congressional process:

> In the spring of 1971, the staff director of a Senate committee dealing with poverty problems urged me to bring CBS cameras to a scheduled hearing. He outlined the "visual appeal" of the panel of witnesses he had arranged, which would include a black, a poor white and an Indian in full headdress. . . .

But Schorr indicated that another assignment prevented him from covering the hearing. The staff director saw Schorr as his

> last hope for network coverage [and] said "I'll get to the chairman and ask him to postpone the hearing." Then, when I objected to being put in the position of influencing the Senate's legislative calendar, he replied that it was not realistic to hold the hearing without cameras—most members of the committee would simply not turn up until informed by their aides that television was present.[67]

This certainly does *not* mean that most members of Congress show up at committee and subcommittee hearings only when the TV cameras are there (indeed, as has been alluded to, most such hearings are not covered).

What it does suggest is how strongly attuned members of Congress are to TV coverage and that this can affect congressional schedules and other aspects of operations.

A Note on Congresspersons' Use of the Media

As has already been mentioned, most Congresspersons make considerable effort to affect how much news coverage they receive and the nature of it. There is, of course, a desire to receive time on network news shows or space in a leading newspaper. But most of the effort is directed at the local media. Several means and methods are used. Important here is the fact that most local media have very limited resources, so provision of a free video segment, a press release that can be used as a news story, or other form of material which is *free* to the news organization and comes from the Congress of the United States is generally welcome. A press release, especially one that requires little rewriting to run as a story in the local paper, is the most common form. Regarding interviews of the local Congresspersons and coverage of events, the press officers of members generally have good working relations with the local media (and more such press officers are working at it, as was noted earlier). With good notice and arrangements, the local media have an evidently bona fide story that is easy to cover. Many Congresspersons also write a regular column for local (usually smaller) papers, and some have their own regular radio or TV program.

The most notable form of such congressional communication through the media is the production of videotape material to send to local stations. This can be either film of a speech on the floor taken from the House or Senate chamber camera and produced in the basement TV studios in the capitol, or can be more full-scale programs (produced in the capitol studios or in more sophisticated private studios elsewhere). Again, for the reasons just noted, most local stations use part or all of this material, often on several news and public officers shows.[68] The result: much more exposure for the incumbent member of Congress—of a largely self-created, positive sort. This does not hurt reelection chances.

The Supreme Court and the News Media

Occasionally, the Supreme Court, directly or indirectly, is the prime focus of media attention, such as when a dramatic decision is handed down (such as *Roe* v. *Wade* or *Regents of the University of California* v. *Bakke*) or when an especially controversial nomination to the Court is made (such as Judge Robert Bork). But overall, mass media coverage of the Supreme Court is not substantial. Richard Davis, in his analysis of coverage of U.S. government institutions in one network news show, an elite newspaper, and a more local paper, found that only 8% of such coverage involved the Supreme Court; the specific network news show (CBS) devoted less than 4% of its stories to the Supreme Court. These findings of rather little coverage of the Supreme Court are in agreement with the (relatively few) other such studies. (Davis did find some evidence of somewhat increased attention to the Supreme Court in recent years.[69]) In practice, this also means that quite a few Supreme Court cases receive no coverage or very incomplete coverage, especially on TV or in nonelite newspapers.[70]

Nature of Coverage; Nature of the Court   Of that which is included in the media, what is the coverage like? Principally, coverage focuses on the ostensible outcome of the court decision, who is involved, and the reactions of interested parties regarding potential impact of the decision. Little of the legal reasoning, legal history, or the process of court decision making tends to receive coverage.[71] Elite newspapers, in the more "important" cases, provide somewhat more information on the legal history and legal reasoning most prominently used, although even such media rarely carry more than the briefest part of the actual court opinion. Far fewer news media assign regular reporters to the Supreme Court than to Congress, so many rely on the wire services to provide most of the stories—with the limitations of standard wire service reporting (i.e., focus on "hard news" (an overt event) and the people involved, brief, punchy writing, emphasis on speed in reporting, etc.).

The nature of the court provides part of the explanation for the relatively small amount of coverage of this institution, which has a large impact on American society. First, we should note that the Supreme Court has occupied a place in the American system rather different from that of Congress and the Presidency. Political scientists have pointed out for years that the Court is, in reality, a policymaking institution with political forces significantly involved in Court operations and their results. But the image of the Court held by most Americans, and most reporters, is of august justices, literally sitting on high, discerning the deeper meaning of law and the Constitution by drawing on their special training in the law, all of which is elevated above "mere politics." The justices have long been well aware of this image and of its value in maintaining the status of the Court, which status is a prime factor in assuring compliance with its rulings by private parties, police, administrative agencies, and so on. The Court's recognition of the value of that elevated image, the aura of specialized authority, is chiefly responsible for its maintenance of a very different relation with the media than those of Congress and the Presidency.[72]

The Court has kept reporters at arm's length, appearing not to need the media, let alone "court it" (so to speak). Reporters have found the inner workings of the court to be heavily guarded, inaccessible. Generally, all reporters are allowed to see are the justices in the ornate main hall of the Supreme Court building hearing oral arguments. The strong tradition at the court is that no interviews are given (only the rarest of exceptions have occurred).

Without access to individuals and their reactions or to proceedings, reporters have tended to treat the court in accordance with the general social image—justices are treated with great deference, the individual justices are little discussed, analysis of political forces is rare, and decisions are usually treated as pure legal interpretation. But without access to sources and with just the opinions of the court, and the occasional reaction of a law professor, the media pay less attention.

The attention has grown some over the past decades, though. And after years of criticism, the Court is a little more accommodating to reporters; reporters "now receive copies of the headnotes, prepared by the Reporter of Decisions and summarizing the main points" of decision. There is an expanded Public Information Office, mainly serving the news media; and "Decision Mondays," where a number of decisions were announced at once, have been abandoned due to criticism of the difficulty of reporters digesting so much at once.[73]

Another factor, on the news media side, makes adequate and accurate reporting difficult—a problem that has been noted in other connections. Many reporters (about half of them[74]) do not have special training in the law. Wading through the legal jargon and sorting out meaning are correspondingly difficult. This situation has improved in recent years, though; all three networks use reporters with legal training, for example. (As Paletz and Entman rightly point out, though, legal education does not guarantee astute *political* analysis of Court process and decision.) It should be added that the network news constraints in particular—one-and-a-half-minute story lengths, visuals, and so on—make adequate Supreme Court reporting even more problematic than other governmental reporting, given the need for careful explanation of legal precedent and reasoning.

One final point in illustration of the need for more adequate reporting: A comprehensive national survey of attitudes toward the courts (in general) found that 34% of respondents, when they could cite more than one source, listed television entertainment programs as a source of information about courts.[75]

The Courts and the Media: The Prior Restraint and Free Press/Fair Trial Issues   Two issues in the relation between the law, the courts, and the media should also be (briefly) discussed. (The second of these issues is also an issue in the making and presentation of the news.) The first issue is called the "prior restraint" issue. The question is: Can the government (national or state) stop a newspaper, magazine, or a news show from printing or airing the entire news or a specific story it does not like, even if officials think the newspaper is engaging in scurrilous attacks or will have other negative impacts? In general, the answer is "no, not prior to publication."

The courts have held that the First Amendment ensures a general right to publish without interference from government. Specifically, the Supreme Court has said: "Any system of prior restraints of expression comes to this Court bearing a heavy presumption against its constitutionality."[76] The "remedy" for injured parties, the court has said, is in use of the libel laws, if and when something authentically libelous is printed or aired. There is some exception to that "heavy presumption against" constitutionality of prior restraint. The principal exception has been in cases where the national security is clearly and substantially threatened, although the "Pentagon Papers" cases indicated that the Court would look very closely at government claims of national security danger and would reject any such claims not exceedingly well justified.

On a sort of "cousin" issue, the news media have not fared quite so well in the courts. This is the issue of whether reporters' notes and other materials from news gathering can and should be subject to use in trials, where information in those materials might be of relevance to the case. If a reporter has information that could help the defense or the prosecution, they are going to want that information. The news media are deeply concerned about the consequences of having to give up their notes or allow the judicial system or police access to other materials (including "out-takes" of film) because confidentiality is vital to maintaining their news role; if sources lose trust in reporters, those sources will "dry up." The important investigative reports done by the news media, including those of government, in the news media's watchdog role, could be seriously impaired if the confidentiality of the news process is lost. Although there has been some hesitancy by the courts to violate the news process, in a number of cases, courts have ordered that reporters' notes be made available for the trial process, and some reporters have gone to jail for holding to the principle and refusing to give up their notes. In 1978 (in *Zurcher* v. *Stanford Daily*) the Supreme Court held that a proper search warrant could be used on a newspaper, just like other organizations, without necessarily violating First Amendment rights.[77] The debate goes on and the news media and civil liberties advocates remain very concerned with that decision. Some states have formally recognized the principle of confidentiality and have enacted "shield laws" which protect reporters' notes and other such material from being exposed in court.[78]

The other basic issue areas concern the conflict between the First Amendment and the Fifth Amendment, that is, between the principle of a free and unfettered press and the right of accused individuals to a fair trial by due process of law—not trial by television news clips or newspaper story. Also, the Sixth Amendment mandates a "speedy and *public* trial," a provision that news people have taken to support their contention of the right to cover trials however they wish. The courts, especially regarding pretrial publicity, have leaned in the direction of restricting media coverage to try to ensure a fair trial for the accused (although this amounts to a special case of prior restraint). "Gag orders" have been issued by a number of courts which have forbidden news coverage of pretrial proceedings and even some trial proceedings. Some suggest that this is a general violation of the First Amendment and of the purpose of the "*public* trial" mandate in the Sixth Amendment, which is intended to ensure exposure of unfair judicial proceedings. But members of the public and reporters could still attend the trial, and news of such judicial practice can be reported immediately *after* the trial, which would effectively raise the same protection without the danger to the fair trial process. The news media also claim the public's "right to know." But this may beg the question: Why do "the public" "need" to know every sensational tidbit if the publicity can affect the chance for a fair trial? Again, this is not an easy issue and the debate will continue.[79]

Administration, Regulation, and the Media: Covering the Bureaucracy

The standard administrative agencies and the regulatory agencies carry out the programs of the government. It is those agencies that turn words on pages of statute books into operating programs that actually serve the public—from determining eligibility and distributing medicare payments to cleaning up toxic waste dumps, to assuring that drugs on the market are safe and effective (at least those are the tasks set out for the agencies). These tremendously important parts of government receive little news coverage on a regular basis, however, and the public's level of understanding of "the bureaucracy" (in general) and, for example, of the regulatory process is very low (or nonexistent).

Scholar Stephen Hess reports a main reason why. He found that 84% of the sample of reporters he interviewed acknowledged that "regulatory agencies are not sufficiently covered and 51% think this is a serious problem." Yet he also found "there is no evidence to suggest that reporters are prevented from doing this work." Says a reporter for a major regional newspaper: "It's drudgery. We've hired four or five people to cover regulatory agencies and they switch to another beat as soon as possible."[80] Editors give little indication of any greater interest in covering the subject.

Respected *New York Times* reporter Tom Wicker has noted the same phenomenon—and its implications:

> The *Times's* failure really to cover the regulatory agencies reflected a major deficiency in every news organization I have known. . . . The dull, the routine, the unexciting, is seldom seen as news, although the dull, routine unexciting clearance of Thalidomide [which resulted in horribly deformed babies], or the dull, routine . . . management of rates and routes for the . . . airlines may affect far more Americans in their daily lives than some relatively more glamorous presidential . . . or congressional action.[81]

A Note on Difficulties and Dangers for Reporters in Covering Government Institutions   Governmental actions are prime news stories week in and week out. Government officers are principal news sources for reporters. Therein lie some difficulties and dangers for reporters in covering those institutions, particularly for reporters on a specific beat. Government officials have what is bread and butter for reporters: information for stories. Reporters need their sources. Also, in Washington, reporters and officials interact in a close environment; there is even a good deal of involvement in the same social activities. Consequently, reporters have strong incentives to avoid stories that anger their official sources, because that may "dry up the source" and cripple the reporter's usefulness on the beat. But officials often wish to communicate a message through the media, as well. Herbert Gans has articulated what often happens:

> As a result, beat reporters are drawn into a symbiotic relationship of mutual obligations with their sources, which both facilitates and complicates their work. . . . Consequently, beat reporters must often practice self-censorship, keeping their most sensational stories to themselves in order to protect their beat [though sources] must occasionally grin and bear it when reporters file displeasing news, especially if they need the reporters' good will—and the publicity.[82]

IMPACT OF THE MEDIA ON POLICY

Media coverage of the institutions of government and officials' efforts to use the media for their own purposes have been discussed. We now need to look at the media–government relation from a slightly different—but vital—angle. The prime product of the efforts of officials in government is public policy. Does news media coverage affect policy itself? Most people probably have that impression. Is there more systematic evidence of such impact, though?

Making a distinct cause-and-effect connection between media coverage and officials' actions which result in policy X is difficult, to say the least. The simple fact that much press attention to a given issue was followed shortly by a policy (or the rescinding of a policy) is not sufficient evidence. (Was the policy process, and the political coalition involved, already well advanced? Were there other factors at work beyond the direct media coverage? . . .) A recent study has provided some good, more systematic evidence of media impact.

Martin Linsky and colleagues at the Kennedy School of Government at Harvard conducted a broad survey of a large number of senior federal government officials who had served from the 1960s through the early 1980s. They also did in-depth interviews of 20 such senior policymakers and 16 journalists "nominated by their peers as having been particularly competent in making policy and covering the federal government, respectively," and they did six detailed case studies. In summary, they found: Many senior officials did think the news media have an impact on the policy process and, depending on various conditions, the policy impact can be substantial. In general, they found something that has been, in effect, a continuing theme of this book: "The press and policymakers in Washington are engaged in a continuing struggle to control the view of reality that is presented to the American people."[83]

Nearly 60% of senior federal officials from the last 20 years felt that the news media had a "substantial effect on federal policy. In fact, over 10% . . . say that the press had a dominant effect." Correspondingly, there was consistent testimony on how constantly aware officials were of how press coverage could affect actions they might take. For example, Joseph Califano (cabinet member in the Carter administration and presidential aide in the Johnson administration) "talked about the regularity with which high policy officials say: 'What will that look like on the evening news or on the front page?' "[84]

Two types of impact on the policy process were most notable in the findings. First, substantial news coverage speeds up the decision-making process. Prominent coverage places an issue actively in the public arena and creates large pressures on officials to do something sooner rather than later, lest they be perceived as incompetent or uncaring or both. Television was seen as having an especially strong impact in this manner. As Linsky noted: "There's no print analog to the reporter standing on the White House lawn live at [evening news time] telling fifteen million people that the president has no response to the crisis the reporter reported the night before."[85]

Inevitably, that compressed time for decision can affect the ability to deliberate thoroughly, as well as the ultimate quality of the decision. Of course, on another side of media impact, an administration that has sought to sweep a problem under the rug or that has dragged its feet on an issue can finally be forced to deal with an important matter, thanks to media coverage. (An example of that was the Reagan administration's (non)-conduct of the toxic waste cleanup program under the "Superfund.")

The second type of impact is that substantial coverage, especially if it is negative coverage of administration actions, tends to push decision-making up the bureaucracy to higher levels of officials, especially to the White House. Again, the White House cannot appear to be letting matters drift; and to preserve its "public prestige" and maintain general influence, the White House must exercise "damage control."

Interestingly, depending on the circumstances and the issue involved, substantial media coverage can either narrow the options effectively available (especially given the brief response time) or it can sometimes effectively force an increase in the options that policy-makers consider (especially if a policy decision has already been made but comes under challenge in a barrage of media attention). As should be evident, the principal impact in the policy realm is on the *process* of policy-making. Policy content is also affected rather directly, at times. Linsky notes a couple of examples of policy reversal due to media coverage (the Reagan administration's position on the tax-exempt statues of Bob Jones University and on reviews of eligibility for disability benefits in the Social Security programs[86]).

Under what conditions is press impact greatest? Three that were found will be noted here. Unsurprisingly, they found "consistently that negative stories have a substantially larger impact on policymakers than positive stories"—"twice as many of the senior officials in our survey believe that positive coverage has no effect as believe that about negative coverage."[87] Second, they found that many executive branch officials (outside the White House) had little experience with or understanding of the news media. The result can be a lack of thought about how an action will "play" in the media—and that can mean disaster (as in the case of the Bob Jones University tax exemption from the political standpoint of the Reagan administration). Correspondingly, the absence of public relations professionals from the policy process can mean that media impact is much greater. Third, which area in the executive branch the policy or issue involves seems to make a difference for media impact. The foreign policy area was that with the highest potential for media influence because so much in the area is considered news, and also, said three Secretaries of State, due to the "sophistication and expertise" of the reporters covering the State Department.[88] (This was also an area in which the Reagan administration made the most extraordinary efforts to influence media coverage, seeking to "put a spin" on the coverage.[89]) Many other departments received so little coverage that media impact is rare.

The media, then, can have a large impact on particular policy matters, and many, if not most, senior officials' actions and decision processes are affected by the constant awareness of what impact the media can have. The impact—and the awareness of it—have also significantly increased in the TV age: "In conversations with distinguished present and former government officials, the presence of television was cited frequently as having made a significant change in the relationship between the press and government over the last two decades."[90]

In one other area of the American political system the change brought about by the TV age may be even greater, however: the election process. To that subject we now turn.

CHAPTER NINE
THE MEDIA
IN ELECTIONS I
Perspective
and Methods of Study

INTRODUCTION AND NOTE ON FOCUS OF CHAPTERS

Elections are intended to be the foundation of the democratic process. In elections, the public (in some fashion) assesses past operation of the government and chooses its future directions, principally through the choice of candidates for public office. Elections are also the realm of the political system where the role of the media is perhaps most strikingly evident. As election day nears it is hard to avoid being exposed to (if not inundated by) pictures and stories of campaign parades and rallies and the sounds and images of campaign ads. Beyond the obvious pictures and hoopla, the fact is that the mass media are an increasingly central mechanism of elections. The study of the media's role in elections is the subject of this chapter and of Chapter 10.

The principal focus of this discussion on the media's role in elections is on presidential elections in the United States. There are very good reasons for that. The Presidency holds a unique place in the American political culture. The president has also been increasingly looked to as the prime leader and mover of government in the American system. In fact, it is probably fair to say that the Presidency is the most important office on the face of the earth. Correspondingly, the way the American people select someone to fill that office is one of the most important subjects to study. The role the mass media play in presidential elections has grown more and more important and is more and more important to understand.

This chapter adds to the discussion in Chapter 1 in seeking to place the media's role in elections in the perspective of a representative democratic system. The unique nature of the presidential nomination process in the United States is then reviewed (as a good understanding of this is vital for understanding the media's role in such elections). Following that, methods used to study the media's involvement in elections are discussed, which discussion includes some critique of two of the most prominent studies of the media in elections, with a note on a third. The discussion of methods is intended to deepen the reader's process of thinking through this vital aspect of the political system (and for students, to give at least a partial "inside look" at how to go about studying this fascinating subject). In Chapter 10 we discuss the findings of the principal studies of the media in elections, presidential as well as nonpresidential. The media's role in elections in another nation is discussed in Chapter 11.

ELECTIONS, THE MEDIA, AND THE POLITICAL SYSTEM

Changes: Parties and the Electoral Process

The electoral process is the principal mechanism of democracy, of linking the mass public with government to enable the people to give basic direction to the government through their electoral choices. But how, in a mass society, can this electoral process be organized? Traditionally, the answer has been: by the political parties. Indeed, a noted political scientist, E.E. Schattschneider, has suggested this striking conclusion:

> The rise of political parties is indubitably one of the principal distinguishing marks of modern government. The parties, in fact, have played a major role as *makers* of governments, more especially they have been the makers of democratic government. It should be stated flatly at the outset that [my thesis is] . . . the political parties created democracy and that modern democracy is unthinkable save in terms of the parties.[1]

The underlying key point is that most people cannot make monitoring government and various candidates in elections a full-time job. For popular control of government to work, the public must have some help in sorting out the choices. For government itself to work in a coherent fashion, and for the public to hold officers accountable for the general direction of government, there must be a force that politically organizes government activity and that can be held collectively responsible for government actions. That force has traditionally been the political parties.

While political parties in the American system have never fulfilled those functions to an absolutely ideal degree, in earlier eras the parties played the major role in organizing the campaign efforts of their candidates and they served as a principal way for the candidates to communicate with the public (through party workers working the precincts, etc.). The vast majority of the public identified with one party or the other and regularly voted for virtually all the party's candidates on the ballot. Parties have provided symbols and general patterns of policy direction which give people cues to help sort out electoral choices. Parties were the principal basis for making voting decisions, then, and they were rather stable, long-term bases.[2]

Over the past few decades, however, things have changed. The parties have declined significantly in the role they play in the American political system. Substantially fewer people identify with a party (from about 80% in the 1940s down to about 65% in the late 1980s), and more people identify themselves as "independents" (about a third). Further, the number who strongly identify with a party has dropped by at least as much, and the number of voters who vote "straight" tickets has declined dramatically.[3] David Broder noted in the results of the 1986 election striking confirmation of this trend: "In an orgy of ticket-splitting, the voters of Maine helped a Democratic governor and a Republican congressman swap jobs. Their counterparts across the country ordained that 26 of the 50 governors face a legislature in which at least one chamber is controlled by the opposition party. . . . And just to certify their fickleness, they even split the governor's and lieutenant governor's jobs between the two parties in 16 states."[4]

Interest groups, on another hand, have greatly increased in numbers, in financing, and in intensity during the period of party decline (1950s through the 1980s). As interest-group scholar Jeffrey Berry points out: "The United States is not just a country with an increasing number of active interest groups, but a country whose citizens look more and more to interest groups to speak for them in the political process. The implications are disquieting."[5] Indeed, Martin Wattenberg pointed to the principal implication when he observed the "growing importance of special interest groups and the dwindling of the principles of collective responsibility. The result, as Morris Fiorina has written, is that we now have 'a system that articulates [a number of] interests superbly but aggregates them poorly.'"[6] The connection with the decline of reasonably strong political parties is evident, and the consequences for organizing government action and avoiding stalemate and policy incoherence are great.

More Changes: The Media and the New Manner of Electoral Politics

What else has dramatically increased, over the same period, is the public's dependence on the mass media for information and impressions on candidates and their campaigns, issues, and institutional performance—

and on the parties themselves. The central way in which campaigns now communicate to the public is through the media. As Thomas Patterson has said: "Today's presidential campaign is essentially a mass media campaign. . . . [I]t is no exaggeration to say that, for the large majority of voters, the campaign has little reality apart from its media version."[7] The same applies to the typical U.S. Senate and governor's election and to many U.S. House elections.

Television gave candidates the means of communicating directly to the public, without using party organizations. Clearly, if that capacity was not the prime *cause* of the decline of parties (as some contend), it was at least a major contributing and exacerbating factor. In any case, two more specific results of the decline of parties and the rise in dependence on and use of TV must be spelled out. First and more obviously, campaigns are fundamentally organized around the mass media, especially television. The schedule, the appearances, the themes, and so on, are geared to the deadlines, need for visuals, and other factors characteristic of the making and presentation of TV news—or of the medium itself in the case of political ads. The same applies, to a somewhat lesser extent, to the print media. Further, the "rise of political consultants," as Sabato has best detailed,[8] has provided expert "hired guns" to enable the candidate (with ample money) to make most effective use of the media in general, and the powerful medium of television in specific. The second result is that elections have become increasingly candidate centered. The principal factor in elections now is the individual candidate and how that candidate is evaluated by the public—as a result of mass media communications. With party identification greatly lessened and with the rather low level of public information on political matters and low levels of opinion coherence (as discussed earlier in the book), information and impressions garnered from the media on the candidates are the prime elements determining many people's votes. These are short-term, unstable factors.

We should note an additional consequence of the decline of parties and the rise of the media and candidate-centered elections: Far more than in earlier areas, candidates are self-selecting. That is, the party organization has had less and less to do with recruiting candidates and providing the campaign apparatus. Rather, individuals who have media prominence and/or have access to ample amounts of money (and time) decide they will run and proceed to form their own organizations and run their own campaigns (with varying connections with the remnants of the local, state, and national party organizations). (It should also be noted that the campaign finance laws adopted in the 1970s channeled public campaign funds directly into candidates' campaign coffers, bypassing the parties, thus adding to the weakening of the parties.) The basic design of the nomination process is what allows this. To an explanation of that we turn next, following a quote that summarizes what has just been discussed. As scholar James

MacGregor Burns has observed: "Parties [once] identified popular wants, defined popular needs, channeled popular hopes and aspirations, organized voters' expectations and demands. So do the mass media today, but in so different a manner as to have helped bring about a transformation of the American political system."[9]

Still More Changes: The American Nomination Process

There are two basic dimensions of the basic design of the electoral process in the United States: presidential and nonpresidential. The dominant form in the nomination stage of both, however, is the nomination primary, a form that has been a major factor in altering the landscape of American electoral politics. But the primary is a very different part of the presidential nomination process compared with the nonpresidential process. In nonpresidential elections (for Congress or for state legislative and executive offices), it is the primary that allows a self-selected candidate to run in the absence of party operations, or in spite of them. As noted in Chapter 1: "The party label has lost significance as candidates of all political colorations, with all variety of relationships with the organization, earn the right to wear [the party label] by capturing primary elections."[10] (A very few states have a modified primary process for nomination, which involves endorsement of candidates by convention of party activists in some fashion.)

The presidential nomination process in the United States is unique in every sense. Although many readers will be familiar with at least the basics of that process, it is important for those who aren't to review it here, and it is a good reminder for the rest. Indeed, a good understanding of the nature of that process is vital for an understanding of the media's coverage.

The first thing to note is the official culmination of the presidential nomination process. It is at the national party conventions that the assembled delegates from around the country, voting by state, nominate the Democratic and Republican candidates for president. How those delegates have gotten selected is a crucial question, though. A historical note is needed to begin the explanation.

Through 1968, the selection of delegates was left up to the individual states. Delegates were principally selected in and through local and state conventions, caucuses, committees of party leaders, and the like. The selection process was a matter for the internal party organization, involving party leaders and prime party activists. A powerful governor or senator (or party boss) would, in various cases, effectively control the entire bloc of the state's delegates.

But following 1968, especially due to the dramatic events involving the Democratic Party Convention, the situation changed (although the seeds of the change were evident in 1968 and even in 1964). There were calls for more popular participation in the process. The Democratic Party, following the loss of the presidency in 1968, was moved to "open up" the process and encourage more participation. The "reforms" the party affected (and later reforms of the reforms) dramatically changed the game of presidential nominations. These spread over nearly all states for both parties, due especially to Democratic dominance of most state legislatures and to some similar impulses in the Republican Party. The principal result of these reforms was to make the process a very public one and to make primaries the dominant way that delegates are selected for the national party conventions. There were other particular changes, as well, which are too detailed for treatment here. In general, the impact of the changes has been great and the consequences profound.[11] And the interaction of the new process with the new dominance of the mass media resulted in perhaps the greatest of those impacts. Chapter 10 presents the evidence on that interaction and those impacts. The next paragraphs concisely review the nature of the presidential nomination process today.

The fact that the American system is a federal one is the reason the nomination for the national office of the presidency is based on the building blocks of the 50 individual states (and the District of Columbia, Puerto Rico, and the American protectorates). The basic design of the system is to allow each of the 50 states to select delegates through one of two basic methods. The primary election is one method. In form a primary election is, of course, like a general election, except that it is intended for all those in the general public who identify with one party or the other to participate in the general process of choosing the party's nominee for president. (Some states have primaries that are not restricted to party members, which muddies the party nomination waters, but that story must be pursued elsewhere.) States differ in exactly how the primary relates to the selection of delegates; this relation ranges from a simple, direct percentage of the vote translating (usually at the congressional district level) to the same percentage of the state's allocated delegate total (the most common approach) to a few states that have a preference primary, whereby the public votes for the candidates to show preferences, while the actual delegates are selected in a different process. For the 1988 election, about two-thirds of the states, selecting over 70% of the delegates, used the primary method.

The second method of choosing delegates for the national conventions is the caucus–convention method. This three-stage method begins with caucuses (meetings) of all interested party identifiers in the precinct, where delegates are selected by vote; then those delegates proceed to county or congressional district conventions, where they are winnowed down, followed by the same at state conventions, where the actual delegates to the national convention are chosen. This method is intended to be one involving a higher level of participation by party identifiers in the public and to produce representatives of those party identifiers who can not only cast a vote for specified candidates at higher-level conventions, but can represent their fellow party "members" more generally. Indeed, delegates can, and a number usually do, run as "uncommitted." (Thus those delegates could deliberate for their party constituency on the platform and on other candidates, as things change, and so on.) Corresponding to that description, the caucus–convention method is *not* inherently undemocratic; in form, it is actually the essence of active democracy. This is important to mention because some members of the media have characterized this method as undemocratic, or at least less democratic than the primary election method. (More people do participate in primaries than in caucuses, but they are not a significantly more representative cross section of the general party, in most cases, and the simple act of casting a primary ballot involves much less meaningful effort and democratic interaction than does caucus participation.)

Looked at as a whole, the presidential nomination process involves a succession of 50 state primaries and caucuses to select the delegates to the national conventions from those states. Traditionally, the precinct-level caucuses in Iowa have been the earliest of the state processes. They take place around February 20. New Hampshire's primary has traditionally been the first primary (since 1984, occurring a week after Iowa's caucuses). The primaries and caucuses in the rest of the states have been strung out from early March through early June, with the national conventions occurring in July and August. It should be added that due to the increased importance of primaries (and caucuses) in the selection of delegates, national conventions are now rarely places where party leaders deliberate and choose a nominee; rather, the great majority of the delegates are already committed to a candidate, and the winner is usually clear beforehand. It is a time for great media attention, though.

This is, then, an extremely long, drawn-out process.[12] The Democrats, since 1980, have sought to shorten the process, recognizing the complaints from many people of the absurdity of such a long, expensive, wearing process, and one in which some delegates are selected five or six months before the convention (during which time much can change). But the stakes are high for the candidates, and also for the states. The latter is because of the pattern of media attention to the early primaries and caucuses which is detailed in Chapter 10. The extreme amount of media attention given the earliest delegate selection events, along with the (rather good) chance the contest for the nomination will be effectively decided in the first half of that long succession of events, thus making later primaries and caucuses unimportant, has led to many efforts by states to move up their primary or caucus to an early position. In 1988, the battle to garner media attention distorted the schedule even more than before. Michigan Republicans moved their unique selection process up to January, the Democrats (DFL) in Minnesota moved the state's caucuses up to February 23, and all the southern and border states with primaries moved them to a common date early in the process (March 8).

Richard Rubin has interestingly pointed out that from 1968 through 1976, television news played a prime role in "legitimating the primary process as *the* genuinely democratic way to choose convention delegates."[13] In general, the impact of media attention, and correlative influence on given state processes of selection of presidential nominees, is striking. Some other details of the nature of the nomination process will be added in the course of the discussion in Chapter 10, as they are notable principally due to the nature of the media's coverage of that process.

Whether all this is a sensible way to choose a presidential nominee is a very different story. More on that in Chapter 10 after we review the empirical studies of the media's role in elections. For the rest of this chapter we review how to go about studying that role.

THE MEDIA IN ELECTIONS: METHODS OF STUDY

How should the mass media's involvement in elections be studied? Since elections are such prominent, public parts of people's lives, especially presidential ones, many people feel that they have a sense of what impact the media have. Mere impressions are not enough, however; the subject is too important, the stakes too high. More systematic study is needed to identify and explain as accurately as possible the nature of the media's role in elections.

The Systematic Study of the Media in Elections: Focus on the Patterson Approach

If the mass media are the principal means of communicating the elements of an election to the public, the logical first question is: What exactly are the media communicating? The news is, of course, the principal source of the public's information and impressions on election subjects (ads are another prime source). In light of those points and in accordance with what was discussed in Chapter 6 on the making of the news, Thomas Patterson has noted: "Election news results from a series of decisions made by news organizations about what to observe, what to report, and what emphasis to place on various parts of the coverage."[14] The method for studying what has been communicated as election news is *content analysis*— the analysis of the number of stories in the news on election-related subjects and of the content of those stories. For a prime exemplification of how to do such an analysis, we will draw on what continues to be the most important study of the media's role in elections: Thomas Patterson's remarkably comprehensive study of the media in the 1976 presidential election (a masterpiece of social science, in this author's opinion).

In doing a content analysis of the news media's communications about an election, especially a presidential election, a practical problem presents itself at the start: It is not feasible to study all news stories in all mass media that reach the entire national public during the entire period of the campaign. Some choices must be made about samples which will stand for all relevant stories in all media. Patterson, for example, analyzed a randomly chosen sample of stories (a large sample of 6567) appearing in the three major network news programs, *Time* and *Newsweek,* and two newspapers each in two locations (one of which was a major paper, the *Los Angeles Times;* others were medium-sized, more local papers). These stories were chosen to cover the entire formal election period: January 1 through the November election day. Regarding the content itself, each of those stories was analyzed for the following: the date of the story, whether it was accompanied by a photo or film, its length, its position in the medium (such as on the front page or later in the broadcast), the principal subject and actor in the story, whether the story "reflected favorably or unfavorably on this actor," and "references to the candidate's personal and leadership qualities, styles, backgrounds, issue stands, values, campaign progress, and similar things."[15]

Further, Patterson recognized that the campaign communication situation involves not only a number of communications through the news, but also receipt of those communications by the public and a public response. Indeed, our ultimate concern, in a democracy, is surely the impact of such campaign communications on "we the people," specifically, the nature of the public's political response. Correspondingly, the second basic dimension of Patterson's study analyzed who was communicated to, by what media, and what their responses were. Patterson's principal method in studying the public's attention and response sought to overcome the limitations of the simple "cross-sectional" survey. Such a survey typically involves a single interview with each respondent at a single point in time (just after election day). But such an approach requires people to recall accurately just how media communications affected their response to candidates and issues, from as much as ten or more months in the past, and to separate media effects from nonmedia effects.

Patterson used the panel survey method to overcome those limitations. In the specific case of his study, a total ("panel") of "1236 eligible voters were questioned as many as seven times in the course of the . . . campaign about their media use, their impressions of the candidates and the campaign, their awareness of the election's issues, their interest in the campaign, and similar topics."[16] But given the post-1968 nature of the presidential nomination and election process, the timing of these successive "waves" of interviews was important. If we are to establish systematically how media communications have affected (*changed*) people's thinking, it is also important to establish people's states of mind *before* they are exposed to such communications. Correspondingly, the first wave of interviews needed to construct a "baseline" of people's orientations, level of interest, awareness of issues and candidates, and so on. Interestingly, while Patterson recognized and incorporated this logic, the new nomination politics and the media age got a little ahead of him. His baseline interviews were scheduled before the first primary (again, New Hampshire), which had been the first delegate selection event to receive significant attention; but in 1976, for the first time, the Iowa caucuses, then occurring in January, received a great deal of attention (as he documented in the section of the study on news coverage). For optimum purposes, in short, his baseline was a little late. (It was still basically adequate, though, as will be evident in the next chapter.) After the baseline wave, Patterson timed the waves of interviews to capture people's attention and responses at the major stages of the process, that is, after the early primaries (April), the late primaries (June), the party conventions (August), and late in the general election (October). As it happened, there were also a series of three debates between the two major party candidates, so telephone interviews were done after the first and second debates. Phone interviews were also conducted after the election to establish whether the respondents had voted and for whom if they had (i.e., what, in the end, was their actual voting behavior?).

But a question could be raised about interviewing the same "panel" of people seven times: Would that repeated interviewing tend to sensitize the people interviewed to the election process in general and the various particular subjects asked about—and hence, alter the very state of mind that was the goal of the study to ascertain? That is, if repeated questioning makes people pay more attention to election news, thereby developing more awareness and knowledge of candidates, and so on, it is not media impact that is being discovered but something artificially stimulated by the study itself. This "reinterview-sensitization" problem, Patterson reports, has not, however, been found to be the significant factor one might expect, in previous studies. And Patterson added new respondents (as control groups) to the second and third waves of interviews and found no significant differences between those people and the original group. The possibility is important to monitor in a study such as this, though.

A final element of Patterson's study method should be mentioned. If it is not feasible to study all media reaching everyone in the nation, choices must be made of what locations and "media markets" to study. Choosing one or a few locations also allows the measurement of virtually the entire significant media environment of those interviewed. Patterson chose the major metropolitan area of Los Angeles, which had a very diverse population, and Erie, Pennsylvania, with a metro population of 270,000 and a more homogeneous, blue-collar, heavily Catholic character. But here we also see a limitation of selecting only two areas and of these two areas in specific: both areas are urban; smaller cities and rural areas are not represented here.

In general, the Patterson study is an outstanding exemplification of how to go about the more systematic study of the media's role in elections. The one notable qualification of that statement is the surprising omission by Patterson of substantial analysis of political ads from his content analysis (especially surprising given Patterson's previous book, which compared the content of ads with that of TV news in the 1972 election).[17] The lack of such analysis, along with questions on responses to ads, makes it impossible to be certain whether the impacts he found were due entirely to news, or whether ads actually accounted for some of the impact, or produced effects not asked about. Patterson also did not specifically analyze the visual dimension of TV news. All things considered, however, Patterson's study remains the prime landmark in studying the media in elections.

Further Explorations in Analysis of the Media in Elections: The Robinson Approach and Campaign '80

Michael Robinson and Margaret Sheehan performed a study that sought to add depth to the analysis of what election news communicates to the public, and to tell us specifically about the media's role in the presidential election of 1980. They produced the most noted study of the media in the election of 1980.[18] In doing so, they have also highlighted some problems in attempting such analysis.

Michael Robinson was a pioneer in the study of the media in politics.[19] In his and Sheehan's study of the media in campaign '80, they did not seek to analyze the impact of communications on the public, only the content of what news was communicated. They were especially interested in comparing print with TV coverage to see if and how they differed. They selected CBS to represent the network news shows (at that time, the most watched and most respected network news), and to represent "traditional" print news, they selected a wire service: UPI (AP refused to rent them a daily wire). By using a wire service, they sought to overcome the limitations of selecting one or a few particular newspapers to represent what people throughout the nation receive from print. But did they also raise problems by this choice? They did. The wire itself is the general feed to newsrooms; which stories among the many editors at actual newspapers select is a very different matter. Thus content analysis of the wire service stories does not tell us what specific communications actually reached the public. As a rough "average" of what is used throughout the nation, perhaps use of the UPI wire is not too bad, though. But what is fundamentally lost using the wires is any *locally* covered and treated stories, a loss that would be more telling with respect to the major papers, which have one or more of their own reporters on the presidential campaign trail. For study of *nonpresidential* elections, the wire selection would not do at all, of course.

The most interesting feature of the Robinson–Sheehan study deals with the aspects of content (or "topics") on which they chose to focus analysis. The prime goal of the study was to evaluate the performance of the news media in their coverage of the election. So what criteria did they use to accomplish that laudable task? They used five criteria (which they "distilled" from several lists of principles enunciated by news media organizations. Those criteria are (1) "objectivity" (more on this below); (2) "equity of access"—did candidates for the same office receive essentially equal time on and in the news media?; (3) "fairness"—beyond simple amounts of time or space received, how balanced and fair was the treatment of candidates for the same office in the "tone" of the stories?; (4) "seriousness"— how much of the news involved the substance of what is at stake in elections, such as policy issues and candidates' qualifications, rather than election event hoopla, speculations about who's ahead and who's behind, personality stories, and the like?; and (5) "comprehensiveness"—by this Robinson and Sheehan specifically mean, how comprehensively were *all* elections covered (i.e., elections other than the presidential one)?

That is certainly a sensible list of criteria, which criteria give promise of taking us a step beyond simply describing amounts of coverage and to construct a composite view of the adequacy of coverage and thereby evaluate it. We must, however, consider the details; how are these criteria spelled out so that they can be used in the operation of analysis? For the purposes of further illustration of methods of study, we concentrate on the first and third of those criteria. (Again, the *findings* of this study, together with those of the Patterson study and others, are discussed in Chapter 10.)

The criterion of objectivity raises some interesting questions. Robinson and Sheehan, after examining several definitions of objectivity in the news, suggest the following as the "best" definition (drawing on the writing of a prominent journalist):

> Objective news: (1) relates only observable facts of an overt event; (2) cites others on matters of opinion; (3) refuses to allow one's own beliefs, principles or inclinations—"or even his own knowledge"—to color raw, overt material for the story. Objectivity includes, above all, a considerable reluctance to go beyond what was actually observed by the journalist, and an even greater reluctance to draw any explicit conclusions or inferences about the events being covered, unless the conclusion or inference comes from another legitimate source, not the journalist him/herself.[20]

From those standards they derived four ways to test for objectivity in news coverage. First, they analyzed what newspeople said to gauge the extent that CBS and UPI "drew explicit and unsupported conclusions about the personal qualities of the candidates." Second, they identified any personal opinions expressed by reporters on the policy issues. Third, they "measured the degree to which both media broke away from 'description' and moved toward 'analysis' in covering candidates or issues, defining objectivity here as a function of basic descriptiveness." Finally, they analyzed the verbs used by reporters to help determine how much "insinuation" was included in reports.[21]

Is a definition of objectivity an adequate one which restricts reporting to "observable facts of an overt event" and which, at the core of the "test" for objectivity, defines it as "a function of basic descriptiveness," and which also disallows use of "even [a reporter's] own knowledge" to "color" material for a story? The discussion in Chapter 6 reviews examples and explains why this is not an adequate definition. The discussion in Chapter 8 of President Reagan's extreme control of news media access, combined with an intensive and comprehensive strategy for presenting a positive picture of the president and for manipulating the news in general, provided further reason for concluding such a notion of objectivity is inadequate, especially regarding incumbent presidents. The Nixon operation, which was the direct precursor to the Reagan one, also made this especially clear.

The 1972 and 1984 elections are the most dramatic illustrations of the problem with such a narrow, "mindless" definition of objectivity. In each of those elections, the incumbent simply did not allow himself to be questioned or challenged, but did appear at a series of carefully staged overt events as part of a general carefully crafted image purveyance. As David Broder has said: "The lessons of the 1972 Nixon campaign—in bypassing the press and refusing to talk about the substantive policy choices ahead— were applied by Ronald Reagan in his reelection campaign in 1984, with even more lopsided and politically satisfying results."[22] Sam Donaldson of ABC News can be credited for repeatedly trying to point out how Reagan was systematically avoiding questions while making lots of quotable speeches and appearances at other media-genic "overt events." An objective coverage of the campaign of 1984 would have centrally pointed out that the substance of the democratic process was being short-circuited and that the campaign-for-the-cameras was calculated image building, not a presentation of the policy record. (It should be noted that Robinson's specific conclusion was that the news media had been "objectivistic": "in the manner of objectivity.")

In Chapter 3 a more specific example was noted which strikingly illustrates the problem (although it took place in the "nonelection year" of 1983): President Reagan's "education initiative." Again, the Reagan operation found public opinion polls registering a public perception of the administration as slighting education. So the president "traveled around the country calling for improvements in educational quality"—that is, a series of overt events were created for the cameras and reporters. Broder describes the news response: "The President's 'education offensive' got massive coverage. The [*Washington*] *Post* carried fifteen stories, totalling 438 column-inches during the nine weeks at the height of his campaign. Almost without exception, the network news shows carried shots of the President at every stop."[23] But no real *policy actions* were taken by the administration. To rate such news as objective because it described a series of (carefully staged) events is to suggest that "the news" need not relate to the actual function of governing. As pointed out in Chapter 6, you cannot be objective without perspective.

That discussion brings us to one other problem with how Robinson and Sheehan have "operationalized" the criterion of objectivity, and with their method more generally. Strikingly, the visual dimension of the news was ignored in their content analysis; only verbal messages were considered. Not analyzing visuals may have avoided a difficult task and made their comparison of print and TV media "cleaner and simpler," but it is a serious omission in the effort to understand fully the objectivity dimension of the coverage of elections, as well as the fairness and seriousness dimensions.[24] Unfortunately, Robinson, along with Maura Clancy, did a study of 1984 election coverage in which the visual dimension was also ignored (although this time, unlike the 1980 study, nonverbal gestures of TV correspondents were analyzed). As they said: "If Reagan smiled warmly on camera or told an hilarious joke we excluded Reagan's performance from our assessment of *news* content. We scored not what Reagan said or did, but instead what Sam Donaldson . . . et al. said or did."[25] The discussion in Chapter 4 explains why this is a serious omission. The lack of visual analysis surely accounts in good part for their rather startling conclusion that "Reagan and Bush received much worse press on network news than the opponents they defeated so handily."[26]

For a little further view of analysis of content for the purpose of assessing the adequacy of news coverage of elections, we can take more brief note of Robinson and Sheehan's "fairness" criterion. To determine how fair media treatment of the candidates was, they settled on assessing how much "positive information" and how much "negative information" each story contained. If a story had three times as much positive information as negative, they considered the story to be "good press" for a candidate, whereas three times as much negative information meant "bad press." If the information in the story was a mix or simply did not add up to the three-to-one ratio, it was considered "ambiguous" in direction of treatment. A story could also be purely neutral.

This is an ambitious effort to look more deeply into the question of fairness in news treatment. This is an extraordinarily difficult issue to enunciate an adequate conceptualization of, let alone measure precisely and objectively. Robinson and Sheehan's effort, while deserving of praise for the effort, illustrates the difficulties. What are the exact criteria for judging which "information" is positive and which negative? Is sheer amount of positive or negative information in a story (measured as lines of words, comments as a unit, or another criterion) a sufficient measure of good or bad press, or should the nature of the subject of the comments and the intensity of them be considered, and if so, what of the three-to-one ratio as the determination point?

Additionally, Robinson and Sheehan did not include "hard news events" in the totals on good press/bad press, "unless the journalist drew or implied a conclusion from those events. Even coverage of an ethnic joke by Reagan or the subject of Carter's brother Billy were not considered bad press in themselves—only conclusions drawn from them."[27] This would presumably mean that the considerable feature news coverage in 1987 of Joe Biden's borrowing from the speeches of other political figures without attribution was not negative press (or, for a nonelection example, the massive coverage of the past occasional marijuana use of President Reagan's nominee for the Supreme Court, Judge Ginsberg). Although there is no reason to conclude that most members of the media in those two cases had bias in mind and *intended* to treat the individuals badly, it is difficult not to conclude that the result in the media was very bad "press" for each. The decision to run a given story at all, and if so, how much prominence to give it, is a news decision, it must be remembered; and the splashy prominence the media did give to those two stories was a guarantee that the individuals would be seen in a much less positive light ("why so much attention if there's nothing wrong," "where there's smoke, there's fire," . . .). The absence of visuals in the analysis, of course, is also a serious problem. Visuals can cast someone in a positive or negative light, depending on which photo of film segment is chosen.[28]

Finally, Robinson and Sheehan "excluded all explicit references made by the journalist as to the candidate's chances of winning."[29] Again, if our concern is the intent of journalists regarding fair treatment, this may make sense; but there are problems if the concern is whether a candidate got "good press" or "bad press," if media treatment itself had a negative or positive impact. (Note: The exclusion is of "references to the candidate's *chances* of winning," not mere recording of actual primary or caucus results.) As political scientists Henry Brady and Michael Hagen sum up regarding evidence they found from the 1984 nomination process, specifically from February and March:

> The electorate during those two months apparently received more information about each candidate's chances of winning the nomination than about his character, his policy goals, or his chances of defeating Ronald Reagan in the general election. . . . John Glenn's chances during those two months were the subject of much more negative press than Jesse Jackson's ever were. The media seemed to focus not on the competition among the candidates but on the competition between each candidate and expectations about his performance.[30]

Richard Hofstetter and Doris Graber have appropriately framed this general problem by noting that we can distinguish between *political* bias or unfairness in news coverage from "structural bias" or unfairness which results from "the circumstances [and orientations] of news production."[31] Those thoughts lead us to a consideration of the findings of various studies of the media's role in elections, which we turn to in the next chapter.

IN CONCLUSION

This discussion of how to go about the study of the media in elections was certainly not an exhaustive review of all noteworthy methods. [One example of a method which there has not been space to discuss here is the interesting "Q-sort" methodology, an approach and statistical method for analyzing people's (quite subjective) possession of images of candidates.[32]] Hopefully, our discussion did illustrate some principal approaches and encourage further reflection on some of the difficulties in studying what the media communicate in elections, what impact those communications have on the public, and how to assess the adequacy of news coverage of elections. A review of the findings of the more notable studies, in effect, carries that effort a few steps further.

CHAPTER TEN
THE MEDIA
IN ELECTIONS II
Evidence
on the Role
and the Impact

INTRODUCTION

Shortly before the 1984 Iowa caucuses and New Hampshire primary, Senator Gary Hart said (in an informal talk with his campaign finance committee): "You can get awfully famous in this country in seven days. . . ." One can, indeed, as Hart proceeded to demonstrate. The reason for this is the nature of mass media attention. Senator Hart continued: "The pattern is: You do better than you were supposed to in early states. That is reported in analyses of the campaign, people begin to talk about you, your polls go up, the money comes in. . . ."[1]

Given what happened to Senator Hart in the weeks after that statement, he would appear to have had a crystal ball. Actually, he simply had followed the patterns of previous news media coverage of presidential nomination campaigns and understood their impact. In this chapter we seek to present those patterns and discuss those impacts, as discovered by various studies of the media in elections. In the first sections we discuss study findings (and other reflections) on the nature of the media's coverage of the presidential election process and on the response of candidates and campaigns to the media. This is followed by review of findings on the impact of media coverage on the public. A special section on debates is added. A further section focusing specifically on campaign ads follows. Finally, the media in congressional, state, and local elections are discussed.

MEDIA COVERAGE OF PRESIDENTIAL ELECTIONS AND CAMPAIGN RESPONSE

Nature of Coverage: The Patterson Evidence

Striking patterns of media coverage of the nomination process have been found. The most comprehensive and systematic study is that reported in Thomas Patterson's *The Mass Media Election,* the method of which was discussed in Chapter 9. This study of the media in the 1976 presidential election process found two patterns of fundamental importance in media coverage: (1) the game and strategy in the process, along with candidate style and image, were heavily covered, but issues and candidate qualifications and leadership abilities received comparatively little coverage; and (2) the basic design and intent of the process (delegate selection through 50 states and a gradual weighing of comparative appeal of candidates to voters and party activists) tended to get lost in the coverage of the game. In fact, the very nature of the process has been altered and the outcomes profoundly affected by the nature of the news coverage. Let us look at the more important specific evidence that Patterson presents. Then, other studies, especially of the 1980 and 1984 elections, are discussed.

The Game: Issues and "Campaign Issues"   Over all the media he studied (again, the three networks, *Time* and *Newsweek,* and two newspapers each in two areas), Patterson found that between 51 and 58% of all the news on elections was about the *game* (i.e., about who was winning or losing, strategy and logistics, appearances and hoopla). Only 28 to 32% of election news involved the substance of the election (i.e., issues and policies, candidates' leadership traits and records, and endorsements). (The *Los Angeles Times* was somewhat exceptional, with 35% of coverage concerning substance.)[2]

It should be noted that the measure of news coverage of "substance" in this study, like most others, does not appear to be terribly demanding. That is (although Patterson is not as specific about this as one would like), news content that included anything more than the briefest mention of the name of an issue or policy was included in the substance column. This does not tell us how many stories involved material that was sufficiently meaningful and substantial that there was a real chance to learn something from it. Patterson did point out, however, that the figures just cited on coverage of the game compared with substance actually understate the media's emphasis on the game. Thus when we look at stories placed in the more frequently read or watched front pages of newspapers or beginning of newscasts, there is an even greater emphasis on the game, style, and image and even less attention to substance.[3]

Patterson also found interesting patterns in the news media's interest in "issues" coverage (broadly conceived of) compared with candidates' interests and efforts. He found that the media preferred to cover "clear-cut" issues, that is, issues that neatly divide the candidates (thus fulfilling the "conflict" news criterion). The candidates generally preferred that more "diffuse" issues be the center of news attention, diffuse issues being those with broad appeal to a general public, which allows a candidate to build a larger set of supporters and offend fewer segments of voters.

To the extent that the media seek candidate discussion of serious policy issues, this tension between a media preference for clear-cut issues versus candidates' preferences for diffuse issues is as it should be; it is a welcome thing for the media to try to "smoke out" the candidates on policy issues. But is that the main emphasis of the media's interest? Apparently not. The media preference is that these issues "produce disagreement and argument among the candidates; rest on principle rather than complex details or relationships; and can be stated in simple terms, usually by reference to a shorthand label such as busing or detente."[4]

Further, one main media focus in "clear-cut issue" coverage is better referred to as "*campaign* issues" than as substantive issues. Campaign issues are those that arise as a result of incidents in the campaign, typically a mistake in judgment by the candidate or his or her campaign principles. The classic example of this was Gerald Ford's misstatement in one of the 1976 debates with Jimmy Carter that Poland was not under the domination of the Soviet Union. This received a great deal of coverage (egged on, of course, by the Carter campaign); but no serious observer of politics thought this represented Ford's view of the Eastern European situation.[5] The misstatement of his law school record by Senator Joe Biden in September 1987 was an excellent example of this phenomenon early in the campaign 1988 process.

Why the absence of coverage of policy issues—and such emphasis on nonsubstantive campaign issues? Newspeople are aware of the idea of democracy. The factors in and orientations of news production, however, push journalists to see policy statements as quickly losing their "newsworthiness," whereas campaign missteps and the tangible events of the election process are "fresh occurrences." As Patterson said, "once a candidate makes known his position on an issue, further statements concerning that issue decline in news value."[6] The journalists who are principally reporting on each campaign also sit through innumerable repetitions (and some variations) of The Speech, the standard campaign speech used at most stops around the country, which normally contains various general statements about the "issues facing our nation today." Reporters, not surprisingly, begin to question the news value of a statement on issues. Does that mean that questions on the policy issues should not be pursued, however? There is a difference between the numbing drone of a standard campaign speech (after the umpteenth hearing) and a serious effort to cross-examine prospective presidents on the significant policy issues and to find out (1) whether they have adequate knowledge about such matters, and (2) whether their general proposals on such things as budget making really add up.

Coverage of Candidates and the Nomination Process   Those are important findings. But even more striking and important is what Patterson found regarding coverage of the candidates and the nomination process itself. The principal Patterson findings have now been echoed in many other sources, even in the media themselves, in their occasional self-analyses. The findings regarding patterns of coverage of the process and the consequences of that coverage remain of central importance for understanding the media's role in elections.

The news media's criteria for news and other news production factors lead them to focus on tangible, official events, especially the earliest such events, in the election process. And following the conflict and drama criteria, it inclines the media to highlight who has "won" and who has "lost." A candidate who did not "come in first" in the voting but who did much better than the media expected can also receive prominent, positive media coverage (under the right circumstances).

In the 1976 Democratic nomination process, for example, Jimmy Carter received about 30% of the votes cast in the Iowa caucuses, the first delegate-selection event (then held in January). (Carter had spent large amounts of time in the state over the previous two years.) Various other candidates received various lower percentages, but also, reflecting the indecision among the citizenry at that early point in time, nearly 40% of the caucus participants cast votes for uncommitted delegates. The media's response to this very mixed result was to pronounce Carter the unequivocal winner and the rest losers: "He was the clear winner in this psychologically crucial test," said network correspondent Roger Mudd, for example.[7] In New Hampshire, Carter received 28% of the primary vote, while Congressman Udall received 23%, with others dividing up the balance of the vote. Of the slightly more than 80,000 people who voted in the Democratic primary, Carter received 4500 more votes than Udall. This meant that Carter received one or two more delegates than Udall in the proportional allocation.

After Iowa and New Hampshire, Carter had a projected total of about 20 delegates out of more than 3000 to be chosen. The media verdict, however, was that Carter was the clear "front runner." He received massive media coverage, while the other candidates received little or virtually none. Thus *Time* and *Newsweek* put Carter on their cover and gave him 2600 lines of coverage, whereas Udall received only 96 lines, and all the other Democratic candidates combined got only 300 lines. In short, the media treated it as if a new President of the United States of New Hampshire had been elected.[8]

Such coverage suggests, in effect, that the results are meaningful for the nation as a whole. But neither Iowa nor New Hampshire were or are now representative of the national Democratic populace or the population in general, since neither state had or has any large cities, much in the way of minorities, and so on. Additionally, by pronouncing clear "winners" and the rest losers, except for an occasional "surprise," better-than-expected "second place" finish, the media have, in effect, reestablished the winner-take-all primary which the Democratic reforms tried to banish in the early 1970s. Actual delegates are apportioned in pure or modified proportional allocations which are based on the percentage of the vote received. But media coverage usually makes it a winner-take-all system in public perceptions. Indeed, even beyond the first caucus and primary, Patterson found that throughout the entire 13 weeks of the primaries and caucuses, in the "typical week following each primary, the first-place finisher received nearly 60% of the news coverage. . . ." The fact that a gradual 50-state delegate selection process was going on, which was of more-or-less proportional nature in nearly all cases, seemed to have been lost on the news media. As Patterson notes, the problem is best illustrated by the New York and Wisconsin primaries:

> In Wisconsin Udall finished second to Carter by less than 1% of the popular vote, gaining 25 delegates to Carter's 29. On the same day, Udall easily bested Carter in New York's primary, receiving 70 delegates to Carter's 35. Thus, Udall collected 95 delegates while Carter received 61, yet Carter got more news coverage and bigger headlines. Why was this? It was because Udall did not "win" either primary.[9]

One further bit of evidence on how the media blow the earliest, "solo" primary and caucus events drastically out of proportion, which includes a huge media buildup of the "importance" of the Iowa caucuses and New Hampshire primary prior to those events: As Michael J. Robinson detailed regarding that 1976 process, the "New Hampshire results received 170 times as much network news time per Democratic vote as the [later] outcome in [the] New York [primary]."[10]

Nature of Coverage: Other Studies and Other Elections

Issues and the Game in the Election of 1980   Other studies of other presidential elections have generally confirmed Patterson's findings. Michael J. Robinson and Margaret Sheehan studied news coverage of the 1980 election on CBS and the UPI wire service. They sought to measure issue coverage a little more precisely than had been done before. To do so, they first assessed whether each news story was "in plurality an 'issue piece' "— was it mostly about policy issues? But they also noted that many news stories weave the issues into coverage of the day's events. Because of that, they felt the first measure, which had been used by most other studies, "understates policy news to some degree." So they additionally measured news content devoted to policy issues "sentence by sentence." Thus their judgment was that other studies understated coverage of policy, and they felt their second measure more fully captured that coverage. Despite that, their conclusion and key data on issues coverage were:

> For both CBS and UPI, the totals for policy issue coverage were not impressive. [W]e found that 59% of the full-fledged presidential campaign news on CBS failed to contain even one issue sentence. On UPI, 55% of the news items made not a single meaningful reference to any one of the ninety-odd policy issues we identified during the course of Campaign '80. Using our less precise measure of general issue coverage, story by story, on CBS, 20% of the news items emphasized issues. On UPI, the figure was 18%.[11]

It is interesting to note that the UPI wire carried even less issues news than CBS. What that also suggests is that readers of local (nonmajor) newspapers receive very little issue news, since those papers rely on the wire services for national news. Further, whether even those stories that "emphasized" issues always, or even usually, were serious, probing pursuits of issue stands and their details is quite questionable.

Meanwhile, Robinson and Sheehan found that "about five of every six campaign stories made some meaningful reference to the competition" between the candidates.[12] Further, in another analysis, Michael Robinson found the game dominant in 1980 election news, while candidate qualifications and leadership characteristics were given short shrift: "There were four times as many explicit references to success or failure [in primaries, caucuses, debates . . .] as there were to all other candidate characteristics combined."[13] These are striking omissions in coverage, particularly as the challenging candidate in 1980 was former actor and governor of California, Ronald Reagan, whose knowledge of policies and issues and general grasp of decision making and administrative process had been questioned. Events, particularly in his second term, rather dramatically brought home the seriousness of inadequate treatment of candidate qualifications and leadership qualities.

One bright spot in 1980 coverage was noted by Robinson and Sheehan, however: the networks (since 1972, in fact) had begun to use somewhat extended interviews with the candidates to make their issue coverage more substantial. As Robinson and Sheehan point out, starting October 20, CBS aired a week-long set of "candidates-on-the-issues reports with five lengthy [by network standards] interviews with Reagan and Carter appearing 'together' on split screen answering Cronkite's questions about the issues of the campaign." In this week, they point out, CBS "did over 1800 seconds (30 minutes) of policy reporting." That was an encouraging development. For democratic concerns however, this was still a literal case of "too little and too late." As the researchers note, that total was the greatest of any *month* for issue attention and constituted, in fact, "10% of the entire year's issue news."[14] Such coverage was too late because by October 20–25, not only had all the (major party) alternative choices been narrowed down to two, but most of the public had already developed some sense of the candidates (especially including some image) and had made up their minds. The 1980 election did happen to have an unusually large number of late deciders; but that was, indeed, *unusual,* and hence such late issue coverage is just that for the typical election: late.

One other pattern reported by Robinson and Sheehan is very interesting and important to note; it can be called: "Whatever happened to the Vice-Presidency?" In the general election of 1980, Carter's vice-presidential running mate, Walter Mondale, "was the featured candidate in a grand total of one story" on the UPI wire; and Reagan's running mate, George Bush, was the subject of only two stories. On CBS Bush and independent John Anderson's running mate Patrick Lucey were the subject of one story each; "Mondale got shut out"—no stories at all. They report that other work found the same pattern in the 1968 and 1972 campaigns. The only reason there were a few more stories on the vice-presidential candidates in 1976 was because of a nationally televised debate between them— which was very acrimonious (conflict news criterion), with Republican Bob Dole in sharp-tongued attack. As Robinson and Sheehan importantly point out, "although four of the last six vice-presidents have become president . . . , the national press consistently ignores the vice-presidential ticket-holders, once they have been selected"; in effect, we "lose" the vice-presidency in national election news.[15]

Issues and the Game in the Election of 1984   Thomas Patterson returned to the fray in 1984, with Richard Davis, and found that it continued to be the case that "election news conveys scenes of political actions, not the values represented by those scenes. . . . Election news concentrates on competition and controversy, not basic questions of policy and leadership."[16]

Further and more specifically, Patterson and Davis considered the election campaign as fundamentally an act of communication between the candidates for leadership positions—most notably the Presidency—and the public. They found that the presidential candidates, especially in the nominating stage, were not able to get through to the public with their leadership and policy themes and ideas because of the news media's fixation on the game. Patterson and Davis did a content analysis of Mondale's standard stump speech and found two central themes: economic fairness and world tensions. Regarding the other prime contender for the Democratic nomination, within Senator Gary Hart's general theme of "a new generation of leadership" they found "a variety of specific proposals relating particularly to economic development, energy, and defense." Indeed, Hart repeatedly said he wanted his campaign to be one of issues; he had prepared a series of substantial position papers on major issues and, over the previous two years, had published several columns in newspaper "op/ed" sections around the nation with detailed discussions of issues such as education and national defense, including proposed solutions. Despite all that, Patterson and Davis found that "neither candidate's themes even appeared in more than a tenth of the articles" on the nomination process in the two newspapers they studied: the *New York Times* and the *Syracuse Post-Standard*. (The exception was Hart's "new generation of leadership" line— just the line itself.) "Nor were the specific issues that contributed to Hart's and Mondale's themes singled out for heavy coverage. In 114 articles about the Democratic campaign, Mondale's charge that Reagan's tax cuts benefited the rich was mentioned only four times; his 'progressive tax plan' was not mentioned once."[17] And so it went.

Interestingly, Michael Robinson offered a very contrasting conclusion regarding the three networks in the campaign of 1984: "[W]hen it came to substance issues, the networks followed the candidates' agenda, not their own. The most frequently addressed issues on TV were the most frequently addressed issues in reality: taxes, religion, U.S.-Soviet relations, deficits, and so on."[18] There are problems with this conclusion, though. The total amount of issues coverage is not documented; there are virtually no data on how much coverage the issues received. If the pattern found in previous elections of minimal coverage of issues continued in 1984, as generally appeared to be the case, the statement above (even if proportionally correct) would make little sense. Further, in the sentence following the statement above, Robinson offers the one bit of hard data on this question (a purely comparative datum): "The networks gave tax issues the biggest play—two and a half times as much as deficits." This was certainly not, however, the priority ranking of the Mondale issue agenda; indeed, taxes themselves were a derivative issue to the budget deficit—they were brought up only because of the deficit. But a serious discussion of the budget deficit was complex, whereas news stories featuring a conflict between Reagan and Mondale over taxes was simple and more dramatic— and had more easily identifiable impact on the general public (news criteria struck again).

To be as complete as possible, though, we should mention some efforts made by the networks in 1984 to add a bit to the usual level of issues coverage. A few specific examples from the general election period: CBS News ran a standard-length piece in August on winners and losers resulting from Reagan administration policy; NBC, in the "Summer Sunday USA" program in early September ran a (half-hour) review of the candidates, including a fair amount of material on qualifications and issues; CBS aired a fairly long segment (by network news standards) distinguishing the "two [different] visions" of governmental policy and society held by Reagan and Mondale in late October. CBS even made three brief tries at coverage of the Reagan campaign's comprehensive, concerted staging of events and manipulation of the media: a short piece in early September on security and control at Reagan campaign events, an interview with Mondale in mid-September allowing him to air complaints about Reagan's staging of events and avoidance of questioning by the media, and Leslie Stahl's analysis piece in October on staging and media manipulation (discussed earlier in this book).

It should finally be noted that Robinson and a colleague found a great deal of coverage of *campaign* issues. Indeed, by their definition "almost 40% of the campaign coverage" was of campaign rather than policy issues. There is good reason to question some of the particulars they include, though, such as "Beruit (as a campaign issue)" (?), "Reagan's availability," and a couple of others, including the difficult question of whether the personal finances of Ferraro's husband (and the disclosure question) were merely campaign issues or legitimate issues of character and perspective.[19] Patterson thought this was merely a campaign issue. In any case, the sheer volume and intensity of the coverage of the Ferraro finances certainly raised questions of balance and perspective in the media's coverage of the substance of election choice.[20]

A Note on Coverage of Minor Parties   In the effort to understand coverage of the substance of campaign choices in the United States the subject of "third" or minor political parties must be considered. Do parties other than the two established major ones have a right to be heard and to offer alternative ideas and compete for votes? As noted in Chapter 1, choice is the essence of democracy—alternative, competing choices. Indeed, various scholars of parties and American political history have pointed out: "As formulators of issues minor parties have been in advance of the major parties. . . . 'Looked at from the social point of view the chief function of third parties has been to bring new policies before the people: they force new policies upon the old parties [after unresponsiveness of the major parties led to third party advocacy and public response] and after accomplishing their work they pass away' [not that all third party ideas have or should have been adopted]."[21]

In the current media age, third parties are nearly invisible, however, especially on network TV. Robinson and Sheehan found in 1980, for example, that minor parties had no significant access to the news. . . . Rounding to the nearest whole number, minor party candidates received 0% of the newstime . . . on CBS and UPI.

In all of 1980, there was only one complete story on CBS weekday news about a minor party presidential candidate [excepting John Anderson's "independent, non-partisan movement"]—a less-than-3-minute piece about Libertarian candidate Ed Clark. On UPI there were two stories featuring Clark, and two featuring Citizens' party candidate Barry Commoner [distinguished biochemist and author of several highly praised books on energy and environmental issues].[22]

These were parties with coherent, intelligent general political philosophies and specific policy proposals (pointed in very different directions), which amounted to intelligent challenges to the status quo of the major parties. But they were virtually invisible to the general public. In 1984, Robinson found the same pattern: "The networks gave practically no time to the minor parties. . . ."[23]

Particularly in the media age, when the mass media so profoundly affect perceptions of what political reality is, including what is legitimate, the question is whether minor parties have an even greater uphill battle for existence with the prime national media almost totally ignoring them. The amount (and respectful nature) of attention that John Anderson received in 1980 was an encouraging sign of news coverage, but Anderson's switch in midelection from Republican to independent, as well as other factors, made his case unique. Indeed, the case of the 1976 independent candidacy of former Democratic senator from Minnesota, Eugene McCarthy, better illustrates the plight of nonmajor parties and candidates. As McCarthy explained, with his usual wit:

> I can see why the media have some trouble . . . giving us time when they have all the other distractions. . . . Walter Cronkite, two or three weeks ago, spent two nights talking about the boy who had been raised by the apes. . . . [F]irst they thought he had, then they retracted two nights later. . . . They found out the child had just watched television too much, and I thought that I might demand equal time with the ape boy, at least for one night.[24]

Coverage of Candidates and the Campaign Process: Other Studies

The Preprimary Period   The first caucuses and primary come early, as we noted in Chapter 9. The real beginning of the presidential campaign process gets under way still earlier in the "preprimary" stage, the "invisible primary" as Arthur Hadley has described it.[25] In these months before the first caucuses, candidates build organizations, seek political support and money around the nation, and seek media attention (which confers a sort of legitmacy on the candidacy and helps bring in money). And how is that media attention gained? As Richard Joslyn points out, a principal way "the press decides who should receive media coverage during the invisible primary is by relying on the support for a candidate in Gallup's or Harris' [polls] of presidential contenders"—those registering higher in the polls receive more media attention.[26] Despite the surface logic, however, there are serious problems with this approach; in fact, such preprimary polls are largely a waste of money and news space. These polls, in most cases, do not measure real support levels for candidates; it is simply too early for the vast majority of the public to be interested in these contests. The polls in this stage measure only name recognition.

Senators John Glenn and Gary Hart in the 1984 election cycle were good illustrations of the mistaken nature of these polls and of the consequences.

According to the media, there were two candidates who were the clear leaders for the Democratic nomination—in fact, prohibitive favorites: Walter Mondale and John Glenn. Glenn was portrayed as the "leader" because he registered high in the polls, well above any of the other candidates other than Mondale in the preprimary stage. But after a few caucuses and primaries were held, where was Glenn? Gone! The "support" he registered in polls was simply a projected name recognition and a vaguely positive image (principally from his astronaut days). Gary Hart, on the other hand, with all his well-articulated issue papers and policy proposals, was generally ignored in the media until his modest, relative success in Iowa and then his "win" in New Hampshire, after which he suddenly received vast coverage and dramatic increases in expressed support, without much public knowledge of who and what he was. This is not a very sensible way to cover potential nominees. (The nature of the coverage of the first caucus and primary also helped sink Glenn's chances.) All of which brings us to coverage of the nomination process.

Candidates and the Nomination Process: In 1980 and 1984   The pattern of primary and caucus coverage Patterson found in 1976 has been amply confirmed in succeeding elections. Robinson and Sheehan found the same severe overcoverage of the Iowa caucuses and New Hampshire primary compared with larger and more representative states. For example, in 1980, Minnesota held its precinct caucuses the same day as New Hampshire held its primary. Although Minnesota's population was more than five times as large as New Hampshire's, the latter received 33 times as many stories in CBS and UPI.[27] (Minnesota's caucuses provided no neat, clear totals for a "winner" and the "also-rans" that night.)

In 1984, the pattern was again repeated—and strikingly so, with a strong impact. Mondale won 45% of the Iowa caucus vote, while Hart received 15% (second best), and Glenn received 5%. This was of the 15% of

Iowa Democrats who turned out. The result has been documented by scholar William C. Adams:

> Despite the tiny size of the electorate, the media verdict was unequivocal, and the self-fulfilling power attributed to the caucuses was monumental: "Senators Hart and Glenn traded places in Iowa. Hart moved up to number two. Glenn became an also-ran. The effect of this surprising reversal already is being felt in their campaigns."—Tom Brokaw, NBC News Feb. 21.

Further, Adams found that in the week following the Iowa caucuses Mondale "actually suffered a decline in his relative share of attention on CBS and NBC newscasts"; Hart was awarded new status as prime challenger, and he received ten times the coverage on NBC and five times the coverage on CBS that he had had the week before. Further, "Hart's coverage was virtually free of any harsh criticism, unflattering issues, or cynical commentary."[28]

And then came New Hampshire. Hart "won" New Hampshire, again upsetting media expectations. The coverage was massive. It was a replay of Carter's coverage at the same stage in 1976. Hart's picture was on the cover of *Newsweek* and *U.S. News* and it shared the cover of *Time* with Mondale (each in chariots—the chariot race, rather than the horse race!). And the prose was purple indeed regarding the epic nature of Hart's victory:

> "In a single dazzling day, he had won the most electrifying upset primary victory in years—and set off a political chain reaction that transformed campaign '84."
> "Suddenly, [Mondale's] entire campaign seemed to be on the fritz."
> "Like the once formidable John Glenn, who stumbled home third in the primary, Mondale was suddenly racing for his life."
> "Reaction to televised accounts of Hart's victory was strong and immediate."
> [And *Newsweek*] "detected an electorate awash in a tidal wave of support for the youthful candidate. . . ."
> "No poll taken amid the white-hot heat of the Hart explosion should be viewed as conclusive. But the dramatic implosion of Mondale's support. . . ."

All this occurred after Hart received 15% of the 15% Democratic turnout in Iowa, while Mondale received 45%, and after Hart won a sum total of under 12,000 more votes than Mondale in the unrepresentative state of New Hampshire (a number of which voters were not Democrats).[29] This was out of the tens of millions of Democrats nationwide.

In general, as Brady and Hagen document, there was some attention to policy issues in the January "flurry of attention to the impending campaign." But "by February, policy issues and all other subjects were buried under a blizzard of speculation about who was winning and who was losing the nomination campaign."[30]

This, frankly, is just senseless; and it seriously altered the nomination process. As journalist Tom Wicker remarked and lamented, the "unexpected" Iowa showing for Hart

> produced a wave of publicity that Hart astutely rode to an upset primary victory . . . among New Hampshire's iconoclastic voters. That generated an avalanche of publicity, under which Mondale was buried in Maine . . . and Vermont. . . .
>
> What's wrong with publicity for the candidate with momentum? The problem is that the publicity *is* the momentum. . . .[31]

What also resulted from such coverage is that many candidates were effectively eliminated after the few earliest primaries and caucuses and people in other states, including such states as New York, Ohio, and California, never got to indicate their preference for a full range of candidates. Effectively, we have a media-elimination tournament, with most candidates being forced to leave the "game" before the sizable majority of the party populace can vote on them.

As Christopher Arterton has described, these and the other patterns of news/media coverage of the campaign process have, in turn, profoundly affected the way candidates and their organizations operate in the electoral process.[32]

And how were the candidates themselves treated in the news? Interestingly, Robinson and Sheehan, in their effort to assess how "fairly" the candidates were treated in 1980, came to a generalization which appears to apply to other years as well (although not without some exception): incumbents and distinct "front runners" receive decidely tougher (at times, hostile) media coverage than other candidates. Robinson concluded that the same was the case in the 1984 general election (although this book has disputed that conclusion because of the visual dimension). In terms of sheer amount of time in the general election, Robinson and colleagues found nearly perfect equality of network and UPI news coverage for the two major party candidates.[33]

. . . And in 1988 In the 1988 nomination process, with no incumbent involved and with "hot races" in both major parties, the temptations of horse-race journalism were at their height. Even in what looked like very encouraging developments for coverage of the substance of election choices, the game, strategy, and speculation on winning and losing consumed journalists. For example, CNN, which had continued its growth and maturation as a news organization, initiated a full half-hour program called "Inside Politics" devoted solely to the 1988 election (beginning in November 1987). They conducted roughly eight- to ten-minute interviews with each recognized candidate in each party during November of 1987. But in the majority of those interviews seen by this author, *most* of the questions

(even before primary/caucus events were in process) were about the game and strategy. Another, quite striking example of the game orientation, as well as of the conflict news criterion, occurred on NBC's special report in prime time the evening of the New Hampshire primary. In the early stages of the Republican nomination race, there was heated disagreement—and some just plain arguing—between Vice President Bush and Senator Dole, the two prime contestants for the nomination. In the last few days of the campaign, the Bush operation ran some very tough ads suggesting that Dole might raise taxes. Election night, NBC's Tom Brokaw got both candidates on live from their headquarters and with a rather insinuating tone in his voice, asked Bush: "Do you have anything to say to Senator Dole?" and then asked the same of Dole with respect to Bush. Brokaw got the sort of reaction he was obviously looking for: Dole, in a harsh tone of voice, said to tell Bush "to stop telling lies about my record."

And that tale leads us to a more fundamental problem in 1988 media coverage. NBC as well as other media organs were very interested in the Bush–Dole conflict (and any conflict they could find on the Democratic side). But in their focus on the game and conflict in the Bush–Dole contest, the media largely lost sight of what should have been a truly central policy issue in campaign '88. In the New Hampshire case, the media focused especially on the conflict over Bush's ads saying that Dole would raise taxes and Dole's angry reaction of denial. But the prime, in fact overwhelming, issue facing American government which caused the tax question to be raised in the first place got lost in the conflict obsession: the monumental budget deficits and what action each candidate would take to (realistically) solve that problem. Bush in particular, during the entire time that Dole was still contesting the nomination, never was seriously cross-examined by the media as to what he intended to do on that problem. This was especially striking in light of Bush's central role in the administration whose policies were a prime cause of the deficits (i.e., the huge 1981 tax cut and the large increase in military spending). (There was a remarkable irony in all this, as well: In the 1980 Republican nomination contest Bush had called just such proposals by Reagan "voodoo economics.") Clearly, this issue should have been at the center of campaign coverage in 1988, with constant efforts to get answers on solutions from candidates in *both* parties. Instead, with the huge "Super Tuesday" set of primaries and caucuses throughout the South and elsewhere, and with the Democratic Party having an active contest through much of the nomination stage, most of what the public got was the game.

On the plus side, major newspapers did continue the trend in recent elections of running special series of articles on the major party candidates, including often good synopses of background, education, career, qualities as public figure and officer, and a fair amount of material on policy positions. The networks did make a more distinct effort *before* the Iowa and New Hampshire events to point out the unrepresentative nature of those states. The networks also made more effort to give the public more information on the politics and demographics of states holding primaries prior to the events—with help from their whiz-bang, computer-generated graphics capacities. Further, both print and TV media did a good job of providing perspective on the candidacy of Congressman Gephardt (D.-Mo.). After trying various themes, Gephardt began to receive good responses to messages of a populist nature which included negative comments about "those politicians in Washington." But especially after Gephardt's success in the Iowa caucuses, the media repeatedly pointed out how Gephardt's actual status as a prime leader and consummate insider in Congress contradicted this "outsider" campaign message.

And the Nominee Is . . .: The Media and the National Party Conventions   As mentioned in Chapter 9, the delegate selection process for presidential nominations was very different in 1968 and earlier, and so were the national party nominating conventions. But the significant impact of television coverage on those conventions came earlier than such impact on the delegate selection process. Gladys and Kurt Lang have described and analyzed the first television coverage of the conventions (in 1952).[34] TV coverage of what was happening outside the 1968 Democratic convention compared with the evidently controlled activities inside was a prime stimulus to the subsequent party reforms. But it was in 1972, the same year the primaries (and coverage of them) became the centerpieces of the delegate selection process, that television's impact on the conventions was most strikingly evident—in very different ways for the two parties.

On the Democratic side the chief impact is best characterized as: "opportunity lost, lesson learned." The turbulence of American society in the late 1960s and early 1970s was evident in the 1972 Democratic convention—there was much wrangling over rules and policies. The result was not just a general disoriented look on TV for that party, but also the fact that nominee George McGovern was not able to give his acceptance speech until long past prime-time hours. This key event of the convention is also the greatest opportunity to present the party nominee to a vast national audience, and it was a blown opportunity. The lesson was learned well by both parties, though: Organize the convention around television for best coverage, and by all means be certain that the acceptance speech is scheduled and is actually given in prime time. The Republicans had already learned this lesson. In fact, as Timothy Crouse told us in his fascinating (and often funny) description of reporting on the campaign trail that year, the GOP had elaborately scripted the entire convention for best appearance on TV—right down to instructions to speakers on "when to pause, nod, and accept 'spontaneous' cheers" and when a "demonstration would interrupt the convention secretary in midsentence."[35] Today the conventions are nearly totally geared to the appearance on TV, with a style at the focal point of the operation well captured by Joslyn: "The podium has taken on the look of a blockbuster talent show, complete with emcees and guest stars."[36]

The audience for these party spectaculars on the tube has, however, steadily declined since the 1950s (presumably because of the general party decline, the typically minimal part played by the conventions in selecting a nominee, since the primary and caucus process has usually already made the holder of a majority of delegate votes evident, and because "Kojak," "Miami Vice," or "Dynasty" have been more exciting). As a consequence, and given the increasing network obsession with the bottom line, the networks cut down on the amount of coverage in 1984—no more gavel-to-gavel coverage in the evening hours.

Speaking of the audience, we now turn to the impact of news coverage of elections on the public. For the best study of that impact, we turn back to Thomas Patterson.

Impact of Election Coverage on the Public

Systematically establishing the impact of election communications on the public's opinions and behavior is a real challenge. That, in fact, is an understatement. As Richard Joslyn has precisely pointed out (to add a note to the discussion of method in Chapter 9): "Empirical demonstration that campaign communication has a particular effect on public opinion would ideally include prior specification of the hypothesized effect, measurement of the relevant opinions both before and after the campaign communication has occurred, a comparison of the opinions of those exposed to the communication with those who were not exposed, and the elimination of all other possible reasons that those exposed to the communication might differ from those unexposed."[37]

This is indeed a challenge—and those requirements of empirical demonstration should certainly be kept in mind whenever statements are made about such effects. Especially considering the final element in those requirements, a perfect such demonstration is nearly impossible in all but rather trivial circumstances. But as described in Chapter 9, Thomas Patterson has provided the closest thing to such demonstration that we have. We turn now to something of a step-by-step look at how he built this overall demonstration of the effects of media coverage of elections on the public.

Interest Patterson's findings on the impact of presidential election news on the public are even more striking than those on election coverage itself. First, given the longer (primary and caucus) campaign process in the post-1968 era, along with the increased media attention, it would seem logical that a higher level of interest in the campaign would have built up compared with past eras. Patterson's findings, however, suggest otherwise, although the *pattern* of increases in interest has changed:

> From February to October, after nine months of intensive campaigning, strong interest among the electorate increased from about 20% to slightly more than 30%. In this respect, today's campaign is not much different from those studied by Lazarsfeld and Berelson in the 1940s. . . . Thus the lengthening and increased activity of the current campaign has not significantly changed the overall level of voter interest.[38]

With the massive early primary/caucus coverage, interest in the nomination *peaks* earlier, but does not ultimately rise to a higher level. We should also note that television contributed the most to that early upturn in interest—although Patterson found newspaper reading to be "about equally responsible for rising interest during the latter part" of the campaign.[39]

One other pair of Patterson findings regarding public interest levels needs to be specially noted. He found that after the primaries and caucuses the televising of the national conventions and the three presidential debates between Carter and Ford actually "replaced the nightly newscasts as the major inducer of public interest. . . . In fact, during the last stages of the campaign the effect of television on voter interest derived almost totally from coverage of the debates and conventions." Further, "interest was particularly likely to increase among weak [party] identifiers who happened to see parts or all of the conventions"—latent party loyalty appeared to be aroused by convention viewing.[40] These findings suggest the importance of televising the conventions and the debates (especially in a time of weakened parties and political disorientation). A series of interesting and important Patterson findings on the impact of televising the conventions and debates are specially noted after the rest of his study results are reviewed.

Thinking and Talking about the Campaign: Media Agenda/Voters' Agenda
And with all the coverage of the sort we have noted, what did the public think was important, and what did they talk about? By this point it should come as no news flash that what the news media emphasized—the game and the horse race—was just what the public thought was important. In fact, the correlation was "more than +.85 at every point once the campaign was under way."[41] This public preoccupation with the game as opposed to the substance of electoral choices appears to be a product of the post-1968 resort to primaries and open caucuses and of the mass media treatment of the campaign. Thus Patterson notes that the premier study of the 1948 election found that "67% of voters' conversations were concerned with the candidates' positions and qualifications," while only one-fourth of them

discussed which candidate was likely to win. But in 1976, "only 34% of people's conversations were concerned with substance" (with a high of only 43% even in October).[42] Is the contemporary democratic electoral choice process being largely lost in a fog of electoral trivial pursuit?

But Patterson also found a significant variation in that pattern of seeing the game as the election's most important feature—a variation of striking importance. He found that the game "was at the top of the voters' lists at every stage of the campaign but one: It fell behind the debates during the general election," and viewing of both the televised conventions and the debates also increased people's sense of the importance of substance in the election: "Indeed, debate and convention viewing was more closely related than either newspaper or evening newscast exposure to a heightened belief in the significance of policy and leadership matters."[43]

Thus people paid more attention to the substance of the election's choices when presented with presidential debates, which have as their essence and purpose the discussion of policy and leadership qualifications. And when presented with the national conventions, involving portrayal of party political orientations and a review of leadership qualifications, along with the debates, people increased their belief in the salience of the substance of election choice—they thought policy and leadership were more important than the game. This suggests that when serious communications about the substance of electoral choice are presented to the public (in an interesting fashion) they respond—and begin to act more like democratic citizenship requires. Networks (and even newspapers) are you listening?!

Jimmy Who? Awareness of Candidates   The nature of the impact of media coverage of the nomination process is perhaps most dramatically evident in people's awareness of the candidates and the consequences for how they vote (our ultimate concern). In the 1976 election Patterson found that most of the public knew little about the candidates for the Democratic nomination at the beginning of the year; even long-time Senate power Henry Jackson, who had appeared in prominent Senate hearings and been a central player in a number of major issues, was unknown even by name to 37% of Patterson's sample, and another 36% "knew him only by name." Even in February, after the Iowa caucuses, only 20% said they knew anything more about Carter than his name. Media coverage following the New Hampshire primary dramatically changed that for Carter. Patterson found that Carter was the only candidate whose public recognition rose dramatically: 20% said they knew something about him in February, 81% said so by June. But the public's recognition of his Democratic opponents increased only modestly. "Recognition levels rose by 14% for [Congressman Morris] Udall, [Governor Jerry] Brown, and Jackson, and by only 9% for [Senator Frank] Church . . . and even declined for [Senator] Bayh and [Sargeant] Shriver."[44]

And most striking of all was the impact of that awareness, from the nature of media coverage, on the vote. Patterson noted the example of Pennyslvania's voters (from the Erie, Pennsylvania, part of his panel study). Of those who voted, 90% said they knew Carter, but only about 50% indicated they knew about Jackson or Udall (the other two candidates still in the race). The result: "Nearly all [voters] picked a candidate they knew something about . . . ." Most specifically, about a quarter of the voters knew only one of the three candidates, usually Carter; he received 90% of those votes. And about 30% knew two candidates, typically Carter and either Jackson or Udall; Carter got 60% of those votes. The nature of campaign coverage, it appears, has a profound impact on the way people vote. This is further confirmed by how people tended to view the candidates—according to who was portrayed as the "winner" and who the "losers."

"Winning Isn't Everything, It's the Only Thing"   That old line of legendary coach Vince Lombardi seems to have been taken to heart by the media, and the public response followed suit in 1976. Who had "won" a primary or caucus event and who was likely to in the future were so prominently and constantly run as news stories that the great majority of the public was certain to have gotten the message. Patterson explained the developments and the impact:

> The first impression that most Democrats had of Carter was that he was doing extremely well in places like Iowa and New Hampshire, an accomplishment that evoked some surprise and a certain amount of admiration. As they heard more about him, most of them also regarded him as an acceptable nominee. This reaction was not based on the feeling that in Carter they had discovered their ideal candidate, for they *knew very little about his politics or abilities.* But he seemed like a sensible and personable individual and, since he had won the acceptance of voters elsewhere, he must have his good points. These were persuasive perceptions [emphasis added].[45]

This impression and the public perception of winners and losers was an especially potent factor in a nomination process where there were no clearly and strongly dominant figures before the process began, as was the case in 1976 on the Democratic side (and as was the case again in 1988). In such coverage, Patterson pointed out, was the making of a bandwagon.

One other aspect of the impact of media portrayal of winners and losers needs to be mentioned. It is an extraordinarily clear and dramatic case. The event involved was the second debate between Ford and Carter (on foreign affairs). In that debate, Ford made his now-famous misstatement about Poland not being under the domination of the Soviet Union. People who were interviewed within 12 hours of the end of the debate saw nothing especially noteworthy in the remark (only 10% mentioning it), and the majority of them thought Ford had "won" the debate. But then the news coverage emphasized the goof or "gaff," featured the question of who "won," and suggested Carter had done so as a result of Ford's mistake. Public opinion reversed itself at that point; a majority then thought Carter had won, and 60% cited Ford's remark.

The media obsession with primary focus on declaring a winner and a loser in presidential debates, along with a penchant for using prize-fight metaphors, has been evident in each succeeding election. In 1984, for example, the *Newsweek* cover after the first debate simply said: "The Debate: Who Won?"—and the subheading for the feature article said "Mondale wins points on style and substance but neither man scores a knockout."[46] Interestingly, and illustrating the standardized thinking in media circles, the covers of *Time* and *Newsweek* after the second Reagan–Mondale debate were virtually identical, with *Time* featuring: "Showdown: Who Won, and Why"; and *Newsweek* featuring: "Round Two: Who Won—And Why." The featured interpretive logic was also identical (and curious): *Time*'s featured story headline read "A Tie Goes to the Gipper," and *Newsweek*'s read "Reagan Wins a Draw" (with the subheading "Mondale lands some punches, but doesn't score the knockout he was hoping for"—was Muhammad Ali or Larry Holmes running for president?). Both *Newsweek* and *Time* also ran stories with the assessments of the "political pros" and "the experts" regarding what transpired—not primarily the substance of what the two said, but "who won," "their performance and its impact." Each magazine did get around to noting some of the policy discussion, but that was a very secondary element.[47]

Images (—and Print Media versus TV)   One brief note is also in order on Patterson's discussion of the images of candidates that people develop from news coverage. Patterson reaches a conclusion about the news medium principally responsible for the people's development of those images which is contrary to much recent discussion: he found that newspapers were "more instrumental in the formation of images" and that newspaper reading "particularly contributes to the fullness of people's images."[48] This, he concluded, was because voters' impressions of a candidate's primary victories, political record, and the like are principally dependent on verbal communication, which is the strong suit of newspapers. Patterson also presents data on correlations of changes in images in various categories ("personality," "leadership," etc.) with newscast and newspaper exposure as empirical backing for that conclusion. The difference between newspapers and TV news in those correlations is, on the whole, quite small, however. And he acknowledges that "when only the voters' impressions about the candidates' personalities and leadership capacities are considered, television's impact is more apparent"—indeed, in the first half of the nomination period especially, "regular viewing of the evening newscasts was strongly associated with the formation of impressions of Carter's personality." He also noted the predominance of stylistic impressions of Carter, along with the fact that "once a candidate's image has been developed, it's unlikely to be altered significantly" by subsequent news—and that the "large majority" of voters had developed an image of Carter by April.[49] Putting those elements together suggests a larger role played by TV in image building. In Chapter 4 we discussed in some detail further reasons for concluding that TV plays a larger role in image building.

Information   On the other hand, Patterson reports convincingly, as have others, that newspaper reading is far more responsible for people's learning of substantive information than is watching newscasts (as was discussed in Chapter 4); in fact, the latter adds little to learning about policies. Two specific forms of TV viewing of election coverage did contribute to people's awareness of the candidates' policy positions, though. Once again, the evidence of the important impact of televising the national conventions and the debates is striking: "Heavier convention viewers became significantly better informed about 63% of Carter's positions and 25% of Ford's [the incumbent and hence already better known]," and "exposure to the televised . . . debates . . . was significantly related to higher awareness of 50% of Carter's and Ford's policies."[50]

Some Additional Thoughts on Debates   Other research on the impact of presidential debates has found less pronounced effects, in other respects, however—even on awareness of candidate attributes. In general, research has not shown a sizable impact on candidates' standing in the polls or on the actual vote.[51] Perhaps, since the debates that have been researched have been those in the general election, held quite late in the electoral season, the reason for the apparent low impact on opinions and the vote is that so many people have already made up their minds (or largely so). In 1980 there was an unusually high percentage of very late deciders; one study suggested a corresponding significant impact of the Carter–Reagan debate, as discussed in Chapter 4.

It may also be that greater substantive impact has been obstructed by the way the debates themselves have been structured and conducted. Certainly, if the democratic principle is to be vigorously upheld, the nature of the conduct of debates (at least as conducted through the nomination stage of 1988) must be altered. The first of two primary problems is the practice of allowing negotiation between the candidates' organizations to determine the structure of the debates and who will do the questioning—that is, *if* both candidates deign to agree to one or more debates (Nixon refused to in 1968 and 1972; Carter balked until the final week of 1980 when polls showed him slipping). The most notorious example of the absurdity of this approach occurred with the first Reagan–Mondale debate in 1984, when it was revealed that nearly 100 journalists were vetoed by the two campaigns (the great majority by the Reagan operation, apparently).

[Commentary!] This is absurd. Clearly, participation in the debates should not be voluntary, and neither the structure of the debates nor the questioners should in any way be determined by the candidates. Proposal: One way to avoid the former problem is to write into the existing campaign finance law a provision that simply says that when the candidate signs the campaign finance agreement, he or she also agrees to appear in a *series* of debates as designated by other parties (perhaps an advisory committee to the Federal Election Commission, with some representatives of the American Political Science Association and the American Bar Association).

The structure of the "debates" is also an absurdity. One-and-one-half-minute answers and one-minute replies to policy matters of importance are utterly ridiculous—and an invitation to the one-liner approach to issues discussion. (Lincoln and Douglas must be laughing—or rather, crying—in their graves.) The three-debate model used in 1976 is an appropriate one (on domestic policy, then foreign policy, then all issues), which *can* then allow for more adequate answer time. Second, there has been little opportunity for questioners to follow-up; some candidates have been able to offer glib replies that do not really respond to the issue—and get by with it. (After the 1980 "debate" between Reagan and Independent John Anderson, for example, questioner Jane Bryant Quinn commented: "John Anderson did answer, in some fashion, every question asked him. . . . But Ronald Reagan's answer count was low. Those who scored the transcript for me gave Reagan anywhere from zero to three answers out of six.")[52] The questioners must be able to follow up—thoroughly—until an actual answer is obtained, or until it is painfully obvious that the candidate is deliberately avoiding the issue—or does not know the information (also important to discover, especially in light of certain events in the later 1980s). Politeness is not required here (the questioners should have the social grace of a Mike Wallace—namely, none). It would also be appropriate to hold part of one debate as a real debate, where the candidates cross-examine one another (as was done, to a limited extent, in a few nomination-stage debates in the 1984 and 1988 election cycles).

Finally, the questioners must be the best and the toughest in the nation. The stakes are too high for anything less. The journalists should be of the caliber of David Broder or Robert MacNeil. Why not also have a political scientist and an economist (who can speak English, not just jargon)? (It should be added that discussions were held in 1987 between the chairs of the two major parties to place the debates under party auspices. As of this writing, final agreement had not been reached.) Interestingly, the importance of debates had become so thoroughly recognized by the 1988 election cycle that more than 50 debates were scheduled in the nomination stage for candidates from both parties—more than 20 of which were held in the later parts of 1987! There was some debate about whether all these debates constituted overkill. (It will be interesting to see any research evidence on whether more people knew more about the candidates' issue positions and qualifications for office.)

THE SELLING OF THE PRESIDENT (AND OTHERS): POLITICAL ADS

Political Ads and Today's Campaign

In his fascinating and revealing "inside" look at the media campaign for Richard Nixon's 1968 presidential election effort, Joe McGinnis made this observation: "It is not surprising . . . that politicians and advertising men should have discovered one another. And, once they recognized that the citizen did not so much vote for a candidate as make a psychological purchase of him, not surprising that they began to work together."[53] And work together they have, as Larry Sabato has excellently analyzed in his review of "the rise of political consultants." The political system is very different as a result: "It would have been difficult for the ward leaders and political bosses [up through the early 1950s] to imagine how completely they would be replaced by professionals independent of the party [organization]"—most notably, the media consultants and the pollsters.[54] This is the case not only in presidential elections but in congressional and principal state elections, as well. Nor are lavish use of TV ads and reliance on non-local professional media people confined to the highly populous states and the big media markets therein, as *Newsweek* illustrated with a story at the end of the 1986 election about the North Dakota U.S. Senate contest. The incumbent, Republican Senator Mark Andrews, ultimately had 52 different TV ads done for his campaign—done by the prominent, veteran campaign consulting firm of Bailey, Deardourff, Sipple & Associates of Washington, D.C. His challenger, Democrat Kent Conrad, relied on his own Washington-based firm of Greer & Associates for his (very clever and successful) ads. As *Newsweek* commented:

> So it went in the battle for North Dakota, a contest fought on the wind-swept northern plains orchestrated from offices 1500 miles away in Washington. . . . More than ever before, the campaign of 1986 demonstrated the encompassing reach and role of Washington's burgeoning legion of vote brokers—media consultants, pollsters. . . . Their [involvement has also] brought national standardization to what used to be the yeasty variety of local brews.[55]

Money is a good indication of the increased emphasis on use of the electronic media to communicate to the public, especially with ads. Nearly 60% of campaign spending for congressional contests in the 1986 election was devoted to media efforts; this compares with 35% as recently as the late 1970s.[56]

The basic communication principles and techniques used in political ads were discussed in Chapters 3 (especially) and 4, so they will not be repeated here. A few other observations are in order on the nature of political ads as communication instruments, though, before we turn to discussion of studies of the effects of ads on the public. The first and more general thing to note is that the formulation and production of political ads has gotten increasingly sophisticated, and a central element of that increasing sophistication is the fact that ads have been made an integrated part of a comprehensive campaign design. Thus, for the most notable aspect, opinion polling is used to find out how people perceive the candidate's attributes and orientations, as well as what the public feels about the issues of the time, and then to design an ad package that best appeals to such public opinion. And tracking polls can be used to make adjustments later in response to the public response to the ad campaign.

Second, TV ads come in various "sizes," namely, 30-second and 60-second "spot" ads or longer 5-minute ads. There are also some different main "types" of approaches to ads and functions they are to perform. As Diamond and Bates point out in their review of the rise of political advertising on TV, the most basic ad is the ID spot—a spot designed simply to build basic recognition of who the candidate is. This is essential for challengers of incumbents and those running for an open seat. Such ads are frequently used as the first stage of a candidate's ad campaign. Diamond and Bates suggest that the typical second phase of the ad campaign involves "argument spots," meaning ads that argue for a particular policy position or general political orientation, or argue against an opponent's position or orientation. They also frequently appeal to people's emotions.[57]

What should also be noted here is that despite the notion common in political commentaries about the empty image mongering of ads, they fairly often contain real, useful information about the candidate's record, qualifications, and issue positions. In fact, in their major study of ads and news in the 1972 presidential election, McClure and Patterson concluded that Nixon's and McGovern's ads, in various respects, actually contained more material on issues than the network news shows![58] (That conclusion should not be carried too far, and the 1972 election may not have been typical; still Patterson and McClure's findings are striking.)

A third thing to note about ads is a revealing characteristic of politics in the media age: It is increasingly rare for candidates' ads to stress—or even mention—their political affiliation (only 12% did so in the 506 ads from many different campaigns that Joslyn analyzed).[59] This certainly encourages the further decline of the party system. Fourth, another type of ad, often used late in the campaign, is the attack spot or "negative ads."[60] There has been much debate over the "increasing negativity" of ads, although little solid evidence of such increases has been presented. The professionals generally use them with care, as they can fairly easily backfire. The specific (local) political culture is a major factor to consider—the "squeaky clean," polite politics of Minnesota makes attack ads that would work fine in some other places hazardous to the perpetrator there.

Finally, we should note that credibility is a central issue in ads—as the "propaganda" of someone's campaign, are they believable? Jimmy Carter's ad-man Gerald Rafshoon articulated another part of the problem in an interesting way, especially regarding the shorter spots: "The environment in which you present the thirty-second spot, sandwiched between deodorants and toilet tissue, doesn't lend enough credibility" to the ads. For Rafshoon, the solution was the longer five-minute ad.[61] Another interesting solution, increasingly used since the mid-1970s, is the "Man in the Street" ad. These look more real since "real" people (average Janes and Joes) are interviewed in natural settings testifying to how good they think candidate X is, or how the reverse is the case for the opponent. An effective variant of this is to make it look as much like a news show as possible, with a reporter-like person interviewing people news-style. This technique was used effectively in the 1976 Ford campaign.[62]

The Impact of Political Ads

Perhaps surprisingly, there have been rather few studies of the effects of political ads on the public. [Clearly, establishing cause-and-effect relations in the political ad area is a great challenge—for the reasons that were noted earlier in the chapter (p. 216).] The evidence is thin for valid generalization. But some material has been gathered.[63]

Patterson and McClure performed the most substantial study (again, in 1972), in which they did "before" and "after" interviews to measure changes in beliefs regarding policy positions taken in the candidates' ads (although they didn't establish specific exposure patterns to the ads). They did find that frequent viewers of television were more likely to change their beliefs in the direction of the ads McClure and Patterson focused on, although the changes were not great. Heavy viewers also learned a fairly substantial amount about candidates' issue positions. Also, people who had low levels of political interest learned more than those with high interest, principally because (1) the latter already knew more from reading and viewing more news, and (2) because the low-interest people did not see much news and were an "inadvertent audience" for ads, which, correspondingly, became a prime source of information for them. Patterson and McClure interestingly conclude:

> Although the issue material contained in spots is incomplete and oversimplified, it also is abundant. So abundant in fact, that presidential advertising contributes to an informed electorate.

[This also happens] because of the powerful way it transmits its issue content. Three basic advertising strategies—simplicity, repetition, and sight-sound coordination—combine to make presidential spots good communicators.[64]

Joslyn, one of the closer students of ads, suggests skepticism is in order about how much meaningful material people learn about candidates' policy positions, however. People may learn some things about the ads themselves, but whether that is accurate, significant, policy-related material is questionable—especially since Joslyn's own review of ads led him to conclude that most contain little in the way of specific policy positions and many tend to be "deceptive, distorted, or so general as to be meaningless."[65]

And what about how candidates themselves are perceived; how are people's perceptions of candidates' attributes affected? Surprisingly, Patterson and McClure found rather little consistent impact on the image people had of candidates. Joslyn, after a closer look at their data, notes that there were particular attributes that were positively affected as perceived by heavier viewers (such as "experience" for both candidates, "forward-looking" for McGovern and "compassion" for Nixon—as well as for "confidence-inspiring" and "trustworthy," interestingly!). In general, taking into account the few other studies, Joslyn concludes that "to date it appears that spot ads have some modest ability to affect public perceptions of both candidates' policy positions and their personal attributes."[66]

Finally, it should be remembered that candidate ads are not the only electoral ad subject. Occasionally, there are ads for political parties as a whole. A particularly effective example of those were the set of ads run by the Republican National Committee in 1979 leading up to the 1980 elections, ads that had the theme "vote Republican, for a change"—and which were unanswered by the Democratic side. These ads appeared to help the GOP in its surprising success in congressional races in 1980.[67]

Campaigns for and against state ballot propositions (initiatives and referenda) in those states which allow them have also increasingly relied on political ads, in many cases with striking results. In three senses, the situation is virtually ideal for maximum impact of ads: no party identification is involved, there is no candidate and hence no human embodiment of policy directions who is more easily perceived and evaluated (although occasionally a public figure comes to play a key role in symbolizing the issue), and public knowledge of the issue involved in a proposition is usually low or very low. Correspondingly, an ad campaign that can effectively "paint a picture" of what the proposition and its consequences are like can often crystallize public opinion and make the difference in voting.

In the absence of party identification and party organization and workers, the key resource is money—lots of money makes a lavish ad campaign possible; the lack of money means the absence of such a campaign. This raises a troubling question for democracy: Can those with lots of money—most notably large corporations and trade associations—largely control the outcome of proposition campaigns that affect them, using massive, clever ad campaigns as their instrument? There is more than a little evidence to indicate a "yes" answer. Sabato reviews two of the more notable and revealing examples. Proposition 15 in California in 1976 sought to limit nuclear power plant construction because of safety concerns and as long as liability for accidents continued to be very limited by a certain law. The electricity industry and the nuclear plant construction industry spent huge sums, hired a top ad agency which produced a very clever series of ads—and the proposition went down to defeat. The same thing happened with a 1978 California proposition to restrict smoking areas—massive spending by the tobacco industry and a top-of-the-line professional ad series led to defeat of the measure. In fact, as Berkman and Kitch have summarily concluded: "[W]here the corporate-backed side significantly outspends the other side, the corporate side usually wins. The tactics used by the nuclear industry are usually successful. Corporate America continues to successfully oppose anti-smoking initiatives, handgun registration initiatives [with much help from the NRA], proposals to increase corporate taxes, . . ."[68]

THE MEDIA IN CONGRESSIONAL AND STATE ELECTIONS

In Chapter 9 we noted that one of the criteria that Robinson and Sheehan had established to assess the adequacy of news coverage of elections (1980 in specific) was "comprehensiveness"—how comprehensively were elections other than the presidential covered by the national media? Their answer: " 'Local' campaigns even at the [U.S. Senate] level make national news only when these stories can be directly pegged to the presidency; or to curiosity candidates; or to high visibility 'politicans' such as Goldwater or McGovern [or Kennedy]. . . ."[69] Thus "governor's races have less newsworthiness than rain in Seattle or blue sky in Santa Barbara" and "congressional campaigns are practically invisible, too. The House and Senate combined accounted for about 2% of the total newstime on CBS."[70]

And what of coverage of congressional campaigns at the local level? Well, there is more of it, but not as much more as one might think—and unlike the case of presidential elections, equality of coverage is *not* practiced. Although there has not been a great deal of research done on the media in congressional elections, what has been done has discovered some striking patterns. We should first remember what was said in Chapter 8: Members of Congress usually find local media very receptive to their efforts to place stories or receive media coverage of events in which they are involved. We should also remember that the general public knows far less about congressional offices and candidates, especially House offices and candidates, than about presidential ones. And regarding elections in specific, as Goldenberg and Traugott summarize, at the *end* of an election; "Although most voters could recognize and [simply] evaluate the incumbents in both the Senate and the House, many more could recognize and rate the Senate challenger than the House challenger. Fewer than half . . . remember learning anything at all about the House challenger in their district."[71]

A prime reason for that low level of learning is the frequent low level of media coverage. Thus a 1978 study of 75 congressional districts "found only about twelve articles and ads per race in the largest-circulation dailies in each area with any mention of either candidate or of the campaign more generally," and TV coverage is equally scarce—or more so.[72] Two prime reasons for this are (1) the fact that House district boundaries are frequently quite different than media circulation and broadcast areas, and (2) "according to Richard Stout, House contests are especially low in priority for media coverage because reporters are unimpressed with the importance of individual representatives. He wrote: 'A House member is not directly responsible for running the town, city . . . or state . . . ; after all, he is just one of a ruly mob of 435.' "[73] Interestingly, though, "because of their higher district efficiency (that is, being entirely within a single congressional district), smaller newspapers tend to cover a particular congressional race more heavily than larger papers."[74]

Additionally, incumbents in Congress tend to receive nearly twice as much coverage in elections as do challengers. Further, incumbents enjoyed a particular advantage "in references to candidate characteristics, such as background and experience, but incumbents also enjoyed substantial advantages in issue coverage."[75]

Finally, Clarke and Evans, reflecting on the general circumstance of the decline of party cues for help in voting, have offered a striking observation on the consequences of the news coverage of congressional elections just noted:

> Where in 1958 just over half of all votes cast *across* party lines went to the incumbent, the figure has . . . edged upward, to stand at about three-quarters in the 1970s. This represents an important shift in electoral behavior.
> Some suggest the pattern of crossover voting is due, in part, to the familiarity that accrues to House members. Current officeholders are well known and well liked; challengers in these elections suffer from low visibility, and few voters display much feeling about them. In fact, party defections would be less loaded toward incumbents if more challengers could make themselves favorably known to voters.[76]

The paradox noted in Chapter 8 of low public ratings of Congress as a whole, while individual members are reelected at rates of 90% or better, is further explained. Whether democracy is well served by all this is quite another matter.

What of the media in state and local elections? The basic answer is: There is exceedingly little coverage of state races other than for the governorship; and serious studies of that coverage are even scarcer. Joslyn, taking into account the point of the quote just above, has offered the best keynote observation about results and consequences: "In such a case the identity of the known quantity is clearly important, and the contribution of news coverage to the visibility of candidates takes on added significance. Furthermore, if this is true in congressional elections, one can well imagine the importance of candidate agenda setting at lower electoral levels, where the information context is generally even poorer [often, much poorer]."[77]

Regarding local elections, evidence on media coverage and its impact may be hard to come by, but developments in candidates' own use of the media (and other "high-tech" techniques) is accumulating, which is interesting. The *National Journal* reports, for example: "Most mayoral candidates in cities with populations of at least 100,000 are using professional polling, radio and TV advertisements and direct-mail consultants to build their images. And there is evidence that modern political techniques are seeping into mayoral and even city council races in smaller cities."[78]

FINALLY, ELECTION NIGHT ("TUNED-IN TV, TURNED-OFF VOTERS"?)

There is one final way that the TV age has notably affected elections—final in a literal sense. Election night is the final act of the election process (the final scene of the election drama). The combination of the competition between the networks and the development of survey sampling techniques (and computers to process the data) has resulted in network projections of a presidential victor well before the polls have closed in some parts of the nation. The election of 1980 was the most notorious case: One network announced its projection of the winner nearly three hours before the polls had closed in most West Coast areas—thereby telling citizens who were preparing to vote during that time, in effect, "your vote is meaningless" (at least for the premier office in the nation). Further, in 1980 a good number of West Coast elections for the House of Representatives were decided by close votes, as will always occur in some number. Correspondingly, if even 5 or 10% of the public which would have voted is discouraged from voting by such projections, the actual outcome of elections can be affected (usually, about 15 to 20% of West Coast voters cast their votes between 6:00 and 8:00 P.M.). There were indeed accounts of voters leaving the voting places after the projections were broadcast in 1980.[79]

The debate over whether this practice has a serious impact and whether such early projections should be allowed has been fairly intense. Unfortunately, systematic evidence (data as well as accompanying logic) has been mixed (what there is of it). Some studies have found a real, though not large impact (just under 3% turnout in one study), whereas others have argued there is no meaningful difference.[80] (Like systematically studying the impact of election news or broadcast debates, studying this subject presents the researcher with thorny problems.)

Ultimately, perhaps, having such "hard data" on precise impact is not necessary. Perhaps there is a basic principle involved. Why should *anyone*'s most basic democratic right of casting a normally meaningful vote be rendered (at least partly) irrelevant because one or more TV networks are seeking to beat the competition and project a winner even earlier? Why is the video version of a high-tech arms race a necessity? Why is it essential to pronounce a winner three or four hours earlier? This tendency is, unfortunately, part of the general pattern of election-night coverage of near total winners–losers coverage, immersed in the constant numbers update. Accurate, meaningful analyses of what the patterns in the election mean have generally been rather few and far between at the national level and the same—or nearly nonexistent—at the local level.[81]

In late 1987, the House of Representatives passed a bill to establish a uniform poll-closing time throughout the nation (7:00 P.M. Western time), and the networks would not be allowed to broadcast projections of winners until then. It is not clear why the election day schedule and the opportunity for citizens to vote must be altered simply because of network competition and lack of responsibility. I cannot resist quoting part of journalist David Sarasohn's response to this action: "Look, if this is too inconvenient for the networks, maybe the West Coast could just give up voting for president entirely."[82]

In these last two chapters we have noted some serious problems in both the contemporary organization of the nominating process, especially for the presidency, and in media coverage of elections, especially of the presidential nomination process. In Chapter 5 some serious questions were also raised about the nature of the ownership and control of the mass media in the United States, and in Chapter 6 some consequences of the private, for-profit basis of the news media were discussed. The logical next question is: Are there alternative ways of doing things? The next chapter provides some answers to that question.

CHAPTER ELEVEN
COMPARISONS
The Media and Politics in Another Nation

COMPARISONS AND THINKING ABOUT PUBLIC AFFAIRS

In the process of thinking about public affairs, considering alternatives to existing ways of doing things can be of great help in both analyzing the existing state of affairs and in identifying ways to improve those public affairs. In fact, a cardinal principle of systematic thought is the consideration of a range of alternative approaches to the solution of a problem or to fulfilling a function (as is spelled out in the classic formulation of the rational model of decision making).[1] In this chapter we seek to do that for the media and politics system by providing a comparison of such a system in a nation other than the United States. Hopefully, seeing other ways of approaching the ownership and control of the media, relations between the media and government, and the media's role in elections will serve as a stimulus to more thorough thinking about elements of the American system. We focus on the media and politics system in Great Britain for comparison.

THE MEDIA AND POLITICS IN BRITAIN: A STUDY IN CONTRASTS

The system of media and politics in Great Britain is a study in contrasts. Before we look at these it should be noted that the British political system has in many ways been a study in contrast with the system in the United States, and so provides many excellent points of comparison. As British political scientist Anthony King, who has spent much time in the United States, has said: "Britain provides an especially useful comparison, partly because it is better documented than most of the others but chiefly because it would be hard to imagine a [Western democratic] system more unlike that of the United States; in most respects . . . the American and British systems are polar opposites."[2] This observation was made just after the 1980 presidential election in the United States, which presented even more stark contrasts than usual, regarding length of election process, public participation, party role, and the like, and also the lack of previous national government experience of the two major candidates (in Carter's case, before taking office in 1977).[3] But the basic statement regarding differences in the two political systems has been valid in general. What is also interesting is that there is now the suggestion that politics and the media in Britain have become increasingly "Americanized" in recent years. For that reason as well, the British system is an interesting one for comparison.

OWNERSHIP AND CONTROL OF THE MEDIA IN BRITAIN

The Print Press: The Good and the Bad, Press Barons, and Partisanship

The first particulars in this study in contrast, both within Britain and between the United States and Britain, concern the geographic scope and the quality of the British newspapers. The daily print press in Britain is dominated by nine newspapers which are based in London and which, unlike those in the United States, are all national in scope; they appear daily throughout the nation. The contrast in quality is striking. As one communications scholar said: "Some of the nine are among the best in the world [namely, *The Times* and *The Guardian*]; whereas some, the sensationalist tabloids, deserve to be ranked among the worst . . ." [namely, *The Sun* and *The News of the World* (which certainly isn't)].[4] (There are also a number of local papers. Interestingly, the British are much more avid newspaper readers than Americans; the circulation of newspapers reaches a much higher percentage of the public (in the 1960s, at least, it was the highest in the world).[5]

On the basic question of ownership, there is no contrast with the United States. Newspapers in Great Britain are privately owned corporations. Further, there has been a trend in concentration of ownership that is quite like that in the United States. A small number of "press barons" and corporations have come to dominate the newspaper industry, such as Rupert Murdock, who owns *The Sun, The News of the World,* and *The Times* (as well as papers and magazines in the United States), and the Thomson Organization, which "publishes at least 55 daily and weekly papers . . . as well as 45 different magazines."[6] More generally, "more than 90% of national daily and Sunday newspaper circulation is controlled by the five leading companies in the sector."[7]

One other point of contrast with newspapers in the United States is important to note: Many of the main papers are distinctly partisan in orientation. And even more than in the United States, the ownership and editorial orientation are towards the Conservative Party and ideology. Quite simply, the Labour Party, as well as the newer Social Democratic and the Liberal Party, are at a distinct disadvantage in the print press; of the nine national dailies, seven more or less favor the Conservative Party.[8] This partisanship can be emphatic—and the "debate" in these papers is often, to put it gently, rather lively. Consider these offerings of a Conservative columnist: on Mrs. Thatcher: "The Prime Minister is the sun around which other politicians orbit"; on the Labor Party leader, Michael Foot: He was "half socialist, half preacher, half politician, half journalist, half writer, half raver, half baked, and half gone."[9]

Broadcast Media: The BBC—Background, Principles, Legend, and Structure

The contrast between the British and American media systems is most notably—indeed famously—stark in the realm of broadcasting. The British Broadcasting Corporation, the BBC, is a veritable legend in the broadcast world. The British took a very different path in development and control of the broadcast media. To set the scene for the current structure of control and BBC's operations, a brief bit of historical perspective is needed, a note that should raise interesting questions for an American readership.

In the 1920s when broadcasting was in its first years in Britain, there was a strong feeling among many influential public officials and citizens that the mass circulation newspapers had largely ceased to fulfill their important function in and for the distinctive British political culture. The feeling was that the "the free market of newspaper competition had produced, not a 'republic of letters,' but a melange of trivia. . . ."[10] Additionally and more formally:

> The BBC was founded at a time when the freedom of the press had begun to shed the absolute quality it once had, and "freedom for what?" was becoming an increasingly pertinent question. Mass-circulation newspapers . . . had sub-

verted the role of the printed word as an instrument of religious, cultural, social and political enlightenment. In a later view, indeed, they had become elements in, and supporters of, the institutional structure of established authority and of political and economic power which it had once been the primary task of the press . . . to expose, discuss and criticize.[11]

Additionally, the British saw the chaos in broadcasting at that time in the United States, and in accordance with what had happened in the newspaper realm, with its increasing dependence on advertising money, "the feeling that to allow financing from advertisements would inevitably lower standards" was strong.[12]

As a result, and to simplify the history a bit, a rather unique public "corporation" was established, which was and is a public entity, yet one of considerable (although at times, challenged) independence. An early House of Commons resolution best stated the principles involved. "The position of the Corporation is thus one of independence in the day-to-day management of its business, and of ultimate control by His Majesty's Government. We find that this line of demarcation has been observed in practice, and we are convinced that no better can be found." And further, regarding that government–BBC "line of demarcation": "Where the interests of the State appear to be at all closely involved, it is open to the Corporation to consult a Minister or Department informally and of its own accord. This method leaves decision and discretion in the hands of the Corporation and is consistent with the independent status which was formulated . . . as the desirable objective."[13]

First in radio and now with the addition of television (or "the telly" as the British call it), the BBC was established as an independent organization, which was to present news and public affairs, culture and entertainment in the public interest, not for private profit. Original conceptions of what the broadcast medium should do are striking. In the radio era, there were three different channels of broadcasting with three different "levels" of culture, sophistication, and "seriousness" making up each of the three "programs." The feeling and intent was that each of these, while cast at different "levels," should contribute to enlightenment and encourage an increasing interest in and benefit from increasingly "elevated" public affairs and cultural programs. As the BBC Director-General said in 1946, this general notion rested on a concept of the "the community as a broadly based cultural pyramid slowly aspiring upward . . .": "Each programme at any moment must be ahead of its public but not so much ahead as to lose their confidence. The listener must be led from good to better by curiosity, liking and a growth of understanding. As the standards of education and culture of the community rise so should the programme pyramid rise as a whole."[14]

These are remarkable expressions of principles intended to underlie British broadcasting, principles that are strikingly in accord with the conception of classic democratic theory, in the sense of tangibly encouraging deeper public understanding and participation. The basic independence, these principles as eloquently and repeatedly enunciated, and the quality of elite schools in Britain which produced the vast majority of the management and production people are the reason the BBC came to be renowned worldwide for the high quality, integrity, and comparatively minimal bias in its public affairs and other programs; indeed, it became a legend in broadcasting. BBC radio news has long been listened to, relied on, and respected throughout the world. And on the whole, the main hour-long BBC-TV news (although a little slow to develop), especially the long-running "current affairs" TV program "Panorama," gained great respect and upheld the tradition of the BBC. However, things got a little more complicated in the TV age. In fact, on a few occasions those high principles were notably forgotten by political figures *before* the TV age. Before we turn to those developments, though, a few more notes on BBC operation.

The hierarchy of the BBC is "topped" by a Board of Governors, which is the body with overall legal decision-making responsibility (rather like a board of directors of an American corporation), but it rarely has gotten involved in ongoing decision making. The top executive position, that of director-general, has been the locus of real, ongoing decisions in the BBC. (A series of very strong directors-general reinforced that pattern.) The director-general has served as chief executive as well as prime spokesman and prime defender of the independence and vigor of the BBC.

Speaking of independence, without advertising, how does the BBC maintain itself financially—obviously a vital question in the discussion of independence? (Remember the Golden Rule: The one who has the gold makes the rules!) The answer is that Parliament has written in law that the BBC receives a "license fee" levied on each radio, then TV set sold (as of 1980, that amounted to $78 for color TV's and $28 for black-and-white sets). (This is, in fact, a method used to generate revenues for public broadcasting in most European countries.)[15]

BBC and the Commercial Challenge In 1954 the BBC situation changed; its "monopoly" was ended and was replaced by a "duopoly." The Television Act of that year authorized the establishment of an Independent Television Authority (IBA) to serve as a competing network and expand the offerings. "ITV" financing would be based on advertising, not TV set "license fees," but the Authority itself would be a public corporation and the arrangements for operation of the network involved a distinct difference from those of the American networks. The IBA

> would own the transmitters and hire them to a group of new companies; these companies would make programmes, transmit them through the corporation's facilities, and collect revenues from advertising to cover their costs.

This was adopted because the government had "decided as a basic principle that there should be no 'sponsoring' and that the responsibility for what goes out on the air shall rest upon the operator of the station, and not on the advertiser."

This, then meant that

> ITV would be in a similar position to the press, who accepted advertisements, but remained responsible for their own news and editorial columns. There the twin principles of private enterprise and effective control could be neatly combined.[16]

Did this mean that ITV was a largely unfettered organization? Not quite. The Television Act charged the IBA to "maintain a proper balance" in the subject matter of their programs and required that "due impartiality [be] preserved on the part of the persons providing the programmes as respects matters of political or industrial controversy, or relating to current public policy." More generally, ITV programs were to include nothing "which offends against good taste [what would be on TV if *that* requirement were enforced in the United States?!], or decency, or is likely to encourage or incite to crime, or lead to disorder, or to be offensive to public feeling, or which contains any offensive representation of or reference to a living person."[17] These are rather serious constraints; and they have apparently been taken rather seriously.

Still, ITV meant serious competition for BBC for the British audience. That competition has been waged vigorously by ITV, including in the news area; and it has had a significant impact. As Philip Schlesinger has commented, by the early 1960s, "BBC had suffered a crisis in the 'battle of the rating,'" and the commercialization of British TV forced the BBC to develop programming with broader audience appeal. This included the news division. As Schlesinger observes, ITV's news program "showed that it could remain within the understood conventions of impartiality and still mediate the news in a more populist [and more "entertaining"] manner," and in so doing, it was "rejecting the BBC notion of news as a solemn ritual." ITV's news program also used the medium of TV more effectively than BBC had.[18]

In sum, the advent of ITV led to a more entertainment oriented, and frankly, a "lower-grade" sort of TV fare. Thus, in some respects, the communication of public affairs, cultural affairs, and even more "purely entertainment" programs are the poorer for it in Britain. But it also served as a healthy stimulus, in some respects, to what had been a rather staid BBC; some admirers of BBC have even suggested that it improved BBC news in its communication to the public over the TV medium.[19]

One other development is of interest, which also illustrates the unique British conception of the broadcast media as important public trusts. In late 1982, the British government decided to create a fourth TV "network" and channel (beyond BBC 1, BBC 2, and ITV), which was intended to be an "experimental" alternative to the existing networks," a channel that would do innovative things in the communication of public affairs, cultural, and entertainment subjects. Channel 4 is supported by receipt of a fixed percentage of ITV's advertising revenue. (ITV can sell commercial time on the channel, but there is no sponsorship connection; it is thus insulated from ratings competition.)

Early on, as *Time* magazine has pointed out, "even in a country where 'highbrow' and 'television' are not mutually exclusive terms, Britain's Channel 4 seemed to be courting disaster." With its heavy doses of arts and politics—and tiny audiences—critics called it "channel snore" or "channel bore." In fact, the chief executive of Channel 4 has said: "If we get more than 10% of the viewers, I know we are *not* doing our job," an appropriate orientation for a channel intended to serve tastes and interests not being satisfied by the other channels.[20]

But by 1986, Channel 4 was considered a great success. In the arts and entertainment, it has not only produced innovative programs, it has also produced widely appreciated and enjoyed works, quite a few of which have been borrowed by American TV and/or brought to American movie houses. "Max Headroom," the computer-generated "talk-show host," originated on Channel 4. Further, the channel's public affairs programming is apparently not as constrained as are the others: "Channel 4's news and public affairs programs often seem calculated to rock the boat." For example, "A series called 'Opinions' gives a public figure 30-min. of airtime each week to expound on a controversial topic." And further: "Channel 4's 50-min. nightly newscast skips crime reports and the doings of royalty in favor of probing political analyses and stories on business, science and the arts. A 1985 documentary touched off a political scandal when it revealed the MI5, Britain's counterintelligence agency, had engaged in illegal wiretapping of union officials and political activists."[21]

Hence it would appear that Channel 4 may be an effort to "live up" to much of the best of those principles of public broadcasting noted earlier. Will they be able fully to do so? Well, there are some fundamental constraints that go beyond the law establishing the channel, constraints that apply to all media in Great Britain. To that we now turn—and once again the striking contrasts in the British media and politics system come to the fore.

MEDIA–GOVERNMENT RELATIONS IN BRITAIN

Constraints: The Law and Reporting

We have noted the remarkable efforts in Britain to establish socially responsible, high-quality broadcasting media, which can more adequately serve the democratic purpose. Even after the commercial challenge of ITV, Britain's broadcasting services remain a striking contrast to those in the United States. On another hand, however, Britain's system involves certain elements—two principal ones—which constrain the serious pursuit of the democratic purpose far more greatly than in the United States.

The most notable element goes by the legal name, "The Official Secrets Act." This act prohibits the airing or publication of any information that government authorities have declared secret. This sounds at first like the American case; but this act, officially intended as protection for defense and national security secrets, actually covers a "draconian width" of subjects, with "the application of military secrecy even to the most innocuous civil information." There are real, immediate teeth in this law, which are actively applied by the government: jail sentences are imposed on those guilty of communicating such information, and the law "authorized the police to search editorial offices and to seize papers or anything 'which is evidence of an offence under this Act, if there is reasonable ground for suspecting that such an offence has been or is about to be commited.'"[22] There is no Freedom of Information Act in Britain. Critics in the United States have complained of excessive secrecy in American government. But the American government focus on secrecy is not comparable to the overwhelming obsession with secrecy in Britain, an obsession of long standing and one elaborately built into the governmental process and civic service.

The overwhelming restrictions imposed by the act serve as a significant discouragement to investigative reporting. So does a second element of the British system: the libel laws. In Britain, the libel laws are much more severe and restrictive than in the United States, and heavy damages are often awarded.[23]

Not surprisingly, the combination of those laws and patterns with the basic charge given to the BBC and ITV, as well as journalistic training and desires to cover public affairs adequately, has resulted in periodic clashes between government officers and the news media. These started occurring long before the TV age (e.g., involving the BBC at the time of the 1926 General Strike), and there were clashes early in the TV era, such as over how the 1956 British invasion of the Suez should be covered. The BBC, with its funding from public law and with the ultimate control over its operations in the government's hands, continually involves the potential for such a clash. Over much of its history, especially in the TV age, the BBC has avoided too much government heavy-handedness and maintained independence and a reasonable amount of reporting vigor by a distinct political balance-wheel phenomenon: "[T]he liberties accumulated by the BBC in political reporting and comment are owing largely to the fact that the Parliamentary Opposition (as potentially the party, or parties, of government) has insisted on the right to have its own views represented in the content of news and public affairs programmes. . . ."

Thus, "what chiefly protects the independence of the BBC . . . is the two-party system, and the fear that something disagreeable done by one party when it's in power would lead to the Opposition, when it was in power, doing something even more disagreeable." But still, given the ultimate control by the government, "broadcasters . . . have to be sensitive to the limit of tolerance of views and points of view allowed them within the brackets of established, Government–Opposition debate."[24]

That balance has gotten more precarious in recent times, however. David Boyce has observed: "The attempt to make the BBC and the IBA conform to ideas of the national interest meant that television in contemporary Britain became embroiled in a series of controversies, especially in the 1960s and 1970s, when television broke new ground in political coverage, in political satire, and professional political reporting."[25] In the 1980s things got more intense, for the BBC especially.

The tension has been particularly great between the Conservative Party, especially the Thatcher Government, and the BBC. The first battle was over coverage of the Falklands war and of Prime Minister Thatcher's trip to the Falkland's immediately after the British victory (more on this case shortly). A second notable case occurred in August 1985 when the BBC's Board of Governors ordered the withdrawal of a documentary on political extremism in Northern Ireland after pressure from the Thatcher Government. An edited version was later shown, but the BBC staff went on a 24-hour strike, leading to the cancellation of news and current events programs for the first time in BBC history. BBC's "Panorama," its prime public affairs program, was successfully sued for libel by two Tory (Conservative) members of Parliament in 1986, which was followed by a carefully prepared charge by a Tory leader of bias in BBC reporting on America's raid on Libya. Most striking was the case in January 1987 when Government pressure led to a decision not to air a six-part documentary ("The Secret Society") which disclosed information about a British spy satellite, a case that involved this event: "Amazed British television viewers watched the BBC cover a police raid on its own Glasgow studios as investigators searched for clues to the identity of government officials who might have leaked information about the satellite." These (and other) cases constituted "an unprecedented assault on [the] independence" of the BBC.[26]

Concern about the freedom of the media is mounting; regarding the last of those cases, as *Newsweek* has reported: "Leaders of Britain's news media and the opposition saw Thatcher's national-security claim as a bald attempt to turn the Official Secrets Act into a political weapon against investigative journalism."[27] This is the profound danger in this realm of the British media and politics system.

The In-Crowd: "The Lobby" and the Coziness of Inside Reporting

Another very different element of the British media and politics system also functions as an effective constraint (or restraint) on probing investigative reporting on government actions. It is called the "Westminster Lobby correspondents" (more simply, "the Lobby"):

> These are the reporters, based in the [Parliament building], who write, not about what happens in House of Commons debates, but more generally about government and politics: they often go under the by-line political editor, political correspondent. . . . They are an organized group with their own rituals. Much of what they do is secret, unknown to their reporter colleagues and often kept even from senior editors on the ground that their sources of information must remain anonymous.[30]

These are the prime "insider" reporters covering the government. But through a long tradition of close involvement with government officials and a custom of the conception of their members as an exclusive, connected "club," these journalists have apparently tended to serve as an extension of the government's communication function, as much as journalists. Very "cozy" relations are apparently the standard. And "off-the-record" is the standard mode. "Lobby journalists . . . depend on briefings that supposedly never take place with government spokesmen who do not officially exist. In fact, the Lobby is the primary conduit for the release by governments of official information. It enables the wheels of Whitehall's [the center of executive operations] news machine to revolve."[31]

In sum, this distinct group of British reporters are the functional equivalent of the White House press corps in the United States except that they work even more completely on a backgrounder basis, they generally have more pleasant relations with the chief executive, and they are even more compliant and co-opted than the White House press corps—apparently, much more. This is also a relic of the old British tradition of an elite that goes to the same private schools, then to "Oxbridge" (Oxford and Cambridge universities), and then maintains a nice, close network of connections and polite, cooperative relations in whatever job they work in.

. . . And Also in Britain: News Management in the Media Age

A final, quite recent development in media–government relations is very important to note. It will remind the reader of the media operations in and of the Reagan administration. It should also raise some profound questions about the democratic implications of government use of the mass media in contemporary society. The development is that of comprehensive news management by the Thatcher Government. As three British writers have pointed out, other prime ministers and their aides have sought to arrange and encourage good news treatment of the prime minister and the Government:

> But no predecessor of Mrs. Thatcher at Number Ten [Downing St.—the prime minister's headquarters] has been so conscious of image and its construction. She has brought in a breed of advertising agent and public relations executive not seen before in British politics. She has become presidential in her use of American techniques of presentation and news management.[30]

Indeed, and she has done so on a scale and with an intensity that matches the Reagan effort discussed in Chapter 8. The prime minister's operation in the trip taken in the aftermath of the Falklands war is an excellent illustration.

Mrs. Thatcher first received (or rather, achieved) remarkably good coverage during the Falklands war. This was not an accident. (The general background of Britain's frustration in the loss of its empire and decline in world influence through this century should be kept in mind.) Partly in combination with and partly in modification of the military, the Thatcher regime comprehensively managed the flow of information and news events in connection with the war to achieve "the good news war," as three British writers put it. There was an extraordinary effort "made to feed the media the 'right' information." And, "throughout the campaign, the bad news was suppressed, delayed or disguised while the good news was trumpeted." In fact, in a later assessment by *The Times* it was concluded that "the reports published in the newspapers in London of the way in which South Georgia was retaken were complete rubbish from beginning to end."[31] On the TV side, the Conservative members of Parliament and the prime minister engaged in a storm of criticism of early BBC treatment of the war—and put enormous pressure on BBC to air the "patriotic" government line. Further, with the smallish pool of journalists allowed to go in the war expedition itself in the effective control of the military, no television pictures were transmitted from the British ship on which the journalists were based: "It is my belief," said the editor of BBC Radio News . . . , "that there was a calculated decision taken by the government not to allow television pictures to come back for fear there might be a Vietnam syndrome. . . . What they wanted to do was to sanitise the worse aspects of it."[32] (This all occurred in 1982. The American invasion of Grenada occurred in 1983. It appears that the Reagan administration and the U.S. military learned something from the Falklands case.)

And then came Prime Minister Thatcher's "triumphal tour" of the Falklands in the aftermath of the British victory—a tour elaborately prepared (in high secrecy). The newspaper coverage was vast, and so was the praise. But in the TV age, the Thatcher operation was most interested in what the TV cameras communicated: "The Prime Minister's itinerary had been carefully considered in order to produce several of what the American's call 'photo opportunities,'" complete with well-calculated settings. A problem arose, however—for Thatcher's purposes. Because of the high secrecy in the preparations for the trip (including some disinformation), the only TV camera crew in the Falklands was a BBC crew; ITV was not represented. For a news person, this meant an exclusive. For the Thatcher regime it meant only part of the all-important TV audience. Correspondingly, the Thatcher operation asked the BBC to pool its film and hence to give it to ITV's news. BBC refused. The Thatcher operation then played hardball (to use an American metaphor). They warned the BBC of "incalculable consequences" if they did not give the film to ITV; and then they played "the card that the government had employed so effectively during the Falklands conflict itself to control the flow of news: its possession of the channels of communication in an age of satellites . . . : 'No film is coming out tonight unless I have [BBC's] absolute assurance that it will be freely available to ITN. . . .'" The Thatcher operation won, and for "five days at peek hours on both networks Mrs. Thatcher's progress through the islands was beamed to millions." This was, indeed, a "considerable media event" as one journalist put it.[33] It was also a striking illustration of comprehensive news management.

It is deeply troubling that the two nations which have often been cited as the two oldest and greatest democracies on earth—the United States and Great Britain—experienced the development in the 1980s of a profound and rather comprehensive control over what picture and general image of the incumbent administration comes across to the mass public. There are some different background customs and specifics of operation, but the basic pattern of use of the TV medium is the same. So are the consequences for democracy and the principle of accountability.

THE MEDIA AND ELECTIONS IN BRITAIN

Britain Compared with the United States

As alluded to earlier, the British party system and electoral process are very different from those in the United States. As noted in Chapter 9, in the United States, the presidential campaign is a year-long process, and with the nominations for president and for other offices primarily resulting from voting by the mass public in primaries, the party organizations are not central to the "party" nominations. The parties have declined in general, and candidates self-select, form their own organizations, and run primarily through the media.

In Great Britain, however, the process has been very different. The British voter does not vote for a long slate of candidates. Only the House of Commons is at stake and voters cast a ballot for only *one* position: member of Parliament from their area (constituency). The prime minister is not voted on directly; the campaign is party based, and whichever party wins a majority of seats (single-member district, plurality elections) in Parliament has its leader installed as prime minister (along with other ministers and leaders). With no majority, a coalition is formed. The candidates for prime minister and Parliament are chosen by the party organizations, basically meaning party activists long involved with the party. There is no set election year other than the maximum term limit of five years; whenever a government (incumbent administration) loses a vote of confidence in Parliament, or when the five-year limit is more-or-less near and the governing party feels that the time is right, the governing party calls a new election. That new election is only three to six weeks long. Further, election financing and organization comes from the parties; individual candidates do not raise their own money and form their own organizations. There are also strict limits set by law on campaign spending. Each party with a substantial following is allocated a certain number of free 10-minute *party* broadcasts (on all channels), but individual candidate ads are forbidden. The number of broadcasts that each party receives is based more or less on general proven following in past elections, but this is debated.[34]

Changes in the TV Age

Such has been the nature of parties and the electoral process in Britain. But things have been changing in the TV age. The first serious study of elections in the age of television, on the 1964 general election, was produced by Blumler and McQuail.[35] But it was British scholar Colin Seymour-Ure who, early on, most effectively spelled out the new trends in media politics in British elections. He found two basic patterns. The first pattern was the increasing dominance of the media in elections, rather than the parties. Parties had long been the centerpiece of the British political system, and it had been the debate between them over policy directions for Britain that had dominated elections—the parties determined what the issues were and how they should be talked about. But by 1970, "There was a major shift in control over the picture of the national campaign from the politicians to the journalists and TV producers." Indeed, "the media would not now accept so readily the parties' own definition of the important issues."[36] And that shift in control over the picture of the campaign meant that media news criteria came to dominate the campaign: "Media liked . . . lively, colourful people having lively, colourful arguments about some thing over which they disagreed and which mattered [according to media values. And] . . . for the media the ideal election issue . . . was a subject which could easily reduce to simple terms; which involved principles more than complex facts . . . ; which was 'fresh and not stale'; which differentiated the parties with tidy polarity. . . ." A prime result, concluded

Seymour-Ure, has been that "the parties seemed to talk *to* and *about* one another yet not so much *with* each other as formerly."[37]

The second basic pattern Seymour-Ure found was, as he called it, the "increasing presidentialism of British elections." That is, the traditional battle between parties and their orientations has been increasingly replaced by a "concentration of attention on the party leader" [candidate for prime minister].[38] This is indeed true, and the trend has continued, if not accelerated. *Newsweek,* for example, appropriately entitled its report on the wind-up of the 1987 election, "Politics American Style: Television Takes Over in the British Campaign."[39] In fact, American-style political marketing has been employed. The Conservative Party "led" the way: In 1979 they "ran their campaign as a single integrated advertising campaign—modelled on the way in which a consumer product would be sold via television commercials. . . . Saatchi and Saatchi [the nation's largest and most successful ad agency] was involved in the entire campaign including the 50 minutes of free network television time (five party broadcasts of ten minutes each) which were built around the format of an ITV news show with commercial interruptions."[40] The same thing was done in the 1983 election, with such additions as having actors present the party's message in the free TV time. Further, Mrs. Thatcher refused to debate her opponents, preferring to rely on the Conservative image machine.

In 1987, the Labour Party joined in the media magic show. As the *Newsweek* report observed: "British politicians are learning the value of showbiz politics. Thatcher's political broadcast featured a futuristic Andrew Lloyd Webber sound track. [Labour leader Neil] Kinnock recruited the makers of 'Chariots of Fire' to script his special."[41] As Jeremy Tunstall has suggested, British elections have "receded further into media land."[42]

Where has all of this led the grand old British democracy? *Newsweek,* borrowing from a venerable British opinion magazine, captured the question and the concern very well: "Horrified at such goings-on, *Spectator* columnist Michael Trend observed, 'Mr. Pickwick and the voters at Eatanswill would have never recognized this as an election campaign.'"[43]

The British case certainly provides some constructive alternative approaches to the ownership and control of the media (although some dangers are also evident). The traditional British approach to political parties and elections is a striking model for Americans to reflect on. But the British case in recent years also raises further profoundly disturbing questions about the survival of authentic democracy and the possibility of healthy, real discussion of issues. It also raises the question of whether a genuine dialogue of democracy tends to be a victim of the TV age.

CHAPTER TWELVE
THE MEDIA
AND THE DIALOGUE
OF DEMOCRACY

THE DIALOGUE OF DEMOCRACY AND THE MEDIA FACTOR

Earlier in the book Bill Moyers' idea of "news as the conversation of democracy" was noted.[1] Considering politically relevant communication in general, perhaps it is better to refer to "the dialogue of democracy." To be more specific, if democracy is to work, especially over the long run, the political communication involved must contain healthy, constant doses of dialogue. That is, there must be significant amounts of real *exchanges* of information, ideas, and opinions between political figures and the public and between different citizens—exchanges in both directions.

Democracy cannot remain healthy without such a dialogue—and the political participation that flows from such communication and makes democracy a reality. If the few who are directly involved in governing primarily talk *at* the many, rather than maintaining a dialogue with them, after a while there will be alienation and distrust, and sooner or later there will be an arrogance of power and then a misuse of power by the governing few. As political theorist Benjamin Barber has said, strong, lasting democracy "requires institutions that will involve individuals at both the neighborhood and the national level in common talk, common decision-making and political judgement, and common action." And as Barber has also pointed out, drawing on the great political thinkers Jean Jacques Rousseau, John Stuart Mill, and Alexis de Tocqueville, authentic exchanges and the political participation that flows from them are the prime way that individuals in a public truly learn what a democracy requires and hence, enable its maintenance: The political learning value of "participation has been noted a thousand times since first Rousseau and then Mill and de Tocqueville suggested that democracy was best taught by practicing it."[2]

But further, "dialogue" means communication. If a dialogue is necessary for an operative democracy, then the essential means of the conduct of democracy is communication. In a modern mass society such as the United States (or Great Britain, for another example), the mass media are the mechanism of communication of prime importance; the public depends, fundamentally, on those media for the stuff of understanding of political matters, and for the material with which to engage in those exchanges. Correspondingly, the character of what is communicated through the mass media, and the impact on the receivers of such communications, are crucial to understand if we are to adequately assess the operation of democracy in such societies today. That is what this book has sought to do.

POLITICS AND COMMUNICATION IN THE TV AGE

Modern Media: Many Contributions

At various points in this book we have taken note of the many benefits brought by the numerous organizations and remarkable capacities of the mass media today. The great amount of information that is provided in the nation's more major newspapers, along with the tremendous contributions of investigative reporting, have been pointed out. Newspaper competition in individual cities has declined dramatically, but the level of ability of journalists, boosted by a higher educational level, as well as better pay and status, has clearly made conditions right for a better quality of news production than in past eras.

The capacity of the medium of television for bringing to the public a vivid view of the area, nation, and world has added a striking dimension to our ability to communicate in mass society. The most dramatic example of this is the capacity to broadcast "live" events of importance and to allow the public to "see for themselves" and judge for themselves, to some extent, the nature of those events and the people involved in them. The fact that this can be done not only for a huge nation of over 200 million people, but even for much of the entire world, is surely one of the most remarkable developments in human history. The pervasiveness of the medium of TV has, correspondingly, made the capacity for communicating through that medium simply awesome, in a variety of ways.

The pervasiveness of TV and the specific capacities of TV for communication have, in fact, been used to bring the public words and pictures to which past ages were not and could not be exposed. Views of faraway lands have been brought to people who could never get there in person— the "window on the world" has indeed been opened some. There have now been many opportunities for the general public to see various candidates for president (and sometimes other offices) in live "debate." The American public has been able to see Soviet spokespersons and various officials in serious, lively exchanges with American officials and experts. And in late 1987, the American people and the Soviet public both saw an hour-long interview with Soviet leader Mikhail Gorbachev. C-SPAN allows a rather direct view of parts of American government in action; and to help explain the congressional process, public television presented a 26-part series called "Congress: We the People." Various other particulars could be added. But this book has also raised a number of serious questions, in fact, troubling questions, about the mass media and political communications in the present age.

Questions

Journalism and Politics   Some analysts have suggested that "straight reporting" and the narrow notion of "objectivity" as giving "just the facts" of an overt event were no longer the dominant mode of operation of journalists by the end of the 1960s, that the news media have "gradually provided more background explanation and interpretation of the news."[3] In Chapter 6 it was pointed out, however, that a major problem remains with "news" that is reported in straight fashion and in the absence of adequate context and perspective. Examples from the 1960s, 1970s, and 1980s illustrated the continuing problem. The news media do not and cannot simply "hold a mirror" up to society and reflect the overt facts of an event. Choices must be made of what "stories" to pursue, which to include in the news, and how to present them. Further, as noted earlier, it must be recognized that the average person is largely preoccupied with his or her work, home, and social lives, and does not have a very elaborate understanding of the political world. Consequently, explanation of the news is required; the news must be put in perspective to make sense of it.

There are also problems with key factors involved in how the news media decide what is news. News criteria, especially as applied within the operating situation of a large, for-profit corporation, often incline news people to choose and focus on news stories that are of little importance for the political system or which distort the realities of it both during elections or during regular governing periods. Former journalist, now professor Lewis Wolfson, places the question in a democratic context and says: "It is time for the news media to move boldly beyond reporting mainly on breaking news, personalities, and confrontation, to tell people more about how

government works, how it affects them, and how they can influence it."
Wolfson quotes noted journalist William Greider, who says the press
should try to "explain more and startle less." Further, Wolfson points out
the consequence of the combination of such news criteria with news people's Progressive-style skepticism in covering government: Various news
people "seem to think that indiscriminate skepticism can substitute for
probing reporting. They tell themselves that exposure of official excesses
and scandals illuminates government, when it actually may distort our
picture of it."[4] Indeed, have we not lost perspective and failed in the basic
purpose of a free press when, for example, in 1980 there were seven times
as many stories on Billy Carter's adventurism than on the prime nuclear
arms control treaty, SALT II (as was discussed in Chapter 6)?

The problem is worse in the prime sphere of the democratic process:
elections. News criteria and the notion of the news as overt events and
tangible end results give the public a view of the election process rather like
that gotten at the Kentucky Derby or at a prize fight, or even that in
"Entertainment Tonight." The substance of what the election process is
intended to be about tends to get lost in the hubbub and hoopla brought to
us by "Action News"; that is, the nature of policy choices on issues, which
candidates and parties stand for (and understand) which policy options,
and candidates' qualifications for officeholding and leadership are largely
lost sight of. As Senator Edward Kennedy was moved to say at the end of
1987, in the middle of the 1988 preprimary process: "My experience in
national campaigns . . . from 1960 to 1980, has left me with a very real
sense of a widening gap between the real issues and the reporting; a feeling
that the voters are not seeing candidates whole or clearly, but through a
journalistic lens increasingly honed to the prism of *People* magazine."[5] That
is precisely the conclusion reached by the *National Journal*'s Richard Cohen
a month earlier. Reflecting on events in the campaign of 1988 and on the
inability of elected officials in the national government to deal adequately
with the budget deficit and other matters, Cohen concluded: "The nation
is paying the price for having tolerated campaign debates [in the general
sense] tailor-made for *People* magazine."[6]

At the front of Kennedy's and Cohen's minds in those reflections was
the news media's binge in coverage of the so-called "character issue," which
led them into a virtual feeding frenzy of "exposés" on Gary Hart's alleged
personal extracurricular activities, Joseph Biden's supposed "plagiarism,"
the premarital activities of GOP candidate Pat Robertson, and so on. These
inclinations, as was discussed in Chapter 6, are products of the media's
news criteria; the inclinations are not basically new, although in the post-
Watergate era, the restraint seemed to have been entirely cast to the wind.
But even some in the major mass media began, by late 1987, to question
these directions and wonder whether perspective had been lost. As *Time*
magazine said: "Last week this trend was prompting some healthy reap-

praisal that might save campaign '88 from runaway triviality. As James Gannon, editor of the Des Moines *Register,* puts it: 'A lot of respected journalistic guts are saying "Whoa!"'" And the magazine quoted the *Washington Post*'s David Broder as saying: "It's time to slow down and take another look at what we're doing, before more damage is done."[7]

But the stakes are higher than the destruction of a couple of presidential candidacies and a Supreme Court nominee due to such reporting inclinations (although those casualties are serious enough); the consequences are great for the conduct of governing itself. As the *National Journal's* Cohen observed further, the

> current political mindset also says something about the decline of substantive dialogue on the major political issues facing the nation. . . .
> Reagan's "morning in America" 1984 reelection [campaign] produced a victory that was perhaps a personal redemption. But it did little to advance, or identify, Reagan's pet causes [or deal with central issues such as the budget deficit].[8]

The *National Journal's* Dom Bonafede is right in saying: "It is no exaggeration to state that this is a critical and confusing transitional period in American journalism."[9] Much more reflection on and systematic review of the patterns of political coverage and the consequences of it are needed.

Cleary, the prime force in many of the patterns that were just reviewed and in the nature of this "transitional period in American journalism" is the medium of television. Special attention needs to be given to TV—to the dominance of its presence, the prime character of its general communication and corresponding basic effects, and its specifically political uses and abuses.

Civilization and Its Contents, Democracy Today and Its Discontents: Politics in the TV Age   This is truly the TV age; indeed, one could call the United States "the first media state."[10] The mass media have become central elements in the electoral process and the conduct of government. Indeed, journalist Dom Bonafede has concluded:

> Changes in the press have reached beyond the news media itself and radically altered the system by which government decisions are made, . . . the picture society has of itself and the way the presidency is conducted.[11]

And Scholar Richard Joslyn has concluded:

> [T]he mass media have contributed to a radical transformation of election campaigns in the United States. This transformation involves changes in how political candidates communicate with the citizenry, in the information journalists provide about election campaigns, and in the flow of available information to the subsequent behavior of the U.S. electorate.[12]

The print media are not the prime reason for these "radical transformations"; it is the newer medium of television which has been the central force in these changes in the political process over the past three and one-half decades.

In the "media revolution" of recent decades,[13] one fact is central and undisputed: the medium of television is truly pervasive. It is pervasive both in the sense that in the developed nations, especially in the United States, nearly everyone has a TV set or has ready access to one and most people watch TV at least several hours each day. In this regard, remember the observations of communications scholar George Gerbner noted in Chapter 2: "Television is a centralized system of storytelling. . . . People are now born into the symbolic environment of television and live with its repetitive lessons throughout life. . . . Transcending historic barriers of literacy and mobility, television has become the primary source of everyday culture of an otherwise heterogeneous population."[14] This raises an important question: With TV so pervasive, has the nature of what it predominantly broadcasts and the nature of people's interaction with it affected the public as political actors in society?

Various observers have suggested the answer to that question is "yes"—a rather ominous "yes." Television is overwhelmingly an entertainment medium (especially in the United States). More specifically, it is a medium whose communications are predominantly diverting amusement and fantasy. Has the pervasive communication of such fare affected people's sense of social and political reality, their interest in, and attention span for discussion of the serious issues the nation faces? Has that remarkable product of "advanced civilization," television, brought with it a tendency for many people, beyond the world of their personal activities, to be contented with amusements and fantasies and to be distracted from the more trying task of understanding the realities of the political world? Communications scholar Neil Postman has argued in detail (and with passionate concern) that we are "amusing ourselves to death," that "public discourse in the age of show business" (i.e., pervasive TV) has steadily declined in the quality and rationality of the discussion of public issues.[15] Political communications scholars Nimmo and Combs have concluded that we have, indeed, been sliding into a fantasy manner of responding to the general world. They note: "The real world is a messy place. . . . Fantasy provides a way out of grappling with [difficult and] contradictory realities." The result: "soap opera politics: the logic of mediated, fantastic reality."[16] Overstated? Distinguished political scientist James David Barber had this observation in the midst of the 1984 election period: "America is drifting into a mode of political thinking that is consciously, even proudly illusory. . . ."[17]

This is a difficult question; we have no definitive evidence that those thoughts are correct. Given much of what was discussed in Chapters 2 to 4 and elsewhere in this book, including recent elections, culminating in the

1984 presidential election,[18] we had better think a great deal harder about this. More research is certainly needed, as well.

Additionally, what of the nature of people's interaction with television? In Chapter 4 we suggested that the character of that interaction is different from that in the case of print media. Political scientist Jarol Manheim has concluded: "Not only is the political content of television generally uninvolving, but the medium itself, in the structure of its interaction with the user, requires a relatively low level of participation in the reception of information." This, in conjunction with the typically shortened, simplified "stories" presented on the dominant evening TV news programs, has some profound implications for democracy. Manheim wondered whether "democracy can survive television" and found this trend: "As the flow of complex information declines apace with the increasing reliance on television as a source of political information, first the perceived need, and later the ability, to perform sophisticated intellectual operations on such information, as well as an appreciation for the complexity of politics itself, will also decline." With regard to that last point, we have certainly seen such a decline in the understanding and appreciation for the complexity of the institution of Congress, as was detailed in Chapter 8. Manheim has suggested that the result of such a general decline in the quality of information and in people's mental processing of it "will be a continuing qualitative reduction of the intellectual content of political discourse among the mass of American citizens which may enable an elite which preserves the requisite knowledge, skills, and resources more effectively to manipulate the polity."[19] In short, is the general public now best characterized as the "telectorate" (as Russell Baker says)?

Manheim also expressed concern about whether many people are not increasingly losing their sense of historical perspective. Wilson Carey McWilliams, writing the perspective chapter in the "report and interpretation" of 1984 election by political scientists at Rutgers University, expressed the same concern. That concern was also joined with note of the nature of the medium of television and the corresponding nature of the potential use of it for political purposes, especially by incumbent presidential administrations which understand the medium and its organizational frameworks and constraints. The implications, he suggests, are troubling. Carrying forward elements of the discussion in Chapters 4, 6, 8, and 10 in this book, McWilliams reports:

> . . . Ronald Reagan's staff realizes that television can be *dominated*. . . . Television can be managed because of its limitations: Reporters can comment only in the context of a picture; the medium is impotent without "photo opportunities" and cannot easily resist a story with good visual possibilities. . . .

McWilliams's conclusion on the end result in the 1984 campaign: "The

President's campaign assertions went largely untested and unchallenged; and the candidate was portrayed, pretty much, in the way his managers desired."[20]

McWilliams then considered the more ultimate implications of the nature of the medium, the tendencies in people's responses to the medium (in the general context of the pervasiveness of the medium), and the uses of the medium. And he reflected on that decreasing sense of history, also suggested by Manheim. McWilliams's conclusion is striking; it should stimulate deeply concerned reflection:

> In one respect, the election of 1984 approximated George Orwell's imagined totalitarianism. Orwell feared that in the future, political regimes would find it possible to manipulate our memory of the past and thereby control the future. Things have not reached that pass, but the possibility is frighteningly foreseeable. Ronald Reagan and his advisers recognize, intuitively at least, that the public has less and less memory, less ability to organize and to recall the past. The old, organic sources of political remembrance in families and communities are breaking up and are being replaced by television's presentation of time as a series of disjointed moments, each a discrete unit, available for reordering at will.[21]

Elections, as McWilliams's thoughts suggest, are the area where perhaps the most troubling questions are raised. The principal ones concern the nature of the news media's coverage of the electoral process, especially the presidential nomination process; the increasingly central role played by political ads (candidates sold with the slickness of Pepsi commercials—and all too often cast in a negativity that seems to increase suspicion and cynicism in general); the increasingly primary role played by professional consulting firms, which in many cases have no tie or commitment to the state or area and its future; and the increasing appeal by self-selected candidates directly to voters through TV—without any connection with the more general political coalition of a political party which could actually move government with some effectiveness in some fairly coherent direction. For those concerned with the health of democracy, these problems are troubling, indeed.

It appeared in 1988 more likely than ever that such a process combined with the nature of the coverage had discouraged some of the most able political figures from running the election gauntlet—Governor Cuomo of New York, for a notable example. It is long past time for more serious review of where the changes of the past three decades have, willy-nilly, taken us. It is hoped that this book has contributed to reflections on that.

Possibilities

We have reviewed principal problems and questions, particularly those involving the medium of TV. Are there, however, some ways in which we might improve media coverage, use of TV, voters' learning about (and interest in) political matters, and so on; are there, in short, other possibilities? There is not space for a thorough review of alternative possibilities, but let a few thoughts encourage further reflection and discussion.

First, a reminder of a basic point of perspective. Earlier in the book it was noted that the news media are the only private industry given special protection by the U.S. Constitution. The principal intent of the First Amendment is the development of an informed and "intellectually vigorous" public. This suggests that expectations of—indeed, demands on—the media should be high.

Various explicit or obviously implied recommendations for improvement have been discussed at various points throughout the book. There is a need for more substantial, specialized training and education for reporters covering the Presidency and other major institutions, as well as foreign societies and political systems (and education for their editors, too). There is a need for longer network newscasts, allowing time for serious treatment of subjects on the dominant news medium. There is also a need for more serious diversity of perspective in prime sources of news—what Gans calls "multi-perspectival news."[22] There is a need to get presidents to hold regular news conferences and to make all possible efforts not to make restriction of access of reporters a successful ploy. There is a need for the news media to spend more time and space covering and critiquing itself (most important, in elections). There is a need to conduct presidential debates (and those for other offices) in a more sensible manner.

An interesting illustration of just how significant an impact good investigative journalism can have was included in a book on Mike Wallace of CBS's vastly successful show "60 Minutes":

> [F]or the most part, their vigilance and probing served the best interests of the commonweal. So much so . . . that many Americans came to regard Wallace as a kind of unofficial ombudsman. As Harry Reasoner put it shortly after he returned to . . . "60 Minutes" in 1978: "Now, when people have a problem, something strange or suspicious going on in their community, instead of writing their congressman, they write to Mike Wallace and demand that *he* fix it."[23]

Considering further the basic purpose of the media in a democracy, perhaps more fundamental questions need to be posed. In a conference of media people, academics, and some political people, political communications scholar Ithiel de Sola Pool said this:

> . . . I want to bring out . . . something about the structure of the way we all think about these problems.
>
> A conference on television and elections could have been organized with an agenda that asked such questions as, how can a television system be designed and structured so as to best raise the information level of the public? How can a television system be organized so as to clarify questions about public policy? What kind of television would change the motivation structure of candidates

and lead them to see an advantage for themselves in talking more about issues and more seriously?

Or one could even ask, what kind of television system would lead to a re-creation and rebuilding of the old type of political parties which involved the public in the political process in a way that nothing now does?[24]

That last question brings us to the final thoughts.

FINAL THOUGHTS: DEMOCRACY AND THE ROLE OF POLITICAL INSTITUTIONS

The American political system has been a troubled one for the past three decades. The governing process in specific has been a rocky road—perhaps increasingly so. The advent and growth to predominance of TV, along with changes in the election process itself and with an increase in organization and aggressiveness of special-interest groups, has increased the particularization and fragmentation of the American political system. The governmental structure in the United States, designed in the 1780s, is "naturally" inclined towards fragmentation, with its separated Presidency and Congress, and the two houses of Congress, all elected for different terms, on different bases. With political parties in decline, with candidates and officeholders increasingly appealing to citizens as individuals directly via the television screen, such fragmentation has been deepened. Changes in American society, from civil rights struggles and the women's equality movement to changes, downturns, and uncertainties in the economy, have made matters still more challenging.

Clearly, the American political system is in a difficult transitional period. The media have been significant elements in creating that transitional condition—both in the form of difficulties and of progress. National news media coverage—especially that of network TV—of the civil rights struggles in the South were clearly central factors forcing America to confront its conscience and to make serious efforts to square its realities with its official principles. The same can be said of the women's movement and, in a little different manner, of efforts to clean up the environment. But social conflict has also been given heavy attention. And, media treatment of what used to be the prime glue holding government operations together and allowing government to move with some coherence, namely, the political parties, has certainly not been constructive—indeed, the treatment of politics and "politicians" generally and of much of government (especially the legislature and "the bureaucracy") has typically been that of "indiscriminate skepticism," to requote Wolfson.

Surely, with the creativity that this society has shown and the talent it has, we can find more adequate ways of better communicating the realities and alternative choices for the future in elections and in the governing process. (Lewis Wolfson's impassioned thoughts and practical suggestions on this are highly recommended reading.)[25] Surely we can make more effective use of the powerful medium of television, in particular, to engage people more deeply in the political process and to understand it better, and to encourage—or demand—more serious discussion of issues by candidates.

Further, surely we can find ways to use the media, especially television, to help bolster and strengthen the political institutions that make a democracy work. The political parties are the most notable example. Can we learn from the British and other systems some ways to enable the parties to play a more vigorous role? Perhaps ten-minute or even half-hour party broadcast time during elections, restrictions on personal political ads, and monthly time between elections on the networks given to the leadership of the parties (perhaps including average citizens as participants for question and discussion) would help.

And are there also ways TV can be used to promote and encourage the public's participation in public affairs? Christopher Arterton has detailed and analyzed a number of efforts around the country to do just that.[26] So has Benjamin Barber, with a thorough grounding in democratic theory. As Barber suggests:

> What strong democracy requires is a form of town meeting in which participation is direct yet communication is regional or even national. Because scale is in part a function of communication, the electronic enhancement of communication offers possible solutions to the dilemmas of scale. Although it brings new kinds of risks, modern telecommunications technology can be developed as an instrument for democratic discourse at the regional and national level.[27]

Such a technique as television town meetings, for example, can be (and on a modest scale, have been) employed, using political figures, scholars, and other "experts" and average citizens to discuss issues, perhaps along with a telephone call-in segment to allow further citizen questions, comments, and participation. Public TV has tried a modest version of this on a couple of occasions. C-SPAN already has political officials involved in periodic call-in programs. Such a program could even be followed up by responses by the public via interactive cable hook-ups such as the (still simple) Warner-Amex QUBE system in place in Columbus, Ohio, and a few other locations. The possibilities for using personal computers in this process are also interesting (although it will probably be a long while until PC use extends sufficiently beyond the upper and middle classes to make that element truly democratic). This and the other techniques discussed by Arterton and Barber[28] should be given more attention.

Noted political theorist Carl J. Friedrich has placed the basic question in historical perspective: "Industrialization brought with it one feature peculiarly favorable to [constitutional democracy], and that is the progressive cheapening of the printed word [which allowed more and more of the general public access to information and ideas]. For the modern press, the channel of mass communication, was everywhere in the vanguard of advancing [constitutional democracy]."[29] The key question now is whether the further product of industrialization of electronic communications is to bring with it a further advance in the historical progress of democracy—or a serious faltering in that progress or even a setback.

There are possibilities if we would but seriously consider them. The future of democracy is at stake, along with such other "incidentals" as the caliber of persons serving as president of the United States.

NOTES

CHAPTER 1

1 Quoted in Doris Graber, *Mass media and American politics,* 2nd ed. (Washington, D.C.: Congressional Quarterly Press, 1984), p. 238.

2 S. Morison and H. S. Commager, *The growth of the American republic,* Vol. 1, 4th ed. (New York: Oxford University Press, 1950), p. 304.

3 Dan Nimmo and James E. Combs, *Mediated political realities* (New York: Longman, 1983), p. 23.

4 This and part of the following draws on Wilbur Schram, *The process and effects of mass communication* (Urbana, Ill.: University of Illinois Press, 1955), especially pp. 3–17.

5 This definition is borrowed (slightly altered) from Dan Nimmo, *Political communication and public opinion in America* (Santa Monica, Calif.: Goodyear Publishing Co., 1978), p. 5.

6 G. Gerbner, Mass media and human communication theory, in Denis Mc-Quail (Ed.), *Sociology of mass communications* (Harmondsworth, Middlesex, England: Penguin Books, 1972), p. 36.

7 See, for example, William Kornhauser, *The politics of mass society* (New York: Free Press, 1959).

8 For a good, concise history of the development of mass circulation newspapers, see Ronald Berkman and Laura Kitch, *Politics in the media age* (New York: McGraw-Hill, 1986), pp. 20–27; for an exhaustive history, see Edwin

Emery and Michael Emery, *The press and America: An interpretive history of the mass media,* 4th ed. (Englewood Cliffs, N.J.: Prentice-Hall, 1978).

9   For a discussion of these and related data, see, for example, Kathleen Jamieson and Karlyn Campbell, *The interplay of influence: Mass media and their publics in news, advertising, politics* (Belmont, Calif.: Wadsworth, 1983), Chapter 5; on the figure for average daily TV viewing time, see Television Bureau of Advertising news release carried over AP wire, February 1, 1986.

10 For a good, concise history of the development of radio and television, see Berkman and Kitch, *Politics in the media age,* pp. 27–41; for a thorough and fascinating history, principally of television, see Erik Barnouw, *Tube of plenty: The evolution of American television,* rev. ed. (New York: Oxford University Press, 1982).

11 Gerbner in McQuail, *Sociology of mass communications,* pp. 37–38.

12 Giovanni Sartori, *The theory of democracy revisited,* Vol. 1 (Chatham, N.J.: Chatham House, 1987), p. 86.

13 William J. Keefe, *Parties, politics, and public policy,* 4th ed. (New York: Holt, Rinehart and Winston, 1984), p. 166.

14 See Kay Lehman Schlozman and John T. Tierney, *Organized interests and American democracy* (New York: Harper & Row, 1986), especially Chapters 4 and 5.

15 See Austin Ranney, *Channels of power* (New York: Basic Books, 1983), pp. 13–14, for a summary of these data.

16 Walter Lippmann, *Public opinion* (New York: Macmillan, 1922), especially Chapter 1.

17 Quoted in Erik Barnouw, *The image empire* (New York: Oxford University Press, 1970), p. 196.

18 On democracy and representation, see Hanna Pitkin, *The concept of representation* (Berkeley, Calif.: University of California Press, 1967), especially Chapter 3.

19 As Robert Lineberry summarized it: The second of the principles of traditional democratic theory is: "Information: Information should be fully available to all. Democracy requires a marketplace of ideas . . . ;" *Government in America,* 2nd ed. (Boston: Little, Brown, 1983), p. 42.

20 Carl J. Friedrich, *Constitutional government and democracy,* 4th ed. (Waltham, Mass.: Blaisdell, 1968), p. 502.

21 Ibid., p. 502.

22 Sartori, *The theory of democracy revisited,* pp. 86–87.

23 Some scholars are very emphatic about this distinction, even suggesting that constitutionalism is the only line which has been seriously developed and that the basic policy-directive role of the public has hardly been developed at all in theory (or is misconceived); see Peter Natchez, *Images of voting/visions of democracy* (New York: Basic Books, 1985), especially Chapter 1.

24 Friedrich, *Constitutional government and democracy,* p. 4.

25 Ibid., p. 32.

26 Robert Dahl, *A preface to democratic theory* (Chicago: University of Chicago Press, 1956), p. 3.

27 Benjamin Barber, *Strong democracy* (Berkeley, Calif.: University of California Press, 1984), p. 4.

28 G. E. G. Catlin, *Systematic politics* (Toronto: University of Toronto Press, 1962), p. 197.

29 Vance Packard, *A nation of strangers* (New York: David McKay, 1972).

30 Kornhauser, *The politics of mass society*, p. 60. It should be noted, though, that some recent research has, to some extent, challenged generalizations about the "atomized man" idea—see, for example, F. G. Kline, Theory in mass communication research, in F. G. Kline and P. J. Tichnor (Eds.), *Current perspectives in mass communication research* (Beverly Hills, Calif.: Sage, 1972). But substantial concern remains about the general phenomenon—for a summary, see, for example, Karen Siune and F. G. Kline, Communication, mass political behavior, and mass society, in Steven Chaffee (Ed.), *Political communication: Issues and strategies for research* (Beverly Hills, Calif.: Sage, 1975).

31 Friedrich, *Constitutional government and democracy*, pp. 520–521.

CHAPTER 2

1   For a more thorough discussion of targeting, see H. L. Nieburg, *Public opinion: Tracking and targeting* (New York: Praeger, 1984).

2   Joe McGinnis, *The selling of the president, 1968* (New York: Trident Press, 1969), pp. 62–63.

3   See George Comstock et al., *Television and human behavior* (New York: Columbia University Press, 1978), p. 5.

4   Ibid., pp. 93–101.

5   Ibid., p. 5.

6   See Comstock et al., *Television and human behavior*, p. 88, for a discussion on this idea.

7   See Comstock et al., *Television and human behavior*, Chapter 3. For a slightly more recent discussion of audience patterns, see Robert T. Bower, *The changing television audience in America* (New York: Columbia University Press, 1985), especially Chapters 2 and 3.

8   See Comstock et al., *Television and human behavior*, Chapter 6, and Leo Bogart, *Press and public* (Hillsdale, N.J.: Lawrence Erlbaum, 1981), pp. 76–79.

9   See, for example, Frederick Williams, Herbert Durdick, and Frederick Horstmann, Where citizens go for information, *Journal of Communication, 27* (Winter 1977), 95–99.

10 See Bogart, *Press and public*, p. 56.

11 Comstock et al., *Television and human behavior*, p. 9.

12 Lawrence W. Lichty, Video versus print, *The Wilson Quarterly, VI* (5) (1982), 49–57.

13 As quoted in Dan Nimmo and James E. Combs, *Subliminal politics: Myths and mythmakers in America* (Englewood Cliffs, N.J.: Prentice-Hall, 1980), p. 7.

14 For an interesting comment on this issue from a Soviet citizen, see Hedrick Smith, *The Russians* (New York: Ballantine Books, 1976/1977), p. 90.

15 Bernard Hennessey, *Public opinion*, 5th ed. (Monterey, Calif.: Brooks/Cole, 1985), p. 4.

16 Walter Lippmann, *Public opinion* (New York: Harcourt, Brace, 1922), p. 31.

17 For a classic discussion of this, see V. O. Key, *Public opinion and American democracy* (New York: Alfred A. Knopf, 1964), especially p. 264.

18 Quoted in Gerald Pomper et al., *The election of 1984: Reports and interpretations* (Chatham, N.J.: Chatham House, 1985), p. 38.

19 See Fred I. Greenstein, The benevolent leader: Children's images of political authority, *American Political Science Review, 54* (December 1960), 934–943.

20 See F. Christopher Arterton, Watergate and children's attitude toward the president revisited, *Political Science Quarterly, 90* (Fall 1975), 477–496.

21 Donald Kinder and Robert Abelson, Appraising presidential candidates: Personality and affect in the 1980 campaign, a paper presented at the 1981 Annual Meeting of the American Political Science Association, New York.

22 See, for example, Hennessey, *Public opinion,* Chapters 9–11, or Richard E. Dawson and Kenneth Prewitt, *Political socialization* (Boston: Little, Brown, 1969).

23 See, for example, full question and data summary in Hennessey, *Public opinion,* p. 256.

24 Comstock et al., *Television and human behavior,* p. 10.

25 Michael Hughes, The fruits of cultivation analysis: A reexamination of some effects of television watching, *Public Opinion Quarterly, 44* (1980), 301.

26 George Gerbner et al., Charting the mainstream: Television's contributions to political orientations, *Journal of Communication, 32* (2) (1982), 100.

27 For a good discussion and critique of this function, which includes an excellent, detailed illustrative example of "legitimizing" media treatment of the Durham, North Carolina, city government, see David Paletz and Robert Entman, *Media–power–politics* (New York: Free Press, 1981), Chapter 9.

28 Austin Ranney, *Channels of power* (New York: Basic Books, 1983), pp. 3–4.

29 See Gerbner et al., Charting the mainstream; see also G. Gerbner and L. Gross, Living with television: The violence profile, *Journal of Communication, 26* (1976), 173–199; and G. Gerbner et al., Cultural indicators: Violence profile no. 9, *Journal of Communication, 28* (1978), 176–206.

30 Gerbner et al., Charting the mainstream, especially p. 101.

31 S. Robert Lichter, Linda S. Lichter, and Stanley Rothman, From Lucy to Lacy: TV's dream girls, *Public Opinion, 9* (3) (September/October 1986), 16–19.

32 Ibid., p. 19.

33 Gerbner et al., Charting the mainstream, p. 120.

34 Paul Hirsch, The "scary world" of the non-viewer and other anomalies: A reanalysis of Gerbner et al.'s findings on cultivation analysis, Part I, *Communication Research, 7* (1981), 403–456.

35 Hughes, The fruits of cultivation analysis, pp. 287–302.

36 See, most notably, Paul Lazarsfeld, Bernard Berelson, and Helen Gaudet, *The people's choice* (New York: Columbia University Press, 1948); and Bernard Berelson, Paul Lazarsfeld, and William McPhee, *Voting* (Chicago: University of Chicago Press, 1954).

37 See, most notably, Joseph Klapper, *The effects of mass communication* (New York: Free Press, 1960).

38 Elihu Katz, Jay Blumler, and Michael Gurevitch, Uses and gratifications research, *Public Opinion Quarterly, 37* (1973), 509–523. For an excellent recent

summary of work in this area (and a good bibliography), see Jack McLeod and Lee Becker, The uses and gratifications approach, in Dan Nimmo and Keith Sanders (eds.), *Handbook of political communication* (Beverly Hills, Calif.: Sage, 1981) (which the discussion here has drawn on).

39   Katz et al., Uses and gratifications research, p. 510.

40   McLeod and Becker, The uses and gratifications approach, p. 74.

41   See Abraham Maslow, *Motivation and personality* (New York: Harper & Brothers, 1954).

42   Most notably, in relation to political matters, see Lee Becker, Measurement for gratifications, *Communication Research, 6* (1979), 54–73.

43   Jay Blumler and Dennis McQuail, *Television in politics* (Chicago: University of Chicago Press, 1969).

44   See, especially, Becker, Measurement of gratifications, pp. 54–73.

45   Harold Mendelsohn and George O'Keefe, *The people choose a president* (New York: Praeger, 1976).

46   Jack McLeod, L. R. Bybee, and J. Durall, Gratifications sought and received as criteria for mass media evaluation, *Journalism Quarterly, 59* (1981), pp. 3–12, 59.

47   Henry Gleitman, *Psychology,* 2nd ed. (New York: W. W. Norton, 1986), p. 191.

48   See, for example, A. M. Treisman, Selective attention in man, *British Medical Bulletin, 20* (1964), 12–16.

49   Gleitman, *Psychology,* p. 194.

50   Ibid., p. 192.

51   See, for example, Lewis Donshew and Philip Palmgreen, A reappraisal of dissonance and the selective exposure hypothesis, *Journalism Quarterly, 48* (Autumn 1971), 412–420; and Michael Miburn, A longitudinal test of the selective exposure hypothesis, *Public Opinion Quarterly, 43* (Winter 1979), 507–517.

52   Thomas Patterson and Robert McClure, *The unseeing eye* (New York: Paragon Books, 1976), pp. 65–66.

53   Most notably, Angus Campbell et al., *The American voter* (New York: Wiley, 1960).

54   See, for example, Stanley Feldman's summation of schema conceptions, first section in Stanley Feldman et al., Political applications of information processing theory, a set of papers presented at the 1985 Annual Meeting of the Midwest Political Science Association, Chicago.

55   Doris Graber, *Processing the news* (New York: Longman, 1984); and second edition (New York: Longman, 1988).

56   Doris Graber, Information processing and the media, p. 1 of Graber section of Stanley Feldman et al., Political applications of information processing theory.

57   Ibid., p. 2.

58   For the most complete exposition of the "state of the art," see Richard Lau and David Sears (Eds.), *Political cognition* (Hillsdale, N.J.: Lawrence Erlbaum, 1986). See also David Kinder, Understanding political understanding in Stanley Feldman et al., Political applications of information processing theory, for cautionary notes on the current limits (and some abuses) of this theory.

59   W. Russell Neuman, *The paradox of mass politics* (Cambridge, Mass.: Harvard University Press, 1986), pp. 15–16.

60   See Neuman, *The paradox of mass politics,* pp. 16–17, for a chart and discussion.

61   From a National Opinion Research Center poll, as reported (along with many other items) in David V. Edwards, *The American political experience,* 2nd ed. (Englewood Cliffs, N.J.: Prentice-Hall, 1982), p. 176.

62   Campbell et al., *The American voter,* especially Chapter 10.

63   Norman H. Nie, Sidney Verba, and John R. Petrocik, *The changing American voter,* enlarged edition (Cambridge, Mass.: Harvard University Press, 1979).

64   For an example, see Arthur H. Miller, Martin Wattenberg, and Oksana Malanchuk, Schematic assessments of presidential candidates, *American Political Science Review, 80* (2) (June 1986), 521–540; and Morris Fiorina, *Retrospective voting in American national elections* (New Haven, Conn.: Yale University Press, 1981).

65   For a brief discussion of this by a prime authority, see Everett Carl Ladd, *The American polity* (New York: W. W. Norton, 1985), pp. 315–328. For a sophisticated—and remarkable—discussion of the status of public knowledge, thinking, and opinion and the implications of them, see W. Russell Neuman, *The paradox of mass politics: Knowledge and opinion in the American electorate* (Cambridge, Mass.: Harvard University Press, 1986).

CHAPTER 3

1   Stephen J. Wayne, *The road to the White House* (New York: St. Martin's Press, 1980), p. 195.

2   Roberta S. Sigel, Image of the American presidency—Part II of an exploration into popular views of presidential power, *Midwest Journal of Political Science, 10* (1) (1966), summary chart p. 130.

3   See, for example, "A view without hills or valleys," *Time,* February 6, 1984, pp. 25–26.

4   Thomas Cronin in E. Sandoz and C. Crabb, Jr. (Eds.), *Election '84: Landslide without a mandate* (New York: A Mentor Book—New American Library, 1985), pp. 37–38.

5   Regarding the "strong leader" perception, see, for example, the summation in Gerald Pomper et al., *The election of 1984: Reports and interpretations* (Chatham, N.J.: Chatham House, 1985), p. 93.

6   Ibid., p. 93.

7   Summarized in the *National Journal,* January 31, 1987, p. 284.

8   For example, in-depth questioning by this author of a small-scale sample (not strictly random, although including a good range of different demographic categories), found fewer than 10% had even the vaguest notion of how the system was supposed to work (simply according to accessible news media accounts). This was a "tag-on" question included in the research reported in Dean Alger, Television, perceptions of reality and the electoral process, a paper prepared for delivery at the 1987 Annual Meeting of the American Political Science Association, Chicago. Regarding the physicists' opinions, see

"Physicists undermine star wars" (an AP story), run in *The Forum* (Fargo, N. Dak.), March 23, 1986, p. A8.

9   Summarized in the *National Journal*, June 13, 1987, p. 1550.

10 W. C. McWilliams in Pomper et al., *The Election of 1984*, p. 163.

11 H. Plotkin in Pomper et al., *The election of 1984*, p. 38.

12 See note 18, Chapter 2.

13 See note 27, Chapter 1.

14 Murray Edelman, *The symbolic uses of politics* (Urbana, Ill.: University of Illinois Press, 1967), pp. 5–6.

15 Ibid., p. 7.

16 Gerald R. Miller, On being persuaded, in Michael E. Roloff and Gerald R. Miller (Eds.), *Persuasion: New directions in theory and research* (Beverly Hills, Calif.: Sage, 1980), p. 19.

17 *Newsweek*, February 22, 1982, p. 19.

18 Steven R. Weisman, The president and the press: The art of controlled access, *The New York Times Magazine*, October 14, 1984, p. 71.

19 Ibid.

20 See Miller, in Roloff and Miller, *Persuasion*, especially p. 18.

21 Gary Cronkhite and Jo R. Liska, The judgement of communicant acceptability, in Roloff and Miller, *Persuasion*, p. 104.

22 See the discussion of this in Cronkhite and Liska in Roloff and Miller, *Persuasion*.

23 See, for example, S. E. Asch, Effects of group pressure upon the modification and distortion of judgments, in H. Guetzkow (Ed.), *Groups, leadership, and men* (Pittsburgh: Carnegie Press, 1951); and M. Sherif, A study of some social factors in perception, *Archives of Psychology, 27* (1935), 187–189.

24 Cronkhite and Liska, in Roloff and Miller, *Persuasion*, p. 107.

25 Ibid., pp. 107–112.

26 Doris Graber, *Processing the news* (New York: Longman, 1984), pp. 161–162.

27 See D. W. Addington, The relationship of selected vocal characteristics to personality perception, *Speech Monographs, 35* (1967), 492–503.

28 This research is reported in Dean Alger, Television, perceptions of reality and the electoral process, a 1987 APSA paper. Also on the Reagan case, see Jeff Meer, Reagan's facial Teflon, *Psychology Today* (January 1986), 18; and Denis G. Sullivan, Facial displays and political leadership: Some experimental findings, a paper prepared for delivery at the 1984 Annual Meeting of the American Political Science Association, Washington, D.C.

29 See Edward Sapir, Symbolism, in *Encyclopedia of the social sciences* (New York: Macmillan, 1930), pp. 492–495.

30 Joyce O. Hertzler, *A sociology of language* (New York: Random House, 1965), p. 28.

31 Ibid.

32 See G. H. Mead, *Mind, self and society* (Chicago: University of Chicago Press, 1934).

33 Hugh Dalziel Duncan, *Symbols in society* (New York: Oxford University Press, 1968), p. 7.

34 Charles E. Elder and Roger W. Cobb, *The political uses of symbols* (New York: Longman, 1983), p. 30.

35 Dan Nimmo and James E. Combs, *Subliminal politics: Myths and mythmakers in America* (Englewood Cliffs, N.J.: Prentice-Hall, 1980), p. 16.

36 Edelman, *The symbolic uses of politics.*

37 Dan Nimmo, *Political communication and public opinion in America* (Santa Monica, Calif.: Goodyear Publishing Co., 1978), p. 75.

38 Selling the candidates, *National Journal,* November 1, 1986, p. 2619.

39 See the discussion of this idea in Edwin Diamond and Stephen Bates, *The spot: The rise of political advertising on television* (Cambridge, Mass.: MIT Press, 1984), pp. 6–10.

40 *Time,* March 30, 1987, p. 29. See also Gary Wills, *Reagan's America: Innocents at home* (New York: Doubleday, 1987).

41 Theodore J. Lowi, *The personal president* (Ithaca, N.Y.: Cornell University Press, 1985), p. 182.

42 See Elder and Cobb, *The political uses of symbols,* p. 36, for a summary and table.

43 Ibid., p. 39.

44 Ibid., pp. 43–47.

45 Ibid., p. 50.

46 Charles Atkin, Political campaigns: Mass communication and persuasion, in Roloff and Miller, *Persuasion,* p. 292.

47 Thomas Patterson, *The mass media election* (New York: Praeger, 1980); see especially Chapters 7 and 10.

48 Atkin, Political campaigns, p. 292.

49 Neil Postman, *Amusing ourselves to death: Public discourse in the age of show business* (New York: An Elisabeth Sifton Book—Penguin Books, 1985).

CHAPTER 4

1 Daniel Schorr, *Clearing the air* (New York: Berkeley Medallion Books, 1978), p. 289.

2 Neil Postman, *Amusing ourselves to death: Public discourse in the age of show business* (New York: An Elisabeth Sifton Book—Penguin Books, 1985), pp. 93–94.

3 From William Schneider, The good, the bad, and the ugly: When U.S. foreign policy becomes covert, *Los Angeles Times,* July 12, 1987, p. 1 of Opinion section.

4 Neil Postman, Critical thinking in the electronic era, *Phi Kappa Phi Journal* (Winter 1985), p. 4.

5 T. Burns as quoted in D. Altheide and R. Snow, *Media logic* (Beverly Hills, Calif.: Sage, 1979), p. 98.

6 Henry Gleitman, *Psychology,* 2nd ed. (New York: W. W. Norton, 1986), p. 191.

7 Ibid., p. 192.

8 Gaye Tuchman, *Making news: A study in the construction of reality* (New York: Free Press, 1978), pp. 109–110.

9   Postman, *Amusing ourselves to death*, p. 70.

10 Ibid., p. 49.

11 Ibid., p. 51.

12 Howell Raines, Reagan appears to succeed by avoiding specific issues, *The New York Times*, September 22, 1984, p. 1A.

13 Daniel J. Boorstin, *The image* (New York: Atheneum, 1962), especially p. 11.

14 Postman, *Amusing ourselves to death*, p. 84.

15 E. E. Schattschneider, *The Semi-sovereign people* (New York: Holt, Rinehart and Winston, 1960), especially p. 71.

16 See, for example, James D. Horan, *Mathew Brady: Historian with a camera* (New York: Bonanza Books), especially pictures 143–154.

17 For a fascinating description, with commentary relevant to this discussion, see Postman, *Amusing ourselves to death*, pp. 44–49.

18 Samuel Eliot Morison and Henry Steele Commager, *The growth of the American republic*, Vol. 1 (New York: Oxford University Press, 1950), p. 628.

19 K. Frankovic in Gerald Pomper et al., *The election of 1980* (Chatham, N.J.: Chatham House, 1981), p. 106.

20 Ibid.

21 Television's blinding power, *U.S. News & World Report*, July 27, 1987, p. 18. See also David Denby, Lt. Col. Ollie North: A face all Americans could love, *Minneapolis Star and Tribune*, July 21, 1987, p. 9A.

22 AP story, Survey finds confidence in republicans, as it appeared in *The Forum* (Fargo, N. Dak.), July 31, 1987, p. A12.

23 Kathleen H. Jamieson and Karlyn K. Campbell, *The interplay of influence: Mass media and their publics in news, advertising, politics* (Belmont, Calif.: Wadsworth, 1983), p. 45.

24 Quoted in Jamieson and Campbell, *The interplay of influence*, p. 47.

25 See, for example, Bernard Hennessy, *Public opinion*, 5th ed. (Monterey, Calif.: Brooks/Cole, 1985), p. 256.

26 Thomas E. Patterson, *The mass media election* (New York: Praeger, 1980), p. 156 and Chapter 12, respectively.

27 J. P. Robinson, Long-term information and media usage, in John P. Robinson and Mark R. Levy (Eds.), *The main source: Learning from television news* (Beverly Hills, Calif.: Sage, 1986), pp. 81–83.

28 J. P. Robinson and Dennis K. Davis, Comprehension of a single evening's news, in Robinson and Levy, *The Main Source*, p. 130.

29 Doris A. Graber, *Processing the news* (New York: Longman, 1984), p. 90. (The second edition of this book is now available.)

30 Ibid., p. 105.

31 Ibid., p. 125.

32 W. Gill Woodall, Information-processing theory and television news, in Robinson and Levy, *The main source*, p. 140. (The original studies were by Findahl and Hoijer.)

33 Ibid., p. 138. (The original studies were by Gunter.)

34 Ibid., pp. 147–148. [The original studies on retention of information were by Pavio (1971) and by Nisbett and Ross (1980), and those on retention of news were by Berry et al. (1982) and Woodall et al. (1983).]

35 Dennis K. Davis and John P. Robinson, News story attributes and comprehension, in Robinson and Levy, *The main source.*

36 Woodall, in Robinson and Levy, *The main source*, p. 148.

37 Gina Garramone, Motivation and political information processing: Extending the gratification approach, in Sidney Kraus and Richard Perloff (Eds.), *Mass media and political thought* (Beverly Hills, Calif.: Sage, 1985), p. 207.

38 See note 26, Chapter 3.

39 Doris Graber, Candidate images: An audio-visual analysis, a paper presented at the 1985 Annual Meeting of the American Political Science Association, New Orleans, La., p. 9.

40 Doris Graber, Say it with pictures: The impact of audio-visual news on public opinion formation, a paper presented at the Annual Meeting of the Midwest Political Science Association, Chicago, pp. 6–7.

41 Ibid., p. 8. On this credibility question, see also Benjamin Page et al., What moves public opinion, *American Political Science Review, 8* (1) (1987), 23–43.

42 Graber, Say it with pictures, p. 7.

43 Jack McLeod, L. R. Bybee, and J. Durall, Gratifications sought and received as criteria for mass media evaluation, *Journalism Quarterly, 59* (1981), pp. 3–12, 59, as summarized in Jack McLeod and Lee Becker, The uses and gratifications approach, in Dan Nimmo and Keith Sanders (Eds.), *Handbook of political communication* (Beverly Hills, Calif.: Sage, 1981), p. 88.

44 Dean Alger, Television, perceptions of reality and the electoral process," a paper presented at the 1987 Annual Meeting of the American Political Science Association, Chicago, pp. 34–37.

45 For a rather enthusiastic discussion of this technology and its potential, see Richard Hollander, *Video democracy* (Mt. Airy, Md.: Lomond, 1985). For a more analytic and comprehensive view, see F. Christopher Arterton, *Tele-democracy* (Beverly Hills, Calif.: Sage, 1987).

CHAPTER 5

1 Quoted in Erick Barnouw, *The image empire* (New York: Oxford University Press, 1970), p. 196.

2 Carl Friedrich, *Constitutional government and democracy*, 4th ed. (Waltham, Mass.: Blaisdell, 1968), p. 502.

3 Ibid., pp. 520–521.

4 Thomas R. Dye and L. Harmon Zeigler, *The irony of democracy*, 6th ed. (Monterey, Calif.: Brooks/Cole, 1984), p. 89.

5 Big firms' sharing of directors studied, *Los Angeles Times*, April 23, 1978, Part 1, p. 33.

6 10 biggest corporate merger deals, *Minneapolis Star and Tribune*, December 12, 1985, p. 18A.

7 Ben Bagdikian, *The media monopoly*, 2nd ed. (Boston: Beacon Press, 1987), p. 4. For more elaborate data and a more cautious interpretive inclination, see Benjamin Compaine (ed.), *Who owns the media?* (White Plains, N.Y.: Knowledge Industry Publications, 1979), although the data are now rather out of date.

8 Gannett goes 3 for 3 in big cities, *Minneapolis Star and Tribune,* May 21, 1986, p. 2M.

9 Compaine, *Who owns the media?,* p. 18.

10 Bagdikian, *The media monopoly,* p. 4.

11 For details of RCA Corp., see, for example, Doris Graber, *Mass media and American politics* (Washington, D.C.: Congressional Quarterly Press, 1984), p. 41. See Dye and Zeigler, *The irony of democracy,* p. 91, for a listing of the largest industrial corporations.

12 See *Newsweek,* April 1, 1985, p. 54.

13 See "Civil war at CBS," and "Tisch: More than a 'squire,'" *Newsweek,* September 15, 1986, pp. 46–51.

14 Bagdikian, *The media monopoly,* p. 4.

15 Ibid., pp. 3–4, including *CJR* quote.

16 Ibid., pp. 24–25.

17 Ibid.

18 GE ends sponsorship of Walters' special, UPI story in the Riverside (Calif.) *Press-Enterprise,* March 1, 1979.

19 See critique, Glowing report on nuclear power was deceptive, by Norman Soloman and Jeff Cohen of the media-watch group Fairness and Accuracy in Reporting, printed in *Minneapolis Star and Tribune,* March 31, 1987.

20 Bagdikian, *The media monopoly,* p. 32.

21 The stars of the bottom line, *Newsweek,* August 26, 1985, p. 42.

22 Cable's biggest leager, *Newsweek,* June 1, 1987, p. 38.

23 Ibid.

24 Ibid.

25 W. John Moore, Tin cup television, *National Journal,* October 25, 1986, p. 2554.

26 Ibid.

27 K. Jamieson and K. Campbell, *The interplay of influence* (Belmont, Calif.: Wadsworth, 1983), p. 24.

28 Moore, Tin cup television, p. 2555.

29 Ibid.

30 Ibid.

31 Ibid.

32 Ibid., p. 2558.

33 Turn on, tune in to public TV, *National Journal,* August 3, 1985, p. 1818.

34 Quoted in Ithiel de Sola Pool, *Technologies of freedom* (Cambridge, Mass.: Belknap Press of Harvard University Press, 1984), pp. 119–120.

35 See Erwin Krasnow, Lawrence Longley, and Herbert Terry, *The politics of broadcast regulation,* 3rd ed. (New York: St. Martin's Press, 1982), especially Chapters 2 and 3, on both presidential and congressional influence.

36 Fred Friendly, *The good guys, the bad guys and the first amendment: Free speech vs. the fairness doctrine* (New York: Random House, 1976).

37 Case of *Central Florida Enterprises, Inc.* v. *FCC,* quoted in T. Barton Carter, Marc Franklin, and Jay Wright, *The first amendment and the fifth estate: Regulation of electronic mass media* (Mineola, N.Y.: Foundation Press, 1986), p. 119.

38 Friendly, *The good guys, the bad guys and the first amendment,* pp. 89–90.

39 Ibid., pp. 95–101.

40 Carter, Franklin, and Wright, *The first amendment and the fifth estate,* especially pp. 92–99, has been drawn on for this section.

41 Krasnow, Longley, and Terry, *The politics of broadcast regulation,* especially p. 223.

42 See Carter, Franklin, and Wright, *The first amendment and the fifth estate,* pp. 99–120; and Krasnow, Longley, and Terry, *The politics of broadcast regulation,* especially pp. 213–231, for a discussion of these points in a legal context.

43 See, e. g., Friendly, *The good guys, the bad guys and the first amendment,* p. 26.

44 See Friendly, *The good guys, the bad guys and the first amendment,* for the most readable discussion of the status of the doctrine up through 1975, including review of the key cases.

45 Ibid., p. 23.

46 Ibid., p. 24.

47 Ibid., p. 27.

48 Ibid.

49 As summarized in "Debate revived over fairness doctrine," *National Journal,* March 14, 1987, p. 635.

50 Friendly, *The good guys, the bad guys and the first amendment,* p. 27.

51 See the fine recounting of the Red Lion case in Friendly, *The good guys, the bad guys and the first amendment,* Chapters 3–5.

52 Graber, *Mass media and American politics,* pp. 109–110.

53 Friendly, *The good guys, the bad guys and the first amendment,* p. 72.

54 For an excellent discussion of this, see Richard L. Rubin, *Press, party, and presidency* (New York: W. W. Norton, 1981).

55 See Rubin, *Press, party, and presidency;* and Neil Postman, *Amusing ourselves to death* (New York: Penguin Books, 1985), Chapter 5.

56 Pool, *Technologies of freedom.*

57 Ibid., especially Chapter 7.

58 Ibid., p. 2.

59 Ibid., p. 138.

60 Ibid., pp. 138–148.

61 See "FCC discovers that carving up the spectrum isn't what it used to be," *National Journal,* May 19, 1984; quote from p. 985.

62 Moore, Tin cup television, p. 2558.

63 See "Cable's comeuppance," *National Journal,* March 26, 1988, pp. 807–811.

64 Quoted (disapprovingly) in Pool, *Technologies of freedom,* p. 134; the case was *FCC* v. *Pacifica Foundation* (1978) and involved comedian George Carlin's "Seven Dirty Words" routine.

65 See, for example, Friendly, *The good guys, the bad guys and the first amendment,* Chapter 12.

66 Newton Minow, A plan to undermine broadcasting fairness, as carried in the *Minneapolis Star and Tribune,* August 28, 1985, p. 17A.

67 Networks send upsetting signal to local station, *Los Angles Times,* December 28, 1986, Part IV, p. 5.

68   FM radio: Real sound investment, *Los Angeles Times,* December 27, 1985, Part I, p. 3.

69   Ibid., p. 29.

70   Edward J. Epstein, *News from nowhere* (New York: Vintage Books, 1974), p. 48.

71   See Krasnow, Longley, and Terry, *The politics of broadcast regulation,* pp. 217–228.

72   For a good review of AIM and the response to it, see Dom Bonafede, One man's accuracy, *National Journal,* May 10, 1986, pp. 1111–1115. Regarding the fallen groups on the liberal side, and other notes on groups, see the discussion in Krasnow, Longley, and Terry, *The politics of broadcast regulation,* pp. 54–61.

73   See Friendly, *The good guys, the bad guys and the first amendment,* pp. 97–98.

74   Ibid., p. 60.

75   See note 28, Chapter 1.

CHAPTER 6

1   David Broder, *Behind the front page* (New York: Simon and Schuster, 1987) pp. 98–99 and 101, respectively.

2   Ibid.

3   Michael Robinson and Margaret Sheehan, *Over the wire and on TV* (New York: Russell Sage, 1983), p. 57.

4   Broder, *Behind the front page,* p. 14.

5   Quoted in Edward J. Epstein, *News from nowhere* (New York: Vintage Books, 1974), pp. 13–14.

6   Herbert Gans, *Deciding what's news* (New York: Vintage Books, 1980), p. 201.

7   On this, see also Gaye Tuchman, *Making news: A study in the construction of reality* (New York: Free Press, 1978); and see W. Lance Bennett, *News: The politics of illusion,* 2nd ed. (New York: Longman, 1988).

8   A. M. Sperber, *Murrow: His life and times* (New York: Bantam Books, 1987), p. 181.

9   Tom Wicker, *On press* (New York: Viking Press, 1978), p. 177.

10   Timothy Crouse, *The boys on the bus* (New York: Ballantine Books, 1974), pp. 268–270.

11   Ibid.

12   *Minneapolis Star and Tribune,* May 7, 1986, p. 1A (state edition).

13   Rich Thomas, Slouching toward a slump, *Newsweek,* May 19, 1986, p. 24.

14   William Pfaff, End the economic-summit shows, as it appeared in the *Minneapolis Star and Tribune,* June 11, 1987, p. 20A.

15   For an exception to this generalization, see the excellent discussion by Bernard Roshco, *Newsmaking* (Chicago: University of Chicago Press, 1975), Chapter 4. For a brief further exemplification and discussion of the manipulation problem in a recent manifestation, see "Making news and non-news," *Newsweek,* September 1, 1986, p. 70.

16   Gans, *Deciding what's news,* pp. 208–209.

[17] Ibid., p. 42.

[18] Ibid., p. 43.

[19] Ibid., p. 51.

[20] See J. Johnstone, E. Slawski, and W. Bowman, *The newspeople* (Urbana, Ill.: University of Illinois Press, 1976); and G. C. Wilhoit, D. H. Wever, and R. G. Gray, *The American journalist* (Bloomington, Ind.: Indiana University Press, 1985).

[21] See Gans, *Deciding what's news*, Chapter 3 and pp. 192–196.

[22] Besides Gans, *Deciding what's news*, see Epstein, *News from nowhere*, and David L. Altheide, *Creating reality* (Beverly Hills, Calif.: Sage, 1976). For fascinating details on four specific media organizations—*Time*, CBS, the *Washington Post*, and the *Los Angeles Times*—see David Halberstam, *The powers that be* (New York: Alfred A. Knopf, 1979).

[23] Testimony describes TV news as "junk," AP story in the *Minneapolis Star and Tribune*, April 29, 1987, p. 7A.

[24] Part two of a series, "Future of network news: Is the signal weakening?," *Los Angeles Times*, December 29, 1986, Part I, p. 16.

[25] Quoted in Sperber, *Murrow*, p. xvi.

[26] Ibid., p. xx.

[27] See, for example, the discussion of these matters in Kathleen H. Jamiesen and Karlyn K. Campbell, *The interplay of influence: Mass media & their publics in news, advertising, politics* (Belmont, Calif.: Wadsworth, 1983), pp. 109–119.

[28] See "A ratings revolution?: The "people meter" may reshape TV's picture," *Newsweek*, September 14, 1987, p. 76.

[29] Future of network news, *Los Angeles Times*.

[30] See the discussion in "Future of network news," *Los Angeles Times*, and in "TV news: Demise is exaggerated," *Los Angeles Times* (the first of the two-part report), December 29, 1986, Part I, pp. 1, 18, 20, and 22–23. The quote is from the former article, p. 16.

[31] See "TV News," *Los Angeles Times*, quotes from p. 18.

[32] Daniel Hallin, The rise of the ten second sound bite: Changing conventions in television coverage of the presidency, 1965–1985, a paper prepared for delivery at the Annual Meeting of the Southern Political Science Association, Nashville, Tenn., November 1985, p. 18.

[33] See Hallin, The rise of the ten second sound bite, p. 11, for a table.

[34] Interview with Bill Moyers, "Taking CBS news to task," *Newsweek*, September 15, 1987.

[35] Koppel raps possible network budget cuts, AP story in *The Forum* (Fargo, N. Dak.), September 25, 1987, p. A12.

[36] See Epstein, *News from nowhere*, pp. 172–173; and Gans, *Deciding what's news*, pp. 171–172.

[37] Epstein, *News from nowhere*, p. 4.

[38] Gans, *Deciding what's news*, p. 167. See also Doris Graber, *Mass media and American politics*, 2nd ed. (Washington, D.C.: Congressional Quarterly Press, 1984), p. 79; and Jamieson and Campbell, *The interplay of influence*, p. 24.

[39] Skipping through the news, *Newsweek*, June 9, 1986, pp. 85–86.

[40] See Graber, *Mass media and American politics*, pp. 78–79.

[41] Ibid., p. 79.

42 See Robert W. Clyde and James K. Buckalew, Inter-media standardization: A Q-analysis of news editors, *Journalism Quarterly, 46* (Summer 1969), 349–351.

43 Graber, *Mass media and American politics,* p. 79.

44 Media overplayed use of cocaine, report says, UPI story as run in *Minneapolis Star and Tribune,* February 8, 1987, p. 22A.

45 Ibid.

46 Jim Fain, A political feeding frenzy on drugs, *Minneapolis Star and Tribune,* September 15, 1986, p. 17A.

47 See, for example, Thomas Collins (of *Newsday*), What did the *Miami Herald* know, and when did it know it?, as run in *Minneapolis Star and Tribune,* May 15, 1987, p. 15A.

48 Anthony Lewis, The bigger story that got away, in *Minneapolis Star and Tribune,* May 13, 1987, p. 18A. See also A. M. Rosenthal (former executive editor, *The New York Times*), Hart story was poor journalism, run in *Minneapolis Star and Tribune,* May 8, 1987, p. 14A. On the general problem, see Jonathan Alter, The search for personal flaw: Where to draw the line, *Newsweek,* October 19, 1987, p. 79.

49 Morality among the supply-siders, *Time,* May 25, 1987, pp. 18.

50 See, for example, "Bush and the 'big A question,'" *Newsweek,* June 29, 1987, p. 6.

51 See "Dan Rather draws a blank," *Newsweek,* September 28, 1987, pp. 47–48.

52 Carl Bernstein and Bob Woodward, *All the president's men* (New York: Simon and Schuster, 1974).

53 See, for example, Gans, *Deciding what's news,* p. 90.

54 Ibid., p. 92.

55 Hallin, The rise of the ten second sound bite.

56 See News media summary, *National Journal,* June 14, 1986, p. 1469.

57 Changing of the guard at Capitol's newspapers and Washington bureaus, *National Journal,* October 5, 1985, p. 2246.

58 Wicker, *On press,* p. 152.

59 Leon V. Sigal, *Reporters and officials: The organization and politics of newsmaking* (Lexington, Mass.: D.C. Heath, 1973), pp. 119–130.

60 Ibid., p. 66.

61 Ibid., pp. 69–70.

62 Epstein, *News from nowhere,* pp. 137–138.

63 Michael B. Grossman and Martha J. Kumar, *Portraying the president* (Baltimore: Johns Hopkins University Press, 1981), pp. 33–34.

64 Tom Brokaw, A network anchorman on the fate of TV news, *The Washington Post,* April 19, 1987, p. D2.

65 Graber, *Mass media and American politics,* p. 81.

66 See Joseph Dominick, Geographic bias in national news, *Journal of Communication, 27* (Fall 1977), 94–99.

67 Brokaw, A network anchorman on the fate on TV news.

68 See, for example, "Hometown TV coverage is booming," *National Journal,* August 29, 1987, pp. 2174–2175.

69 Graber, *Mass media and American politics,* p. 97. For more specifics, see, especially, George Comstock and Robin Cobbey, Watching the watchdogs:

Trends and problems in monitoring network news, in William Adams and Fay Schreibman (Eds.), *Television network news: Issues in content research* (Washington, D.C.: George Washington University Press, 1978).

70 See Halberstam, *The powers that be,* for a good review of the interesting history of *Time* magazine's dominant political orientations and their impact on its news decisions.

71 Data from National Opinion Research Center surveys, as reported in "Journalism under fire," *Time,* December 12, 1983, p. 79. Gallup poll data on the same question showed a similar drop from 1979 to 1984 in those who expressed a great deal or "quite a lot" of confidence in "newspapers"—51% down to 34%—and in "television"—38% down to 26% (4% margin of error). See, for example, "The media in the dock," *Newsweek,* October 22, 1984, table on p. 68. A more recent poll by the Gallup organization, commissioned by the *Los Angeles Times,* came to more optimistic conclusions; see "The people, press & politics," Times Mirror Company, Los Angeles; see Dom Bonafede, Believability, *National Journal,* February 22, 1986, p. 480, for a comment on this poll.

72 Journalism under fire, *Time,* p. 76.

73 Ibid., pp. 76–77.

74 The media in the dock, *Newsweek,* p. 68.

75 Journalism under fire, *Time,* p. 79.

76 Gallup poll reported in "The sudden fall of Gary Hart," *Newsweek,* May 18, 1987, p. 25 (4% margin of error).

77 Journalism under fire, *Time,* p. 77.

78 Journalism under fire, *Time,* p. 83. On *Westmoreland* v. *CBS,* see, for example, "Westmoreland takes on CBS," *Newsweek,* October 22, 1984, pp. 60–66; on *Sharon* v. *Time,* see, for example, "Absence of malice," *Newsweek,* February 4, 1985, pp. 52–57.

79 The media in the dock, *Newsweek,* p. 68.

80 For one latter-day account, see "The saga of Kathleen Morris," *Sunday Magazine, Minneapolis Star and Tribune,* September 6, 1987.

81 The original study (and origin of the term) was that of M. E. McCombs and D. L. Shaw, The agenda-setting function of the media, *Public Opinion Quarterly, 36* (Summer 1972), 176–187. For a good summary, specifically including evidence on the cumulative effect and some unpublished studies, see L. B. Becker, M. E. McCombs, and J. M. McLeod, The development of political cognitions, in Steven Chaffee (Ed.), *Political communication* (Beverly Hills, Calif.: Sage, 1975).

82 See the brief but astute critique on findings, conceptualization, and methods in Denis McQuail, *Mass communication theory* (Beverly Hills, Calif.: Sage, 1987), especially pp. 275–276.

83 For an excellent example, see Part 1 of Michael B. Mackuen and Steven L. Coombs, *More than news* (Beverly Hills, Calif.: Sage, 1981).

84 Becker, McCombs, and McLeod, The development of political cognitions, p. 46.

85 Shanto Iyengar and Donald Kinder, *News that matters* (Chicago: University of Chicago Press, 1987), p. 33 (with inserts from p. 113).

86 Ibid, pp. 114–115.

87 Ibid, p. 115.

88 Alex Schmid and Janny de Graaf, *Violence as communication: Insurgent terrorism and the western news media* (Beverly Hills, Calif.: Sage, 1982), p. 16. Also see Chapter 1 in this excellent study for a review of the definitional issues in the concept of terrorism and for some good relevant history.

89 Brian Michael Jenkins, The psychological implications of media-covered terrorism, Rand Corporation paper, June 1981, p. 1.

90 Manipulation of the media, section of "Unmasking terrorism," pp. 11 and 10, respectively, in reprint of stories appearing in the *Christian Science Monitor*, May 13–16, 1986.

91 Does TV help or hurt? *Newsweek*, July 1, 1985, p. 32.

92 See, especially, Dan Nimmo and James Combs, *Nightly horrors: Crisis coverage in television network news* (Knoxville, Tenn.: University of Tennessee Press, 1985), Chapter 5.

93 Jenkins, The psychological implications of media-covered terrorism, p. 6.

94 Manipulation of the media, *Christian Science Monitor*, p. 12.

95 William Pfaff, The media's role in terrorism, Los Angeles Times Syndicate in *Minneapolis Star and Tribune*, September 18, 1986, p. 17A.

96 Jenkins, The psychological implications of media-covered terrorism, p. 2.

97 Lessons for the networks, *Newsweek*, July 15, 1985, p. 24.

CHAPTER 7

1 James F. Larson, *Television's window on the world: International affairs coverage on the U.S. networks* (Norwood, N.J.: Ablex Publishing Corp., 1984), p. 1.

2 George Gerbner and G. Marvanyi, The many worlds of the world's press, *Journal of Communication*, 27 (Winter 1977), pp. 52–66; see pp. 56–57 for aggregate data quoted.

3 Larson, *Television's window on the world;* p. 40.

4 Doris A. Graber, *Mass media and American politics*, 2nd ed. (Washington, D.C.: Congressional Quarterly Press, 1984), p. 308.

5 As noted in "Foreign correspondents: America's overseas eyes, ears," *Los Angeles Times*, June 29, 1986, part I, p. 23.

6 Foreign correspondents: It's on-the-job training (second in series), *Los Angeles Times*, July 2, 1986, part I, p. 15.

7 The program "Dateline: Moscow," appearing in spring 1983 (a revised and updated version of an earlier program).

8 Ibid.

9 Gerbner and Marvanyi, The many worlds of the world's press, pp. 56–57.

10 "Dateline: Moscow," spring 1983.

11 Foreign correspondents: America's overseas eyes, ears, *Los Angeles Times*, p. 23.

12 Drawn from the summation by John A. Lent of several surveys by John Wilhelm and by Ralph Kliesch, in "Foreign news in American media," *Journal of Communication*, 27 (1) (Winter 1977), p. 49. Others have suggested different specific totals; see, for example, Graber, *Mass media and American politics*, p. 309, on totals for Vietnam in the war and immediate postwar years. In any case, there is agreement on the decline in numbers.

13   Foreign correspondents: America's overseas eyes, ears, *Los Angeles Times*, p. 23.

14   Ibid., p. 24; and "Covering foreign news," *National Journal*, December 14, 1985, p. 2864.

15   Foreign correspondents: America's overseas eyes, ears, *Los Angeles Times*, p. 24.

16   Larson, *Television's window on the world*, p. 46.

17   Mort Rosenblum, *Coups and earthquakes: Reporting the world to America* (New York: Harper Colophon Books, 1981), p. 2.

18   Foreign correspondents: America's overseas eyes, ears, *Los Angeles Times*, p. 23.

19   Rosenblum, *Coups and earthquakes*, pp. 5 and 8, respectively.

20   "Dateline: Moscow," Inside Story, 1983.

21   Larson, *Television's window on the world*, p. 53.

22   See Herbert Gans, *Deciding what's news* (New York: Vintage Books, 1980), pp. 32–33; and Sophia Peterson, International news selection by the elite press: A case study, *Public Opinion Quarterly*, 45 (Summer 1981), 143–163.

23   Gerbner and Marvanyi, The many worlds of the world's press, pp. 57–60, including comparative maps depicting news coverage of the regions of the world.

24   Larson, *Television's window on the world*, pp. 55–57.

25   On elections and royalty, see Gans, *Deciding what's news*, p. 35.

26   Taking CBS news to task, *Newsweek*, September 5, 1986.

27   Graber, *Mass media and American politics*, p. 309.

28   Rosenblum, *Coups and earthquakes*, p. 8.

29   Foreign correspondents: America's overseas eyes, ears, *Los Angeles Times*, p. 24.

30   Covering foreign news, *National Journal*, p. 2864.

31   Rosenblum, *Coups and earthquakes*, pp. 10–11.

32   Ibid., pp. 11–12.

33   Larson, *Television's window on the world*, p. 103.

34   Testimony before subcommittee on International Operations of U.S. Senate Committee on Foreign Relations, June 15, 1977, as quoted in Larson, *Television's window on the world*, p. 95.

35   In 1967, Leo Bogart, found 80% of reporters in Western Europe claiming that they read and spoke the respective language with native fluency or at least, "easy facility" and found similar totals for Latin America. These are self-reports, however, and subject to some exaggeration. The reports of noted journalists and editors, some related here, are strong testimony to the effect that lower totals are more realistic. Bogart did find admission of a dramatically lower level of language competence in Asia, Eastern Europe, and so on. See "The overseas newsman: A 1967 profile study," *Journalism Quarterly*, 45 (Summer 1968), especially p. 300.

36   Foreign correspondents: It's on-the-job training, *Los Angeles Times*, p. 14.

37   Andrew Nagorski, News from Moscow: Covered in caution, *Los Angeles Times*, October 27, 1985, Opinion section, p. 1.

38   Rosenblum, *Coups and earthquakes*, p. 38.

39   Interview in "Dateline: Moscow," Inside Story, 1983.

40 Ibid.

41 Foreign correspondents: It's on-the-job training, *Los Angeles Times,* p. 14.

42 Ibid.

43 Foreign correspondents: America's overseas eyes, ears, *Los Angeles Times,* p. 23.

44 See, for example, "End of a shadow regime," *Time,* February 20, 1984, p. 16.

45 For example, *Newsweek* on various issues under discussion between the United States and the Soviet Union: "But Soviet obstinacy on minor matters seemed deliberate . . ."; and on "Reagan's initiative on regional conflicts": "Tass described it as an 'effort to whitewash the undeclared wars unleashed for the purpose of suppressing people's struggle for freedom and progress'—conveniently neglecting to mention the Soviet Union's 118,000-man occupying force in Afghanistan or the 35,000 Cuban troops in Angola" (as if Angola were a simply obvious situation). "Obstinacy" and "conveniently neglected" are words charged with editorial comment. "Road to the summit," November 4, 1985, p. 19.

46 See "Dateline: Moscow," Inside Story, 1983, for a sharp analysis of the media's treatment of Andropov.

47 Seymour Hersh, *The target is destroyed: What really happened to flight 007 and what America knew about it* (New York: Random House, 1986).

48 Summary by Anthony Lewis, Reagan's deal for Daniloff, as it appeared in *Minneapolis Star and Tribune,* October 5, 1986, p. 17A. See also Thomas Hartman, KAL: The missed stories, *Washington Journalism Review,* 5 (9) (November 1983), p. 12.

49 Disarming charm, *Newsweek,* October 14, 1985, pp. 30–31. See also "Psy-war games," *Newsweek,* September 16, 1985.

50 Strobe Talbot, The Gorbachev era, *Time,* July 27, 1987, p. 29.

51 The great war of words, *Time,* September 9, 1985, p. 32.

52 Ibid., p. 33.

53 In "The wary warlord," *Newsweek,* May 11, 1987, p. 5.

54 See, for example, Dom Bonafede, Moscow's media thaw, *National Journal,* June 13, 1987, pp. 1526–1529.

55 Moscow's vigorous leader, An interview with Gorbachev, *Time,* September 9, 1985, pp. 16–29. See also "The Gorbachev era," etc., *Time,* July 27, 1987, pp. 28–45; and *Newsweek's* cover stories under the general and cover title "Moscow's new generation," March 25, 1985, pp. 22–53, and second, under the general title "Gorbachev's gamble: Opening a closed society," January 5, 1987, pp. 12–33.

56 See the discussion in Robert L. Stevenson and Donald L. Shaw (Eds.), *Foreign news and the new world information order* (Ames, Iowa: Iowa State University Press, 1984), Chapter 1, quotes on pp. 7–8.

57 Quoted in Stevenson and Shaw, *Foreign news,* p. 7.

58 See Stevenson and Shaw, *Foreign news,* pp. 13–20, for a summary discussion; quote, p. 17.

59 Quoted in Graber, *Mass media and American politics,* p. 307.

CHAPTER 8

1 Richard Neustadt, *Presidential power* (New York: Wiley, 1980).

2 Doris Graber, *Mass media and American politics* (Washington, D.C.: Congressional Quarterly Press, 1984), p. 221.

3   For a good, concise discussion of this, see George C. Edwards III and Stephen J. Wayne, *Presidential leadership* (New York: St. Martin's Press, 1985), pp. 6–11 and various later chapters. For an interesting view of some problems stemming from these factors, see James MacGregor Burns, *The power to lead: The crisis of the American presidency* (New York: Simon and Schuster, 1984).

4   Theodore Lowi, *The personal president* (Ithaca, N.Y.: Cornell University Press, 1985), pp. 69–70.

5   Samuel Kernell, The presidency and the people: The modern paradox, in Michael Nelson (Ed.), *The presidency and the political system* (Washington, D.C.: Congressional Quarterly Press, 1984), p. 233. See also Samuel Kernell, *Going public: New strategies of presidential leadership* (Washington, D.C.: Congressional Quarterly Press, 1986).

6   Kernell in Nelson, *The Presidency;* See also Roderick P. Hart, *The sound of leadership: Presidential communication in the modern age* (Chicago: University of Chicago Press, 1987).

7   George E. Reedy, *The twilight of the presidency* (New York: A Mentor Book— New American Library, 1971), quotes from pp. 100 and 105, respectively.

8   David Halberstam, *The powers that be* (New York: Alfred A. Knopf, 1979), p. 388.

9   Stephen Hess, *The Washington reporters* (Washington, D.C.: Brookings Institution, 1981), especially p. 98.

10 See Graber, *Mass media and American politics,* pp. 238, 221–222.

11 Ibid., p. 238.

12 Richard Davis, News coverage of American political institutions, a paper prepared for delivery at the 1986 Annual Meeting of the American Political Science Association, Washington, D.C., pp. 3–4.

13 Ibid.

14 See especially Elmer E. Cornwell, Jr., Presidential news: The expanding public image, *Journalism Quarterly, 36* (Summer 1959), 275–283; and Alan Baluthis, Congress, the presidency, and the press: The expanding presidential image, *Presidential Studies Quarterly, 7* (Fall 1977), 244–251.

15 Davis, News coverage of American political institutions, p. 4.

16 Michael Baruch Grossman and Martha Joynt Kumar, *Portraying the president* (Baltimore: Johns Hopkins University Press, 1981), pp. 254–257.

17 Ibid., pp. 259 and 258, respectively.

18 Ibid., p. 255.

19 Ibid., p. 256.

20 David Broder, *Behind the front page* (New York: Simon and Schuster, 1987), pp. 181–182.

21 Grossman and Kumar, *Portraying the president,* p. 28.

22 Quoted in Grossman and Kumar, *Portraying the president,* p. 45.

23 Ibid., pp. 274–298; quote from p. 274.

24 Hess, *The Washington reporters,* pp. 15–16.

25 Ibid., especially pp. 18–19.

26 Grossman and Kumar, *Portraying the president,* p. 183; see also Hess, *The Washington reporters,* pp. 63–66.

27 Grossman and Kumar, *Portraying the president,* p. 183.

28   Ibid., p. 181.

29   Reedy, *The twilight of the presidency,* Chapter XI; quotes from pp. 150 and 158, respectively.

30   Hess, *The Washington reporters,* p. 61.

31   Quoted in Grossman and Kumar, *Portraying the president,* p. 181.

32   Ibid., p. 187.

33   Reedy, *The twilight of the presidency,* p. 104.

34   Drawn from White House Phone Directory, 1985 edition, as published by the *National Journal.*

35   See, for example, "A new team of stage managers maximizes Reagan's star quality," *National Journal,* January 18, 1986, pp. 162–163.

36   Reedy, *The twilight of the presidency,* pp. 155 and 156.

37   For a tabulation of presidential press conference from Herbert Hoover through Reagan as of May 1987, see "Thank you, Mr. President," *National Journal,* May 2, 1987, p. 1068 (updated from Kernell, *Going public*).

38   Reagan: Running from the press, *Newsweek,* December 19, 1983, p. 25. On the news media's role in press conferences, and on why they have not more vigorously sought to overcome (Nixon's) and Reagan's practices, see "The White House press: Public watchdog or megaphone for president's messages?," *National Journal,* November 16, 1985, pp. 2580–2585.

39   Reported in Dean Alger, Television, perceptions of reality and the electoral process, a paper prepared for delivery at the 1987 Annual Meeting of the American Political Science Association, Chicago, pp. 36–37.

40   Quoted in Stephen Hess, *The government/press connection: Press officers and their offices* (Washington, D.C.: Brookings Institution, 1984), p. 75; see the rest of Chapter 7 for a more complete discussion of leaks and related techniques.

41   *Time,* September 9, 1985, p. 34.

42   Quoted in Broder, *Behind the front page,* p. 181. See also the discussion of this situation in the interview with Sam Donaldson in *Playboy* magazine, March 1983, especially pp. 59–63. See also Grossman and Kumar, *Portraying the president,* pp. 112–113, on the White House photo operation.

43   See, for example, the discussion of the Nixon control efforts in Broder, *Behind the front page,* pp. 80–93.

44   The cocoon strategy, *Newsweek,* September 17, 1984, p. 38. See also Steven Weisman, Reagan builds wall of isolation through TV, *New York Times* analysis article, as run in the *Kansas City Times,* June 10, 1982, p. A-16. For an interesting analysis of Reagan White House management, in a very effective manner, of news relating to the 1981 assassination attempt and Reagan's hospital stay, see Robert Sahr, President Reagan's use of the news media: Exploiting media methods of operation, a paper prepared for delivery at the 1986 Annual Meeting of the Western Political Science Association, Eugene, Oreg., pp. 9–10 and Appendix.

45   See Broder, *Behind the front page,* pp. 180–181.

46   See, for example, "An off-the-record war," *Newsweek,* November 7, 1983, p. 83.

47   See Dom Bonafede, Muzzling the media, *National Journal,* July 12, 1986, pp. 1716–1720, quotes from pp. 1717 and 1716, respectively. See also Jack Nelson, Information act comes under siege, *Los Angeles Times,* March 23, 1986, Part V, pp. 1 and 3.

48   See, for example, "A bodyguard of lies," *Newsweek,* October 13, 1986, pp. 43–46.

49   Broder, *Behind the front page,* p. 199.

50   Richard Davis, News coverage of American political institutions, p. 4 and table 2 on p. 16.

51   Greg Schneiders, The 90-second handicap: Why TV coverage of legislation falls short, *Washington Journalism Review,* June 1985, pp. 44–46, data from p. 44.

52   See Davis, News coverage of American political institutions, p. 7.

53   See Michael J. Robinson, Three faces of congressional media, as reprinted in Doris Graber, *Media power in politics* (Washington, D.C.: Congressional Quarterly Press, 1984), p. 216. See also Arthur Miller, Edie Goldenberg, and Lutz Erbring, Type-set politics: Impact of newspapers on public confidence, *American Political Science Review, 73* (March 1979), especially pp. 70–71.

54   Quoted in Schneiders, The 90-second handicap, p. 45.

55   Michael J. Robinson and Kevin R. Appel, Network news coverage of Congress, *Political Science Quarterly, 94* (Fall 1979), pp. 407–418, especially p. 412.

56   See, for example, Michael Robinson, Three faces of congressional media; and Ben Bagdikian, Congress and the media: Partners in propaganda, in Robert O. Blanchard (Ed.), *Congress and the news media* (New York: Hastings House, 1974).

57   Timothy Cook, Determinants of media strategies in the House, a paper prepared for delivery at the 1986 Annual Meeting of the American Political Science Association, Washington, D.C., p. 4.

58   See the discussion in Stephen Hess, *The ultimate insiders: U.S. senators in the national media* (Washington, D.C.: Brookings Institution, 1986), Chapter 1; quotes from Norman Ornstein and Michael Robinson, respectively, both cited on p. 4.

59   Ibid., Chapter 2, tables on pp. 11 and 14–15; see notes on p. 7 for other recent studies by Timothy Cook and Joe Foote and David Weber confirming these patterns for the House and for both houses, respectively.

60   Cook, Determinants of media strategies in the House, p. 3.

61   Hess, *The ultimate insiders,* p. 91.

62   Quoted in Martin Linsky, *Impact: How the press affects federal policymaking* (New York: W. W. Norton, 1986), p. 62. See also Hess, *The ultimate insiders,* pp. 17–19, for some evidence supporting these conclusions (e.g., of 33 top newsmakers in 1983, 10 were "nonleaders").

63   Martha Kumar and Michael Grossman, Congress: The best beat in town, a paper prepared for delivery at the 1986 Annual Meeting of the American Political Science Association, Washington, D.C.

64   See Susan Miller, News coverage of Congress: The search for the ultimate spokesman, *Journalism Quarterly, 54* (1977), pp. 459–465.

65   See Hess, *The Washington reporters,* pp. 104–105; and Hess, *The ultimate insiders,* Chapter 3.

66   See Rich Cohen, Covering Congress, *National Journal,* November 12, 1983, p. 2376; or, for a more complete review of the conference (at Harvard's Kennedy School of Government, involving media people, academics, and congressmen) see Stephen Bates (Ed.), *The media and the Congress* (Columbus,

Ohio: Publishing Horizons, 1987). Also on this subject, see David L. Paletz and Robert M. Entman, *Media–power–politics* (New York: Free Press, 1981), Chapter 5.

67 Daniel Schorr, *Clearing the air* (New York: Berkley Medallion Books, 1978), p. 289.

68 See the good summary of these means and methods in Ronald Berkman and Laura Kitch, *Politics in the media age* (New York: McGraw-Hill, 1986), pp. 235–239.

69 Richard Davis, News coverage of American political institutions, pp. 7–8, table on p. 16. See also David L. Grey, *The Supreme Court and the news media* (Evanston, Ill.: Northwestern University Press, 1968); David Ericson, Newspaper coverage of the Supreme Court: A case study, *Journalism Quarterly, 54* (1977), 605–607; David Leslie, The Supreme Court in the media: A content analysis, a paper presented at the 1976 Annual Meeting of the International Communication Association, Portland, Oreg.

70 See especially Leslie, The Supreme Court in the media.

71 Ibid.; see also Stephen Wasby, *The Supreme Court in the federal judicial system* (New York: Holt, Rinehart and Winston, 1984), pp. 292–296.

72 For an excellent discussion of this, see Paletz and Entman, *Media–power–politics,* pp. 99–104.

73 See David M. O'Brien, *Storm center: The Supreme Court in American politics* (New York: W.W. Norton, 1986), pp. 282–283.

74 Ibid., p. 284.

75 Cited in Paletz and Entman, *Media–power–politics,* p. 106.

76 Stated in *Bantam Books, Inc.* v. *Sullivan* (1963), affirming *Near* v. *Minnesota* (1931) and cited in *New York Times* v. *United States* (to name the three key cases). See, for example, Donald Gillmor and Jerome Barron, *Mass communication law,* 3rd ed. (St. Paul, Minn.: West Publishing, 1979), pp. 110–144; quote from p. 120.

77 See Gillmor and Barron, *Mass communication law,* pp. 373–401.

78 Ibid., pp. 362–373; see also the brief discussion in Graber, *Mass media and American politics,* pp. 124–127.

79 See Gillmore and Barron, *Mass communication law,* Chapter VI, for a thorough discussion of this; or Graber, *Mass media and American politics,* pp. 122–124, for a brief discussion. On each of these media and the law issues, see also Kenneth S. Devol, *Mass media and the Supreme Court,* 4th ed. (New York: Kampmann & Co., 1987).

80 Hess, *The Washington reporters,* p. 64.

81 Tom Wicker, *On press* (New York: Viking Press, 1978), p. 44.

82 Herbert Gans, *Deciding what's news* (New York: Vintage Books, 1980), p. 133.

83 Linsky, *Impact,* p. 36.

84 Ibid., p. 84 (both quotes).

85 Ibid., p. 65.

86 Ibid. See pp. 95–104 and 49–60, especially regarding the respective cases.

87 Ibid., p. 142.

88 Ibid., p. 129.

89 See, for example, "Duel of the spinmeisters," *Newsweek,* October 27, 1986, p.

23 (a good example of the better perspective that a *weekly* news magazine can give).
90   Ibid., pp. 59–60.

CHAPTER 9

1   E. E. Schattschneider, *Party government* (New York: Rinehart, 1942), p. 1.

2   See the excellent discussion of the conception of the role of parties, along with current realities, in the concluding chapter of William J. Keefe, *Parties, politics, and public policy in America*, 5th ed. (Washington, D.C.: Congressional Quarterly Press, 1988). See also Walter Dean Burnham, *The current crisis in American politics* (New York: Oxford University Press, 1982), Chapters 1 and 3 regarding past eras.

3   See the discussion of this in Keefe, *Parties, politics, and public policy*, Chapter 1; or for a detailed analysis, see Martin P. Wattenberg, *The decline of American political parties: 1952–1984* (Cambridge, Mass.: Harvard University Press, 1986).

4   David Broder, As destiny smiles on the Democrats . . . , as appeared in *Minneapolis Star and Tribune*, November 9, 1986, p. 38A.

5   Jeffrey M. Berry, *The interest group society* (Boston: Little, Brown, 1984), p. 18.

6   Martin Wattenberg, *The decline of American political parties*, p. 2.

7   Thomas Patterson, *The mass media election* (New York: Praeger, 1980), p. 3.

8   Larry J. Sabato, *The rise of political consultants* (New York: Basic Books, 1981).

9   James MacGregor Burns, *The power to lead* (New York: Simon and Schuster, 1984), p. 150. See also Martin P. Wattenberg, From parties to candidates: Examining the role of the media, *Public Opinion Quarterly, 46* (1982), 216–227.

10   Quoted from Keefe, *Parties, politics, and public policy*, p. 166.

11   For an outstanding review and analysis of the party-election reforms and their consequences, see Nelson W. Polsby, *Consequences of party reform* (New York: Oxford University Press, 1983). See also Stephen J. Wayne, *The road to the White House*, 3rd ed. (New York: St. Martin's Press, 1988), Chapter 4, for a more recent review.

12   See Wayne, *Road to the White House*, for a good review of this process and schedule. For a fascinating critique of the current presidential nomination system and detailed suggestion of an alternative approach, see Terry Sanford, *A danger of democracy: The presidential nominating process* (Boulder, Colo.: Westview Press, 1981).

13   Richard L. Rubin, *Press, party, and presidency* (New York: W.W. Norton, 1981), pp. 191–196.

14   Patterson, *The mass media election*, p. 9.

15   Ibid., pp. 11–12. On the method of content analysis, see Klaus Krippendorff, *Content analysis* (Beverly Hills, Calif.: Sage, 1980); and William C. Adams and Fay Schreibmen (Eds.), *Television network news: Issues in content research* (Washington, D.C.: George Washington University, 1978).

16   Patterson, *Mass media election*, p. 14–15.

17   Thomas E. Patterson and Robert D. McClure, *The unseeing eye* (New York: Paragon Books, 1979).

18 Michael J. Robinson and Margaret A. Sheehan, *Over the wire and on TV: CBS and UPI in campaign '80* (New York: Russell Sage, 1983).

19 See, for example, "Television and American politics: 1956–1976," *The Public Interest, 48* (Summer 1977), 3–39.

20 Robinson and Sheehan, *Over the wire and on TV*, p. 40.

21 Ibid.

22 David Broder, *Behind the front page* (New York: Simon and Schuster, 1987), p. 92.

23 Broder, *Behind the front page*, p. 204.

24 Robinson and Sheehan, pp. 21, 26–27.

25 Maura Clancy and Michael J. Robinson, General election coverage: Part I, in Michael J. Robinson and Austin Ranney (Eds.), *The mass media in campaign '84* (Washington, D.C.: American Enterprise Institute, 1985), p. 33.

26 Ibid., p. 27. See also Dean Alger, Television, perceptions of reality and the electoral process, a paper prepared for delivery at the 1987 Annual Meeting of the American Political Science Association, Chicago, for analysis of the positive media attention, through visuals, gained by Reagan and the impact of such attention.

27 See Robinson and Sheehan, *Over the wire and on TV*, especially pp. 94–95.

28 For excellent demonstrations of this, with a discussion, see Harold Evans, *Pictures on a page: Photojournalism and picture editing* (Belmont, Calif.: Wadsworth, 1978).

29 Robinson and Sheehan, *Over the wire and on TV*, p. 95.

30 Henry E. Brady and Michael G. Hagen, The horse-race or the issues?: What do voters learn from presidential primaries?, a paper prepared for delivery at the 1986 Annual Meeting of the American Political Science Association, Washington, D.C.

31 See Richard Hofstetter, *Bias in the news* (Columbus, Ohio: Ohio State University Press, 1976), Chapter 1; and Doris Graber, *Mass media and American politics* (Washington, D.C.: Congressional Quarterly Press, 1984), pp. 192–194.

32 For a good example of use of this technique as part of a more general study, along with a good, concise (but not simple) explanation of the Q-sort technique, see Dan Nimmo and Robert L. Savage, *Candidates and their images: Concepts, methods, and findings* (Pacific Palisades, Calif.: Goodyear Publishing Co., 1976). For the principal full-scale exposition of the method, see Steven R. Brown, *Political subjectivity: Applications of Q-methodology in political science* (New Haven, Conn.: Yale University Press, 1980).

CHAPTER 10

1 From a film of Senator Hart in the (remarkably well done) PBS "Frontline" program, "So you want to be president?" Judy Woodruff, correspondent/moderator, aired summer 1984.

2 Thomas Patterson, *The mass media election* (New York: Praeger, 1980), p. 24.

3 Ibid., p. 25.

4 Ibid., Chapter 4; quote from pp. 31–32. See also Colin Seymour-Ure's original discussion of the "clear-cut issue" preference of the media in a British context, in *The political impact of mass media* (Beverly Hills, Calif.: Sage/Lon-

don: Constable & Co., 1974), especially p. 223. Quote on pp. 31–32 in Patterson. Also, see Benjamin I. Page, *Choices and echoes in presidential elections* (Chicago: University of Chicago Press, 1978) for a detailed discussion of candidates' preference for diffuse issues.

5   Patterson, *Mass media election,* pp. 34–37.

6   Ibid., p. 30.

7   Ibid., p. 44.

8   Ibid., pp. 44–45.

9   Ibid., pp. 45–47, quotes from pp. 45 and 46 (footnote), respectively.

10   Michael J. Robinson, The TV primaries, *The Wilson Quarterly* (Spring 1977), p. 81.

11   Michael J. Robinson and Margaret Sheehan, *Over the wire and on TV: CBS and UPI in campaign '80* (New York: Russell Sage, 1983), pp. 145–146.

12   Ibid., p. 148.

13   Michael J. Robinson, A statesman is a dead politician: Candidate images on network news, in Elie Abel (Ed.), *What's news* (San Francisco: Institute for Contemporary Studies, 1981), p. 161.

14   Robinson and Sheehan, *Over the wire and on TV,* pp. 146–147.

15   Ibid., p. 168.

16   Thomas Patterson and Richard Davis, The media campaign: Struggle for the agenda, in Michael Nelson (Ed.), *The elections of 1984* (Washington, D.C.: Congressional Quarterly Press, 1985), p. 113.

17   Ibid., p. 116.

18   Michael Robinson, The media in campaign '84, Part II, Wingless, toothless, and hopeless, in Michael J. Robinson and Austin Ranney (Eds.), *The mass media in campaign '84* (Washington, D.C.: American Enterprise Institute, 1985), pp. 36–37.

19   Maura Clancy and Michael Robinson, The media in campaign '84: General election coverage, Part I, in Robinson and Ranney, *The mass media in campaign '84,* p. 30.

20   Patterson and Davis, The media campaign: Struggle for the agenda, in Nelson, *Elections of 1984,* pp. 118–119.

21   Pendleton Herring, The significance of third party activities, in John R. Owens and P. J. Staudenraus (Eds.), *The American party system* (New York: Macmillan, 1965), p. 94.

22   Robinson and Sheehan, *Over the wire and on TV,* p. 73.

23   Michael Robinson, The media in campaign '84, p. 35.

24   Quoted in Jim McClellan and David E. Anderson, The making of the also-rans, as reprinted in *Annual editions—Readings in American government 79/80* (Guilford, Conn.: Dushkin, 1979), p. 200 (originally published in *The Progressive* magazine).

25   Arthur Hadley, *The invisible primary* (Englewood Cliffs, N.J.: Prentice-Hall, 1976).

26   Richard Joslyn, *Mass media and elections* (Reading, Mass.: Addison-Wesley, 1984), p. 121.

27   Robinson and Sheehan, *Over the wire and on TV,* p. 34. See also Jeff Greenfield, *The real campaign* (New York: Summit Books, 1982).

28 William C. Adams, Media coverage of campaign '84: A preliminary report, *Public Opinion* (April/May 1984), pp. 10–11.

29 *Newsweek,* March 12, 1984, pp. 20–21; see also Otis Pike column (Newhouse News Service) as run in *The Forum* (Fargo, N. Dak.), March 4, 1984.

30 Henry E. Brady and Michael G. Hagen, The horse-race or the issue?: What do voters learn from presidential primaries, Center for American Political Studies, Harvard University, Occasional Paper (1986 APSA Annual Meeting Paper), p. 8.

31 Tom Wicker, Hart's well-managed windfall, as run in *Minneapolis Star and Tribune,* March 11, 1984, p. 17A.

32 See F. Christopher Arterton, *Media politics* (Lexington, Mass.: Lexington Books, 1984).

33 On candidate treatment in 1980, see Robinson and Sheehan, *Over the wire and on TV,* pp. 115–134. On toughness on the incumbent in 1984, see Clancy and Robinson, The media in campaign '84; on equality of news time, see Robinson and Sheehan, *Over the wire and on TV,* Chapter 5, and Robinson, The media in campaign '84, p. 35.

34 Gladys E. Lang and Kurt Lang, *Politics and television re-viewed,* (Beverly Hills, Calif.: Sage, 1984), Chapter 3.

35 Timothy Crouse, *The boys on the bus* (New York: Ballantine Books, 1974), pp. 176–180 (including a review of how the networks treated this highly orchestrated event).

36 Joslyn, *Mass media and elections,* p. 135.

37 Ibid., p. 159.

38 Patterson, *Mass media election,* pp. 69–70.

39 Ibid.

40 Ibid., pp. 71–72 and 73.

41 Ibid., p. 98.

42 Ibid., p. 105.

43 Ibid., pp. 98 and 103.

44 Ibid., pp. 109–110.

45 Ibid., p. 126.

46 *Newsweek,* October 15, 1984.

47 *Newsweek* and *Time,* October 29, 1984.

48 Patterson, *Mass media election,* p. 142.

49 Ibid., pp. 143 and 134–135, respectively.

50 Ibid., p. 157.

51 For an excellent summation of the research, see Joslyn, *Mass media and elections,* pp. 203–214; for a good overview as of 1979, see Austin Ranney (Ed.), *The past and future of presidential debates* (Washington, D.C.: American Enterprise Institute, 1979) and/or Sidney Kraus (Ed.), *The great debates: Carter vs. Ford, 1976* (Bloomington, Ind.: Indiana University Press, 1979); for a more recent review, with analysis of the impact of the 1984 Reagan–Mondale "debates," see James Endersby, There they go again: The impact of televised presidential debates on voter choice, a paper prepared for delivery at the Annual Meeting of the Southwestern Political Science Association, San Antonio, Tex., 1986.

52 Jane Bryant Quinn, A reporter's complaint, *Newsweek,* October 7, 1980, p. 32.

53   Joe McGinnis, *The selling of the president, 1968*, (New York: Trident Press, 1969), p. 27.

54   Larry J. Sabato, *The rise of political consultants* (New York: Basic Books, 1981), p. 112.

55   How the vote brokers operate, *Newsweek*, November 10, 1986, pp. 22–23.

56   Larry Sabato as quoted in "How the vote brokers operate," pp. 22–23.

57   Edwin Diamond and Stephen Bates, *The spot: The rise of political advertising on television* (Cambridge, Mass.: MIT Press, 1984), pp. 302–315.

58   Thomas E. Patterson and Robert D. McClure, *The unseeing eye* (New York: Paragon Books, 1979), Chapter 5.

59   Richard Joslyn, Television spot ads and the origins of candidate appeals, a paper prepared for delivery at the 1985 Annual Meeting of the American Political Science Association, New Orleans, La., p. 19.

60   See Diamond and Bates, *The spot*, pp. 326–344, for a discussion and examples.

61   Sabato, *The rise of political consultants*, p. 126.

62   See the discussion in Stephen J. Wayne, *The road to the White House* (New York: St. Martin's Press, 1980), pp. 206–207. For a detailed review and analysis of presidential political advertising, see Kathleen Hall Jamieson, *Packaging the presidency* (New York: Oxford University Press, 1984).

63   See Joslyn, *Mass media and elections*, pp. 196–203 for a good review of work up to 1984.

64   Patterson and McClure, *The unseeing eye*, Chapter 6, quote on p. 117.

65   Joslyn, *Mass media and elections*, pp. 199–200.

66   Ibid., pp. 201–203, quote on p. 203.

67   See Michael J. Robinson, The media in 1980: Was the message the message?, in Austin Ranney (Ed.), *The American elections of 1980* (Washington, D.C.: American Enterprise Institute, 1981), pp. 185–186.

68   Sabato, *The rise of political consultants*, pp. 135–138. For another excellent discussion, see Ronald Berkman and Laura W. Kitch, *Politics in the media age* (New York: McGraw-Hill, 1986), pp. 293–303, quote on p. 303.

69   Robinson and Sheehan, *Over the wire and on TV*, pp. 172–173.

70   Ibid.

71   Edie N. Goldenberg and Michael W. Traugott, *Campaigning for Congress* (Washington, D.C.: Congressional Quarterly Press, 1984), p. 110.

72   As summarized in Joslyn, *Mass media and elections*, p. 173.

73   In Goldenberg and Traugott, *Campaigning for Congress*, p. 11.

74   Ibid., p. 125.

75   Ibid., p. 127, table on p. 128.

76   Peter Clarke and Susan H. Evans, *Covering campaigns* (Stanford, Calif.: Stanford University Press, 1983), pp. 55–56.

77   Joslyn, *Mass media and elections*, p. 174.

78   Mayoral candidates enter big time using costly TV ads and consultants, *National Journal*, April 6, 1985, p. 737.

79   See the summary in Joslyn, *Mass media and elections*, pp. 150–152.

80   See Raymond Wolfinger and Peter Linguiti, Tuning in and turning out, *Public Opinion, 4* (1) (February/March 1981), 56–60; Laurily K. Epstein and

Gerald Strom, Election night projections and West Coast turnout, *American Politics Quarterly*, *9* (4) (October 1981), 479–491, and Percy Tannenbaum, *Turned-on TV, turned-off voters—Policy options for election projections* (AEI Book) (Beverly Hills, Calif.: Sage, 1983).

81 See the analysis of this in Richard Joslyn, Marc Howard Ross, and Michael M. Weinstein, Election night news coverage: The limitations of story-telling, *PS*, *XVII* (3) (Summer 1984), 564–571.

82 David Sarasohn, A poll-closing scheme designed to keep Westerners from voting, Newhouse News Service, as run in *Minneapolis Star and Tribune*, November 18, 1987, p. 17A.

CHAPTER 11

1 The first three steps of the model (as usually spelled out) are: (1) identify the problem, (2) clarify goals and rank them, and (3) list all alternative means and methods of achieving those goals. See, for example, Charles E. Lindblom, *The policy-making process* (Englewood Cliffs, N.J.: Prentice-Hall, 1968), especially p. 13.

2 Anthony King, How not to select presidential candidates: A view from Europe, in Austin Ranney (Ed.), *The American elections of 1980* (Washington, D.C.: American Enterprise Institute, 1981), p. 307.

3 See the discussion in King, *How not to select presidential candidates*, pp. 308–320.

4 Paul S. Underwood, Europe and the Middle East, in John C. Merrill, *Global Journalism* (New York: Longman, 1983), p. 63.

5 See David Butler and Donald Stokes, *Political change in Britain* (Harmondsworth, Middlesex, England: Penguin Books, 1971), pp. 281–282.

6 Underwood, in Merrill, *Global journalism*, pp. 64–65.

7 Philip Norton, *The British polity* (New York: Longman, 1984), p. 331.

8 Ibid.; see, e.g., pp. 330–331.

9 As quoted in David Butler and Dennis Kavanaugh, *The British general election of 1979* (London: Macmillan, 1980), p. 207.

10 David G. Boyce, Government and the news media: The British experience, in Dan Nimmo and Michael W. Mansfield (Eds.), *Government and the news media* (Waco, Tex.: Baylor University Press, 1982), p. 81.

11 Tom Burns, *The BBC: Public institution and private world* (London: Macmillan, 1977), p. 180.

12 Boyce, in Nimmo and Mansfield, *Government and the news media*, p. 80.

13 Quoted in Burns, *The BBC*, pp. 12–13.

14 Director-General William Haley as quoted in Philip Schlesinger, *Putting "reality" together: BBC news* (London: Constable/Beverly Hills, Calif.: Sage, 1979), pp. 33–34.

15 See, for example, Everette M. Rogers and Francis Balle (Eds.), *The media revolution in America and Western Europe* (Norwood, N.J.: Ablex Publishing Corp., 1985), pp. 25–26.

16 Boyce, in Nimmo and Mansfield, *Government and the news media*, pp. 83–84.

17 Ibid., p. 84.

18 Schlesinger, *Putting "reality" together*, pp. 40–41.

19   Ibid.; see, e.g., pp. 40–44.

20   "Channel snore" to the fore, *Time,* September 1, 1986, p. 73.

21   Ibid.

22   Michael Cockerell, Peter Hennessy, and David Walker, *Sources close to the prime minister: Inside the world of the news manipulators* (London: Macmillan, 1985), pp. 17, 18.

23   Boyce, in Nimmo and Mansfield, *Government and the news media,* p. 87.

24   Burns, *The BBC,* pp. 187–188.

25   Boyce, in Nimmo and Mansfield, *Government and the news media,* p. 84.

26   New head of BBC faces big challenge, *Los Angeles Times,* April 10, 1987, Part VI, p. 10.

27   The blowup over the BBC, *Newsweek,* February 16, 1987, p. 43.

28   Michael Cockerell, Peter Hennessy, and David Walker, *Sources close to the prime minister,* pp. 9 and 10, respectively. See also Jeremy Tunstall, *The Media in Britain* (New York: Columbia University Press, 1983), pp. 13–20.

29   Ibid.

30   Cockerell et al., *Sources close to the prime minister,* p. 11.

31   Ibid.; see Chapter 8 in general; quotes from pp. 148, 149, and 150, respectively.

32   Ibid., p. 160.

33   Ibid.; Chapter 7 in general, quotes, pp. 117, 118, and 119, respectively.

34   See, for example, Norton, *The British polity,* Chapter 5 on this.

35   Jay G. Blumler and Denis McQuail, *Television in politics* (Chicago: University of Chicago Press, 1969).

36   Colin Seymour-Ure, *The political impact of mass media* (London: Constable/Beverly Hills, Calif.: Sage, 1974), p. 235.

37   Ibid., p. 223.

38   Ibid., p. 234. For a partially contrasting view, see David Morgan, Media and British elections, a paper prepared for delivery at the 1985 Annual Meeting of the American Political Science Association, New Orleans, La.

39   Politics American style, *Newsweek,* June 8, 1987, p. 41.

40   Tunstall, *The media in Britain,* p. 13. See also Morgan, Media and British elections, especially p. 13 on the similar effort in 1983.

41   Politics American style, *Newsweek,* p. 41.

42   Tunstall, *The media in Britain,* p. 13.

43   Politics American style, *Newsweek,* p. 41.

CHAPTER 12

1   See Bill Moyers interview, "Taking CBS news to task," *Newsweek,* September 15, 1986, p. 53.

2   Benjamin Barber, *Strong democracy* (Berkeley, Calif.: University of California Press, 1984), pp. 261 and 235, respectively.

3   See, for example, Lewis W. Wolfson, *The untapped power of the press: Explaining government to the people* (New York: Praeger, 1985), p. 2.

4   Ibid., quotes from pp. 2, 5, and 6.

5   Kennedy assails campaign coverage, *Twin Cities Star Tribune*, December 6, 1987, p. 37A.

6   Richard E. Cohen, Congressional Focus section, "People politics," *National Journal*, November 14, 1987, p. 2940.

7   Rethinking the fair game rules, *Time*, November 30, 1987, p. 76.

8   Richard Cohen, People politics, *National Journal*, p. 2940.

9   Dom Bonafede, Media Focus section, "Self-examination," *National Journal*, September 7, 1985, p. 2020.

10   Ibid.

11   Ibid.

12   Richard Joslyn, *Mass media and elections* (Reading, Mass.: Addison-Wesley, 1984), p. 5.

13   See, for example, Everett M. Rogers and Francis Balle (Eds.), *The media revolution in America and Western Europe* (Norwood, N.J.: Ablex Publishing Corp., 1985).

14   See note 26, Chapter 2.

15   Neil Postman, *Amusing ourselves to death: Public discourse in the age of show Business* (New York: An Elisabeth Sifton Book—Penguin Books, 1985).

16   Dan Nimmo and James E. Combs, *Mediated political realities* (New York: Longman, 1983); quotes from pp. 9 and 14, respectively.

17   James David Barber, As voters consent to a politics of illusion,. as run in *Minneapolis Star and Tribune*, May 1, 1984, p. 11A.

18   See the outstanding book on the media and the manipulation of political perceptions of reality by journalist Martin Schramm: *The great American video game: Presidential politics in the television age* (New York: William Morrow, 1987).

19   Jarol Manheim, Can democracy survive television, in Doris Graber, *Media power in politics* (Washington, D.C.: Congressional Quarterly Press, 1984), p. 134.

20   Wilson Carey McWilliams, The meaning of the election, in Gerald Pomper et al. (Eds.), *The election of 1984: Reports and interpretations* (Chatham, N.J.: Chatham House, 1985), pp. 161–162.

21   Ibid.

22   Herbert Gans, *Deciding what's news* (New York: Vintage Books, 1980), Chapter 10.

23   Mike Wallace and Gary Paul Gates, *Close encounters: Mike Wallace's own story* (New York: Berkley Books, 1985), p. 380.

24   Quoted in Martin Linsky (Ed.), *Television and the presidential elections* (Lexington, Mass.: Lexington Books, 1983), p. 114.

25   Wolfson, *Untapped power of the press.*

26   F. Christopher Arterton, *Teledemocracy* (Beverly Hills, Calif.: Sage, 1987).

27   Barber, *Strong democracy*, pp. 273–274.

28   Ibid., Chapter 10.

29   Carl J. Friedrich, *Constitutional government and democracy*, 4th ed. (Waltham, Mass.: Blaisdell, 1968), p. 29.

INDEX